HYPE

HYPE

Steven M. L. Aronson

WILLIAM MORROW AND COMPANY, INC. • NEW YORK • 1983

Copyright © 1983 by Steven M. L. Aronson

Grateful acknowledgment is made for permission to reprint the following:

The selection from *Lunch Poems,* copyright © 1964, by Frank O'Hara, reprinted by permission of City Lights Books.

The excerpt from *Swanson on Swanson* by Gloria Swanson, copyright © 1980 by Gloria's Way, Inc., reprinted by permission of Random House, Inc.

The excerpt from "Fern Hill" by Dylan Thomas, in *Poems of Dylan Thomas,* copyright 1945 by the Trustees for the Copyrights of Dylan Thomas, reprinted by permission of New Directions Publishing Corporation; and in *Collected Poems,* published by J. M. Dent, reprinted by permission of David Higham Associates Limited.

The excerpt from "Sailing to Byzantium" is reprinted by permission of Macmillan Publishing Co., Inc., from *Collected Poems* of William Butler Yeats. Copyright 1928 by Macmillan Publishing Co., Inc., renewed 1956 by Georgie Yeats; and by permission of Michael Yeats, Anne Yeats, and Macmillan, London, Ltd.

The excerpt from the February 14, 1982 "Suzy" column, reprinted by permission of Tribune Company Syndicate, Inc.

The excerpts from Mimi Sheraton's reviews of La Coupole and McDonald's, copyright © 1981 by The New York Times Company. Reprinted by permission.

Lyrics from "Love for Sale" by Cole Porter, 1930 (renewed), Warner Bros., Inc. All rights reserved. Used by permission.

Library of Congress Cataloging in Publication Data

Aronson, Steven M. L.
Hype.

Includes index.
1. Advertising—United States.   2. Fashion.
I. Title.
HF5813.U6A76   1983   659.1'0973   82-21679
ISBN 0-688-01228-0

Printed in the United States of America

First Edition

1   2   3   4   5   6   7   8   9   10

BOOK DESIGN BY LINEY LI

For Finn Guinness, years later

Acknowledgments

I would like to thank the many people who appear in these pages for the time they gave me.

I would also like to thank the following friends for their eclectic contributions to the writing of this book: Charles Addams, John Appleton, Pearl Bailey, the Duke and Duchess of Bedford, Paula and David Blasband, Patricia Bosworth, Joel Carmichael, Elvire Connery, Paulette Goddard, John Grimond, Pat Hackett, Jerome Hamlin, Simon Head, Clifford Irving, Katharine Johnson, Jesse Kornbluth, Kenneth Jay Lane, Viscount Lewisham, Gael Love, Gail Lumet, Charles Maclean, Robert Mapplethorpe, James Mellon, Charles Michener, Caterine Milinaire, Barbara and Stanley Mortimer, Victoria and Robert Pennoyer, Doria Reagan, John Richardson, Natalie Robins, Princess Alexander Romanoff, Ethel Scull, Maureen Simmons, Lionel Tiger, Sidney and Brian Urquhart, Shelley Wanger, Jeannette Watson, and Jacqueline and Matthew Weld.

I am especially grateful to Karen Lerner for the suggestion that hype was a subject worth exploring, to William Jovanovich for his faith in me, to my agent, Lynn Nesbit, for her unfailingly good advice and enthusiastic support; to Hillel Black, former editor-in-chief of William Morrow, for his acumen, tenacity, and abiding goodwill, and to Jane Cavolina Meara of Morrow, a born editor and spirited professional dedicated to the principle of words fervently used, of ideas coolly presented.

Always in the history of a book there is the friend who "bolsters our courage and approves, or sometimes disputes, our ideas." I thank Virginia Tiger for years of uncommon friendship and hours of fruitful discussion; her bracing skepticism steeled me for this journey through the landscape of excess.

Contents

The Girl Who Cried Hype

• A TRUE FABLE •

The film director dropped his wife and daughter off at a shabby brownstone in Greenwich Village and went to find a parking place. It was a blowy Sunday afternoon in spring.

He was not looking forward to the occasion: earnest parents and nervous offspring meeting one another for the first time three months before the start of summer camp. The sorry high point of the afternoon would be the showing of the camp's promotional movie.

When the Film Director walked in the door, his spirits sank afresh. Four mothers and one father sat sipping coffee and eating cake. He realized he would have to make awkward small talk with the other father, a total stranger. At the sound of the doorbell, his spirits lifted.

A woman with a small girl in tow entered the room. She had on monstrous dark glasses and a scarf knotted so tightly at the throat it was a marvel she could swallow. The scarf was wrapped so completely around her head that not a hair was visible.

The Film Director recognized her anyway, although nobody else in the room seemed to.

Just as he was about to say hello to the Mystery Woman, someone from the camp rushed over and introduced her to him as Barbara Guber. She held out her hand and repeated, "I'm Barbara Guber," her tone of voice indicating in the sternest possible measure: Don't give me away; I haven't come here in disguise for nothing.

The Film Director, musing on the mode of the Mystery Woman's disguise—dark glasses and taut scarf—was amused: To appear conspicuously anonymous, she had dressed herself in the paraphernalia of a Jackie Onassis or a Garbo announcing privacy as publicly as possible.

Going along with the charade, the Film Director said, "Glad to meet you, Mrs. Guber."

13

As a matter of fact, he had met Mrs. Guber before. He had run into her at least half a dozen times over the years, and twice he had been a guest on her talk show.

Now, during this game of non-recognition, he had to smile watching her play the Little Mother as though she were just another doting parent whose daughter was going off to summer camp.

The lights dimmed and as the blank screen jumped alive to scenes of rackety-packety girls playing volleyball, diving, canoeing, laughing, giggling, and toasting marshmallows, the Film Director ducked out to the corner bar for a beer.

When he returned twenty minutes later, the movie was over. The PR had obviously worked, for the room was busy with talk of the splendid summer ahead. His wife was sitting on a couch deep in enthusiastic conversation with another mother.

As he walked toward the couch, Barbara Guber, who had been standing alone on the other side of the room, intercepted him. "Which one is yours?" she asked.

Pointing out his daughter, *he* asked, "Where's yours gone?"

"She's in the bathroom," she said. Then, adjusting her dark glasses, she added, "Having a kid . . . it's the best thing in my life."

At that moment, the Film Director's wife joined them. "Honey, this is Barbara," he said, "Barbara . . ." and stumbled, having forgotten the perfectly forgettable surname she was using that afternoon (as it happened, the name of her former husband). "What did you say your last name was?" he innocently asked.

Offended, she replied, "Come off it. *You* know I'm Barbara Walters."

What *Is* Hype?

Were the worthy schoolmaster on whom James Hilton modeled the hero of his novel *Good-bye, Mr. Chips* around today, he would probably be hosting a morning talk show called *Hello, Mr. Chips.*

Hype would have had its way even with this shy, essentially serious person, using all the contemporary techniques of marketing and packaging at its command—sales gimmicks, publicity stunts, promotional junkets, ad campaigns, and public relations—to inflate him into just another macrostructural phenomenon. You can bet your bottom buck there'd be Mr. Chips T-shirts, Mr. Chips rulers, Mr. Chips chalk, and—*some* marketing whiz would be sure to come up with it—chocolate Mr. Chipses.

"Hype." A word aggressively in tune with the times. Its very sound—sharp, shrieky, cheap, belligerent, predatory—alerts us: A hard sell is in the works.

Available to common usage as either noun or verb, hype can be most usefully defined as the merchandising of a product—be it an object, a person, or an idea—in an artificially engendered atmosphere of hysteria, in order to create a demand for it or to inflate such demand as already exists. Its object is money, power, fame.

The provenance of "hype," like that of most coined monosyllabic words, is murky. Some say the word is derived from the hollow hypodermic needle; that in the narcotic addict's argot, "hyped up" meant "high." Others argue that "hype" is derived from "hyperbole," the Greek word for excess or exaggeration. Hyperbole is also a figure of speech not intended to be taken literally; the great Roman rhetorician Quintilian defined it as "an elegant straining of the truth."

There is nothing elegant about hype. And very little truth in it. But not all hype is unattractive, not all hype is bad. There are exaggerations that are unobjectionable, and some that are properly enhancing. Others, however, are outrageous and duplicitous.

Hype routinely debases language, the currency of communication, thus making the coin worth less; in a universe where *everything* is *"FABULOUS!,"* nothing is anything.

And most invidiously, hype manipulates taste as it vitiates our power to discriminate. An item may be inferior or superior—that, we often can't discern; all we can tell is whether the hype is first- or second-rate. The competition for our dollar is really a contest between one hype and another. Since we're buying the hype when we buy the product, hype is a product, too.

Hype differs from advertising—which it employs, along with public relations, as accomplices—in that it is not directly paid for. Its clear first principle is to attract as much *free* publicity as possible—news stories, magazine covers, talk-show appearances, gossip-column mentions, and editorials.

The objects of hype's hard sells have included intellectuals, journalists, architects, and—now that the great take-over battles and proxy fights take place in the financial press where investor confidence can most skillfully be manipulated—big businessmen with their public relations advisers, Flitter, Flatter, Hatter, Patter, Patter & Sklom. And serious artists. The distinction between high art and popular entertainment collapses when a Pavarotti performs with a Sinatra. And Pavarotti is not the only classical artist working with press agents to become a pop hero whose every appearance is an instant "event." It's hype that created Pavarotti's need and made possible its sleazy fulfillment.

Perhaps the most nefarious feature of hype is that it is not billboarded as a species of advertising and therefore enjoys greater credibility. We distrust ads and press releases because we know where they come from; we don't always distrust hype because very often we can't see it for what it is. Its inner workings are as invisible as its results are visible.

Hype, like propaganda, is a conspiracy against the public. And the public not only tolerates it but unconsciously encourages it.

Why are we so gullible?

In America we have a long history of being hoodwinked—and just as long a history of hoodwinking. Hype is no novelty. It may have come to fulfillment in our time, but it can be traced all the way back to our earliest origins as a mercenary people. Americans are consummate con artists, tricksters, confidence men.

Melville was writing about deception—about hype—in *The Confidence-Man* . . . the riverboat swindler who could sell anyone anything. "No man is a stranger. You accost anybody. Warm and confiding, you wait not for measured advances."

Whitman, arguably our greatest American poet, was a shameless promoter of his own work. The author of "Song of Myself" had the supreme audacity to write—and publish anonymously—articles about himself that amounted to psalms of self-aggrandizement.

And Mark Twain reveled in hype, told the tallest of tall tales. In the nineteenth century, the tall tale was a popular form of literature. It was done with humor, to amuse and entertain, and not intended to be taken seriously. Then something new came into the world—people began to take tall tales seriously. They began to believe them.

What easy marks we Americans were—and are. "Hello, Sucker!" could well be our national anthem.

Gore Vidal, who has thought long, hard, and profitably about his country, replied with Olympian confidence to a query about the essentially American origins of hype: "America is a nation of hustlers, a bunch of Europeans who came over, killed the Indians, enslaved the blacks, told each other lies. Everybody was on the lam. One of the reasons Americans had such difficulty with conversation is that it was really not considered good form to ask anybody where he was from or what he did or even what his name was, because he was probably 'wanted.' "

This book will not return to those early days. If it were to make such a journey into American history on the grounds that hype applied to any and all exaggerated claims and efforts, the term would lose its meaning. *Hype* will not go back beyond the invention and use of the word.

Because we live in the age of hype, the process demands inspection, if not evisceration. How does a movie get to be a box-office hit? How does an ad campaign completely rejuvenate an industry? How does a book become a best seller? How does a rock star sell out Madison Square Garden? How does a hairdresser get to be as famous as the high-status people he serves? There's work involved. And hype is that work.

How does a politician become a winner? *That* we don't need to be told. Politics is dramaturgy. Adlai Stevenson said once, of American election practices, that a candidate has to render himself unfit for office in order to obtain it. A book recently appeared with the discouraging title *The Duping of the American Voter: Dishonesty and Deception in Presidential Television Advertising.* A politician is simply the PR advice he gets. The first thing political consultant David Garth does when he takes on a candidate is order him to lose weight. And the first thing out-of-office Presidents do, after turning in their hype slogans ("Why Not the Best?" and so on), is sign up with talent agents who package them like Vegas acts.

Hype, it might seem, is the only world in town. People no longer do anything with respect to what they're doing; they do everything with respect to that third eye, which is the eye of *People* magazine.

The world of hype is interlocking. At a certain level, everything connects. Indeed, there's an international daisy chain of hype. "International Daisy Chain" is a game that Truman Capote invented one rainy Sunday. The link was sex. One had to get from, for instance, Tennessee Williams to Cardinal Spellman in two moves—just through bed. *That* was easy. In fact, it was easy to get from almost anybody—from, let's say, Louis B. Mayer—to almost anybody—to, let's say, the Duke of Windsor—by going through one particular woman who had slept with so many men and so many women—so many prominent women—that she was a kind of junction; one could get to almost anybody in two moves through *her*. We could play the same game with hype, changing the link from sex to promotion.

Hype is a small enough daisy chain. Though today we inhabit an electrically charged and electronically connected planet, we remain creatures atavistically committed to the small scale. It's not surprising that we should adopt as our heroes only a few dozen men and women. Call them celebrities, call them gods and goddesses, they are the embodiment in our time of classical heroes.

We don't have the luxury the Greeks had of a set of gods firmly in place. We want heroes, and there are so few natural ones. Perhaps that's why we have to keep inventing them—or rather, having them hypecast for us. Perhaps that's why we let ourselves be hyped into believing in unnatural ones. Strip them of their trappings and they flail about as piteously as Soraya, who as Empress of Iran had grown so accustomed to having crowds make way for her that as a private citizen she kept crashing into people on the streets.

Hype is about both those who do the inventing and those who are invented, and suddenly emerge to inhabit our collective consciousness.

If the book strikes some readers as variously buoyant, frivolous, playful, irreverent, indignant, and at the odd moment scatological, that is intentional—form must marry content. The subject, after all, is a perfectly mercurial one.

Each of the following chapters is an X ray of hype, which this book has defined as "the merchandising of a product—be it an object, a person, or an idea—in an artificially engendered atmosphere of hysteria, in order to create a demand for it or to inflate such demand as already exists." Together, the chapters reveal a persistent pattern that speaks of a sorely menaced culture.

Perhaps, hidden somewhere behind this harlequinade of hype, there is an antidote sufficiently vital to combat a force that makes a mockery of the human essence.

HOW A
STAR IS BORN

CHERYL TIEGS:
CHEESECAKE SERVED AS APPLE PIE

Wou'd ye have fresh Cheese and Cream?
Julia's Breast can give you them:
And if more; Each *Nipple* cries,
To your *Cream,* here's *Strawberries.*

—ROBERT HERRICK, "Fresh Cheese and Cream"

I nduction is the systematic reasoning from a part to a whole, from the particular to the general, from the individual to the universal; the process of demonstration in which the general validity of a law is inferred from its observed validity in particular cases by proving that if the law holds in a certain case, it must hold in the next and therefore in succeeding cases.

Let us inductively arrive at a model of hype.

1

Body Incomparable,
Body Incorporated

This is the U.S.A., the United States of Advertising. Pompon daughters of Quaker undertakers win prized places on American Presidents' energy councils. Pop-out pinups parade up to platforms and address annual shareholders' meetings of 27.36-billion-dollar corporations.

Because, in the United States of Advertising, anatomies that can be marketed determine destinies that can be franchised.

Cheryl Tiegs, born, like Beatrice in *Much Ado About Nothing,* under a star that danced, grew up to become the illustrative model of hype, which may be defined as much more ado about something than that something is ever worth. The girl who was raised under the star-spangled banner of the California skies by a mortician father and a housewife mother would one day find her name on everybody's lips and her body on everybody's mind. Including that of a President of the United States who had famously admitted to lusting in his heart after women other than his wife—*he* would appoint her a member of his Council for Energy Efficiency at a time when energy was the world's burning issue.

Then, one other day, she would find herself mounting the dais to report to the annual shareholders' meeting of Sears, Roebuck—the first time in the corporation's ninety-three-year history that somebody other than a company director had been so honored.

You've come a long way, Cheryl Tiegs, from that lubricious photograph in *Sports Illustrated,* where your nipples stared out of the imprisoning fishnet of your bathing suit like convicts' eyes.

Now wait just a minute. How did forces in the culture conspire to inflate an already inflated body, transfiguring it into a secular icon of energy, warmth, health, happiness, and wealth?

In any sort of success there's an element of smiling fortune—such as being in the right face and the right body in the right place at the right time.

There's usually driven ambition: stopping at nothing in order to grab everything.

And there's always good management. Behind every celebrity stands a retinue: hairdressers, makeup artists, cameramen, plastic surgeons, press agents, business managers, accountants, lawyers, drivers, bearers, beaters, beards. And managing these managers is yet another manager. Often he's been in on the ground floor of the celebrity's career, sometimes even laying the bricks and mortar. Always he holds the metaphoric edifice together. He stokes the boiler, fixes the plumbing, does the painting and the plastering, oversees the reconstruction. Usually he lives on—if not off—the figurative premises. He's called the super.

Cheryl Tiegs was beautiful, ambitious, and lucky—and *very* lucky in the beautiful managing of her career by her ambitious supers.

"Cheryl's not just a star," judges Jerry Ford, co-owner with his wife, Eileen, of Ford Models, the world's largest and most successful modeling agency. "She's the biggest star that's ever come out of this business. We've represented Jean Shrimpton, Suzy Parker, Candice Bergen, Ali MacGraw, Lauren Hutton, Cristina Ferrare, Brooke Shields, and every other big name over the years, and none of them came even close to the size and scope of Cheryl. It's not only the money I'm talking about, although she single-handedly changed the pricing structure in the industry. It's that the public sees her not as a model but as a personality. You can imagine what a great thing it is for us just to say we represent her."

("Jerry Ford talking about what Cheryl means to his business," laughs Tiegs's current husband, photographer Peter Beard, "is like a cattleman telling you how much a prize Charolais or Limousin means to him. No one outside the beef business can possibly understand how one dumb cow can be worth a million bucks!")

"Yes, Cheryl's been an incredible asset," Ford says, diplomatically adding, "as well as a very dear friend."

Cheryl Tiegs was neither Jerry Ford's very dear friend nor his agency's incredible asset when, at the age of twenty, she first moved to New York all fired up from having won a "Miss Rocket Tower" beauty contest in California. After catching her in a double-page Cole of California ad in *Seventeen* (the first bathing suit of her career), *Glamour* booked the body and sent Cheryl on assignment to Fort Lauderdale, where celebrity hairdresser Kenneth was waiting to take her hair in hand. Back in

Manhattan, a fellow model, Lauren Hutton, took Cheryl's face in hand, showing her how to put it on. Exaggerated makeup, she saw, was not for her—it only masked the natural beauty she was working overtime to cultivate. Besides, false eyelashes were so heavy they made her act sultry—and she was smart enough to know her future lay in acting sweet.

Sweet girls get married, and at twenty-two Cheryl did, to a man fifteen years her senior, the director of an ad agency, Stan Dragoti. Just as Kenneth in Fort Lauderdale had taken her hair, and Hutton in Manhattan had taken her face, so now in Los Angeles, to which the newlyweds had sped, Dragoti took her whole body in hand.

Thus did Cheryl Tiegs obtain her first super.

Dragoti, with his street smarts and his network of ad-world connections, was fully equipped to superintend the bathing beauty. He was—in the language of the avenue that had fashioned him, and would soon fashion her—the right guy for the job.

"You can imagine how I felt," Dragoti reminisces, "when Cheryl came to me a few weeks after we were married and said, 'Stan, I don't want to model anymore.' She spent the next couple of years just puttering around, shopping, feeding the dogs—*and* herself, just going down jelly-roll lane. Little by little she blew up. When she hit one-fifty-five, she came to me and said, 'Stan, I've lost my ego,' and I said, 'Sweetie, you'd better start losing some weight.' So a year later, she came to me and said, 'Stan, I have to get back to work now.'

"So I gave her some good positioning advice, told her the right way to get back in, because going back was kind of scary, she'd been out of there for three years and a lot of young girls had come up—big, young, y'know. She listened to me. One thing—she was never terribly verbal, but she always listened real good."

Along with the extra pounds, Tiegs had shed the baby skin of the ingenue. There was, she would now discover, a world beyond Fort Lauderdale. Modeling regularly for *Harper's Bazaar* and for a cornucopia of *Vogues*—English, Australian, French, Italian—she enjoyed the nomadic prestige of the professionally rootless; one week she flew to Honolulu with the decadent photographer Helmut Newton, another week to Rome—to model the collections—with David Bailey who, she'd heard, had been the inspiration for the shallow fashion photographer in *Blow-Up,* wherein Antonioni had taken the movie-going public for a symbol-riddled ride through the swinging London of the sixties.

This baby had come a long way, cooed the Virginia Slims ads she was also modeling for.

The ride was made satin-smooth when *Sports Illustrated* booked her for their annual high-circulation swimsuit issue. She posed as a sex kitten in a bathing suit designed by "Alley Cat"; the shot was captioned, in the rib-poking language of a man's magazine, "sitting pretty in six inches of ocean."

In subsequent "girlie" issues of *Sports Illustrated* there were fewer inches of ocean—and more inches of Cheryl—showing. Until, in 1978, she posed for the magazine wearing a see-through fishnet bathing suit. She was, for all practical purposes, naked.

This issue was banned in Boston. But second to success, nothing succeeds like controversy, and it went on to become *Sports Illustrated*'s "No. 1 letter-provoker" of the year.

The fishnet bathing-suit shot was to make Cheryl Tiegs's career: a career in which processed cheesecake, beautifully packaged, would become homemade apple pie. For the all-but-naked woman would, a fast three years later, become the spokesperson for that most conservative of American corporations—Sears, Roebuck.

With the politician's awareness of a constituency, Tiegs had elected to show off in *Sports Illustrated* rather than in *Playboy*, realizing that if she were to be marketed as the girl next door, she couldn't afford to sit in the center of *Playboy:* A *Playboy* bunny does not live next door. "When I realized I could control my own career," she says *now*, "I decided never to do nudes. I could have made a lot of money that way. Lots of people offered me, but I always said no."

Last year, when five major American corporations had millions invested in Cheryl Tiegs's new apple-pie image, *Harper's Bazaar* dug up from its files a ten-year-old photo of a topless Tiegs and used it without her consent to illustrate an article titled "Fitness Tips from More Top Models." "How dare they!" Tiegs fumes. "I did that before I was anybody. But what can I do? I'd signed a release."

If this scenario sounds familiar, well, it is. Marilyn Monroe's nude calendar was also dug up after *she* had shot to fame, and then leaked to the press by producer Jerry Wald to hype his Monroe movie *Clash by Night.* And so, too, in 1981, were color photos of a ten-year-old Brooke Shields naked in a tub—taken before she became an international star— which her super/mother went to court to prevent the photographer from peddling.

One of Tiegs's Middle-American fans was provoked by the fishnet bathing-suit photo to send her a postcard, the contents of which confirmed the correctness of her strip strategy:

Last month's *Sports Illustrated* featuring you semi-nude was great. One request, Cheryl—don't pose in the nude. I'd love to see you naked same as any guy but I feel it'll ruin you. You've worked hard to get where you are today and it would be a crying shame if anything happens. If you do pose nude, I'll still love you, only I'll hate people if they refer to you as just another Miss March or April.

"Yeah, those *Sports Illustrated* items got a helluva huge reaction—the first one she did and all hence," comments Dragoti, not very much a superintendent of the Queen's English. "Some people got very irate about them. There was global controversy."

Tiegs, with her instinct for the bigger, brassier brass ring, understood that now was the time to take her bathing suit off the magazine racks and into the supermarkets and headshops. There was, she calculated, a much more profitable way to sell and distribute good cheesecake.

Dragoti intones: "Cheryl came to me and said, 'Stan, I want to do a poster. Farrah did a poster, and *hers* worked.' I said, 'Sweetie, you want it, we'll make it happen.' At this point I think she was seeking a new avenue of expression. Remember, she's not an actress, and she wasn't a celebrity yet, let alone a household name, and she wasn't into editorial reportage yet, either, so it was, like, what could she explore next. Here was a girl who basically just had her looks, searching for maybe a new dimension on *that*. I contacted Pro-Arts, the outfit that put out Farrah's poster. They said they were always interested in having a pretty girl come out with a sexy poster."

"An *interesting* poster," Tiegs corrects.

"Bill King," Dragoti continues, "the photographer who takes the pictures of the 'Legends' for those fabulous Blackglama ads, shot her in a tight red T-shirt. Then I hired a PR firm, Rogers and Cowan, to push her. She doesn't like the pushy PR system, but I've got to hand it to her—she was able to separate gossip PR from meaningful PR. So they got her on the talk shows. Here's this girl who's known to millions upon millions—her face and body had been around for years—but nobody had ever heard her say a thing. But remember, she's not terribly verbal, so I mean, what the hell was she going to talk about? It was a problem, believe me. So I invented this issue, women's potential, for her to talk about."

Negligent, if not ignorant, of the great feminists of the past—Mary Wollstonecraft, Charlotte Perkins Gilman, Carrie Chapman Catt, the

Grimké sisters—Tiegs took in her super's issue, believing as she listened to him that Stan Dragoti had invented the first female spinning jenny.

"Everybody across America just responded to that face when it opened its mouth," Dragoti marvels. "Cheryl delivered this combination of real warm beauty and issue, and it was just a one-two punch that's total Americana."

What Cheryl Tiegs was busy really doing on the talk shows was selling a poster that would sell *her*.

Us magazine gave her a hand in the selling when it featured her in the red T-shirt with the words "Number One" stenciled across her capacious chest. The story inside proclaimed her America's highest-paid model. In truth, she wasn't, but hype operates to make life rise to inflation, and so, soon enough, she *would* be the highest-paid model in America—with a little help from another friendly magazine.

Over in the Time & Life Building in Rockefeller Center, it had rolled round to the time of year when the editors of *Time,* like their counterparts at *Sports Illustrated,* sat down to put together that year's pretty package of upbeat limbs and fresh faces. One can almost hear the wires between *Time* and Manhattan's modeling agencies buzzing with, "Quick, give *us* cheesecake too!"

Jerry Ford says, "Cheryl's biggest break came when *Time* asked me to nominate four or five pretty Ford models for a bathing-suit story." By now Ford had a thick file on Tiegs—a stack of newspaper and magazine articles featuring her, fan mail about her talk-show appearances, and printouts of the substantial sales figures on her poster—and with this he was able to persuade *Time* to devote the bathing-suit story exclusively to Tiegs.

The piece ran in the July 4, 1977, issue as part of a cover package titled "Here Comes Summer." That week's European edition, which often has a different cover from the American edition, featured Tiegs on its cover, illustrating "The Joys of American Summer" and portioned out symbolically in a bathing suit of red and white stripes and stars. Jerry Ford sees the European cover as paving the way for Tiegs's more "meaningful" appearance on *Time*'s domestic cover eight months later. Dragoti, however, gives credit for the domestic cover to the man who had been instrumental in publishing Tiegs in *Sports Illustrated* and who today is the managing editor of *Time:* Ray Cave.

"Ray saw this thing with Cheryl about to happen, so he grabbed it and shot it onto the cover of *Time.* He just said, y'know, 'Supermodel. The All-American Model.' "

The March 6, 1978, cover of *Time* read "The All-American Model," and showed Cheryl Tiegs wearing her by-now regulation outfit—a bathing suit and a smile.

Time tailored its prose to dress the scantily clad figure on its cover, describing Tiegs as "the nation's muse, our new moon . . . a splendid beacon in the mind of every wistful teen-age buyer of eye enlarger and cheekbone sharpener."

From there *Time* marched on to celebrate one of its own magazines, for the far-flung empire of Time Inc., contains *Sports Illustrated:* "Two poses in a recent issue of *Sports Illustrated* show why she is a rarity. One has the model facing the camera in a wet, white fishnet suit that is, of course, transparent. Her full breasts show clearly. Most women would look like a sack of potatoes. Tiegs' body is awesome, and her face is so fine and strong and unembarrassed that questions of taste do not arise."

Questions of taste *do* arise. They always arise. And not only in Boston. We must remember that for all practical purposes, this is a picture of a naked woman. *Time,* reproducing the *Sports Illustrated* photo in the context of its cover story on a rising fashion model, was simply taking advantage of the opportunity to have some cheesecake without appearing to eat it.

The Cheryl Tiegs *Time* cover rated Number Two in newsstand sales for all *Time* issues in 1978, eclipsing such cover subjects as Ali (Number Three), Pope John Paul I (Number Four), Pope John Paul II (Number Eleven), John Travolta (Number Five), Burt Reynolds (Number Nine), Prince Charles (Number Twelve), Super Bowl (Number Sixteen), and Cyrus Vance (Number Fifty-two out of fifty-two). The Tiegs cover had been edged out of first place by "Cult of Death," the story of the Jonestown massacre—proving, one might suppose, that if it's sex and violence that sell best, violence outsells sex.

Time's cover not only featured Cheryl Tiegs, it also endorsed her. And with the name recognition its cover story conferred—"A famous face is now a name" was the title of it—she could endorse products as well as advertise them. And in a very short time the products she advertised, and then endorsed, would begin to advertise *her.* The hype process goes like this: Tiegs had been working anonymously for Cover Girl cosmetics, one of the hundred largest advertisers in the United States of Advertising, for thirteen years, but after the *Time* endorsement, Cover Girl advertised not just its "clean, fresh, Cover Girl look" but its promoter—"If you want to make the most of your eyes, do what Cheryl Tiegs does . . ." the ad copy read.

"This fine-looking, tough-minded California lady has packed her makeup kit and her tennis racket and taken a deep breath," *Time* exhaled, "and is ready to move on."

With a send-off of such magnificent disproportion, Cheryl Tiegs could have gone out and sold cockroaches in the South Bronx.

Because, in the words of her friend, the producer Robert Evans, "the cover of *Time* or *Newsweek* is the only surefire publicity left." As it happened, *Newsweek* did a feature story on Tiegs in its "Life/Style" section the same week that *Time* did its cover story. That week was Cheryl Tiegs's week in America.

That week her second poster—Tiegs in the skimpiest, pinkest of bikinis—was distributed. *Time* had given its readers a heady preview, predicting that the poster would be a "knee-weakening challenge" to Farrah Fawcett's, which had sold some seven million copies.*

"I was dissatisfied with my first poster," Tiegs explains today. "That red T-shirt was not unusual enough. It was tight, a *bit* wet, and I had a flower in my hand, a red hibiscus, but they cropped me at the waist. It just wasn't a pop-out. I didn't jump out like Farrah jumped out of the picture at you. The photographer of the second poster, Albert Watson, squirted water on the back of the picture to make the blue background shiny, and it also made the pink bikini shiny—and the body was gold against the shiny blue. That's how my second poster got that healthy sex look that it needed to get into conservative stores like Sears, Roebuck."

---

* In September 1982, Cheryl Tiegs would make the cover of *Time* for the third time. Headlined "The Inmate Nation: What Are Prisons For?" the cover featured an angry young man in his penal cell, supine on his monastic cot. On the wall over his head is Cheryl Tiegs's hot, pink poster, which *Time* had so strenuously pushed—far, far from the all-American headshops and into the all-American jails.

2

Corporate Intercourse,
Corporate Affairs

In the two years that passed between the week the cheesecake was delivered to Sears and the week Sears served it up to its annual shareholders' meeting as apple pie, some four or five additives, consisting of some six figures each, would be included in the package. Tiegs's supers would get her some very big deals.

"Cheryl had been working for Cover Girl cosmetics without the right kind of contract," Jerry Ford says. "For years I'd been telling them, 'Hey, you can't do that!' The week of the *Time* cover, Cover Girl made an honest woman of Cheryl and gave her the right kind of contract."

That week Cover Girl called a press conference to announce that it had signed Cheryl Tiegs to what was then the largest cosmetics contract in the history of the industry, one that would pay her 1.5 million dollars over five years. Thus did Tiegs with one fast fist wipe out Lauren Hutton, whose much-ballyhooed contract with Revlon called for her to receive a million dollars over three years; Margaux Hemingway, whose contract with Fabergé stipulated that she flog its Babe perfume exclusively in order to receive her million dollars over five years; and Shelley Hack, who had a million-dollar deal with Charlie perfume.

Clairol jumped in as well that week, signing Tiegs to endorse its brand-new hair-color product, Clairesse, at an annual salary of the now-obligatory six figures. On the occasion of the signing, Lois Wyse, president of Wyse Advertising, which handles the Clairesse account, accurately predicted that women would buy the hair tints because "Cheryl is a believable beauty—'natural' is a byword for her; women won't feel phony following Cheryl's lead." Cheryl Tiegs didn't feel phony herself, however dishonest it might have struck some for her to be broadcasting

31

natural beauty by unnatural "natural-looking" means; she's been with Clairesse since the signing.

The week of the *Time* cover, Tiegs was inundated with all sorts of offers—guest appearances on television series, featured parts in movies—all of which she had her lawyer, Russell Goldsmith—who, conveniently, carries his function in his name—refuse. Tiegs realized that, although she was now a celebrity with instant name recognition, were she to go on stage or screen, she would have to be more than naturally beautiful; she would also have to be naturally talented.

"I knew I couldn't be Bette Davis," Tiegs admits. "I probably couldn't even have been Lauren Hutton. And what if I were as bad as Lee?* Besides," she adds, outraging the spirits of Artaud, Meyerhold, Stanislavski, Vakhtanghov, and Brecht, "to be an actress, you have to be a really good liar. You have to change personalities. And I can't—what you see is really me. Theoretically, the reason why people like you is because of yourself."

Though Tiegs had refused all calls to the stage and screen, she was still accepting telephone calls. One of them, from Bill Hayes, the head of the Los Angeles-based Executive Business Management, began, "Cheryl, you may be bigger one day, but you'll never be hotter than you are right now." She listened, feeling gold syrup inside herself. "Let me make a couple of calls for you to ABC," the voice continued. Now she listened harder—the kind of TV contract Hayes was talking guaranteed that she could go on playing Cheryl Tiegs.

By the end of that week Hayes had clinched a two-million-dollar deal with ABC, whereby Tiegs would receive four hundred thousand dollars each year for "three years solid with a two-year option." (Instead of charging her a straight fee for the leading role he had played in "introducing" her to ABC, Hayes proposed that he become her business manager, taking 7 percent of her total annual income for his super's services. For the one year he superintended her, she paid him one hundred eleven thousand dollars, 7 percent of the roughly $1.6 million she earned.)

---

* Tiegs is recalling the acting debut of Princess Lee Radziwill, another celebrity with no natural talent. The princess's once-upon-a-time full-time friend Truman Capote had emboldened her to re-create—on national television—the eponymous role of Laura, which Gene Tierney, by virtue of her green-eyed, self-possessed beauty, had made her own forever in the 1944 Preminger movie. Millions were positively exhilarated by the magnitude of the princess's failure. When Truman had adapted *Laura* as a "vehicle" for Lee, he had in mind a private jet. The vehicle, alas, turned out to be an unmechanized wheelchair.

For ABC, the former "silent sphinx," Dragoti's proud phrase for the pre-talk-show Tiegs, opened her mouth each week on *Good Morning America* to deliver a three- to four-minute tip on fashion, fitness, or health. She spoke in a voice whose lack of melody, resonance, and spontaneity did not go unremarked. One wit quipped, "Cupid dies every time she opens her mouth," Tiegs herself told friends she wished she had "a voice I didn't mind listening to," and *People* reported that she was taking "thrice-weekly coaching sessions to modulate her voice to some listenable timbre."

The former *Sports Illustrated* illustration, whose only previous athletic credit was her season as a pompon girl in high school, conducted interviews, lasting thirty-seven seconds each, with the stars of tennis, track, soccer, prize fighting, and football. But the appeal of her sports reportage owed more to "healthy sex" than seasoned commentary; Tiegs nibbled at the athletes, acting impressed with how tall and sweaty they all were.

The former *Glamour* glamour puss also made three featured appearances on ABC's *The American Sportsman,* sponsored in part by her future employer, Sears, Roebuck. "We match the stars up with our shows very, very carefully," explains associate producer Bob Nixon. "There was this program we wanted to do on the critically endangered whooping crane that we thought Cheryl would be perfect for, because the whooper is a long, lanky, beautiful bird, and Cheryl is long and lanky, too."

Tiegs, whose only previous connection with wildlife was an ad she'd done for Cougars, the Lincoln-Mercury species, asked and answered for the television audience the question: "Why are whooping cranes rare?"

Persuaded by the high Nielsen ratings that Tiegs received for her performance as the friend of "whoopers" and hoping to tap the consumer appetite for exotic Africa, ABC sent the pinup deeper into the bush. "Model Cheryl Tiegs photographs the big five of Africa on foot, encountering bull elephants at distances of less than five yards!" read the promotional copy for her next *American Sportsman* appearance.

"I've never been so exposed," Tiegs reminisces. "An elephant charged me. We actually looked at each other face-to-face for a second." In the show's wintry coda Tiegs and Nobel Peace Prize Laureate Dr. Norman Borlaug, father of "The Green Revolution," engaged in an on-camera colloquy about the relationship between human and animal population densities. In Dr. Borlaug's scholarly words: "too many people, too large animals, too little space, Cheryl."

Now wait just a minute. Let's take away the veil, the all-enveloping veil of hype, and reconsider the above. Is it not absurd? Is it not a tawdry trivialization of issues that have had the lifelong attention of first-rate minds? When *National Geographic* or *Natural History* features a photograph of, say, primatologist Jane Goodall with a chimpanzee in Tanzania or of Scottish zoologist Iain Douglas-Hamilton with an elephant in Uganda, we are not offended, because the connection between the person and the animal is genuine.

But Cheryl Tiegs's fond embrace of all things African is an act. *Her* work is selling cars, cameras, cigarettes, cosmetics, and clothes.

When the opaque veil of hype is lifted, Tiegs's espousal of whooping cranes and elephants can be seen in its full, luminous incongruity. It's as silly as if a giraffe were to come down a runway in New York for Cover Girl mascara, or as if a tiger that had had its stripes successfully retouched were to roar "Clairesse Hair Coloring!," or as if a rhinoceros were to wiggle its hips wrapped in Cole of California swimwear.

"Animals bring us back to the basics," the fashion model lectured, yet in the end few in the television industry found Tiegs convincing in her role as concerned ecologist. (When her contract with ABC expired in March 1981, the network decided not to renew.) But how could she have been ecologically convincing when her natural world was the world of products?

Significantly, the biggest thing Cheryl Tiegs was ever to do on television was a commercial about a camera, an intimate and very dear friend to which she owes her career. For another intimate and very dear friend to whom she also owes her career had stepped into the picture again as a super—Stan Dragoti.

"*I* got her that famous Olympus commercial with the guys all falling off their bikes over her looks," Dragoti boasts. "She was the perfect solution to the particular advertising problem this camera had. It needed an identity—a celebrity who was tied to photography. We had to sell the operating simplicity of what people perceptually perceived as a complex camera." What Dragoti is saying is that the way to sell complexity is through somebody the public perceives as being simple.

"That commercial was my best performance performing as myself," Tiegs says today, "and Stan directed it. I say, 'Hi, I'm Cheryl Tiegs, and I feel at home in front of the camera.' See, I'm struttin' along, and then I turn to the camera and say, 'But *behind* the camera I don't know the difference between a Broadway opening and a lens opening, so I use the Olympus OM-10.' You wouldn't *believe* the flack I got from that last line. People said, 'Don't you realize it makes women appear stupid when you say things like that?' I said, 'Gosh, do you *really* think I don't know the difference between a lens opening and a Broadway opening?' " But since Cheryl Tiegs is supposed to mean everything she says in the ads, people can be forgiven for believing that she cannot distinguish between the two apertures.

With Tiegs's endorsement, Olympus camera rose in national market share from Number Six to Number Two. This additive to her cheesecake career produced—for her three days' work in 1980—almost half a million dollars. In 1981 she signed a five-year contract with Olympus, which, in return for seven days of her time every fifteen months, will net her almost two million dollars—repeat, two million dollars.

Ah, the world of hype, where, since the formula's the same—the grafting of inflated words onto simple images—the Dragoti who took an unconversant woman, put an issue in her mouth, and made a talk-show guest out of her, then put a camera in her hands and made her, his, and the camera's fortunes soar, was also able to take a bankrupt state and help to make it solvent. "New York had a helluva charley horse there," Dragoti grins. He and his ad-world colleague Charles Moss co-created—and Dragoti directed—the "I Love New York" theater commercial for television, featuring actors from Broadway shows singing the four-note phrase "IIIIIIII Love New Yoooooooork," over and over and over and over again. (Dragoti knew that if people heard "I Love New York" sung enough times in enough places with enough canned ardor, they *would* come to love it.) Then a telephone number was flashed on the screen, selling a complete "I Love New York" package: Broadway show, Manhattan hotel, hot meal.

Theater sales boomed, the restaurant business flourished, and one couldn't find a New York hotel room—indeed, tourism became the second largest industry in the state. The "I Love New York" ad jingle went on to become the official state song. New York also flirted with the idea of offering the slogan on license plates, which would have entailed convicts upstate stamping the legend onto a set of lugubrious numbers, thus hyping the state that perhaps even they had been sung into loving.

Dragoti's commercial, having hyped the Broadway theater, was awarded Broadway's most coveted prize, the Tony. The commercial is now enshrined in the permanent collection of New York's Museum of Modern Art—a tribute to that more profitable of modern arts: promotion.

*   *   *

If in the commercial arena of his life Dragoti was rewarded for his skill at promotion, in the personal he was punished. For in deepest, darkest Africa, Cheryl Tiegs had not been traveling alone.

Among those on location for her *American Sportsman* special, "Africa: The End of the Game," one man was on a very special footing with her. It was he who had given her the new issue—wildlife—which made the issue Dragoti had given her look pretty tame by comparison; and it was he who had persuaded her to persuade ABC to produce the special, based on a book he had written and costarring her and him. He was a pagan who worshiped nature in all her sensuous guises; an outdoorsman who times beyond number had slept beneath the stars; an irresistibly handsome adventurer who times beyond number had slept on top of them. He was also a fashion photographer, an ecologist, and the heir to an all-American fortune (his great-grandfather was James Jerome Hill, the nineteenth-century railroad magnate and financier). His name was Peter Beard. Their affair was inevitable.

They did not, as legend has it, meet in Africa. The story of the all-American way they did meet can now be told. Tiegs, having just aced *Time*'s cover, was playing for *Time* in the annual *Time*-vs.-*Sports Illustrated* baseball game in Central Park. It was June, and Peter Beard was ambling along as the lady came up to bat. "I was only up to bat once," Tiegs recalls, "but I got a run in. My batting average was a thousand." For sure: She batted the ball—*and* her eyelashes—and got the guy.

A few hours later, they were having drinks in an outdoor café, and a few hours later still, they were dancing to the drums at Studio 54. That night Beard would have *his* turn at bat.

It was a whole new ball game now.

The next morning Tiegs broke the love connection with Dragoti. (But not the super connection—to this day she calls him for advice on every business move she contemplates.) She left the adman for the adventurer and moved from Los Angeles to New York. The fifth-generation-American, Yale-educated Beard would give Tiegs "class" —introduce her to "class people," involve her in "class projects." And *she* could give him clout as a photographer in the marketplace.

The press was quick to perceive that Cheryl Tiegs was much more interesting copy as Peter Beard's Shana of the Jungle than as Stan Dragoti's homing pigeon of the L.A. pad. *Look* magazine proclaimed "CHERYL TIEGS: THE NEW AFRICAN QUEEN." The cover photo, taken, naturally, by Beard, showed Tiegs sporting two unusual pieces of jewelry.

Having touched the primitive world with her perfect body and her mind, she had come back to civilization wearing a small gold elephant charm on a chain around her neck. She nicknamed it "Willy" after a young elephant she'd gotten to know in Kenya, and later she had Tiffany imprint it on her stationery. She also sported a copper and gold African tribal bracelet around her wrist, the identical twin to the one on Beard's wrist. "Peter went to this Masai village to find that bracelet," recounts *American Sportsman*'s Bob Nixon. "He pulled it right off some poor shrunken wrist. He was actually yanking!"

Life magazine featured Tiegs on its cover as *Time*-tested cheese-cake in a leopard-print Valentino bathing suit. All the *Life* photographs of Tiegs were by Beard, who would also be taking most of her photographs for the beauty book she was working on with a silent collaborator. (One of today's sanctioned ways to hype a career is by writing a hard-cover book in one's field of expertise. But since there's not usually a great deal of expertise outside the expertise, books are often ghostwritten or quote-unquote coauthored.)

People headlined "CHERYL TIEGS: HER NEW LIFE AND NEW MAN," while the *National Star* screamed "CHERYL TIEGS TORN BETWEEN TWO MEN IN AGONIZING LOVE TRIANGLE EXCLUSIVE INSIDE STORY."* The story inside suggested that Peter Beard had a rich romantic past.

For all that, Cheryl Tiegs's public light was shining steadily, drawing to it all the moths that hype attracts. Wherever she went—head-shops, bookstores, supermarkets, radio and TV stations—she was plucked at by fans. In Milwaukee a young man with a wedding ring on his finger presented her with a white pillow case and some sheets to sign. Somebody in her entourage whispered a retort in Tiegs's ear and she quipped, "I don't want to come between you and your Mrs." At every whistle-stop, the siren heard wolf calls: "I bought your camera." "I buy your eyeliner." "I love your hair." "You have the cutest smile." "I'm your Number One fan."

---

* One night Beard, from the suite he was sharing with Tiegs at Manhattan's Carlyle Hotel, confused two telephone numbers in his address book; he thought he was phoning his friend Terry Southern, coauthor of *Candy,* in Connecticut, but reached Los Angeles instead. When he asked for Southern, there was a gasp, and then a long pause followed by *"you motherfucker"* and a torrent of similar abuse. "I used more profanity in those two minutes than I ever used in all my fucking forty-eight years," the curser recalls with the deepest satisfaction. "I just kept fucking Beard over, and the terrific thing was, he didn't hang up, he just kept on taking it."

The curser was, of course, the precurser; the voice three thousand miles of telephone wire away from the Carlyle belonged to Stan Dragoti.

Back at the Carlyle there were snowdrifts of mail to plow through: a letter from Johns Hopkins University informing her that in its annual charity turtle derby, a turtle dubbed "The Model T" in her honor had come in first; a letter on the slightly lower-grade stationery of Wayne State University in Detroit asking her to help raise funds for its ecological project, "The Elephant Interest"; a bizarre letter from a girl who said she had had an encounter with a UFO and who had read in *Modern People* that Cheryl had had a similar experience.

And there were other letters, all battening on her famous name with their requests: Would she—would she—would she? Would she co-host a women's basketball association event in Newark, New Jersey? Would she lecture to the U.S. Air Force Academy on the subject of leadership? Would she and Rory, the curly-coated, chocolate-colored, lion-eyed, Queen Anne-legged American Water Spaniel—"Rory over the Reggenbran," "ol' Rory rippin' through a field of cocklebur!"—with whom she had made a much-aired public service commercial for the ASPCA, attend a gala luncheon in their honor sponsored by Gordon's Vodka? And finally, from Olivia, the corn capital of Minnesota, the state where Tiegs was born: "We want to invite you to be our honored guest at the annual CORN CAPITAL DAYS CELEBRATION. Last year we started something very unique when Olivia Newton-John came to Olivia to help us celebrate our centennial."

Celebrities often speak of how tiring all this is. They do, however, oil the hype machine themselves. When the newly liberated Iranian hostages were being honored by New York, Tiegs, uninvited, rushed over to the Tavern on the Green in Central Park, brushed past "New York's Finest," and bussed each hostage on the cheek. One has to call this a publicity stunt. But in charity one must assume that the complaint celebrities make—"It's not all champagne, sunglasses, and limos," Tiegs grumbles—is, in part, a legitimate one. In order to put up with being consumed by a hungry public day in and night out, they need to be renewed in places of private comfort.

In the early seventies Peter Beard bought six acres of wild woodland in the easternmost Long Island village of Montauk. He then purchased a fifty-three-year-old replica of an English windmill and had the fifty-foot-high structure moved cautiously four miles along the busy Montauk Highway. It was later reassembled on a cliff sixty feet above the pounding sea. Beard spent two years gutting and rebuilding the interior. When the mill was finished, he installed his art collection, consisting of gifts from such friends as Andy Warhol, Richard Lindner, Salvador Dalí, Andrew Wyeth, and Francis Bacon, who at the time was painting a triptych of Beard which would subsequently be sold for the highest price ever paid for the work of a living artist. Also his collection of rare African books, his complete photographic archives, and twenty years of his idiosyncratic scrapbook/diaries—collages composed of his own photographs, newspaper and magazine cuttings, lipstick imprints, ink-pad footprints, dead bugs, cigarette butts, snakeskins, feathers, elephant eyelashes, dried blood, phone numbers, motel keys, and miscellaneous fragments and remnants of a very contemporary life indeed. At last Peter Beard and his hitherto scattered possessions were united in—he thought—indissoluble matrimony.

Beard's mill, the easternmost house in that easternmost village on Long Island—there was nothing between it and Portugal but the Atlantic Ocean—became a lodestar for the famous and infamous. There they all came to play: Andy Warhol, who himself had recently purchased a long, low, white, nautical Montauk beach house for a shrewd quarter of a million dollars cash (it's worth more than ten times that today); such other Montauk neighbors as playwright Edward Albee, with two of his Irish Wolfhounds; former talk-show host Dick Cavett ("Tricky Dick," Beard dubbed this media brat, freezing him with the phrase); Elia Kazan, who took to calling Bianca Jagger "Vampira," not only because she looked to him "like a bloodsucker" but because once, after she gave him a kiss, he broke out in blood (she had accidentally nicked his face with the sharp edge of her dark glasses); and Richard Avedon who, after buying the property on the other side of Beard's mill, was unnerved to discover several unmarked graves on his land; top black model Beverly Johnson, who impressed the pants off fearless adventurer Beard by plunging into a cold November sea; supermodel Lauren Hutton, who brought red to some jaded cheeks by swearing a blue streak and giving everybody the finger; the German model Veruschka, above whom the fashion photographer had thrashed with his camera clicking in *Blow-up,* and who with her Watusi body, with its high breasts, long waist, and long, long limbs, was a decadent dream in motion as she ran up and down the steps wearing a white bantam cape.

And there came Halston, to rent the mill for the summer of 1976 in exchange for furnishing it. His entourage, with patriotic perversity, painted the boulders on the beach red, white, and blue with scenes of gay graffiti. Beard was not amused.

To the mill came Elizabeth Taylor, too, who with her dog and hairdresser sat up all one night on the octagonal deck watching the falling stars with a certain sense of sympathetic identification; Truman Capote (Beard had come back from a trip they'd made to San Quentin unaccountably calling him "Trudy"), the only visitor to the mill too timid to climb to the widow's walk that afforded one of the East Coast's most panoramic views; Keith Richards ("He slept a lot," Beard knowingly nods); Mick Jagger, who had taken Beard along on the 1972 Rolling Stones American concert tour. In Montauk, Beard, to his amused contempt, would discover that Jagger, despite the waves of women he had rolled through, could not swim in simple water.

Roy Lichtenstein came. And Maud Adams. And Carole Bouquet, who would soon be mystifying audiences with her beauty in Buñuel's *That Obscure Object of Desire*. And Candice Bergen, Beard's companion for several months. "For some obscure reason Candy put a lot of importance on her nose," Beard fondly recalls. "I had to always be careful not to nuzzle it too hard. She commented to me on several occasions that her nose is the reason she's a star. It's like Betty Grable and her legs, I guess."

Lee Radziwill came. Her Polish émigré nobleman husband, Prince Stanislas Radziwill, universally known as "Stash," had just divorced her, naming Peter Beard as corespondent. "Lee sure liked those flashbulbs," Beard remembers. "She was like a moth to flame, she had to feel the heat, but she got burned more than she got the pleasure of the heat."

And Jacqueline Onassis came. She was working on a movie with Beard and the filmmaker Jonas Mekas about the disintegration of Long Island as seen from the eccentric perspective of her cousin and her aunt, two recluses who would later be featured in the documentary *Grey Gardens*. Beard had spent a recent summer divided between Skorpios and the *Christina*. "I hang about as the court jester," he wrote a friend, "and divert his maj with such pranks as—yesterday—winning a $2,000 bet staying underwater for over 4 minutes, breaking my ankle on an olympic trampoline Ari has set into concrete, and bagging stitches in my lip, etc.—they love it and so do I."

And here to this bright cliff came Iman, Iman of the impossibly long neck. Fresh from the dusty bush. From the thump of *nyama* drums to the tinkle of champagne glasses. From the thud of a *rungu* and the whoosh of a *makuki* to the click of a camera shutter. "I was driving in Nairobi one day and saw this amazing spectacle walking down the street," Beard recounts. *"We've* forgotten how to walk, but of course Africans at their best are brilliant at this. I stopped the car and I got out and said to her, 'Listen, I just hope you're not going to waste that incredible visual appearance of yours.' "

A few weeks later Beard was introducing Iman to the world at a press conference in a borrowed Fifth Avenue apartment. He said he had "discovered" her in the northern frontier of Kenya. He said she came from the African *bundu*, that her father was a cattle dealer. "He actually *was*," Beard states, "but he used modern equipment to transport them. He was really in the diplomatic corps. But you see, we had to simplify her origins because we needed to make an impact quick. The idea was that she was a spectacular fresh ingredient from a so-called primitive source coming into a very sophisticated field—modeling—that had gone so far that it needed to go back." (In other words, bushblack is beautiful.) "When people found out that she really wasn't from the bush," Beard explains, "we got a second wave of press, and the second wave is what put her on the map." Beard, meanwhile, had taken Iman straight to model agent Wilhelmina, who calculated how much she was worth and "sold" her. Today Iman is the top black model in the world. She recently signed an exclusive long-term contract with Revlon to be its Polished Ambers Girl. She is also hard at work on a collection of African fables. One wonders wildly whether she will include The Fable of Iman.

Models, film stars, painters, photographers, socialites, and their inevitable appendages all milled around on sun-shot summer afternoons and sultry summer evenings, sniffing the sea air, sipping champagne, peering down into the open, fully stocked snakepit, and gawking up at the world's largest female elephant tusk, a trophy that Beard's old friend, the sportsman Jay Mellon, had given him for his deck.

Beard's celebrity cliff-hangers didn't always all get on with one another. After all, as Beard himself said cheerfully, "Who can stand somebody who's richer or more famous?"

Two summers before Cheryl Tiegs entered the picture, one July evening between 9:30 and 9:45, Peter Beard's uninsured mill—and all that was in it—with biblical conclusiveness burned to the ground. The lurid flames could be seen clear across the water in Connecticut. "Shit," Beard quipped, grimly cavalier in extremity, "at thirty-eight hundred degrees Fahrenheit my stuff gave up."

Perhaps Beard's museum of memories had to burn before Cheryl Tiegs could fully penetrate his life. At the end of Tiegs's favorite novel,

Daphne du Maurier's *Rebecca,* the brooding, romantic protagonist returns from a day in London to find his ancestral home going up in flames. Symbolically, the burning of Manderley is the burning away of Maxim de Winter's past, tenanted as it is by the memory of his dead first wife, Rebecca.

Had Tiegs's reading extended to *Jane Eyre,* she might have recognized in the culminating blaze that engulfs the novel's Thornfield Manor the same symbolic pattern, for the house with its secret passion must go up in flames before Jane can in conscience marry Rochester. "Reader, I married him" runs the triumphant opening line of the novel's conclusion. The true-life story of Cheryl Tiegs and Peter Beard would imitate gothic romance—for, Reader, after his house burned, she moved in with him.

All that remained on Beard's property after the fire was a simple farmhouse in the woods, which caught Tiegs's fancy as a country seat. In time she turned it into a gingerbread cottage so Hansel-and-Gretelish that one half-expected Peter to come bouncing out in lederhosen and Cheryl in a dirndl.

It was there, while Stan Dragoti languished wifeless in L.A., "alone with the stars," that Cheryl Tiegs and Peter Beard constructed a parody-romantic world of their own, complete with lovers' quarrels and tender reconciliations. There were times when they reminded friends of those novelty barometers out of which pop a gloomy boy when the weather is foul and a beaming girl when the outlook is fair. Once, in a driving rainstorm, Beard threw Tiegs's entire wardrobe out the window onto the lawn. A few days later, Tiegs locked Beard out of her suite at the Carlyle in the early hours of the morning. He repaired to a bench in Central Park—that night's sleep was a *real* adventure, a lot more dangerous than the wilds of deepest, darkest Africa.

On a dark, rainy night in the dead of spring, as memory mingled with desire and lilacs embalmed the air, as the lovers lay languidly abed gazing into the eye of *General Hospital,* a telegram slipped under the door. The bold type jumped out at Tiegs, the three words like fists punching her into semiconsciousness: STAN WAS BUSTED.

Dragoti, en route to Cannes to promote the Dracula spoof *Love at First Bite,* which he had directed, was arrested during a layover in the Frankfurt Airport for possession of twenty-one grams of cocaine. The coke was discovered wrapped in foil and taped to the inside of each of his Fiorucci-draped thighs. As he was led away to the dingy, red-brick Preungesheim jail, he cursed Tiegs, shouting that it was his wife's affair with Beard, plus her refusal to help him hype *Love at First Bite,* which had driven him to drugs.

"I sent my wonderful, wonderful parents over to be with Stan through the trial," Tiegs says. ("Cheryl adores the idea of adoring her parents," scoffs Beard who, once asked by an interviewer if his parents were still living, answered, "Physically.") "I knew my pop particularly could help Stan a lot." (Isn't Theodore Tiegs a mortician?) "I'd slipped into Frankfurt myself for a weekend, pretrial, but I had to slip right back out, because the last thing we wanted now was publicity, and with me around there would be a million flashbulbs."

Imprisoned by hype, Cheryl Tiegs could not remain by her jailed husband's side. She could, however, use hype to find important people to help her help him. "The minute I heard that Stan had been busted, I started spending twelve hours a day on the phone trying to get him out," she explains. *"That* was my career for three whole months. I contacted important people all over the world—lawyers, politicians. Wonderful Bob Evans introduced me to Kissinger and Teddy Kennedy, who both said, 'I'll help you but please don't ever tell anybody.' "

Providentially, Dragoti's eight-and-a-half hour trial took place on Independence Day, 1979. The judge suspended his sentence and ordered him released. "Not that I got off scott-free," Dragoti bitterly comments. "I got a $54,350 fine, which is not exactly a drop in the bucket. But the jail experience was a real educative one for me. There were a lot of American kids in there who'd been busted—most of *them* for dealing. They made me rather proud to be an American."

Everything is potential grist for the hype mill, including a criminal act. Jail was Stan Dragoti's big break. At long last *he* was the lead in *The Cheryl Tiegs-Stan Dragoti-Peter Beard Story.*

"I didn't get my real notoriety," Dragoti says, betraying his belated understanding that a super's priority job is to superintend himself, "till right after the bust-up and the bust. When *Time* was doing the cover on Cheryl, they came up to my agency, a four-hundred-million-dollar ad agency, and ate in my executive dining room, and their article made me out to be some guy who just lucked out with his wife. In one of the *People* stories on us, there was a shot of me on the telephone, and the copy read: 'From their home pool, hubby Dragoti does the wheeler-dealing.' I mean, a wheeler-dealer is someone who's on the phone all day creating hype out of nothing. I'm from the *East,* man—I'm a very substantial human being. I'm from a very structured life back East here. Just deal with who I am. I could never understand it. I already had Cheryl's success, Alka-Seltzer 'Try It, You'll Like It,' 'I Love New York,' and a hit movie all going for me, but it took a broken marriage and a drug bust!" To his very great satisfaction—for fame, he discovered, is the most soothing narcotic of them all—Dragoti had become a public personality himself.

When the suspended Stan arrived at the L.A. airport—thighs clean as a hound's tooth—Cheryl was there to greet him—accompanied by fifty-six reporters. After spending the weekend welcoming him back, she flew to Africa to join her lover, Beard. In the future whenever Dragoti, in S. J. Perelman's redolent phrase, "skyed in" to Manhattan from the City of the Angels, he and Tiegs would have a late dinner at Elaine's, the restaurant where public people go to be private in public. Now that both of them had name recognition, they could enjoy their spaghetti and veal chops twice as much.

Over one of their publicly private dinners at Elaine's, Dragoti reassured Tiegs that their separation would not hurt her image provided they could show the American public that they were still the best of friends. "Look at it this way," he explained to her, "women will say to themselves, 'Cheryl Tiegs was married ten years and loved her husband *deeply,* but then she went off with another man because she'd gone through one life and she needed to have another. And look, she and her husband are still the *best* of friends, they even work together.' And then, hon, they'll identify with you—'Cheryl is a *lovely* girl and tragedy has even happened to *her* and she's overcoming it, so hey, maybe *I* don't have to spend a whole lifetime with one man, either, maybe I can fall in love, too, and be happy for five, six, seven years, and then someone else'll come along." Moved, Dragoti reached out and took Tiegs's left hand—her ring hand—and held it. At that precise moment a photographer snapped.

Naturally, the photograph of Dragoti and Tiegs holding hands appeared the next day in the *New York Post*—captioned "Getting Back Together." The *National Star* spun a more elaborate confection: "The couple's rekindled love for each other burst into the open when Dragoti flew to New York recently and took Cheryl to a romantic dinner for two at Elaine's. They were pictured kissing, hugging and holding hands . . ."

Tiegs bristled—she always had at any hint of inimical publicity—at the newspapers' implication that there were still two romantic leads in her life.

Dragoti, on the other hand, wasn't a bit fazed by the photograph.

He was already in the future, superintending another Eliza Doolittle, as the *New York Post* posted:

> **Stan Dragoti,** in town to sign a major TV deal, has flipped for ingenue supermodel **Carol Alt.**
>
> Dragoti, the former ad exec who masterminded the highly successful *I Love New York* campaign, is also the Svengali who guided his ex-wife **Cheryl Tiegs** to the pinnacle of modeling stardom.
>
> So he knows what he means when he tells our man **Alan Markfield:** "Carol is a young **Gene Tierney.** This girl is going to be a major, major star."
>
> He will be testing Carol, 20, for the starring role in his new TV movie.
>
> But Dragoti has more than a professional interest in the beautiful young brunette.
>
> Earlier this week, they were spotted huddling at the posh Elaine's.

If the above passage seems repetitive, well, it is—hype patterns *are* repetitive. So if the episode that follows seems repetitive . . .

Suddenly, Tiegs's other great and good friend, producer Robert Evans, was busted for possession of $19,000 worth of cocaine, a mere pinch of the spoon compared to Dragoti's $54,000 non-drop in the bucket.*

Evans's judge sentenced him to a year's probation, decreeing that his record would be expunged if "Mr. Evans used his unique talents"— had he not, after all, produced *The Godfather, Love Story, Chinatown, Marathon Man, Urban Cowboy,* and *Popeye?*—"to look for a breakthrough where others have failed in this horrible thing of drug abuse to children."

Thus was born one of the most cynical hypes of the American century: Bob Evans's "probation project"—court-ordered humanitarianism at its most disproportionate.

Evans talked NBC into sponsoring a week-long alternative-to-drugs campaign with the catchy, ad-smart tag: "Get High on Yourself Week in America." He then talked into participating in an hour-long kickoff spe-

---

* In 1982, another good friend of Tiegs, John DeLorean, husband of her great friend, model Cristina Ferrare, would get caught in a similar snowstorm.

cial sixty of his celebrity friends, each of whom had to sign a statement that he or she was drug-free and intended to stay that way. Among them: Muhammad Ali, Carol Burnett, Farrah Fawcett, Andy Gibb, Rosey Grier, Dorothy Hamill, Bob Hope, Julius (Dr. J) Erving, Cheryl Ladd, Mary Tyler Moore, Paul Newman, Olivia Newton-John, Victoria Principal, Christopher Reeve, Burt Reynolds, John Travolta, Joanne Woodward, and, naturally, Cheryl Tiegs, who also offered to help raise money to buy TV time. Tiegs would never forget that it was Evans who had helped her get Dragoti sprung by introducing her to Kissinger and Teddy Kennedy. Now she could repay her debt to Evans by helping him pay his debt to society, and at the same time she could do some well-publicized philanthropy of her own.

A "Get High on Yourself" song was commissioned from the man who composed the "I Love New York" theme song, Steve Karman, the nation's premier jingleman. In the event, it was sung with unflagging animation by the sixty-odd stars. Then, high on themselves and each other, they proceeded to torture the sixty-two million children of America with a sappy caveat about a serious subject: "Reject a foreign substance that will screw your brains around."

The show added up to a full soporific hour of hype. A hype of itself—"This is the most major campaign ever done," it persistently reminded us. "A song was written, a commercial was made, a spirit was started, this is how it happened." (No mention was ever made of Evans's bust although in effect he was doing time on prime time.) A hype of all the participating stars. And, especially, a hype of Bob Evans: The "special" could qualify as the entry in the *Guinness Book of World Records* under "Most Shameless Self-Promotion"—"Bob Evans," the stars kept repeating, to a beat that sounded suspiciously like "IIIIIIII Love New York."

"Get high on yourself,/ You can set your own style, . . ./ You can make yourself get higher than you have ever known," Cheryl Tiegs sang, jumping up and down beside Bob Hope, who jumped high to whisper in her ear an invitation to appear on the forthcoming Bob Hope special.

3

Corporate Nuptials, Corporate Matrimony

When Cheryl Tiegs returned to New York, ABC was waiting for her with the heady news that soon she *would* be able to set her own style. The ABC merchandising division was negotiating a deal with Sears, Roebuck that would be the biggest coup of her career: her own signature clothes line.

Dressed in their corporate livery, three ABC executives had approached Allen Fredman, vice-president of Colonial Corporation of America, a division of the Kayser-Roth Corporation and one of the major producers of apparel for the chain circuit, the rag trade's equivalent of fast food. "I only deal with three customers: Sears, Penney, and K-Mart—I *am* Middle America," Fredman says grandly.

Cheryl Tiegs, the nation's most natural beauty, and Sears, the nation's most national retailer, were made for each other, Fredman saw. "Female apparel had the greatest growth potential at Sears as well as at Penney and K-Mart," he explains. "Sixty percent of all children's clothing in the U.S. is bought at Sears, Penney, and K-Mart, and thirty-five or forty percent of all men's wear. But in female apparel my three big clients weren't accounting for more than ten percent of market share, because most women shop in ego-intensive areas like department stores and specialty shops."

Fredman predicted that Tiegs would be the perfect Pied Piper for his crusade. He smacked his lips as he pictured the women of America abandoning the boutiques and specialty stores, the fashion floors of Field's and I. Magnin's, and marching after Cheryl Tiegs into Sears.

"Cheryl is the *best* example of the girl next door," Fredman announces. "She *can* look sexy but she *always* looks cute. She strikes that perfect balance right in the middle. The Bible Belt, as we refer to many

47

of our customers, were very offended by the type of ad campaign that Calvin Klein carried on with Brooke Shields—nothing comes between her and her Calvins, my ass!*—which has a high connotation of sex.

"But Cheryl was just right—she was even *born* in Middle America. And her taste level has never really gotten too far above it. She doesn't have a very high awareness of high fashion. That made her perfect in my books."

Fredman advised ABC Merchandising to push for a Sears deal. Sears, however, decided to commission a market-research study before offering Tiegs a contract.

Sears's female customers were asked to rank the following list of celebrity names in terms of which one they'd prefer to have stitched on their bottoms: Doris Day, Bo Derek, Cheryl Ladd, Suzanne Somers, Cheryl Tiegs, and Gloria Vanderbilt ("They wanted to see how Cheryl would rank against Gloria," Fredman explains, "even though Gloria was already positioned with Murjani").

Sears found that the majority of women interviewed preferred Cheryl Tiegs; Bo Derek and Suzanne Somers were apparently "too threatening," Cheryl Ladd "too young," and Doris Day, the original Miss Middle America, "too unknown."

Sears had long been attracted to Tiegs—back in 1966, she was the

---

* Fredman doesn't know what it was exactly that did come between Brooke Shields and her Calvins. One day in May in the middle of the night Calvin Klein's phone rang and his answering service picked up. The operator, hearing only a whine, asked, "Who is this?"

"It's Brooke! I've got to get ahold of Calvin right away. My zipper's gotten stuck halfway up, and part of my skin from my stomach is stuck in the zipper. What am I going to do? Calvin's always told me what to do before. And I can't ask my mother to help me, 'cause she's not here. And I can't go to a neighbor, 'cause I'm having problems getting up and down the stairs. So, see, there's no one here but me. Please, please, call Calvin. It hurts *so much.*"

The answering service operator, who had thought she'd heard it all, told Brooke Shields, the ideal of feminine beauty, the idol of millions, and multimillion-dollar one-woman conglomerate, "Lie down on your back, suck in your stomach, and pull your zipper down."

"Wait a minute. Okay, I'm lying down. *Now* what do I do?"

"Suck in your stomach and release the zipper."

"*Ohh*, it worked," squealed the girl who had to be told what to do in order to get out of her pants—the pants that Calvin Klein paid her three quarters of a million dollars a year to get into.

Saying good night, the answering-service operator filed a message for Calvin Klein that at 1:57 A.M. Brooke Shields had called.

company's catalog cover girl. Now, thirteen years later, her credibility pretested, she signed a letter of understanding with Kayser-Roth which guaranteed her a seven-figure annual income from Sears as well as a substantial share in the profits. Kayser-Roth/Colonial would manufacture the clothes and sell them to Sears; Tiegs would receive a royalty on whatever Sears sold.

"It was my lawyer, Russ, who did it," Tiegs says of her Goldsmith, celebrating yet another super. "He toppled the Sears Tower." (The tower in question, 110 stories and 1,450 feet high, is the world's tallest building.) "He got me the most fantastic merchandising contract—design control, quality control, control over type of garment, and a strong say in the advertising. I have final approval, which is something no other celebrity in this business has—including Gloria Vanderbilt. But I couldn't have signed the contract unless I really believed in jeans.

"Somebody once offered me a doll to endorse. See, Farrah had a doll. They were willing to give me fifty percent of my doll. *Plus* I could have had control over her hair, her face, her wardrobe, her accessories, and the box she came in." (The real Cheryl Tiegs had had to have Kenneth take her hair, and Lauren Hutton take her face, and Stan Dragoti take her whole body in hand, but the Cheryl Tiegs doll would have just one super, Tiegs herself, to take her hair, face, and little plastic body in hand.) "Little girls like me, and that means a lot, because if they're jealous of you, if they *don't* like you, your doll will never make it. But I said no—a doll isn't serious, a doll isn't *dignified*. Dolly Parton has a doll, but Phyllis George doesn't.

"I said no to the first jeans offer I got," Tiegs goes on, " 'cause they were going to put 'Cheryl Tiegs' all over them without giving me any design input. It's a whole different ball game with Sears. My only tiff with them was over the logo. I wanted a rabbit, or an elephant." It's no wonder that Sears balked. Catherine the Great might have allowed a horse on her, but the average Middle American woman would no more allow an elephant on her than she would a hippo—or, for that matter, a bunny, given *its* reputation for fornication. A less objectionable logo would have been a camera. But Sears, rejecting the funny bunny and the inelegant elephant, persuaded Tiegs that her own initials were enough: CT.

The company proceeded to put double the amount of money into the Tiegs line than it had ever put into a new product line before, in the process transforming cheesecake with its Cover Girl, Clairol, Olympus, and ABC additives into all-American apple pie.

Contract and logo were in place; now the Sears store managers and regional officers had to be hyped so they would hype the "CT" line. A clip of Tiegs's Olympus camera "bike commercial" was doctored up for showing at Sears regional meetings—with the faces of top executives in the women's fashion division superimposed on the faces of the Olympus bike riders.

Very soon thereafter, the Sears in-house organ announced the birth of Cheryl Tiegs jeans—trumpeting value, styling, and quality ("Our quality standards equal or even surpass designer label standards"—inferring that the rich-little-poor-girl Cheryl might throw a curve at the poor-little-rich-girl Gloria in her spacious Vanderbilt jeans).

In every Cheryl Tiegs Shop at Sears across the nation, there would be a "point of purchase video" machine featuring Cheryl Tiegs taking the unpracticed customer "through the signature collection showing her how to put the items together for TOTAL OUTFITS."

"Over $35 million in advertising will be spent on Cheryl Tiegs products in the next 18 months," the in-house organ shrilled. On its last glossy page there was a collage of the career additives, all the products Tiegs had had to hype before she could capture Sears: photographs of Cheryl Tiegs selling Cover Girl, Cheryl Tiegs selling Clairol and Clairesse, Cheryl Tiegs selling Olympus, and Cheryl Tiegs selling Cheryl Tiegs with her own picture on her own beauty book—all leading up to and illustrating the last three words of the brochure: "CHERYL TIEGS PRE-SOLD."

Post-sales would show that preselling sells, but meanwhile there was skepticism in the best jeans circles. Allen Fredman recounts: "Paul Guez—he's one of the three brothers who own Sasson jeans—bet me that the Cheryl Tiegs line was never going to fly." (Not fly? When every single pair of zippered jeans was singing "I'm Cheryl, fly me!"? *Sasson* jeans were certainly flying, saying "I'm *Sassoon*, buy me!" At least that's what Vidal Sassoon heard; he took Sasson to court, forcing it to alter the way it was pronouncing its name.) "Well, a few months later, Guez admitted *publicly* that Cheryl Tiegs was the most desirable of all designer lines. That didn't come as news to *me*, because—but don't tell anybody this—*I* make the big three. I make Sasson jeans, I make Calvin Klein jeans, and I make Jordache jeans, and they're *all the same*. You bet your ass they are! The only difference is Cheryl's retail for twenty and the rest of them retail for forty and up."

That Tiegs was flying national and commercial wasn't thanks just to Goldsmith, Fredman, and Sears. In the old Hollywood tradition in which the star gets work for the men in her life, Tiegs had had Sears hire Dragoti to direct her television spots and Beard to take the photographs for her print ads and the Sears, Roebuck catalog. "It *is* all a bit incestuous," she admits, though so far she hasn't included her father, the mortician, in the act.

"We have sort of a family chemistry going here," Fredman confirms. "We've achieved an astounding photographic standard with Peter."

"If Sears only knew how fucking easy it was to do those photos!" Beard expostulates characteristically. "Photography is a parasite field, because all you have to do is squeeze your index finger, and you've got yourself a profession. I made forty thousand bucks for a few days' work. Sears wants quality? They can give me another four grand a day."

Promotional gimmicks tend to be repetitive. This time it was Beard who proposed the inevitable poster, suggesting that Sears distribute to its eight hundred stores give-away posters of Tiegs and a photogenic animal. Sears, influenced perhaps by the fact that Tiegs had once advertised Cougars, suggested one.

With immense difficulty (cougars, also known as pumas or mountain lions, are extinct in the eastern United States), a puma was located, and booked for a half-day's work. The animal, which hailed from a Rocky Mountain state, had an agent but no New York license, so the shoot had to be delayed while the agent flew to Albany to secure the puma's papers.

The rescheduled shoot began auspiciously. Tiegs lay on the floor modeling her "CT" signature jeans, the puma beside her, modeling its own unpurchased fur, and purring (mountain lions cannot roar but they can purr continuously—*that's* their roar). Then in one wild—that is, natural—moment, having had enough of all this namby-pambyhood, the puma pounced and bit. Beard leaped to his feet and shot the animal. With his Olympus OM-10.*

"The energy was so high I got a great shot," Beard says. "Cheryl

---

* It's not just pumas that pounce. Predictably, there were other predators stalking the prey. Olympus, having gotten wind of Beard's shot for the Sears poster, asked him to reenact it. A puma was booked again, Cheryl Tiegs put on her jeans again, and Beard held his Olympus OM-10 again, but this time the puma had no fangs and the camera had no film. The crew from Olympus, however, did have film in *their* cameras. The promotional film thus made was then shown at a photography trade-group convention to demonstrate that quality photographer Peter Beard uses an Olympus camera when photographing superstar model Cheryl Tiegs.

was okay—just a couple of tiny puncture marks, nothing that a dab of Mercurochrome couldn't cure."

The Sears poster turned out to be well worth the tooth marks on Tiegs's bottom. Millions were run off; rolled together for national dissemination, the posters filled four trailer trucks. Beard was thrilled. Tiegs was thrilled. Sears was thrilled. Olympus was thrilled. Even the puma had had its jollies. Everybody was thrilled.

Except . . .

The Sears Customer Relations Department received an epistle from a minister from the very middle of the Middle America Sears so assiduously serves.

Dear Gentlemen,

I'm writing to voice my protest to your extremely tasteless decision to allow Cheryl Tiegs posters to be freely given away in your retail outlets across the country. In this particular poster, Miss Tiegs is pictured as becoming physically involved with some member of the cat family. Semi-nudity and semi-vulgarity are the seemingly bedrock principles of contemporary ad philosophy, but Miss Tiegs's poster adds the suggestion of sexual relations between humans and animals to the adman's bag. I'm not blinded to the professed freedoms of our hour. I am shocked and sorely disappointed that your fine company would have anything to do with such a program. I find it ironical that Miss Tiegs, gifted and talented as she must be, would have ever been convinced that she needed to indulge in this type of suggestive ad campaign in order to hock her wares. Truly, beauty is as beauty does. In conclusion, your poor judgment in this matter has cast a shadow over any future dealings that I might have with your store . . . Methinks that your operating procedures are solely based on financial considerations. Scripture speaks to the one who gains the whole world. In the end *he* is the big loser.

Yours in Christian ministry.

In justice, it could be argued that the reverend's is a valid reading. Our eyes *are* scaled: We live in a time of wanton images, yet we see no evil. And when a voice from the wilderness cries out to be heard, all the supers of hype, closing their ears, hear no evil.

But questions of taste do arise—and not only in Boston.

* * *

Now that Cheryl Tiegs's jeans had realized their commercial potential, Sears grabbed the opportunity to display its recent blue-chip acquisition to the annual meeting. For the first time in its ninety-three-year history, Sears was inviting someone other than a company director to address its shareholders: Cheryl Tiegs.

A private jet was dispatched for her by Kayser-Roth, which owns the Colonial Corporation of America, which manufactures Tiegs's line and which itself is a wholly owned subsidiary of Gulf and Western Industries, which owns Simon and Schuster, which published Tiegs's beauty book.

Accompanying Tiegs to Minnesota ("They try and pick a quiet place in the middle of America," Cheryl explains) were her secretary, Barbara Shapiro, Allen Fredman, Jim Spiegel, the chairman of Kayser-Roth, and Howard Stringer, the president of Colonial. Tiegs had been born in Minnesota, so it was just like going home again—this time to be born rich.

At a company dinner in a Minneapolis hotel banquet room, Tiegs was seated between Sears's chairman and chief executive officer, sixty-two-year-old Edward R. Telling, whom the *New York Times* had just described as "white-haired and fatherly," and Sears's president, forty-seven-year-old Edward A. Brennan, whom the *Times* had described as being "built like a wrestler." Across from her was Sears's former chairman, lanky, aristocratic sixty-nine-year-old Arthur M. Wood. ("*God* what a nice man!" she recalls.) Tiegs was the only woman at the head table.

At the shareholders' meeting the next day, Tiegs listened backstage as strapping President Brennan introduced her. Her line of clothes, he said, was representative of Sears's recommitment to merchandising—in fact, looking across the valley of the economy, he saw that Cheryl Tiegs fit right into Sears's long-range strategic plan. The night before, white-haired, fatherly Chairman Telling had told her that she had already been so successful in changing Sears's image in women's apparel that that image might well be the one the entire company should project: "solid, very conservative, very exciting." Backstage, waiting to go on, Tiegs broke into a grin, then smiled—as well she might have, hearing that the ninth largest corporation in America was planning to reshape its image entirely in terms of her image of herself.

She stepped up to the dais. In her minute-and-a-half speech, which Sears had written for her, she thanked them all for being there, told them all how gratifying it was for *her,* a former Sears catalog girl, to be back at

Sears, and how nothing in her whole career had given her more pleasure than working with Sears on a line that was solid, *very* conservative, and so *exciting*.

Then the curtain went up on ten beautiful models who performed Tiegs's line. Naturally, Tiegs herself did not model, although only a few years before, she might have been one of the clotheshorses prancing about up there.

The applause greeting the finale was reassuring. Tiegs could see President Brennan wrestling with a smile, and white-haired Chairman Telling—*in loco patris*—beaming with pride. Impulsively, she blew them both a kiss.

As the kiss drifted toward them, were these two captains of industry thinking of her solid line or of her curvaceous line? Even they, in the presence of this pulsating female, must have had a moment of being male; even they, as they looked across the valley of the economy, must have stolen a glance at the delectable mountains.

"We knocked 'em dead," Tiegs, as she came off stage, whispered to Barbara Shapiro. "We're knocking 'em all dead, because the line is really solid, *very* conservative, very *exciting*." Her secretary smiled.

Six May days after the Sears annual meeting, on May 25, 1981, Cheryl Tiegs married Peter Beard. The wedding took place in the quietude of Montauk. Back at the house, Tiegs was being made up by free-lance makeup artist Sandy Linter. In the next room her betrothed was having his hair cut by free-lance hairdresser Maury Hopson; Beard had already been made up by Tiegs, who on nonnuptial mornings as well applies liner and mascara to his eyes.

Tiegs arrived at the Montauk Community Church, a place of Presbyterian worship, in a stretch limousine preceded by a security car livid with flashing red lights. A private guard force to the number of thirty manned all the entrances to the chapel; there were private times when a public person had to be protected from her public. The bride wore white, even though it was her second marriage (in 1970 when she married Dragoti, she had worn black). Clothed in a dress custom-designed by Oscar de la Renta—tulle top, full sleeves, full organdy skirt, ruff collar, crinoline petticoat, and an imitation nineteenth-century bustle—her beauty lay at its meridian.

Carrying an antique lace handkerchief, Cheryl Tiegs walked down the aisle to the strains of "Here Comes the Bride." The wedding accent was so squarely on tradition—later there would be the throwing of rice and the cutting of a three-tiered wedding cake and the dancing of the first dance to a lilting "Blue Danube"—that it seemed almost as though Cheryl Tiegs were marrying Sears, Roebuck with its Middle American consumers rather than the swashbuckling philanderer Peter Beard.

Then the newlyweds hied themselves home for the reception. A white tent had been pitched on the edge of the cliffs, with pink and white tables inside; and as the daylight faded, a favoring moon came out, turning the light to silver, and a soft wind blew from the sea. The world was "their oyster, their champagne, their caviar." A few feet from the tent where the champagne freely flowed, holding in its elephantine grasp oysters, mussels, caviar, and crabs, was—in the wedding-cake words of the story that would appear the following week in *People* magazine—"an effigy in ice of an elephant, a symbol of Beard's lifetime devotion to the preservation of African wildlife. It dripped until dawn."

Halfway through the reception, Peter Beard's aristocratic mother sailed over to greet her son's new in-laws. "This is such a happy day for both our families," she chirruped, perhaps in her heart remembering an even happier wedding day, back in 1962, when Peter joined the name of Beard in holy matrimony to that of Cushing, linking arms with Minnie, the most beautiful debutante in America, before five hundred guests in Newport's historic Trinity Church. To Mrs. Beard's gracious remark Mrs. Tiegs responded bluntly. "*We* think it's terrible," she said. "We really love Stan, and we don't believe in divorce." Later in the evening Peter's aristocratic father rejoined his wife and, lowering his voice slightly, said, "I've just been talking to Mr. Tiegs and you'll never guess what he does."

After such a traditional wedding ceremony, one would expect the newlyweds to fly off on a very traditional honeymoon. But Tiegs was too busy working with a decorator on her new apartment—a two-bedroom duplex with six walk-in closets on upper Park Avenue. Taking one look at the decorating job, which had just cost his wife about half a million dollars, Beard described it—accurately—to a close friend: "The carpets are gray, the walls are gray flannel ultra-gloom. The lighting is dim. There are *Easter* lilies and rhododendrons. And sprayed shade trees. But if I were an undertaker's daughter, that's exactly what I would have. Up in the bedroom there's a Jap cabinet that opens like a coffin. It's like *being* in a fucking coffin, man."

"I love my nest," Tiegs says. "It's so *quiet.*"

Within the year Beard could be heard complaining: "Cheryl's put a reality blanket over the windows and door, and she's got *towels* stuffed under the cracks. She won't even subscribe to newspapers, because she doesn't want to see them stack up in the sanctuary of the mortuary. It's full-time suffocation. She imposes a *curfew*—locks the door at midnight. I can understand my not being allowed to talk about Lee Radziwill, Barbara Allen, Candy Bergen, Andy Warhol, and Mick Jagger. I don't understand my not being allowed to play a Stones tape. I'm talking about heavy-duty censorship, man. *I* don't stop *her* from mentioning Ron Duguay, George Hamilton, Chevy Chase, Jack Nicholson, Bob Evans, Vitas Gerulaitis, and Nastase. Her life is total bullshit nothingness by the pool—where swimming doesn't even take place. She's a public figure from Pasadena, but everyone around her can't be a Pasadena patsy. The tragedy is she's at the borderline of being a marvelous person. It's a very sympathetic case."

And within the year Tiegs was introducing Beard, only half in jest, as "the second best husband I've ever had," and confiding to friends, "I don't think it's going to last." Indeed, newspaper copy read: "It's splitsville for the couple, who wed less than a year ago. Tiegs, one of the world's most beautiful women, is dating other men with relish while Beard is in Africa, ostensibly on a photography mission." But despite the shaky foundations of that first year of marriage, the couple is still together—and rebuilding on the charred ruins of Beard's old mill.

The inevitable question arises: How long will Cheryl Tiegs last? "She'll be proving that you can still model at whatever age," Jerry Ford predicts. "She will show that a woman can be goddam attractive at age forty and fifty and sixty."

F. Stone Roberts, senior vice-president of the ad agency for Nox-L, the manufacturer of Cover Girl makeup, and the professional who has worked with Tiegs the longest, assesses her future in the business: "One of the advantages she has is that she's right in the generational move with the seventy-five-million people who made up the baby boom. As she grows older, so do they, and so does the image that most modern marketers are looking for to appeal to their target audiences. A thirty-seven-year-old woman is probably going to feel more comfortable seeing a thirty-seven-year-old woman rather than a nineteen-year-old girl endorsing a product. There's one thing Cheryl has to guard against, though—like everyone else in this business—and that's overexposure."

Jerry Ford disagrees. "I think every ad she does helps fortify who Cheryl Tiegs is," he explains. "Some hundred million people will see it. There's still a few of them out there who don't know who she is. I don't buy this theory of wearing out images by overexposing them. I don't think there's any such thing as overexposure—there's only *bad* exposure. I hate to bring up other names, but I don't think Farrah Fawcett, for instance, was overexposed; I think she was incorrectly exposed."

By all accounts, Cheryl Tiegs will be no flash in the pan. (The point of successful hype, after all, is to extend the flash as long as possible and to make the flash as bright as possible.) As long as she is correctly exposed, as long as the aura she projects is that of Mason-jar Middle America, as long as she stays with quality mass products that are mutually compatible, she will work—and be disproportionately rewarded for that work. (Cheryl Tiegs takes home at least five million dollars a year from Sears, Roebuck alone.)

"Evolution," Peter Beard expounds, "favors certain creatures. The ones that survive, the ones at the top of the food chain, are the ones that happen to work. In Cheryl's case it isn't the natural world that favors her survival, it's the artificial world, which eats up her combination of blond hair, blue eyes, height, and health."

By any estimation, her career has been an altogether extraordinary one. First, there was the bust, her natural one. Then came Stan, the posters, and the PR firm. Then there was "the issue." Then along came Ray Cave of *Sports Illustrated,* followed by Ray Cave of *Time.* Then there was the bust-up. Then there was *the* bust, the drug bust.

And through it all, Tiegs succeeded in keeping together all the different aspects of her public image. For Cover Girl, which has her face, lips, and nails under contract, and Clairol, which has her hair, she's had to be *soignée;* for Olympus, which owns her smile, dumb-blonde; for Sears, which retails her name, small-town-down-home. Like a good politician, she found the way to appeal to different constituencies without ever appearing to lie.

Thanks to the sweetness and guilelessness of her image, Cheryl Tiegs has been able to give the lie to all the truisms in the modeling business:

1. Models don't get fat.
2. Models who do get fat don't get back.
3. Models who've done cheesecake can't sell angel cake.
4. Models over thirty can't sell any kind of cake, certainly not pancake.
5. Middle American role models don't live in sin.
6. Middle American role models who do get fat and yet get back, and do do cheesecake and can still sell angel cake and even pan-

cake over thirty, and do live in sweet sin, and do have husbands who get caught with coke, don't get made the spokesperson for the ninth largest corporation in America. Not even the ninety-ninth largest.

Tiegs is wedded to Sears, Roebuck now. She has promised to love, honor, *and* obey. A tenacious social convention—one whose strength has not grown less with time—holds that when a woman marries, her veil, lifted for the ceremonial kiss at the altar, comes down again, effacing her sexuality: She can still be provocative, but she must not actively provoke men other than her mate. She must be an exemplary wife and loving mother.

Several months ago, two of the children of the union of Cheryl Tiegs and Sears, Roebuck—CT Nylon Tricot Nightie ($23) and CT Nylon Tricot Robe ($29)—were christened with a *People* magazine cover.

What stimulated the cover was some heated auction bidding for a swatch of Tiegs's lingerie. When a former Tiegs super, model agent Nina Blanchard, asked Tiegs's secretary to donate, in aid of some West Coast charity, a pair of her employer's jeans (Mother Sears's first-born), Barbara Shapiro offered her employer's underpants instead (Mother Sears's newest-born). The panties fetched such a disproportionate sum when they went under the hammer that the L.A. papers profiled them. And that's where *People* picked them up.

The article described Tiegs as a "fashion mogul," whose "CT"-labeled clothes annually account for one hundred million dollars in Sears sales. Indeed, the *People* cover headlined: "FASHION'S $100 MILLION LADY."

"Finally," Tiegs confided to a friend, "I've been labeled a lady—I mean, *officially.*"

Lady? Now wait just a minute. The *People* cover shot of Mother Sears showed her seated on her bed, mouth provocatively open, "Willy" elephant locket wrapped round a thrusting throat, Nylon Tricot Robe positioned slipping off a shoulder, Nylon Tricot Nightie seductively revealing a not-very-matronly bosom.

"The *People* cover will double my sales and lock me in even tighter with Sears," commented Tiegs, who, we no longer need Dragoti to remind us, knows "meaningful PR" when she gets it.

But *we* know that, once again, cheesecake has been passed around America's coffee tables—and been passed off as apple pie.

HOW SUPERSTARS ARE REBORN—

DIETRICH, CRAWFORD, BACALL, BARDOT, NUREYEV, AND OTHERS REDRESSED FOR LEGENDHOOD

—AND STAR SUPERS BORN

Lana Turner has collapsed!
I was trotting along and suddenly
it started raining and snowing
and you said it was hailing
but hailing hits you on the head
hard so it was really snowing and
raining and I was in such a hurry
to meet you but the traffic
was acting exactly like the sky
and suddenly I see a headline
LANA TURNER HAS COLLAPSED!
there is no snow in Hollywood
there is no rain in California
I have been to lots of parties
and acted perfectly disgraceful
but I never actually collapsed
oh Lana Turner we love you get up

—FRANK O'HARA, "Poem"

Hype is a full-time job. Stars can't afford to be unemployed. Even if they can pay their supers' salaries, stock their cellars with vintage wines, their garages with vintage cars in mint condition, and their pools with musk-oiled bodies in spearmint condition, in the eyes of the bankers of hype they have insufficient funds when they're not performing in the public eye.

The only way they can stay solvent is to get themselves newly minted—again and again and again.

Stars understand that their immortality is as fragile as the fickle flick of a finger on a dial, as evanescent as the beam of an usher's flashlight in a movie house. Hollywood, which has produced more royalty than White Russia, has seen the kings and queens of the silver screen fizzle and fade out of the picture.

When stars can't be reborn anymore, there are supers to manage them all the way to the grave—witness Dr. Thomas T. Noguchi, the medical examiner of Los Angeles County, who has been called "coroner to the stars" and accused of routinely turning the aftermath of many celebrity deaths into a "circus to grab the headlines."

But sometimes stars *can* be reborn. In 1950 former silent-film star Gloria Swanson, who had not worked profitably in Hollywood in years, made one of the great comebacks in screen history. Her vehicle of rebirth, a movie ideographically titled *Sunset Boulevard,* could just as effectively have been titled *A Star Is Reborn,* for in it Gloria Swanson impersonated herself, playing a former silent-film star unfiguratively dying to make a comeback. *Sunset Boulevard* dramatized a Hollywood home truth: Some stars—indeed, most stars—will be extinguished. As the all-wise Shakespeare wrote, "golden lads and girls all must,/As chimney-sweepers, come to dust."

There aren't always movie roles to bankroll overdrawn or underdrafted careers. Stars must therefore drive themselves in their vintage cars to do something more determined than window-shop for new vehicles.

Fortunately, there are other instruments than movies for career resuscitation and recovery, other vehicles of renovation and revival, other agencies of rebirth.

1

Blackglama Mink:
New Skins for Old Stars

One of the smoothest vehicles of revival—one of the glossiest agencies of rebirth—is the Blackglama mink "What Becomes a Legend Most" advertising campaign. Overnight, in the split of a fingernail, it made Blackglama the star among furs, giving it that prerequisite of stardom: name recognition.

How? By taking the principle of face recognition and hyping it for all it's worth. Overnight, in the split of a hair, the Blackglama campaign resuscitated the once-successful sales gimmick of the star endorsement.

When advertising was in its adolescence, the superstars were not film stars but aristocrats, whom such beauty companies as Pond's Cold Cream tried to lure into endorsing products. Usually, the company had to settle for some debt-ridden duchess or a contessa who'd been born in Buffalo.

Now that advertising has reached its monstrous adulthood, genuine bluebloods are no longer in demand to endorse products. Advertisers go after overachievers—redblooded athletes, movie stars, and supermodels, who become our bluebloods by way of hyping products that in turn hype *them*. In times past, endorsing a product would have meant that one tarnished one's impartial place in the world. Today, it's one way of maintaining one's place in the world.

Hype is the new way to social status, the new breeding ground for aristocrats. And everybody still wants to be an aristocrat—*that* hasn't changed. What has changed is that our old-line aristocrats are all littered with labels. Even Gloria Vanderbilt has been driven to take one of the most illustrious names in American social history and sew it on her ass.

There are also redbloods—athletes—out there shaking their label-littered asses. Historically, athletes have always been America's great

63

mythic heroes—second only to cowboys. Thanks to television, these redbloods are able to keep their place in the sun of public adulation longer than their torn muscles and worn sinews will allow. Their physiologically brief careers can now be telegenically extended—but at a cost. *They,* of course, make money; the cost is to the culture.

Athletes are role models, not models. It's a pity when children worship heroes who themselves worship products. Reggie Jackson idolizes Panasonic; O. J. Simpson, Hertz; Suzy Chaffee, Chap Stick; Bruce Jenner, Minolta; Sugar Ray Leonard, 7-Up; Jack Nicklaus, American Express; Cathy Rigby, Stayfree Maxi Pads; Wilt Chamberlain, Volkswagen; Mickey Mantle, Natural Light; Pete Rose, Aqua Velva; Peggy Fleming, Trident. And, in the most successful athlete ad campaign of them all, Jim Palmer, Jockey underwear. The hero of old was crowned with laurel leaves; the apotheosis of Palmer's heroic stature, his eight twenty-win seasons and two thousand strikeouts notwithstanding, is a poster spun off from his Jockey ad, which displayed him magnificently callipygian in briefs a good deal briefer than his career might have been without his endorsement of these tight top drawers. Palmer's ad—beefcake dressed as sirloin steak—quadrupled the underwear company's fan mail, and his poster pushed Cheryl Tiegs's out of some headshop windows and nudged Farrah Fawcett's from others.

If we live in a litter of labels and brand names pitched to us by stars, then we have the Blackglama ad campaign partly to thank.

At the end of the sixties the fur industry was lackluster and needed a hypodermic to give it back its health. Retail sales of fur coats had plunged from $600 million a year to $279 million.

Environmentalists and conservationists who, when they looked at fancy furs, saw not lustrous garments but pelts hanging together like ropes of mackerel, skinned and split, had joined together to get a landmark piece of legislation passed, the Endangered Species Act, making it illegal to capture, kill, transport, sell, buy, possess, import, or export exotic jungle animals.

So furriers started to think mink—thinking it to such an extent that soon 80 percent of all fur garments *were* mink. The only catch was the scarcity of young women who wanted to *buy* mink. They were sick to death of their mothers' old-fashioned status symbols.

Desperate, the Great Lakes Mink Association—made up of four hundred ranchers producing among them thirty thousand black mink pelts a year—turned to adwoman Jane Trahey to remodel the public's perception of mink, especially dark ranch mink. (By 1975 the figure for retail sales of fur coats would be back up to $525 million, and by 1980, $944.2 million.)

Trahey had always been put off by traditional fur ads, which tended to depict beautifully kept women nuzzling their sugar-daddies' Cadillacs. Herself a self-made woman tuned in to the women's movement, she was determined to show autonomous, forceful females in her ads.

First, however, playing on the word "glamour," she named the dark ranch-mink pelt "Blackglama." But since the mink is not truly black— it's many shadings of all the natural mink colors—the moment Trahey named the fur Blackglama, she was committing the ad campaign to artifice rather than to truth.

Seeing that natural dark ranch mink, lustrous as it was, photographed as blandly as dark wool, Trahey ingeniously decided to make the focus of the ad not the mink pelts but the face in them—and to make sure that that face was so lustrous with fame as not to need to be identified by name. The tagline would read simply "What Becomes a Legend Most."

The most radically clever aspect of Trahey's concept was that the star would not be paid for lending her star status to the ad. Instead of the large fee she could command, *she* would get to choose a coat for herself, and if the one she wanted was over budget, *she* would have to make up the difference.

By Trahey's calculations, the production of each "Legend" ad would cost the Great Lakes Mink Association a modest twenty-five thousand dollars. The ad would run during the prime mink-buying months of September through December—one each in *The New Yorker*, *Vogue*, *Town & Country*, *W*, *Harper's Bazaar*, *The New York Times Magazine*, *Women's Wear Daily*, and fur trade publications. The range of magazines would be extended to include *Los Angeles Magazine*, *Chicago Magazine*, *Architectural Digest*, *People*, *Glamour*, *Cosmopolitan*, *L'Officiel*, and *Mademoiselle*.

And while the ad was running, posters made from it would be distributed to furriers for window displays, and also offered to the public for free—as a publicity gimmick.

But how the hell was Trahey going to persuade a superstar, and preferably one whose name had never been associated with a product before, to endorse a product in exchange for a dumb fur coat? The star would of course have the tickle of being photographed by one of the handful of photographers in America who needed no tagline, Richard

Avedon. The problem was she had probably been tickled by Avedon before, just as, surely, she already had a closetful of furs.

Trahey, however, had an agent friend at MCA named David Begelman. He agreed to "deliver" Lauren Bacall, Melina Mercouri, Barbra Streisand, and Lena Horne in exchange for a free mink coat for himself. (Garbed in that free fur, Begelman rose to the presidency of several major Hollywood studios. But fur wears badly at the elbows, pockets, and other stress points. . . .)

Next, Bette Davis joined Trahey's lineup of stars. They were ceremoniously tagged "What Becomes a Legend Most" and processed, one by one, in *The New Yorker* and *The New York Times Magazine*. After that, Trahey and a young associate of hers, Peter Rogers, didn't have to make any more calls. It was the agents who would be doing the phoning now, pushing their clients as "Legends."

What magnet was it that drew stars to the Blackglama ad? As pleasant as the gift of a coat and the cachet of an Avedon might be, it was the word "Legend" that seduced—the certification implicit in being included in a species whose first property was instant recognition. Within a couple of years the "First Lady of the American Theater," Helen Hayes, upon being invited to become a "Legend," would exclaim, only half jokingly, "I thought you'd never call!"

By that time it was Trahey's young associate, Peter Rogers, who was taking the "Legends'" calls. In the years that followed, he would superintend enough "Legends" to refashion the Blackglama campaign as *his* vehicle to star superdom.

Peter Rogers has been fast on his feet, rapid on the road. He came to New York in 1959 from Hattiesburg, Mississippi—a nice-looking boy clutching three sketches that had won him prizes from a kids' magazine, *National Scholastic,* but carrying his true skills in his initials: P.R. He had worked his way through the University of Mississippi dressing windows at the local J. C. Penney, but to get to New York he'd had to borrow five hundred dollars from his sister Merle.

Rogers's first job in town was running messages for a pharmaceutical agency for forty dollars a week; his next, working in traffic for fifty dollars a week. One evening, having come to an unaccustomed standstill, he was introduced to the adwoman of his life at an industry dinner party. Jane Trahey offered him a job and, putting his early apprenticeships behind him, Peter Rogers turned the sharp corner that would lead him to a bigger parking space on Madison Avenue.

"Jane didn't even know what traffic *was,*" Rogers recalls, his account racing even faster than the traffic. "Within two weeks I'd set up a traffic department for her." Within two years Rogers had become executive vice-president.

When the agency's art director, Norman Sunshine, suffering from a serious case of life copying climate, moved to California, Rogers took the opportunity to knock at opportunity's door. "Jane," he said, "I've done just about everything else—let me be art director." She nodded approval.

In 1974 Trahey, swept along by the stream of current events, decided to devote all her time to NOW, the National Organization for Women, and other feminist groups. Rogers bought her out and, by then no mean adman—he understood the PR power of having name recognition—rechristened the agency Peter Rogers Associates. Today, as president and creative director of PR Associates, he makes *all* the window-dressing decisions in the firm. While the company remains a small one (twenty employees, twenty clients), billings run thirty million dollars fat (an increase of 400 percent since Trahey's days)—making Peter Rogers Associates one of the largest advertising agencies specializing in fashion. Rogers's accounts have included Bill Blass, Geoffrey Beene, Charlotte Ford, Halston Sportswear, Mary Quant, Pauline Trigère, Yves St. Tropez, Mark Cross, Bulgari, and Bottega Veneta.

Trahey's departure made Rogers the sole custodian of the Blackglama campaign. Now he was *the* super behind all the "Legends."

Behind every successful man, there is a woman, the saying goes. (That she may be screaming to get out goes without saying.) It is an open secret that the woman behind Peter Rogers not only was but always will be Jane Trahey. Rogers must live forever with the fact that it is she who invented the campaign with which he is universally associated.

Despite this fact, at every stage Peter Rogers has worked—and he *has* worked every stage—to hype Blackglama. One of his hype tools was a book.

In 1979 Simon and Schuster published *What Becomes a Legend Most? The Blackglama Story* by Peter Rogers. "I thought that if I finally put it all into print," he comments, much too ingenuously, "people wouldn't need to ask me all these questions about what it's like to hang around all those legendary ladies."

The ninety-five-page book is a patchwork quilt of photographs by Avedon and Bill King, who succeeded Avedon as campaign photographer in 1975, and text by Peter Rogers: his own—embroidered—stories about thirty-eight of the "Legends" whose passage to eternity has been furred by Blackglama. Whatever else it may be, *What Becomes a Legend*

Most? The Blackglama Story is not the inside story it pretends to be. Oh, we do get to peek through Rogers's portraits in prose at the cobwebbed wrecks of Judy Garland, now of the defenseless dead, and Rita Hayworth, now of the distressed living. And wherever Rogers was crossed by some old hoofer or young filly of a "Legend," the book betrays it—the bobcat in him hisses, the coyote in him coils, the bitch in him bites. "I was surprised to see her in that red sequined pant suit she'd performed in so often," he writes of one "Legend." But mostly the book sighs and simpers, oohs and ahs. "Colbert radiates sex appeal, and has the energy of a teenager," the adman writes—of an eighty-year-old woman.

The idea that *this* could be a book! The idea that a campaign aimed at selling pelts could be transformed into something that would both sell the campaign and be sold itself! That's a hype to hype a hype. ("If I'd written the truth," Rogers admits today, "I'd have a lot of lawsuits on my hands right now." An odd slant on the truth: Most authors get their hands slapped with lawsuits when they write *lies*.) And, uncoincidentally, a hype to hype the super behind the hype.

For all its gush and gloss, *What Becomes a Legend Most? The Blackglama Story* is a sober document—the history of a milestone in the life of hype. For those who can decode its subtext, the book is a tract for the times.

The Blackglama campaign demands extended examination. In its carefully plotted artificiality it is to real life as the terrarium is to the living moss and tangled grass and trampled stones and insuperable anarchy of nature. Stuck under glass like merchandise on display, the "Legends" in the Blackglama terrarium hold the mirror up, not to nature but to artifice.

And "artifice" is a highfalutin word for "fake." Pitifully few of Peter Rogers's "Legends" resemble their Blackglama photographs. "They may be old and horrifying if you meet them after just having seen one of their old movies on TV," current campaign photographer Bill King admits, "but at least they've studied all their pictures and still know what to do in front of a camera."

During one Blackglama shoot, Marlene Dietrich, after composing her face, insisted on arranging, combing, and plucking at every other hair on the Blackglama coat she posed in. Then she directed Avedon to photograph her with her legs casually crossed. "My legs aren't so beautiful," she told Rogers. "I just know what to do with them."

"Of all of my 'Legends,' " Rogers confides, "it was Dietrich who demanded the most retouching. After we'd done a thousand dollars' retouching ourselves, she sent the proof back with a staggering number of corrections. She'd even marked the creases on the gloves she was wearing in the photo."

If Marlene Dietrich handles her own image with kid gloves, it's because she's been around long enough to know—better than any super—when her photograph is presentable enough to be presented to the public. She is still a serious student of her own image, the glittering image that Josef von Sternberg created for her in *The Blue Angel*. As she recently said to a friend, "I look at my face on the television screen, and I remember how every tooth was capped, how every hair in that head was dyed and shaped, how every inch of skin on that neck and face has been pulled and shaped, and in spite of knowing all that, I sit back and say to myself, 'That is *still* the most beautiful thing I've ever seen in my life.' "

But what happens when Rogers, who is often meeting the "Legend" for the first time when he arrives to escort her to the photographer's studio, takes a close look and sees that she is grossly unpresentable?

"After seeing some of the more recent 'Legends,' " he replies, "I intend to do a lot more investigating before I give out contracts for the campaign. On the other hand, I know that my makeup people and my hairdressers and Bill King with his magic strobe can transform anyone into anything. But I have to admit I *was* shocked when I met Rita Hayworth—I guess I'd been expecting Gilda in that strapless black satin, and not a chunky middle-aged woman with close-cropped hair.

"And I was really *startled* to see Lana Turner, who couldn't have weighed more than eighty pounds. She told me she'd dried out—hadn't had a drink—*or* sex—in years. She goes around with her hairdresser/bodyguard. This Lana Turner didn't sound like Lana Turner. My problem was she didn't *look* like Lana Turner, either. But," Rogers grins, "she looked like Lana Turner when *I* got through with her. The first thing I did was send out for old photographs of her, and when they came in, I told the retouchers to copy them."

Some of the photographs Rogers requested were stills from the Lana Turner film *Imitation of Life,* so saccharine a story about a black girl who passes for white that *Imitation of Soul* would have been an apter title. In the end, Peter Rogers and Retouching Associates worked a miracle of mimetic reconstruction: imitative art—that is, photography—copying a film that is—and was titled—*Imitation of Life*.

"To be quite fair to Turner," Rogers says today, "the bones were there."

Whatever, the Lana Turner Blackglama photograph is hardly an example of "truth in advertising." On the label of a can of peaches, the manufacturers are required by law to list the ingredients and the weight. But on the Lana Turner can that Rogers falsely labeled luscious, he neglected to mention that the fruit inside was dried—and dried out—apricot.

As rotten a lie as the doctored photograph of Lana Turner represents, Blackglama's photographic falsehoods have had their lighter side.

Amusingly, to this day Paulette Goddard refuses to accept the fact that in her Blackglama photograph she is simply not herself from the waist down. Avedon had shot her sitting in a yoga position, her legs crossed under her, but when Rogers submitted the photo for the furriers' approval, they rejected it—the coat didn't show up well enough. Rather than go through the rigmarole of photographing Paulette Goddard again, Rogers and Associates photographed the coat on Avedon's assistant, then spliced her bottom and Goddard's top so seamlessly that no one could ever guess that under the coat there lurked a little secret.

"The whole *thing* is me," Paulette Goddard insists. Incidentally, the Blackglama coat she received for her performance was not the coat she had posed in. "I took a gorgeous, long, slim, evening-formal, full-length Blackglama coat. And you wanna know what I did with it? I gave it to my mother. 'Cause I don't wear black." (Goddard's daughterly gift confirms our speculation that the "Legends" don't do the ad for the free mink— they do it for the hype.)

Have any other Blackglama "Legends" not kept the coats their images earned them?

"Legend" Aileen Mehle, who as "Suzy" is America's leading society columnist, when informed that one of her sister "Legends" won't wear black and gave her Blackglama coat to her mother, expostulated, "Well, *I* wear black and I *don't* give mine to my mother and I *won't* sell it and I like it *very* much," adding, "but it wasn't the coat I coveted. I did the ad for the prestige."

One wonders if she also did it for the publicity—the publicity that she would, somewhat uncharacteristically, give herself when she featured her non-pseudonym in her Suzy column: "If you want to see legend **Aileen Mehle,** better known as **Suzy,** and described as 'gorgeous and trustworthy,' all you have to do is look on pages 78 and 79 of **Peter Rogers's** book."

One legendary mother gave her Blackglama coat to her daughter. "Legend" Lena Horne's very talented child, Gail Lumet, former wife of the very talented director Sidney Lumet, confides: "My mother already owned a Blackglama when she did the ad, but she's always said a girl needs more than one mink to keep her warm. She wore her new coat for a year, then gave it to me. To my generation, mink is an old-lady fur— I'd feel much more luxurious in lynx—but I sure as hell wasn't going to say no to a free fur."

The hype astuteness of using a black woman in the Blackglama campaign wasn't lost on Peter Rogers. "Horne was one of the *first* 'Legends' I did," he points out. "Not that Lena Horne is really black." (This may come as news to Miss Horne, whose career stands as a triumph over a life of racial slurs.) "And I've used other blacks—Leontyne Price, for instance. *I* call her 'LP.' She's from Laurel, Mississippi, just thirty miles north of my hometown. I've also used Diana Ross and Pearl Bailey, and one thing's for sure—black women don't show their age. That's the *least* retouching we've ever had to do."

2

Circus Animal Stunts

A terrarium needs watering to keep it growing; an advertising campaign needs refueling to keep its hype flying. So Peter Rogers plunged into his bag of promotional tricks and publicity stunts.

The first stunt he pulled was with a redblood-blueblood, Joe Namath, to whom he gave a rather unmacho mink coat. (Namath's was a relatively inexpensive redblood-blueblood body to cover. Covering an athlete on the order of Wilt Chamberlain would have entailed draping twelve or so additional human inches with pricey pelts. Since between fifty and sixty pelts—that is, between fifty and sixty *animals*—make up a full-length Blackglama coat, for the 7′1″ Chamberlain, roughly 120 animals would have had to be sacrificed.)

"Let's get one thing straight," Rogers says. "I wasn't inviting Namath to be a 'Legend.' I was just giving him a coat—strictly for PR. Blackglama got a million-dollar blitz of free publicity out of it. *Sports Illustrated* ran three pages, *Time* and *Newsweek* both did stories, and when the coat was stolen from Namath's apartment a year later, we got so much more free publicity, including the cover of *Esquire,* that everyone accused *me* of lifting it."

So bo-hunk a redblood as Joe Namath, who clearly got off on performing on the cover of *Esquire* as the playboy of the Western World in his female fur, could not have survived an appearance in the actual Blackglama ad. Male "Legends" Rudolf Nureyev and Luciano Pavarotti both flourished amid the fur, but they were protected by the idiosyncratic social status of their respective callings, ballet dancer and opera singer. While Namath had already lent Brut cologne the stink of uncontested virility ("I'll go all the way with Brut," he teased in the ad)—an endorsement for which Fabergé still pays him roughly $250,000 per year—there was a real difference between endorsing cologne, which men traditionally put on to attract women, and endorsing fur, which they probably put on to attract other men. (Namath was later to do an ill-considered panty-hose spot, which ran only once on each of the three networks.)

If Joe Namath was Rogers's athletic feat, Lillian Hellman would be his cerebral stunt, his exercise in intellectual calisthenics.

During one of Rogers's almost daily telephone conversations with his favorite "Legend" (and therefore the only "Legend" to be featured twice in the campaign), Claudette Colbert mentioned casually that Lillian Hellman was coming to lunch that day.

"A couple of minutes later," Rogers recalls, "I picked up the *New York Times* and right there, on the front page, was this story about a juicy lawsuit that Lillian Hellman was having with some writer called Diana Trilling, and I said to myself, 'This Hellman dame is too good to pass up—she's obviously a magnet for publicity and there could be a lot more of it.' I called Claudette right back and asked her to help me out and get me Hellman for the campaign, and she said, 'Send over my poster so I can show it to her.' Within a couple of hours Claudette was on the phone saying, 'Peter, there's a legend here who would like to speak with you.' After I put the phone down, I said to my art director, 'You'll never believe this, Len, but Lillian Hellman is going to do the Black-glama campaign.' He said—I'm not kidding—'Is she from the mayonnaise family?' "

Lillian Hellman appeared in print for Blackglama, authoritatively dragging on a cigarette, and many more people than Len failed to recognize the "Legend." As a playwright and pundit of note, Hellman had name recognition, but in most circles she didn't enjoy face recognition. Indeed, when her Blackglama ad ran, some mistook the roaring literary lion for the cowardly cinema lion, Bert Lahr; others mistook her for George Washington, a Jewish George Washington at that. (Later in the campaign, "Legend" Diana Vreeland would be mistaken for Richard Boone by those who had not already mistaken her for *Le Stryge,* Charles Méryon's fierce etching of a medieval gargoyle on top of Notre Dame.)

"Hellman was a real shot in the arm for this campaign," Rogers declares. "Hundreds of letters poured in from women all around the country saying that, who*ever* the 'Legend' was, she looked glamorous, and that it was high time old people were recognized as being glamorous."

In truth, *most* of the Blackglama "Legends" are old. Lillian Hellman was a campaign first only in that she was allowed to look her age— to appear in print looking as lined as the Blackglama coat she posed in and as travel-worn as any of the good leather bags Peter Rogers Associates also traffics in.

"You won't accuse our bags of turning into old bags," runs Rogers's ad copy for another of his accounts, Mark Cross leather goods. "Instead of losing their looks in time, our bags in fact become even more beautiful with age." Says art director Len, speaking of yet another Rogers leather-goods account, Bottega Veneta ("When your own initials are enough"): "We try to get the grain and any imperfections in the leather into the shots to show how really beautiful the goods are. Retouching is just beside the point. It couldn't add anything to the product's own beauty."

Rogers and Bill King together had made the quality decision not to airbrush the adamant Hellman wrinkles. "What would have been the point of doing Lillian Hellman without the character lines?" Rogers asks rhetorically.

The Hellman photograph brought national and even international attention to the campaign. "As well as over a million dollars' worth of free publicity for my client, the Great Lakes Mink Association," Rogers adds.

But for the sentinels of culture, Lillian Hellman's appearance in the Blackglama campaign proved once and for all that she had her price. Some of her friends felt that she had betrayed her class. Some of her enemies felt that finally she had revealed her true lack of class.

After all, would Diana Trilling ever stoop to Blackglama's blandishments?

When the question was put to Mrs. Trilling recently, she replied: "You say the Blackglama man says he decided to ask Lillian to do the ad when he saw the account of our lawsuit on the front page of the *Times* and said to himself, 'Oh, gee, this Hellman woman gets so much publicity.' You see, he didn't say, 'This Trilling woman gets so much publicity,' and he was *so* right. In 1976 I submitted to my publisher, Little, Brown, the manuscript of a book in which I took issue with *Scoundrel Time,* Lillian's account of the McCarthy years, which had also been published by Little, Brown. They asked me to remove certain passages that were critical of Lillian, and when I refused, *they* refused to honor their contract with me to publish my book, which I then took to Harcourt Brace Jovanovich. Anyway, at some point during the time Lillian was suing me, she said to me that she hadn't even *read* my book, and so she didn't know *what* I had written about her book that caused Little, Brown to refuse to honor its contract with me, and I said, 'But, Lillian, if *my* publisher ever put *me* in this position, the first thing I would do is say, let me see what scurrilous things have been written about me.' And Lillian said, 'You're you and I'm I.' And that's it. Because if that man had asked *me* to pose in a Blackglama coat, I would have burst out laughing and said sorry. I just *couldn't* do a thing like that. You see, in my book *Mrs. Harris* I talk about moral style, the relation of taste to large moral issues . . ."

Would Madame Curie have succumbed to Blackglama's blandishments?

Would Doris Lessing?

Would Margaret Mead have? She once said that there was just as much fashion in Samoa as anywhere else, that when the smart set raised their grass skirts from ankle to knee, the dowdy ones took so long to catch up that, by the time they did, the smart set had the hemlines of their grass skirts somewhere else; the dowdy ones always had them at the wrong length—which was wonderful coming from *her*!

Yet here, posing uproariously in a fur coat, was that figure of moral rectitude of the fifties, the very woman who had taken that high-class position before the House Committee on Un-American Activities. "I cannot and will not cut my conscience to fit this year's fashions,"* she wrote, dressed at the time in the latest fashion. Roy Cohn, chief counsel for HUAC and a respectable cloth-coat—not a fur coat, and certainly no Blackglama—Republican, delights in reminding Hellman's allies that in one of her own books she mentions that the Balmain outfit she purchased to wear for her "talk-show" appearance before his committee cost one thousand 1952 dollars. "I've also seen her at the Pierre Hotel swathed in furs and leading a team of Mark Cross luggage bearers," Cohn goes on. "Why doesn't she use the money she spends on clothes to feed the poor? How come she talks like a Communist and lives like a capitalist?"

When Lillian Hellman accepted Rogers's offer to flog Blackglama mink, she did so fully realizing that she would probably be punished for it. After the photo session she said to a good friend, too coyly for a woman of her very certain age, "I just did something very naughty."

"She must have said that as a throwaway line," Rogers counters, "because she loved doing the campaign. She loved every single succulent minute of it. She loves controversy. And she loves clothes. She's one

---

* That line would become very fashionable—indeed, after twenty-eight years, fashionable enough for Hellman's fellow "Legend," Liza Minnelli, dressed for the occasion by Halston, to deliver it in a show about the blacklist days, *Are You Now or Have You Ever Been.*

of the vainest women I've ever met, and believe me, I've met plenty."

Bill King adds: "I've photographed a lot of prima donnas in my time, but she was the worst." Evidently, it was ages before Hellman was satisfied with the way her hair looked and agreed to collaborate with King's camera.

The Blackglama ad was not the only "very naughty" thing that Lillian Hellman had recently done. Officially "forgiven" by the Hollywood that once upon a time had blacklisted her, she was invited to make a presentation at the Academy Awards ceremony. Instead of reciprocating with her own forgiveness ("Forgiveness is God's job, not mine," she was subsequently quoted as saying), she retaliated on national television with her by-now-familiar blend of pretentious self-righteousness and moral indignation. She dressed Hollywood down for being materialistic and corrupt—only to appear a short while later in the most splendiferous of advertisements. This about-face was seen by the charitable as silly, and by the morally indignant as downright decadent.

Richard Avedon shook his head in dismay, commenting to the friends he and Hellman shared, "It's so stupid of Lillian to do a chichi ad right after that moral performance she gave at the Academy Awards."* Ironically, many people assumed that it was Avedon who had taken the Blackglama portrait of Hellman.

In true hype fashion, the Hellman photo went on to appear in magazines where Blackglama would never pay to advertise. Gore Vidal gossiped delightedly to a friend that "the kids on *The New York Review of Books* staff have stuck the poster of Lillian in that Blackglama contraption on a wall and they've been adding fake jewelry to it—little earrings and brooches and trinkets. They just keep gluing away, pasting all this cheap junk jewelry on her."

Soon Hellman would find herself vilified from all political directions. If *The New York Review* on the left had smeared her with glue, *National Review* on the right would brand her with derision. "William F. Buckley, Jr., clipped the Blackglama ad right out of *Vogue*," Rogers says, his voice rising indignantly, "and put it on the cover of *National Review*, and in *our* typeface, which he *stole*, he headlined—well, just the most un-

---

* Moral indignation from the photographer who a few years later would be marketing an expensive poster of his prurient *Vogue* photograph of a nude Nastassia Kinski supine on a floor with a thick python wound between her legs, across her hips, and along her back? We don't need Sears, Roebuck's pen pal, the minister from Middle America, to ask the question, "What is the significance of the snake?"

speakable shit you've ever read." The legend accompanying Lillian Hellman's Blackglama photograph on the cover of *National Review* read: "And Who Is The Ugliest Of Them All? Lillian Hellman." Inside was a review of *Scoundrel Time* by William F. Buckley, Jr.

The poster resurfaced in 1979, when Samuel W. Wagstaff, Jr., a former museum curator of painting and sculpture, and now one of America's leading collectors of photographic art, was invited to be a guest curator for a show titled "Photo Politik" at P.S. 1, a former Long Island City public school now utilized as an "alternative space" for art and artists. "I just had to have America's most distinguished Stalinist in her Blackglama coat in my show," Wagstaff explains, "as a preview of what a commissar's wife will wear next season."

Obtaining a tearsheet of the Hellman poster directly from Bill King, Wagstaff used it as the focal photo for a mandala of famous images. Around Hellman in her Blackglama coat he positioned the Mussolini of the twenties, in business suit and bowler hat, crouching inside a cage with a half-grown tiger; the blood-spattered tunic of Archduke Franz Ferdinand of Austria, whose death at the hands of an assassin in the frontier town of Sarajevo was the improbable provocation for World War I; a gruesome-looking old man with a cigarette hanging out of the corner of his mouth—juxtaposed with Marlboro's "Smoking is so glamorous" ad; and finally, the face of Marilyn Monroe, scissored from a Salvador Dalí-Phillipe Halsman photo collage and superimposed on a poster of Mao Tse-tung—Monroe's face circumscribed by Mao's minimal mane and ample neck—America's White Goddess now made a political gargoyle.

Lillian Hellman in her tiresome fur coat was the very omphalos of this parodic universe.

So many things become a legend most, inspired satire among them.

As effective as both the Joe Namath athletic stunt and the Lillian Hellman intellectual blow-up had been in spotlighting Blackglama, an even more spectacular publicity play, featuring many actresses, would contribute to the long run of the campaign, though itself closing after the opening night performance.

To conduct the first "Blackglama 'Night of the Legends' Dinner Dance Gala," former traffic manager Rogers assumed the persona of a speeded-up *vigile* in front of Rome's Monumento Vittorio Emanuele, for the evening's honorees were to be a tourist's postcard of "Legends."

Rogers would charge a hundred dollars a head—which is what he thought the traffic would bear—with all proceeds going to the very promotable Police Athletic League, a charity affectionately known as

PAL—according to the "Blackglama 'Night of the Legends' Dinner Dance Gala" dinner program, "the best friend of the less-privileged youngsters of New York City."

The gala for the over-privileged was held at the elegant Four Seasons Restaurant in the sleek bronze Seagram Building, itself a monument to the no-expense-be-spared aesthetic that prevailed at the "Night of the Legends" gala. Rogers had managed to persuade Lauren Bacall, Claudette Colbert, Joan Crawford, Paulette Goddard, and Leontyne Price to perform as "Legends" and model their coats in a Blackglama style show. He didn't know that Paulette Goddard may have had to borrow her coat back from her mother for the evening.

That many leading ladies on one stage would surely cause an evening's drama: Who would get top billing? Who would go on first?

For one "Legend," having top billing meant making a *final* entrance. "The day of the night of the 'Night of the Legends' gala," Rogers recalls, "Joan Crawford called to ask me who was going to be on last, and, knowing how *she* always had to make the final splash, I of course said, 'Darling, *you* are.'" (Meanwhile, back at the PAL precinct, the kids were still rattling their chains and pleading, "Send this kid to camp. Please, sir, can I have a baseball bat? Can I go for a swim?")

3

Revolt of the Performing Pelts

All the Blackglama stunts turned out to be worth their weight in publicity. Everyone was scrutinizing Peter Rogers's terrarium, his artificial world under glass.

One day, looking down into other terraria, as any good gardener of PR must, Rogers saw an ad in the *New York Times* that shocked him. Lauren Bacall, his very first "Legend"—his first-born, so to speak, and the campaign's first *reborn*—was featured walking along Fifth Avenue carrying a bag that said "Fortunoff, the Source."

Fortunoff! The Source!! The source of *what?*—Peter Rogers must have asked himself. Bad taste? Why, it was the sort of vulgarly ornate store one would expect to find on the boardwalk of Atlantic City after the advent of gambling.

"Bacall's classy face launched our campaign," Rogers had gushed in the fanzine prose of his book, "and established Blackglama as one of the world's great status symbols." But now, as far as he was concerned, Bacall was a Fortunoff bag lady.

Rogers's distaste for Bacall's wholesale merchandising was shared by other merchants—and regulators—of taste. Walter Hoving, Tiffany's then longtime chairman, indelicately remarked to an associate: "She *looks* like she should be doing those ads for Fortunoff."

"And Bacall's not the only 'Legend' who let me down by running off and endorsing any old thing that came along for a buck," Rogers fulminates. "Joan Fontaine did those tacky Lebenthal ads. And she's just become the spokeswoman for Hummelwerk, an outfit that distributes porcelain plates and figurines. She made her Hummelwork debut the other day at Gimbels talking to hundreds of housewives. Gimbels! Housewives! Can you imagine! The heroine of *Rebecca*, the mistress of Manderley, the star of the best picture of 1940!!!"

Yet Joan Crawford's tireless flogging of Pepsi-Cola—opening not only plants but individual bottles the world over—didn't distress Rogers, perhaps because, while she was prying open all those Pepsi tops, she was no Pepsi popsy; she was a director of the company, and the wife of its chairman of the board. Still, distill it as Rogers will, Pepsi-Cola is no more Perrier than Fortunoff is Tiffany. (One can only wonder what black thoughts raced through Rogers's mind as he sat in some darkened movie theater watching one of his Blackglama "Legends," Faye Dunaway, ferociously embodying another, Joan Crawford, in the horror movie *Mommie Dearest.*)

If Crawford was one "Legend" who never disappointed Rogers, others, as we've discovered, did. But then, as Thackeray shows in *Vanity Fair,* the puppeteer can master but cannot always control every inch of his puppet's being. While Thackeray prefers his little Becky puppet to his Dobbin Doll and his Amelia Doll *because* Becky gets out of hand and steals the show, Rogers denigrates his Becky puppets when they take on lives of their own. He'd like to keep them all under wraps—furry ones.

But Peter Rogers's "Legends" are not puppets, there are no strings attached—they fight back.

THE ROGERS-BARDOT FIGHT

Brigitte Bardot insisted that she be photographed for Blackglama not by Avedon but by French photographer Jean-Louis Sief, her lover at the time. She also insisted that Rogers not be present at the shooting. Rogers submitted to both of her demands. Bardot's was to be the only photograph in the history of the Blackglama campaign not fashioned by either Avedon or Bill King.

"The Sief shot was the disappointment of all time," Rogers says, smugly pleased. "I'd envisioned very little Blackglama, a *lot* of Bardot skin, and all that mad hair. What I got from Sief was Bardot's hair as manicured as Dietrich's gloves. Americans mistook Bardot in the ad for Jane Fonda, who was then married to Bardot's former husband, Roger Vadim, who had perpetrated the same number on Fonda that he had on Bardot—the manicured-hair number. It serves Bardot right for not letting *me* supervise the shoot."

If Rogers gloats over the confusion of identity of the nonidentical twin superstars Bardot and Fonda, he positively breaks into a grin as he recalls the embarrassment the ad would cause Bardot over the years: "She did the campaign before she went marching all over Europe as a friend of the French Animal Protection Society. God, just the other day she appeared on French TV holding one of the hundred eighty dogs she'd saved from starvation during the Christmas season and urging the people of France to adopt forty-five dogs in forty-five minutes. But now, every time she speaks out against killing animals for pelts, all the furriers in Paris," he gleefully explains, "stick her Blackglama poster in the windows of their shops." And posters, we know, sell products, so that while Brigitte Bardot marches, Blackglama pelts walk out the doors of the fur salons.

THE WINNER BY DECISION: ROGERS

THE ROGERS-CHANNING FIGHT

Rogers traveled to Washington, D.C., to supervise the Blackglama shoot of Carol Channing, who was being reborn there as the star of *Lorelei,* a remake of *Gentlemen Prefer Blondes,* the show where her stardom was first born. The price for Channing's participation in the campaign was a full-length *white* mink. While the price was not quite right (Blackglama is synonymous with dark mink), Rogers paid it. ("Naturally," he lowers his voice, "I can't afford to have anyone find out about this.")

Months later, Rogers was home watching *The Tonight Show* when, to his enduring discomfort, out walked Carol Channing in her white mink coat. Johnny Carson squealed, "What a great coat!" and Carol Channing squeaked, "*Isn't* it beautiful!" as she scurried around displaying it to the program's umpteen million viewers. Then Rogers heard her speak the words that would ring forever after in his imagination of disaster: "Blackglama gave me this luscious white mink for doing the 'What Becomes a Legend Most' ad."

The first thing in the morning Rogers called Carol Channing's manager/husband, Charles Lowe. "You may tell your wife for me *never* to wear that white coat again on television or make any reference to it whatsoever, *if* you please," he commanded.

But when big stars are partial to white, they wear white. One night years later Rogers stationed himself backstage at *The Dinah Shore Show,* on which Carol Channing was scheduled to make an appearance as a Blackglama "Legend." Channing swept in late—naturally, in her white mink. "I grabbed her just as she was going on," Rogers grimaces. "I said, '*Miss* Channing, appear like this and I'll lose my client.' " Rogers then did some pretty fancy cape-work, throwing the spare Blackglama he'd brought with him over her as she wriggled out of the white fur. As he saw dark mink closing on her like a trap, he breathed a sigh of relief.

THE RESULT: A DRAW

THE CHAMPIONSHIP MATCH: ROGERS VS. NUREYEV

For years Rogers had been trying to entice the world's most fabulously romantic dance couple into doing a *pas de deux* for Blackglama. His yearly pleadings had met with yearly spurnings. Then, one electric day, Martha Graham's agent called to say that Miss Graham would "deliver" her friends Nureyev and Fonteyn in exchange for a free fur coat and the promise of being included in the picture. Rogers readily agreed.

At the shoot, Nureyev was excessively eccentric. He rejected the catered lunch Rogers offered him with, "I don't eat your food. I don't know you." Then he ordered his good friend, the bulging Belgian starlet Monique van Vooren, to fetch a box lunch from the Russian Tea Room.*

After his Russian lunch, Nureyev tried on half a hundred capes and coats before finding one he would consent to pose in. Unhappily, it was the fur coat Rogers had chosen for Miss Graham: a high-collared number blazing with jewels and embroidered in gold. Only when Rogers dangled a furry Daniel Boone-type hat in front of Nureyev was he able to coax him into giving back Miss Graham's coat to Miss Graham.

Then, at last, Bill King could shoot the triad of fur-maned prima donnas.

When Rogers was preparing to recycle the campaign by publishing his book about it, he asked each "Legend" to sign a release giving him permission to reproduce the photograph. Of the thirty-eight "Legends" he approached, only one refused: the stubborn Russian. And his refusal meant that the book would lose *three* "Legends"—the Nureyev-Fonteyn-Graham triptych, considered by many to be the epiphany of the whole campaign.

Rogers appealed to Monique van Vooren to intercede with Nureyev on his behalf. She readily agreed, stipulating that should she be successful, she would receive a free Blackglama coat. Rogers readily agreed.

---

* Van Vooren's fetching days are done. In 1982 her novel, *Night Sanctuary*, about a temperamental Slavic ballet dancer, was published; she is now trying to launch a perfume of the same name.

Nureyev told Van Vooren that he would sign the release provided he receive a second free Blackglama coat.

Just as Rogers was prepared to accept Nureyev's terms, the Russian escalated his demands, stipulating that the fur be sable and the length be floor. Incidentally, that would bring the number of floor-length sables in the dancer's closet to two. Impresario Sol Hurok had given him one, to help make the opening night of their film *Don Quixote* warmer.

Rogers put his foot down: *no*. And Nureyev put *his* foot down, refusing to give permission for the photo's use.

A year later, Rogers retaliated with a rage all the more peevish for its long suppression. The cost-conscious adman squandered an expensive double-page spread of *What Becomes a Legend Most?* to window-dress his petulance. The photographless pages read: "A Note from Peter Rogers: For unknown reasons, Mr. Nureyev refused permission to reproduce the photograph." In a book that is nothing if not a testimony to the skills of photography—that amounts, in fact, to a work of fiction written by a camera—it is startling to come upon two pages whose blankness is relieved only by sixteen words.

Peter Rogers in his pique has drawn an unknowing self-portrait. His note succeeds mostly in revealing the put-out prepubescent in his post-pubescent self: "If-you-won't-play-the-game-*my*-way-*I'll*-show-you!"

As a super aspiring to star superdom, Rogers should be stroking stars. But his arrogance is so uncircumscribed, his presumption so uncircumcised, that he dares to walk onstage and actually take the place of Nureyev, positioning his own name in the book exactly where, had the triptych been reproduced, the dancer would have stood in all his furry-hatted fame.

Presumably, the only thing that stopped Rogers from getting Bill King to photograph him in Nureyev's Daniel Boone fur cap so that he could step into the picture himself is that he knew the PR value of a few pointed words. The note from the adman—that P.S. from P.R., a man whose business, after all, is graphic images—makes it graphically, even iconographically, clear that in Peter Rogers's view what becomes a "Legend" most is the "Legend"-maker.

But it's Nureyev who wins, because in his absence from the book we want to see him more than ever.

THE WINNER BY DECISION: NUREYEV

4

The Trainer
Gets Into the Act

It's one thing for a super to be engaged in battles with stars—win or lose, he can hype the outcome. It's another thing when a super has no tapered fingers to tap, or even hands to hold.

What does a "Legend"-maker do when he can't make a "Legend"? When the "Legend" of his choice rejects his proffered hand?

Rogers had long been eager to bag sculptress Louise Nevelson. "To continue this campaign," he once explained, "I'm going to have to open some new doors." Finally Nevelson said yes. But then, to Rogers's dismay, she firmly shut the door on him and locked it.

Ages later, Bill King was assigned to photograph Nevelson for a profile in Italian *Vogue.* Although the shoot had nothing to do with Blackglama, the fur was flying anyway: Prancing about her studio in a floor-length chinchilla, the sculptress said, out of the blue, "I could never get away with doing 'What Becomes a Legend Most.' It's fine for show-biz people, but I'm a serious artist." King nodded, knowing that, like other serious artists he could name—Picasso, Dalí, Warhol, Wyeth— Nevelson owed a large part of her success to the arty way she'd sold herself. "She's no purer than Lillian Hellman," he comments, predicting that Nevelson will one day do the Blackglama ad. What makes King so sure she's going to unlock her door and open it to Rogers? "When you talk about something that much," he answers, "it must really be on your mind." So, that chinchilla in Nevelson's closet may have a mink mate yet.

Nevelson is not Rogers's only "Legend" to say yes, then no. "I lost Shirley Temple," he sighs. It seems that, one nonwhite California Christmas, Shirley Temple Black's hairdresser gave her *The Blackglama Story.* Thumbing the pages of Rogers's book as she looked through the portholes of the good ship *Lollipop,* she recognized some old Hollywood hands on deck—whereupon the former Little Miss Marker, alarmed that this time she had missed the mark, cried out, "Why have they never asked *me*?!" Whereupon her hairdresser super cooed back, "Listen, I know how to get to Peter Rogers."

"When her hairdresser called," Rogers says, "I told him to tell her to consider herself asked. But just as she was about to sign the contract, Ronald Reagan was elected President. That blew it."

It seems that Shirley Temple Black, Richard Nixon's ambassador to Ghana and Gerald Ford's Chief of Protocol, delegated her hairdresser to call Rogers with the news that she was stepping back for the moment— hoping as she surely was for another Republican presidential appointment. Alas, she didn't get one, despite the fact that then-Secretary of State Alexander Haig, asked by the *New York Times* to name his favorite actress, nominated *her*.

There is one legend whom Peter Rogers has always longed to have sweep through the doors of his campaign, as she used to sweep weekly through the doors of *The Loretta Young Show* into the living rooms of America in her chiffon fantasies. "When I first approached her," Rogers recounts, "she asked for twenty-four hours to think it over. After forty-eight, she said, 'I'm willing to do it, but mine has to be different from all the others.' She wanted to wear a white mink *in* the ad. I explained to her very patiently that she'd kind of missed the point—that Blackglama was *dark* ranch mink. It's called *Black*glama, for chrissake! And that wasn't all she wanted, either. She wanted the Blackglama photograph of her in a white mink coat plastered across *two* pages!"

Elizabeth Taylor demanded the longest, freest Blackglama coat there ever was for being plastered across one. During Taylor's much-hyped Broadway run as the greedy Regina Giddens of "Legend" Lillian Hellman's *Little Foxes,* Rogers received a call from costume designer Flossie Klotz, Taylor's custom tailor for the play. "Peter," she said, "I can get Elizabeth for you. She'll do it for a floor-length sable."

"I told Klotz to tell Taylor to forget *that*," Rogers states. "I don't play that game—not even for the Number One female box-office draw of all time. I offered instead to give her the same mink deal as everybody else, *plus* I would donate money to that thingamajig hospital she's got in Africa."

Like many other stars who are deluged by torrential annual incomes, Elizabeth Taylor uses philanthropy to make palatable to the public her conspicuously extravagant way of life. Her bio in the program notes for *Little Foxes* read: "She has begun to dedicate more and more of her personal life to the needs of the unfortunate . . . Israeli war victims, Botswana Clinics in Africa, the arts, children of the world, Vietnam war veterans, senior citizens, the mentally retarded. . . ." Taylor's philanthropic gestures are but a public doffing of a Halston hat to the envy that percolates in the world outside her privilege.

"I said to Klotz to go through the hospital angle with her and see if it works," Rogers explains, "and Klotz said, 'Peter, it *won't* work. She wants the sable.' "

Few things are safe to say. It is safe to say that Elizabeth Taylor needs another fur coat like the late Joan Crawford needs another adopted daughter.

Whatever Rogers's defeats in his skirmishes with "Legends" and his failure to sign some of the "Legends" he wants most, he continues to operate like a four-star general directing a winning campaign.

Queried about future "Legend" possibilities, he's able to make instant decisions as to various stars' potential for Blackglama rebirth.

"Garbo! She'd still photograph like a dream. And if she knew what was good for her, she'd do the campaign—get it all out of her system.

"Nancy Reagan? I was told by a close friend of hers that she wanted to do it. *I* didn't. I didn't think she was a legend. She wasn't a President's wife then. I simply wasn't willing to risk twenty-five thousand bucks to have her shot and positioned for the campaign on the *off*-chance she might be elected. Anyway, even if I *had* done her, I'd have had to put her on hold till the election, and then the Department of the Interior or somebody would have stopped me from running her." (Still, Rogers couldn't have been especially pleased when he viewed the First Lady on Inaugural night sweeping to her coronation ball in her regal Lunaraine mink.)

"Elaine? Absolutely not! Too déclassée.

"Jackie Onassis? First class! Someone asked her for me, and for a while there, it looked positive.

"Liberace? I'd rather have Annette Funicello. She's not being sued for palimony by an animal trainer.

"Gloria Vanderbilt? She's endorsed too many products—all of them carrying her own name.

"Billie Jean King? Well, I actually considered her a couple of years ago. Don't get me wrong, I never thought she was glamorous. But a woman athlete would have been a new twist for the campaign.

"Picasso? I thought about asking him, then decided not to. Of course, that was way before the big Picasso exhibition at the Museum of Modern Art. It's too late now. I did want to do Hitchcock—imagine that profile in a Blackglama cape! It's too late there, too.

"Dolly Parton? I've asked. The tragedy is she doesn't even know it—she's protected by as many people as Muhammad Ali. Talk about what becomes a legend *least*! He's pushing roach-killer.

"Joy Adamson? *Born Free?* Her image is lion—we could never use her. Anyway, it's too late now—somebody murdered her.

"Barbara Walters? When I asked her, at the time of all that publicity over her million-dollar-a-year salary, she *had* to refuse. She wanted to do it, but it was just the wrong time for her to break in six magazines dripping in Blackglama and being called a 'Legend.'

"Mary Tyler Moore? Bill King asked her for me years ago. She admitted to owning a mink coat, but she said she thought she should distance herself publicly from controversial issues like killing animals and putting them on your back. Later she did go and endorse furs—fake furs—and that ad had severe repercussions for our industry. That's how I lost Paul Newman and Joanne Woodward, by the way. One year I was considering doing couples, and *they,* Lord knows, are a natural couple. Woodward wanted to do it, but their kids are totally against anybody wearing fur, and that killed it.

"Vidal? Sassoon? Oh, you mean *Gore* Vidal? *No!*" (That, when it comes to Vidal, the Blackglama king is more familiar with the bottled slick of Sassoon than with the true grit of Gore is as it should be: Rogers has the Vidal Sassoon account, and created for his client the clever slogan: "If you don't look good, we don't look good." Informed of Rogers's *"No!,"* Gore Vidal issued a put-down of his own: "There are some things like Blackglama that are *too* sleazy to do.")

"Avedon? Only if he'll take his own photograph—and he can't, 'cause Bill King's got the Blackglama contract now!

"Greer Garson? I'm considering her. She looks terrific, to judge from the glossy her agent just sent me, which is *not* from 1934. The only trouble is the Great Lakes Mink Association has begun to grumble about the lack of youth in the Blackglama campaign. So I'm trying to find some younger 'Legends,' only they seem to be nonexistent. I did ask Bette Midler—after *The Rose.* I thought that she'd get right on her unicycle and pedal across town to score on *this,* but she said no. You can have the younger ones. The old ones are used to being on movie sets—they arrive at the shootings on time, all ready to go. The younger ones are still asleep at noon.

"Cheryl Tiegs? She's come a long way from a Danskin model, but she's no 'Legend.' Now don't get me wrong, I've got nothing against models. There was a time when I would have done Shrimpton. There was a time to do Twiggy. But I can't see that there will ever be a time to do Tiegs. Much as I *like* Cheryl. Much as Middle America *loves* Cheryl."

What Rogers is saying, significantly, is that if you're Sears, you can't be Blackglama. Indeed, Tiegs's "target customers" at Sears don't even buy the magazines where Blackglama pelts are advertised. Rogers's words will come as a disappointment to Tiegs. Recently, when a friend congratulated her on her stupendous success with Sears, saying, "Now the only thing that's left for you to do is Blackglama," she replied, "Yeah, it's a stamp. It's the official recognition that you've done something lasting. It's like leaving your footprints outside Grauman's Chinese Theater." There is an irony in Tiegs's wish to participate in the Blackglama campaign: Having achieved face recognition, and then driven herself to achieve name recognition, she now craves to be back in the fashion magazines—nameless and modeling a coat.

We didn't have to learn from Peter Rogers that stars are constantly looking for new hype techniques by means of which they can be professionally reborn. What's instructive here is to watch Rogers himself at work and to chart the steps taken as the super becomes the star super. For, inevitably, there comes a time when the star, anxious as she is to be reborn, as her competitors have been, needs the super more than the super needs her. This is the point at which the super becomes the star super.

In true synergetic hype fashion, *What Becomes a Legend Most? The Blackglama Story* won Peter Rogers the nod of approval from his own hometown. A local newspaper article actually headlined "LOCAL BOY MAKES GOOD." The "Alumni Profile" column of *Mississippi Magazine* also trumpeted: "From Hattiesburg he set out, New York and the worlds of Glamour, Fashion and Advertising to conquer. And he has. His clients are the elite, his friends the famous, his address on Fifth Avenue, New York, his name often in the society columns of town, his appointment book like a White House register of Who's Who, and," the column concluded mercilessly, "his roots are in Hattiesburg."

What Becomes a Legend Most? The Blackglama Story, while it did enlarge the Blackglama empire, also served to place Peter Rogers on the emperor's throne. *People* magazine, that barometer of celebrityhood for the millions who stand in supermarket lines, pointed its arrow directly to the super. The three-page article was ostensibly on the book—of course, it also celebrated the campaign—yet it was titled "Who Becomes a Blackglama Mink Legend? Nobody Without the Nod of Advertising Ace Peter Rogers." The photographs of the thirty-eight "Legends" in the book were all reproduced postage-stamp size; the photograph of Rogers was accorded a whole half-page.

The book worked to insure that Rogers would occupy his throne for a long time. His client, the Great Lakes Mink Association, was delighted when requests for copies of many Blackglama posters quadrupled after the book's publication.

The battle with Nureyev still rankling, Rogers revised the standard Blackglama contract to include a clause giving him permission to reprint the "Legend's" Blackglama photograph in a book. "Now I'm free to add new 'Legends' to the book and publish an updated edition," he explains. And so the book itself will one day be reborn.

Would we really be surprised were Rogers to franchise a Legend School—like a charm school or a modeling school—where men and women who crave a free Blackglama coat could be taught how to become a "Legend"? All the old "Legends" could give courses. The school could be based in Rogers's hometown of Hattiesburg, then franchised to all the "Legends' " hometowns—Leontyne Price could lecture in Laurel, Mississippi, Paulette Goddard in the Bronx, Lauren Bacall and Barbara Stanwyck in Brooklyn, Bette Davis in Quincy, Massachusetts, Lena Horne in New Orleans. And Nureyev could start the Continental franchise, lecturing on mink in Minsk. All of them giving the lie to Thomas Wolfe by proving that, with the proper packaging, you *can* go home again.

Finally, in true synergetic hype fashion, Peter Rogers's book got him on the air.

Now wait just a minute—talk shows are for *stars*. Peter Rogers has been the legendary escort, helping stars in and out of long black limousines. But now the limousines were pulling up for him. Chauffeurs were holding doors open and Rogers was stepping in. Then, before the stares of envious onlookers, Rogers was stepping out—and into television studios in Milwaukee, San Francisco, Boston, Baltimore, Washington, D.C.—escorted, of course, by his own PR person, his own fawning super.

In New York Rogers was allotted the entire ninety minutes of *The Merv Griffin Show*. The theme for the day was—God help us!—"What Becomes a Legend Most."

Rogers was introduced at the beginning of the show, followed by the five "Legends" he had persuaded to appear with him: Lillian Gish, Myrna Loy, Ethel Merman, Renata Scotto, and Ann Miller. Each as she came on pecked Peter on the cheek. When the group was in place on stage, they who had been reborn saluted Rogers with applause. Then he stepped back, and the five "Legends" modeled their Blackglama coats. Then Merv talked with each "Legend" about her "fantastic" career.

At the end, Rogers was reintroduced, and all the superstars once again congratulated the star super on his super campaign.

During the show, Ann Miller had enthused, "Peter Rogers is the gourmet of beauty." Unwittingly, she had stumbled on an appropriate metaphor—one drawn from eating. From the first Blackglama ad to the latest, Rogers has been processing "Legends" as commercially as the multibillion-dollar food industry processes food. He's taken old dishes, spiced them up, and supplemented them.

And they all come on like breakfast cereals: Country Corn Flakes, Frosted Rice, Body Buddies, Lucky Charms, Sugar Smacks, Puffed Wheat, Kix.

Good Morning, America, this is the United States of Advertising!

III

STAR SUPERS

THE MEN WHO PRIMP AND PROP
THE PEOPLE AT THE TOP

The world kindly imagined that Angelica Early's beauty was deathless and that it lived its charmed life without support. If the world could have seen the contents of her dressing table and her bathroom shelves! If the world could have known the hours devoured by the matutinal ritual! . . . The slightest alteration in the color of a strand of hair caused Angelica to cancel all engagements for a day or two, during which time a hairdresser was in attendance, treating the lady with dyes and allaying her fears. A Finn daily belabored her with bundles of birch fagots to enliven her circulation; at night she wore mud on her face and creamed gloves on her hands; her hair was treated with olive oil, lemon juice, egg white, and beer; she was massaged, she was vibrated, she was steamed into lassitude and then stung back to life by astringents; she was brushed and creamed and salted and powdered. . . . If my talent goes, I'm done for, says the artist, and Angelica said, if I lose my looks, I'm lost.

—JEAN STAFFORD, "The End of a Career"

The Blackglama "Legend" needs a Peter Rogers once and once only: for a mink coat.

But legends—or superstars—need *some* star supers over and over again. To maintain the glossiness of their corporeal pelts. To comb their hair and curl it. To pat their skin and cleanse it. And, if that skin tatters, to sew it up—or maybe even redesign it.

Star supers have their operations carried on the backs—or faces—of their celebrity clients, who function as walking advertisements for their skills. Superstars promoting star supers are an American variation on the ultimate in British business cachet, the royal warrant: "By Appointment to Her Majesty the Queen." So Elizabeth Taylor is the logo for Halston just as much as Halston is the logo for her.

In hype, everything filters down: down, down, down. Hype bulletins, like laser beams, travel great distances at great speeds—to us, the willing receivers. And we, when we receive information, act on it: We *want*—we *buy*.

Invariably, the hype product—be it an object, a person, or an idea—becomes crude as it filters down, often by way of imitation. It's not that the animating hype image loses any of its power or luster; it's that the duplication—the copying—makes the product cruder. Elizabeth Taylor in a Halston, limelighted by publicity strobes, is—to wallow for a moment in the kind of excess which it is the business of the critical mind to stem—the hype bulletin to end all hype bulletins. The receivers are the women who go out and buy copies of Elizabeth Taylor's Halston and request replicas of her hairstyle; and, lower down, the home sewers who copy that Halston on their own machines and that hairdo in their own plain mirrors. Back at the top, the star supers who work on the superstars know that the image business is big business only because it *does* reach the bottom—the most humble home sewer humming Halston on her Singer.

In any business other than the image business, this many workers lined up to finish a single product would be called an assembly line. The superstar, we know, is assembled as methodically as any top-of-the-line Detroit car. What we might not know is that each worker on the assembly line—the hairdresser, the plastic surgeon, the makeup artist, the fashion designer—has an attached self-promotion machine, which sends out hype bulletins about its own "extra-special read-all-about-it uniqueness."

We receive these hype bulletins wide-eyed, not stopping to examine the strategies by which, say, hairdressers and plastic surgeons—in a word, supers—become merchandisers of the intimate, then merchants of taste, and then—if and when they go public with their private practices and franchise—very prosperous landlords indeed, and sometimes even empire-builders.

HOW HAIRDRESSERS FONDLE OUR FEARS TO FASHION OUR FANTASIES

One of Mr. De Mille's assistants next led me to the hairdressing department and turned me over to Hattie, a tiny black woman who was standing at an old-fashioned ironing board ironing a long switch of dark-brown hair. She was wearing a narrow-brimmed black straw hat, beneath which she seemed to have very little hair of her own, and she kept a watchful eye on the ten or fifteen girls who worked under her. "This is your hair I'm ironing," she said with an enormous smile. . . . Hattie blended my own hair with the switch and tied the creation with a ribbon band. While she worked I did my make-up and we talked. . . . "Don't feel bad about being famous," Hattie said. "That's what everyone out here wants to be. Why, I'm famous myself on Central Avenue now, just because I work with you."

—GLORIA SWANSON, *Swanson on Swanson*

1

Kenneth:
The Celebrity as Servant

In 1954 the Helena Rubinstein beauty salon on Fifth Avenue boasted thirty-two booths. The newest haircutter had been assigned the last booth. It was minimally decorated, some would say stark—a chair, a sink, a plain mirror, a counter with a couple of brushes on it and five sizes of scissors.

One afternoon around three, the manager sent an assistant over to Booth 32. "Lawrence is out with a cold," the assistant told the haircutter, "and one of his clients, a lady from Boston, has just arrived without an appointment. She can't always make appointments, because she never really knows how long she's going to be in New York. You're free, Kenneth—will you take her?"

The lady from Boston was ushered into Booth 32. The young cutter studied her head and said that in his judgment her hairdo was much too short for her body size; also that she would look better if her hair were a little smoother and not quite so curly—perhaps if she let it grow a bit longer, the weight of the hair would stretch out some of the curl.

The next time the lady from Boston came to the salon, she'd made an appointment. But not with Lawrence. With Kenneth.

The name on the appointment book read Mrs. John F. Kennedy.

The young cutter was gratified to see that she had followed his advice and let her hair grow a little bit.

"You can look at it today and say, 'Oh, my God, Jackie Kennedy!'—I mean, I just read about a man in Atlanta, a hairdresser, who said he'd give a million dollars to get Jackie as a client—but in those days it was just a lady from Boston," Kenneth explains, having in the thirty years that have passed since that serendipitous afternoon at Rubinstein made millions, not alone on his measured judgment of head and hair but on the dazzling dizzle of his clientele.

As Kenneth discovered early on, fashion is made and sustained by fashionable people; a hairdresser's fame rests on the women who wear his hairdos—if they're the most photographed women in the world, their heads are bound to be carbon-copied. The 1961 Inaugural bouffant hairdo that Kenneth contrived for Jacqueline Kennedy's fine, thin hair— a style *he* described, generously, as "uncontrived fullness"—became a national institution.

Back in the sixties, any style Jacqueline Kennedy adopted, whether from Seventh Avenue, the Avenue Georges Cinq, or the Via Gregoriana, was duplicated and distributed on all the Main Streets of America—from the Inaugural pink pillbox hat designed by a mad hatter at Bergdorf-Goodman named Halston Frowick (those were the days when Halston had to use a surname), to the Somali leopard coat and mink sweater, to the lace mantilla so piously perfect for church-going, to the sari dress and low-heeled shoes and gold chain-handle purse, to the mammoth dark glasses so indispensable for conspicuous anonymity. The day after she married Aristotle Onassis, wearing a staggeringly expensive beige lace top and skirt custom-confected for her by Valentino, the designer received thirty-eight orders for the identical item, which he describes today as his "most famous dress." Why, even now, one sees clones of Jacqueline Kennedy circa 1961.

Kenneth will never forget the first lady who walked into his salon and announced, "I want my hair done just like the First Lady's." She was a woman from the Midwest, from the staid state of Indiana, and Kenneth saw at once that the style wouldn't be right for her. She persisted, becoming the first victim of the nation's newly minted hair bulletin.

A little later, Kenneth was summoned to Washington to script a newer hair bulletin (in those heady days of the New Frontier, the press made it seem as if, whenever Mrs. Kennedy was not en route to New York for an appointment with Kenneth, he was en route to the White House to style her hair). With witty sobriety he created for the First Lady a caplike hairdo that featured a smooth sweep of bangs across the forehead and the back swept up from the neck, puffed out at the crown. Thus did the big head tumble, and with it a whole era in hair.

"Kenneth and Jackie, Jackie and Kenneth—that was as big as hair could ever get," drools one of Kenneth's competitors, adding that "Nancy Reagan and Monsieur Marc don't stand a chance."

Jacqueline Kennedy was the style-setter—the client always is—but like a good star super, Kenneth was the man who set her style.

Over the years he would set the style for style-setters beyond number—among them Gloria Vanderbilt; Lauren Bacall; "Jan" (Mrs. Gardner) Cowles; "Bunny" (Mrs. Paul) Mellon; "Happy" (Mrs. Nelson) Rockefeller; "Missy" (Mrs. Thomas) Bancroft; "Babe" (Mrs. William) Paley; "Pam" (Mrs. W. Averell) Harriman; "Marella" (Mrs. "Gianni") Agnelli; "Slim" (Lady) Keith; Anita "The Face" Colby; Mia "Frank Sinatra/André Previn/Woody Allen" Farrow; and Princess Lalla Nezha, the sister of the King of Morocco, who told society columnist Suzy that what she liked best about New York cultural life was the way Kenneth did her hair.

And for such other style-setters as Joanne Woodward; Rosalind Russell; Dinah Shore; Lucille Ball, who reduced the salon to giggles by posing at the top of Kenneth's stairs and delivering the line, "Where's God?"; Carol Channing, whom Kenneth prepared for her role in Shaw's *Millionairess;* Elizabeth Ashley, whom he taught to take down a hairpiece seductively on stage; Barbra Streisand; Judy Garland; Kay Kendall, for whom he created the distinctive piquant hairdo that sent yet another hair bulletin zizzling through the air; Charlotte Ford; Faye Dunaway; Princess Lee Radziwill; Katharine Hepburn who, forced by her role in the Broadway musical *Coco* to exchange her famous "concierge" hairdo for a Chanel, went to Kenneth for her first haircut since 1955; and the Queen of Thailand, who waived the royal court custom forbidding anyone to stand above her so Kenneth could set her long, coal-colored hair.

And for such other style-setters as Marilyn Monroe ("I met her when she was just finishing *Some Like It Hot* and was having problems with her hair, which had been overbleached and was, *she* felt, too curly," Kenneth recalls. "And she became my favorite steady client. She had *wonderful* hair, she had wonderful *everything.* She was one of the greatest people I've ever known"); and Christina Onassis, of whom syndicated columnist Eugenia Sheppard once wrote, rather too ingenuously: "It looks as if Jackie Onassis has a devoted fan in her stepdaughter Tina O. Tina has been following in Jackie's footsteps at Kenneth's. And she ordered a fur coat at Maximilian, because Jackie shops there too."

Kenneth is the star super keeping all these mighty heads held high. How does he do it? What actually is the relationship between the star-super hairdresser and his superstar clients?

"You have to know enough not to get carried away," says the self-protective Kenneth of today. "You have to know enough not to misuse your association with your clients. You can make terrible mistakes. You know, *I* almost did. When Jackie was in the White House, I allowed *Glamour* magazine, which was doing a big story on me, to photograph me going through the White House gates. I was too stupid to understand that this could be offensive to Mrs. Kennedy," adds the post-political Kenneth of today. Indeed, it was the aftermath of that *Glamour* impropriety that gave Kenneth what he calls his "first perception of what a two-headed snake publicity was."

Again and again, Kenneth closed the door on journalists who came snooping around for a Jacqueline Kennedy hair scoop. The *New York Times* reporter who called to check out the portentous tip that "Jackie's" hair would soon be snipped was summarily dismissed; and the news magazine that offered Kenneth money to demonstrate on a model how he cut the First Lady's hair was coldly rebuffed.

"It gave me a new dimension as a person to be able to do her and resist saying anything about her," Kenneth says. "To do her without wearing a Jackie button. This is basically a private service where people wish to be protected. You are standing over a client with her hair wet and it doesn't really matter whether you're in her bedroom in the White House or in your own salon."

Perhaps not, because wherever the hairdresser works from, he has power over his clients. After thirty years of superintending them, Kenneth knows better than anyone that women live through their hair. "Façade or not," he explains, "it's one of the ways they feel they're judged. Now a new hairstyle *can* make a big difference. The trouble is I've had so much publicity that any woman coming into my salon expects a miracle."

We refuse to let Kenneth just do his job; we insist on transforming him into the God that Lucille Ball so antically invoked. *Vogue,* a core distributor of hype bulletins, years ago delegated an authority to Kenneth that still makes him uneasy. "Kenneth," the magazine sighed, "is a kind of hair psychiatrist who not only changes women's looks but their lives and careers."

Kenneth has been consistently hyped in the press as "the Svengali of the Silver Scissors," "the Rembrandt of the Ringlets," "the Picasso of Coiffure," "the Herod of Hairdressers," "a diplomat," "the Secretary of Grooming in Mrs. Kennedy's fashion cabinet" (Louisville *Courier-Journal*), "an artist with a scissors" (*The New Yorker*'s Lillian Ross), "the artist every woman dreams of 'just one appointment' with" (the *Detroit*

Free Press), and "that famous wizard of witchery" (Stillwater, Oklahoma, *News-Press*).

Kenneth prefers a one-word description—"hairdresser."

A hairdresser does have power over women. Although female hairdressers outnumber male hairdressers thirty to one, all the well-known hairdressers, those who attract media attention—indeed, most of the better-known figures in the fashion industry—are men. Why?

First of all, there is society's patriarchal plot, which goes: Through time, men have been in positions of power, and women have been subordinate to them.

But this alone can't account for the intimate relationship that exists between a male hairdresser and his female client, a relationship that traditionally has been the subject of mockery—there's a Joan Rivers routine involving a hairdresser named "Mister Phyllis"; there's Danny Kaye's immortal "Anatole of Paris" ("I reek of chic"); there's even a Jimmy Breslin column beginning "Mr. Tony, formerly of Mr. Frank's of, the window sign claimed, Palm Beach."

What, then, accounts for the intimacy? With her hairdresser a woman works almost as hard to be charming as she does at the start of any love affair. A relationship inevitably develops, which the hairdresser feeds because he wants her to come back. And which *she* feeds because by now she's dependent on his skill with her. She knows it's essentially a dramaturgical universe she lives in; she realizes that, however much such present-day slogans as "Dare to be great" and "Look out for number one" have vulgarized the notion of self-enhancement, she must look her best.

But why does her hairdresser have to be a man? Perhaps she feels that from the standpoint of pure design, a man can be more objective than a woman; perhaps a female hairdresser would be too subjective and impose her own self-image on her client.

Or is it just sympathetic magic? If the man who is doing her hair thinks she looks beautiful, other men will think so too.

Whatever, it is a fact that fashionable women are not as willing to give other women the authoritative role in grooming them that they give men.

"In hairdressing, it *has* to be a man-woman relationship," Kenneth pronounces. "But a man who doesn't like women can't do women's hair well. I recently had to fire one of my hairdressers because he was just rotten to his clients, he beat them up inside."

Yes: In a relationship based so intimately on domination and subordination, the hairdresser has power.

Certainly we need no special instruction to see that today women's presentation of themselves is posited in part on how their hair looks. But has it always been this way?

Well, in the forties, for example, the shape, the flattering line on a head, all the fantasy—indeed, the formal finishing touch for a costume—was some species of hat. Milliners were kept busy making hats for morning, noon, tea, cocktails, and evening. Women went to the hairdresser's simply to get their hair washed and ironed, since it would only be hiding under their hats. Hair was the accessory, the hat the focus.

Even after Dior came along in the late forties with what America called the New Look—a twentieth-century version of a mid-nineteenth-century fashion: wasp-waisted, voluminous skirts worn low-calf with quantities of petticoats—the hat did not disappear. The fabric restrictions of World War II had recently been lifted, and women giddily swathed themselves not only in dresses and gloves, but in frivolous hats as well.

In the fifties, the technique of setting hair went from pin curls to rollers; later, the Italian cut came in, lifting hair off the scalp, giving it volume. Because hats would crush their hair, some women thought twice about wearing them. But if hair was generally freer then, it was thanks also to American sportswear, which had begun as a reaction against that impractical New Look of waist-cinchers and upholstery, and was liberating fashion throughout the world. No longer obsessed with looking ladylike, women were finally adopting the styles of hair and dress which suited both their social and their physical needs.

But what really destroyed the hat was Kenneth's bouffant hairdo. Only when bouffant hairdos came in did hats go for good—all except that vestigial hat, Jacqueline Kennedy's Halston pillbox, whose shrunk size could perch contentedly on a bouffant head.

Round about this time came Brigitte Bardot, saying with her own sane lyricism, "I don't like hats. I prefer my hair. It is part of my personality." That was the last straw for hats. By 1972 they were fit only for musical comedy songs, such as the one Elaine Stritch sang in *Company:* "Does Anybody Still Wear a Hat?"

In a world now hatless, women paraded about wearing their fantasy lives in their hair. By the sixties they were spending even more time and money on their hair than on their clothes. Industry had naturally moved in to manipulate the pretty fantasy with an urgent array of potions and products. The beauty business of yore was now a two-fisted, ten-billion-dollar-a-year affair, serviced by senior vice-presidents of creative marketing and executive vice-presidents of creative merchandising, who were on no account to be confused with senior vice-presidents of package design and executive vice-presidents of corporate marketing and design.

The elevation of hair had elevated—and inflated—the hairdresser. "He's zoomed into his own," roared a typical *Harper's Bazaar* hype bulletin of the day. Indeed! Everybody was saying that he was the sociological phenomenon of his time, moving on almost equal terms with his clients.

In London, Vidal Sassoon set up shop on New Bond Street and became the self-styled sultan of the swinging sixties; in Paris, Alexandre ensconced himself on the Faubourg St. Honoré and was soon in a position to place his daughter in the Grand Deb Ball at Versailles; in New York, Lupe, one of the celebrated hairdressers of his time, who is now forgotten, opened a salon on East Seventy-second Street and was shortly announcing to the fashion press that "I don't socialize with other hairdressers, only with my clients and their husbands"; and Marc Sinclaire, a hairdresser who was even more celebrated than Lupe, and who today is even more forgotten, was remembered in Dorothy Kilgallen's will.

So where was Kenneth, *the* sociological phenomenon of his time?

In Osterville, on Cape Cod, at the small party Mrs. Paul Mellon, universally known as "Bunny," was giving at one of her country houses "in honor"—the invitation read—"of Jacqueline Kennedy's birthday." All the guests had fabulous last names—Whitney, Paley, Harriman, McNamara, Bruce. All except Kenneth, that is; had a gossip columnist dropped his last name—Battelle—no reader would have known who he was. But Kenneth had first-name recognition. (In the tradition of hairdressing, hairdressers are known by their first names only: Norbert, Sebou, Pierre-Henri, Daniel [pronounced Don-yell], Gregory, Adrien, Enny of Italy, Mr. Ronald, Mr. Edward, Mr. Hugh, Mitchell, Suga, Maury, Miguel, Mr. William, Mr. Butch, Wayne, Gary, Mr. Michaeljohn, Vidal—not Gore but Sassoon, who quickly retrieved his surname to empire-build; the man who used to scissor geometric cuts and who today oversees thirty-one salons in six countries, three hairdressing schools, sportswear boutiques in London and Beverly Hills, a line of jeans, and an assembly line of hair-care products, brushes, hair sprays, combs, and scissors is known internationally as Vidal Sassoon.)

But for an incident that occurred shortly after Bunny Mellon's party for Jacqueline Kennedy, Kenneth might well have become the lap-dog of the rich, licking guests at one grand dinner after another. At a party given by socialite interior decorator Diana Phipps, author of the recently published and oxymoronically titled *Diana Phipps's Affordable Splendor,* Kenneth encountered two of his superstar clients, Mrs. H. J. Heinz, universally known as "Drue," and Marion (Mrs. Jacob) Javits.

Drue Heinz, who has spent much of her life fruitfully moving people about at parties, took Kenneth by the hand and said, "You're coming with Marion and me—I can't let on where, but you'll have fun."

Mrs. Heinz's car ferried the three of them to the Seventy-ninth Street boat basin, where a tender was waiting. Minutes later Kenneth was being received in the main salon of the *Christina,* which, he was startled to see, contained a fake El Greco* and a larger-than-life Maria Callas (Jacqueline Kennedy's marriage to Onassis lay deviously in the diva's future). The next day Kenneth would rue his recklessness in escorting a client, when he saw a gossip column headlined "PICKLE QUEEN GOES TO YACHT PARTY WITH HAIRDRESSER."

"That was one of the last things I ever went to—my life since that night could be called 'Winding Down from There,' " says the party-pooping Kenneth of today.

All through the hairdresser-permeated sixties and increasingly throughout the seventies, we couldn't twist a dial, flip through a magazine, or saunter through a department store without being saturated with the "seriousness" of hair. It's no wonder that today when we describe someone—when we're asked, "Tell me about Mary Smith" or Arabella Bingham—we're apt to begin, "She's a brunette," or "She has red hair," or "She's dark," or "She's a blonde, a statuesque blonde." Even when we answer more generally—"She's very stylish" or "She's rather sloppy"—it's probably hair we're thinking of, whether or not we realize it.

"We probably do think first of what goes on up there," Kenneth reflects, adding that "*finally* people are establishing some *individual* style when it comes to their hair. Fashion, you see, is dead. 'Fashion dictates,' as they were once known, are finished—at least in the sense of what's-new-this-fall-this-winter-this-spring-this-summer," says the Kenneth who won a Coty Award—the Oscar of the fashion world, which normally

---

* "It's a *sincerely* fake El Greco," elucidates Peter Beard, who spent two summers on the boat. "At least Big Ari bought it thinking it was real. All the paintings on the *Christina* were sort of what you'd see in a Greek restaurant. I once heard Ari say that the Impressionists were so named because they wanted to make a big impression. But he was a wonderful person."

goes to dress designers—for having helped to make hairdressers "a key factor in current fashion, for the first time since French Court days."

"We have a national uniform now called Levi's," Kenneth continues. "People look around and say, 'Well, gee, everybody's got the Levi's—and the crêpe shirt and the good belt and the skinny body and the boots or the high heels—so what's going to make me *me?*' And then they realize that they're going to have to make their big impression from the neck up, because from the neck down it's really pretty much the same."

Now obviously, somebody who designs heads is going to say it's hair that confers identity, just as somebody who designs boots or belts will claim a disproportionate status for *his* wares. Still, at a time when most of us are covered with initials so graphically not our own ("YSL," our scarves scream; "CC," our sheets shake; "G," our belts blare and our handbags honk; "CT," our jeans jerk), perhaps hair *is* our first-last-only advertisement for ourselves—at least until some hairdresser is able to work out a design that forms *his* initials in *our* hair.

It is precisely because Kenneth has always represented hair—what hair will do and what hair won't do—and not fashion that his salon is still thriving. It is, in fact, the only salon in America of its size and quality which pays for itself, as opposed to being sustained by franchises or a product line.

Today, Kenneth is superintending his second and even third generation of clients. "A client was in today with her daughter," he says. "She's about sixteen now and has been coming here since she was eighteen months old."

The continuing success of Kenneth's salon is an anomaly in a business notorious for its fickle clientele, particularly in a city like New York; Manhattan's urban jungle is one of those places where fashionable women often prefer hunting for hairdressers to hunting for men. A name appears for the first time in *Vogue* or *W* and, pouf!, the ladies who want to look like a page from the current issue of their favorite magazine will materialize at the new salon.

A fashion, when it has lasted long enough, becomes a tradition. For twenty years Kenneth has been the most celebrated and sought-after hairdresser in the world. His may be the only proper name that the woman on the street—and even the man—can associate with the word "hair."

If Kenneth is an anomaly in the profession in terms of the durability of his salon, he is an anomaly also in terms of the sobriety of his person.

Carrying the tools of his trade in an outsize black-leather Hermès attaché case, he looks like a banker or a general practitioner.

"Most Americans automatically assume that male hairdressers possess high, squeaky voices, walk with an odd gait, and talk with fluttery gestures," Kenneth says, living proof that these are not necessarily the conditions of his calling. His voice is as modulated as his manner is mild. His smile is modest, and his eyes, which an Australian reporter once hype-bulletined as "having a brooding James Dean look," are a genial gray-blue. He is of medium build and height, though a midwestern columnist once high-hyped him as being "about six feet six inches, a tower of a man."

Kenneth is fifty-five years old, and his steel-gray hair is disappearing. Whenever a client asks him for his solution to baldness, he shakes his head and says, "If I had one that worked, do you think I would look like this?" And then he laughs—a nice laugh. He is, and everyone says so, a nice man.

Born and bred in no-nonsense upstate New York, a child of the Depression, Kenneth went into hairdressing indentured to the American work ethic. Shortly after moving to Manhattan, he got a job at Helena Rubinstein, at the time the most publicized beauty salon in America. Models, beauty editors, assistant beauty editors, and assistants to the assistants to the assistant beauty editors, all tittuped into it to be tinted and tressed. It was the Rubinstein policy to do all fashion industry types gratis. The salon knew that a small freebie here could mean a big freebie there, that the editors who had been given a good free cut would be sure to tell the readers of their magazines how good—but not how free—a Helena Rubinstein haircut could be.

"I had no clue whatsoever about money in those days," Kenneth remarks. "I never paid the slightest attention to the fact that after your basic salary, your money came through commissions, which were twenty-five percent on each paying customer. The other hairdressers were all more street-smart moneywise than I was; *they* realized that every time they did a client gratis they weren't going to take home a commission, so they would do the free people that they couldn't get out of doing—*badly*—so they wouldn't come back. Now that never occurred to me. I was on a one-to-one basis with somebody in the chair and I was there to do my best."

Nor did any of the other hairdressers enjoy being sent out on assignment to arrange models' hair for magazine and newspaper sittings, since there was no tip or credit involved (the hairdresser's name wasn't even mentioned). Kenneth volunteered for these assignments—"for the experience," he says. And that way, he came to know more beauty editors even better. Before long, almost every beauty editor in New York was going to Kenneth at Helena Rubinstein.

In 1956 two of Kenneth's customers, the fashion models Gillis McGill, later Mrs. Bruce Addison, and Melissa Weston, universally known as "Missy" and later Mrs. Thomas Bancroft, Jr., introduced him to Lilly Daché, the most fashionable milliner in New York.

Miss Daché was looking for a talented hairdresser to be the style director of the second- and third-floor beauty parlor she had recently added to her millinery establishment in a narrow building on East Fifty-sixth Street. She hired Kenneth on the spot. Ironically, given the contest between hair and hats for the trophy of a woman's head, the whole time Kenneth worked there designing hair, Miss Daché was upstairs frantically designing hats.

At Daché, Kenneth only cut hair—which is still all he does today (sets, perms, dyes, and so on are done by others at the salon)—that is, when he isn't giving television and newspaper interviews, making store appearances, lecturing, or doing photographic sittings (at Daché, Kenneth made it his policy to give the stylist who worked on a magazine or newspaper sitting name credit).

Mrs. Kennedy and most of Kenneth's other clients followed him to Daché, and in a very short time it became the most important salon in New York. It was while he was there that Dream Client Number Two started coming to him: Bunny Mellon, famous for her taste and refinement; so attractive, so beautifully dressed (in those days by Balenciaga, today by Givenchy), and so often seen in all the best places.

"She came just by word of mouth," Kenneth says. "Because somebody had told her I was sympathetic and wouldn't cut her hair too short, and hairdressers had always cut it too short before." They were soon to discover that they had two passions in common: gardens and paintings.

Kenneth was well prepared, we can speculate, for his second most substantial dream client. We can even speculate that he had been well prepared for the first. Surely he didn't go into his cubicle at Helena Rubinstein each morning without understanding that at any moment a whirling dervish could appear. Inevitably, he'd been reading the unwritten hairdresser's handbook. "Your customers are rich," it said. "They have husbands who provide them with the money to have their hair done by you, and with the pocketbooks to put that money in, so you can be sure it's a certain kind of pocketbook they're carrying. Oh, and customers here aren't *just* rich, they're well placed, too. And they have rich, well-placed friends."

So what did Kenneth do when Dream Client Number One came floating into Booth 32? He gave her some very down-to-earth advice. And since any kind of criticism from a hairdresser hurts, or at least alarms (the client is just like Silly Putty in the stylist's hands), Kenneth got Jackie Kennedy for a client.

But all Kenneth wanted was to serve her. He has always had the set notion that the hairdresser should be a good servant to the women of the world. "We are completely service-oriented here," he says today of the house of profit that he built on this principle. "We're craftsmen, too, but basically we're servants. This attitude is not very widespread anymore. Just look at the pseudo-snootiness, the pseudo-snooty *rudeness* you get in a lot of salons in this country, where clients are made to feel ill-at-ease. And that's because those hairdressers aren't truly servants. All they're trying to do is make an instant atmosphere. They think they're all bigger than their clients, they all carry on like stars—whether or not anybody's ever heard of them outside of the place they work in.

"The other day I was told that at a very well-known midtown salon a lady went in at nine A.M., and the girl behind the desk was having a glass of white wine, and the guy who was going to color her hair came out on roller skates. Hairdressing is a very silly business and a very serious business at the same time. I think that I can separate the two and most hairdressers cannot.

"I think they concoct this kind of presentation to cover up something: a lack of respect for what they're doing and for the people sitting in the chair. I don't think they *like* their clients. You can't be a good servant when you behave like that," Kenneth concludes. "You just get in the way."

The word "servant" has not been heard on human lips in America for a good quarter of a century. Americans in service steadfastly do not see themselves as having been born to serve. Waiters go on saying they're actors long after they haven't made it; taxi drivers can't wait to tell you that they're really painters or sculptors, poets or playwrights; the soda jerk of yesteryear calls himself a fountain attendant; maids are now house managers, and housekeepers, domestic technicians, while housewives are home economists, domestic scientists, and human ecologists; and hairdressers have been known to hang out a shingle saying "Personal Appearance Consultants." And now here is Kenneth, the elder of the hairdressing tribe and himself the master of a teeming household staff, describing himself as a servant.

He knows, of course, that the servant is the master, that, as George

Steiner has told us, "It is only the servant who can underwrite the master's self-recognition." In Kenneth's business, where one puts one's hands in clients' thinning, graying hair and where one's eyes see and one's fingers touch the ineradicable, not very honorable scars from plastic surgery, mastery is given; the only question is—Is the hairdresser going to be a malevolent or a benevolent master?

This servant, Kenneth, has made it his business—and a very good business it is—to be a kind master. Like the butler or nanny of the past, he lives comfortably enough in his vocation, having understood that by serving faithfully one was actually ruling.

2

The Servant Commanding
His Sumptuous Salon

Whether servant-master or master-servant, Kenneth understood from the beginning that rich women expect—and women less rich want—to be pampered. Not for them a beauty parlor decorated with ticky-tac travel posters.

Kenneth left Daché in 1963 to open a salon of his own. With backing, he purchased a baronial five-story town house on Fifty-fourth Street between Fifth and Madison avenues, which had been built and decorated in the Edwardian manner by a rich woman in the mistaken belief that she would one day be entertaining the Prince of Wales there. Kenneth, too, dreamed of building a beauty palace.

How is it that such an understated man came to have such a Technicolor dream?

"My ideas for the salon all came out of my sitting in the movies every Saturday in the thirties, a child of the Depression," he explains, "and seeing those fantasy 'Houses of Beauty' on the screen—complete with mudpack rooms and mysterious doorways and masseuses and fantasy-rich customers running up and down the halls with clay masks all over their faces, and Russian wolfhounds."

To substantiate his dream, Kenneth approached William Baldwin, universally known as "Billy," the most sought-after American decorator since World War II.* ("When 'In' interior people get together," *Vogue* puffed, "Billy's the Kid.") Kenneth did not know Billy Baldwin person-

---

* Closing his decorating business in 1973, Baldwin continued for a time to attend New York's "Gay Nineties" parties, where the men are all gay and the women are all ninety. But after moving permanently to Nantucket Island, he began complaining about the social side of decorating. "All my clients absolutely *made* me go out with them," he snipped. Asked by an interviewer if he had a manicurist, he answered, "I do it myself at

ally, but they had a number of clients in common, including Jackie Kennedy, Babe Paley, Missy Bancroft, Diana Vreeland, and fashion designer Mollie Parnis.

The decorating of Kenneth's salon was Baldwin's first commercial job—commercial in the sense that he was working, as he put it, "not for any one person but for a million women"—and would mark a milestone in interior design. "As Billy and I walked into the building together for the first time," Kenneth recalls, "I said, 'I cannot bear oak as a color,' because the whole place was paneled in that awful yellow Frank Lloyd Wright kind of wood. Then I said, 'I want a Chinese lamp on every newel post going up the stairs.'

"Well, Billy looked absolutely shocked. Here he was just meeting me, and the first and second sentences out of my mouth amounted to my telling him how to do his job. He said, 'Exactly how *do* you see this place?' and I answered, 'Amusing.' And he said, with that little edge of his, 'Just what do you mean by *that*?' And *I* said, 'Well, I've been to a marvelous pleasure palace—the man who did it must have been mad, totally mad, but he had a great sense of humor—the Brighton Pavilion.' "

Billy Baldwin got the message, and went ahead, using pattern with unheard-of abandon: pattern on pattern on pattern on pattern on pattern on pattern. About Kenneth's salon Baldwin has written some lines that would make a totally plausible entry in any anthology of prose hysteria:

> Paisley on paisley splashed on. The material is cotton—yards and yards of it, used really on a mammoth scale. We swagged it, draped it, tented it, all of it richly colored—scarlet, blue, butter yellow—and filled and surrounded with layer upon layer of pattern. I thought it would be great fun for a woman to have her hair dried under a paisley tent, her fingertips manicured on a Porthault pillow, her hair curled by the light of a palm-tree lamp, as she sits in a lacquered bamboo chair.

Where on earth is the woman in Baldwin's description sitting, anyway? If she appears to be sitting on some South Seas island, we should

---

home, I can't bear to have a woman hold my hand that long." Yet many of Baldwin's former clients—remembering, as they read his acrid remark, hands held, faces pecked, and hugs exchanged in the fond flush of decoration acceleration—genuinely believed, quite wrongly, that they were "the one exception." They didn't even stop to ponder whether Billy could bear to shake the paw of a dog if it were a bitch.

know that it took five hundred yards of paisley print fabric and nine hundred yards of Indian jungle flower fabric to transport her there.

She *is* sitting—or lounging around or puttering about—in what would soon become the world's most publicized beauty parlor. "The Kingdom of Kenneth," the press lost no time in styling it.

The Kingdom of Kenneth: The indigo awning carries no name, simply the street number—Nineteen. Inside the massive black-iron fretwork doors—huge, pagodalike armoires covered with bamboo and roofed with straw cloth, wicker chairs with cushions covered in a black crocodile-patterned linen available only to the trade (that is, through decorators), brass standing lamps, potted palms, Oriental mirrors in red lacquer frames, a drying room in yellow, red, orange, and black paisley, draped high to the ceiling in a tent and lighted by a Regency chandelier that shares the same paisley for a shade, and male stylists all dressed in dark double-breasted suits and sober ties—bankers or general practitioners all!

Not a manicuring table or a washbasin in sight. Not even a bobby pin or a roller.

The social historian Cleveland Amory has described Kenneth's salon as "archrevolutionary." To the eye of the eighties it may not smack unduly of revolution, arch or otherwise, yet no beauty salon like it had ever existed before. It immediately created its own conviction of taste—amusing, exuberant, above all comfortable. The product of a collaboration between America's best-known decorator and her best-known hairdresser, Kenneth's salon could never be exactly copied.

"Within the first six months after we opened," Kenneth laughs, "a woman remarked that the place looked like a very grand Chinese restaurant, and another woman said it looked like a wonderful bordello."

A chintzy Chinese restaurant? A Billy Baldwin bordello? It may strike us as uncharacteristic that so humble a servant and so sincere a craftsman as Kenneth would choose to assault people with this kind of space. But this was the one brilliantly calculated step Kenneth took to enhance his already flourishing career. With a certain craftiness of purpose, he grasped the value of having his salon decorated in a style wildly disproportionate to his perception of his craft. Though relocating himself in an atmosphere of excessive excess, he's been able to remain true to his core principle of moderation. Kenneth's salon is—as the French structuralists would say, decoding the contradiction—Kenneth's "antitext."

The influence of the salon on decorating was considerable. Clients went home with their coifed heads stuffed full of voluptuous new ideas; a few of them even had their own houses done in some version of the manner in which Kenneth's had been decorated by that great fantasist for domestic life, Billy Baldwin.

To Kenneth's, then, they all came: beauty and fashion editors, matrons, divorcées, rich widows, women between husbands, debutantes, and career girls, to see and be seen—for there was always the hope of sighting a messy Jackie padding around the place in paper shoes, cotton batting between her newly painted toes.

To Kenneth's they all came, not only to have their hair dressed, set, styled, stretched, straightened, sheared, shaded, shampooed, shorn, puffed, pulled, cut, combed, colored, curled, frosted, streaked, brushed, braided, and highlighted, but to avail themselves of the full array of beauty services offered by the salon—facials, massage, sauna, wax treatments, makeup with instruction, manicure, pedicure (a dollar-fifty per toe), pedicure with hot gloves and boots, waxing, wig cleaning, fall conditioning, scalp treatments, "Kenneth" (a sufficiency in itself), and virgin hair. ("There ain't much of that around," Kenneth laughs, explaining that virgin hair is hair on the head which hasn't undergone any chemical process.)

Kenneth may be Kenneth of the House of Kenneth but, very democratically, he will cut anybody's hair. "Anybody," he says. "Absolutely anybody. They don't need an introduction, they don't need *any* of that. All they have to do is pick up the phone and make an appointment. But not if they want it next week. It's usually a three-month wait."

But there is sadness in store for the client who, having waited three months to be cut better than she's ever been cut before, makes an appointment to be cut again three months hence, and discovers that Kenneth will cut "absolutely anybody's" hair *once*—he won't give her a second appointment. Being the main source of new clients for the other hairdressers in the salon, Kenneth has had to make it his policy to pass clients on—otherwise, they would all stay with him.

But because the salon also functions as a status-theater, we shouldn't be too surprised to learn that Kenneth continues to cut the hair of his favored customers—the Jackies and Jans and Bunnys and Pams and Slims and Missys and Happys and Bessies and Babses of this world—which he does in the third-floor space hyped in hushed tones throughout the house as "Kenneth's room." But remember, anybody, "absolutely anybody," can walk through the front door.

3

The Master-Servant as Moderate Savant

Against the salon's hysterical opulence, Kenneth has worked out his own way of being Pygmalion to the good bourgeoisie. As we have seen, his way of exploiting the system is by not embracing the style that attaches to it. In the hype world of hairdressing, Kenneth Battelle is exotic by virtue of his steadiness. Let others call for madder music and for stronger wine at 9:00 A.M. Kenneth will call for bigger rollers and darker pins. Let others bring their roller skates to work. Kenneth will be that most unconventional creature—a hairdresser with both feet planted firmly on the ground.

But the culture abhors such understatement. So it pins on Kenneth such ribbons as "Rembrandt of the Ringlets," "Picasso of Coiffure," "artist."

"I don't think of this business as an art," he protests. "I think of it as a craft. A high craft. It's very American to turn things into art. *That's* hype. But I never got carried away with the flamboyance of the *art* of it all—the way Alexandre did, for instance. He thinks he's an artist, and if you think of French hairdressing through the centuries as great art, then you would have to say he's right. I think that even in its time it was not necessarily an art. But there's no question he's the great French coiffeur of our time, complete with the Marie-Antoinette attitude."

Alexandre is the master of the elaborate coiffure, and he has a diamond barrette, France's most illustrious hairdressing award, to prove it. He is credited with creating—for while Kenneth cuts, Alexandre "creates"—such hairstyles as the artichoke and the beehive.

He was "discovered" at the shampoo bar in the Cannes salon of the Paris-based hairdresser Antoine in 1944 by Miss France of 1930, who was shortly to marry the Aga Khan. She introduced Alexandre to her friend the Duchess of Windsor, whom he followed to Paris, and there he coifed her unruly hair daily until the morning her head swiveled right around, as it were—fixed indeflectibly on the past. (The senile eighty-six-year-old duchess, approaching the eleventh anniversary of the duke's death as a "sleeping beauty," according to her staff, is still dressed and made up each morning by a maid so that, when she's awakened by our first creator, she can enter eternity with pride.) It was largely thanks to the style-setting duchess's patronage that whenever a ball was given in pre-Mitterrand Paris, cars conveyed Alexandre in a "relay race from one great house to another."

After the duchess, Alexandre's most exalted client was Jacqueline Kennedy, for when the President quipped famously during his 1961 state visit to France "I am the man who accompanied Jacqueline Kennedy to Paris," the man behind the woman behind the man was Alexandre, not Kenneth.

Alexandre has also coifed Garbo, Audrey Hepburn, and Elizabeth Taylor. Taylor took him across the Steppes to Moscow, and then across the Rubicon to Rome to do not only *her* hair but also her fourth and fifth husband Richard Burton's for the 1966 film *The Taming of the Shrew,* in which she diplomatically wangled the part of the Spanish ambassador for the man who tames her tresses.

At about this time, Alexandre arrived in America dressed in a green-suede body stocking and canary-yellow tie. Last year when he came to New York as the spokesman for L'Oréal conditioning products, which includes Alexandre's Marrow Treatment, he was dressed, like the businessman he's become, in a three-piece pin-stripe suit and dark foulard tie.

Today he oversees hairdressing establishments in Milan, Madrid, Rome, and Tel Aviv from his eighteenth-century town house-salon on the Rue du Faubourg St. Honoré, where a frenzied retinue of unpaid apprentices, paid assistants, and paying visiting hairdressers crowd around as he emerges from the high-wrought wash room. With hands protected by a million-dollar insurance policy, Alexandre reaches for his gold scissors, and the work begins: the work of "art."

Not quite Kenneth's style. Kenneth lives alone while Alexandre lives with his super. Kenneth describes himself as a "hairdresser" while Alexandre hypes himself as an "industrialist." Kenneth's bed is flanked by—nobody knows; Alexandre's is flanked by photographs of the Kennedys, the Windsors, and Elizabeth Taylor and Richard Burton.

When Kenneth started out, extravagant behavior was what Americans expected of hairdressers, thanks in large measure not to Alexandre but to Alexandre's former employer. The Polish-born Antoine affected lavender hair, having first experimented on his poodle to get the right lilac tint, and went on to invent the wind-blown bob as well as that insignia for proper little old ladies—tinted blue hair.

During World War II he was rescued by Adam Gimbel, a great Francophile and the chairman of Saks Fifth Avenue, who installed him in a salon of his own at the store. Antoine in America persisted in his eccentric ways. The bathroom of his house on Fire Island—tub, toilet, and washbasin—was located outdoors; he slept in a white coffin like Sarah Bernhardt; and he arranged for Girl Scouts to strew rose petals in his path when he got off the plane in Dallas en route to a strategically moonstruck "personal appearance" at Neiman-Marcus. And this is the way Americans think hairdressers still behave.

As dramatically different as Kenneth is from Alexandre and Antoine, he has had to swim through the effluvia of the *Shampoo* world. Kenneth is a past master in the art of obtaining and creating publicity. What distinguishes him from the others is that he is able to disentangle his ego from his craft. He lives by his skill, not in his image. When he appears on television, he doesn't hold forth on political problem areas or on the state of our sexual mores—he talks about hair. Vidal Sassoon, on the other hand, was introduced on *The David Susskind Show* as "a public figure passionately involved in some of the leading issues of his time," and proceeded to expound appropriately—or rather, inappropriately. Publicity means nothing to Kenneth except as a source of business.

Kenneth's clients come back, although, unlike most hairdressers, he refuses to be an instrument of the culture's image bulletins—at least, of the ones he hasn't scripted himself. "Over and over again," he says, "I have to say, 'You *can't* do that with your hair, your *hair* just won't do that,' or 'You've already done this, that, and the other thing, and none of it has worked—you've just told me all these horror stories,' because people come to me with a list of twenty years of what's happened to them at hairdressers'—all hateful, terrible stories."

Kenneth has his own horror stories to tell. "Faye Emerson," he divulges, "went to Michel of Helena Rubinstein, and he gave her a permanent wave on bleached hair, and her hair came off with the curlers. Thus was created something called 'The Poodle Cut.'" He laughs that nice laugh. "Then another hairdresser gave somebody else a permanent on top of double-process color and the same thing happened: The hair came off with the curlers. And somebody else gave somebody else a permanent on top of a permanent—and her hair was glue for a year and a half. Not everybody realizes that permanent-wave lotion is chemically the same as a depilatory, which breaks down the molecular structure of the hair, softens and melts it till it takes the form of the rod and makes a curl or wave and is hardened on the rod by neutralizer. That's what makes it permanent, so to speak."

Though he's scripted so many image bulletins, Kenneth prefers editing hair to writing it. "For the most part I suggest, I don't insist," he explains. "After all, it's the client's money." Most clients submit to the servant Kenneth—making him the master of the matrons. Deny it as he will, in the narcissistic vistas of life Kenneth wields power.

"I *suppose*," he concedes, "that in terms of what people come to *me* for—given the hype of hairdressing in general and whatever belief in my particular powers they've brought with them—with all of that, there's a power I *could* have if I wished to, a kind of power over them for a moment or two until they discovered that that's not what I'm about. It's a vulnerable time, an *intimate* time. I mean, how many people besides your hairdresser have ever touched your hair *wet*? It's not something we *do* with one another. And I try not to take advantage of the situation."

4

The Hairdresser as Confidence Man

One of the hypes about hairdressing has always been that women confide in their hairdressers—or rather, good women confide, bad women confess. Thus, perhaps, the slogan: "Only her hairdresser knows for sure."

But why is it he of all her supers who knows for sure?

She can't confide in her dentist—her mouth's full of gear. She doesn't feel especially comfortable talking intimately to her internist—he's going to say she'll only make herself sick with all that carrying on. She certainly can't tell her PR man the truth, the whole truth, and nothing but the truth—he might go out and publicize it; she has to give him a hyped version so he can hype *that*. And finally, she *can't* confide in her terminal beautician, her mortician—unless she's Cheryl Tiegs and he's her dad.

So she confides in her hairdresser: "Mr. Edward, I have three children, two sons and a daughter, and my daughter is the only one who likes girls." She finds the beauty salon the perfect setting for the shifting of covert information. (Amusingly, Washington's most fashionable salon, the Watergate, has been nicknamed the "Gossip Salon.") Her eyes look at the mirror reflection of her hairdresser's eyes—it's a looking-glass world.

In the matter of client confidentiality Kenneth is particularly rigorous, understanding as he does that customers may nurse a wish, however unconscious, to be patients as well as clients. Once, when he suggested to a first-time customer, as he ran his hand over her head from right to left, that she comb her hair a certain way, she resisted with a violence that surprised them both. "But I always comb it the *other* way! Don't *make* me comb it this way!" she whined, subsiding into preanalytical infantilism: "Oh, God, do I comb it that way because that's the way my mother always combed my hair?" Kenneth answered honestly that he didn't know.

"I cut people off who begin telling me intimate things," he says. "Some of them want to talk only as an excuse or explanation for looking the way they think they look—as *bad* as they think they look." Kenneth's aversion to being made the repository of clients' secrets makes him, once again, the benevolent master. "Only a hairdresser who wishes to be mean to his clients will permit confidences," he pronounces. "Only a hairdresser who hates them."

But surely, Kenneth, in your thirty-odd years of hairdressing, there must have been confidences you haven't been able to close your ears to!

"I had a woman in here," he begins, uncomfortably, "a woman of about thirty-eight—never saw her before in my life—who started to tell me a story that just put me away. I mean, it just knocked me out, it was so *embarrassing* to me."

Something sexual, Kenneth?

"In a sense, probably, yes. And it frightened me. She was an Austrian, she said; her father had been a Nazi with black hair, her mother was a blonde, and her children were blond, and she'd just gotten her father out of her system by locking herself away from the world for the past several months and writing a book. Her father had done something *terrible* to her mother, she said; and what she wished to do now was look exactly like her mother had looked in the year 1931—she showed me this faded photograph—and she wanted *me* to help her. She wanted *me* to make her into this pale-blond, white-blond, Harlow-blond Austrian creature. I just knew something more was coming.

"I tried to stop her from going on. I said, 'None of this is going to make any difference in the decision about what to do with your hair. If you wish to become a blonde, you do that for your own reasons, but I don't need to know what they are.' I begged her not to become a blonde, by the way, even though she had blond coloring, because—here we go again, same old technical thing—she had very fine hair, and the particular color blond she wanted to be cannot be achieved with single process, it requires double-process—bleaching *and* tinting—which is much less easy on the hair. Hardly anybody goes into double-process color today if they can avoid it. So, just technically, for what it would do to her hair, I said, 'I wish you wouldn't do this.' But she insisted, insisted, *insisted.* I came terribly close to sending her away, but I have to confess she did go out of here a blonde—and very happy. I'm still not sure I did the right thing. It's obviously bothering me."

But why was this encounter so disturbing for you, Kenneth? Why does it *still* trouble you? Can you be more specific? What exactly happened between you and that woman in the chair?

"Well, this woman had on probably the most expensive pair of shoes I have *ever* seen, bar none. I'd never seen anything quite like them. They were brogues. Wing-tipped. Black. Almost like men's shoes. And she was wearing a pair of beautiful flannel pants, I mean the *most* expensive—she was dressed in the most *incredibly* expensive way. Quiet—like the Duke of Windsor. As she was leaving the salon, people in the dressing rooms stopped her, people stopped her on the stairs, everyone turned around and looked at her, she looked so extraordinary. She looked like Dietrich in her tuxedo—not mannish, just very German mid-thirties: hair shorter in the back, longer in the front, finger-waved almost. She'll be a hit in the Mudd Club, I remember thinking—no question about that."

This is the sole occasion—one wants to say case—when Kenneth felt he went beyond his professional ethic. A woman comes in asking to be transformed. At first he has trouble locating this particular organism in history, finding a context for it. But then, before he can stop her, she's telling him her obfuscatory tale, and by the time she's finished, it seems to *him* she's all but told him that she was trying to get involved in the sexuality of her *parents*! It is a measure of Kenneth's measure, also of his premonitory sensitivity, that this story haunts him so. He takes no comfort from the fact that the woman left his salon, everyone said, looking terrific. The point is, he doesn't want craziness around him.

This customer had managed to outrage not only his canon of taste but every one of his gospel truths. That she hadn't wanted to be given an appropriate uniform, like all the ladies he was used to quietly commanding, was one thing, but that she'd wanted to be given stars and stripes like a general . . . ! She had behaved not like the good women of his constituency but like a decadent, wicked woman—and in a salon whose values, whatever the decadent appearance of the *space,* were solidly bourgeois. This Valkyrean blonde was a most improper client.

A year later, the woman reappeared—neither in Kenneth's salon nor in the Mudd Club, but in the good, gray pages of the *New York Times.* Turning one morning to the book page, Kenneth was arrested by a nostalgic photograph of a dark-haired woman which accompanied a review of some memoirs. The picture had the authoritative elegance of a Hoyningen-Huene photograph from the thirties. It was the hairstyle that drew Kenneth's eye. He thought—what a wonderful shape to the head, people don't look like that anymore—and began reading the review.

When he came to the reviewer Christopher Lehmann-Haupt's words, "And so she began the long search she describes with such stunning intelligence and sensitivity in *Ghost Waltz: A Memoir,* and by slow and painful degrees she discovered her father's history. He had joined the Nazi party. Voluntarily. With enthusiasm, even. And also the S.S. . . ." Kenneth looked again at the picture in the paper and realized with a shudder that the dark-haired woman was the Valkyrean blonde; then, with a second shudder, that the memoir must be hers.

The story is so strange—indeed, the critic for *The New York Review of Books* described it as "one of the most curious rebellions of the unconscious I have ever read in a memoir"—and bears out Kenneth's intuitions to such an uncanny degree that it demands detailed attention. The book's eighty-one diarylike entries describe a daughter's love for a father about whom she learns the unsavory truth when she is seventeen and an Austrian exchange student in the United States. The author's search for time past is a search for that father, is a ghost waltz with that father, though we never find out—as Kenneth might have—what the "terrible" thing is that her father did to her mother.

Two years before the publication of *Ghost Waltz*, the talk of the New York literary world was a sexual confession titled *Nine and a Half Weeks: A Memoir of a Love Affair* and published under the pseudonym "Elizabeth McNeill."

"Unlike *The Story of O,*" the publisher's jacket copy informed us, *"Nine and a Half Weeks* is not fiction or fantasy; it is a true account of an actual experience, a sadomasochistic episode in the lives of a real man and a real woman. From the beginning, their sexual excitement depends on a pattern of domination and humiliation." The publisher's special letter to reviewers went on to claim for the book a universal significance, describing it as "a metaphor for the relationship of domination and humiliation that exists between all men and women."

The book, having no biographical ballast and therefore little emotional accuracy, seemed as unreal as someone else's bad dream. Lehmann-Haupt ended his review of *Nine and a Half Weeks* in the *Times* with some prescient questions: "What had the author's previous life been like? *Why* was she this sort of person? Fatuous as it may be under the circumstances, one can only hope that on another day, she will have a different story to tell."

The publisher described Elizabeth McNeill only as "a young woman who lives in New York, where she works as an executive for a large corporation." Despite persistent attempts on the part of journalists and critics to uncover her identity, it has remained—until now—a secret.

The woman hiding behind the innocuous-sounding pseudonym Elizabeth McNeill is the Valkyrean blonde of putative Mudd Club fame: Ingeborg Day, the author of *Ghost Waltz: A Memoir*. And so, in retrospect, her story of sexual domination and humiliation becomes plausible.

Ms. Day does indeed live in New York, where for many years she was on staff at *Ms.* magazine. *Ms.* may be startled to learn that one of its own wrote such a book—being not only a magazine but the house organ of a movement whose abiding thesis is that women must resist being dominated in any arena, that they must break the bonds of servitude—cast off, in Wollstonecraft's phrase, "the yoke of sovereign man."

Ms. may be startled. Kenneth will be confirmed in his uneasy intuition.

Another *Ms.* editor—a cofounder of the magazine, in fact—the feminist icon and idol Gloria Steinem, once served the mythology of hype, disseminating from New Grub Street hype bulletins about hairdressers.

In a *Glamour* magazine article on Kenneth titled "Man with a Mission," the woman whose own mission would make her synonymous with the women's liberation movement (she would soon be convening the National Women's Political Caucus and helping to found the Coalition of Labor Union Women) telegraphed those buzz words of hairdressing hype—"analyst," "change your life," "transformations," etc.—which in an enemy context also happen to be the buzz words of consciousness-raising.

"Because he knows us so well, a trip to his salon is a little like going to see an analyst or a plastic surgeon or a beau. It's quite likely to change your life. . . . If he sees a client who is beginning to look 'set,' he tells her, 'Shake your head three times.' Why three? 'Well,' he smiles, 'I find that women like to be told something *definite*.' Almost all his customers are so happy with their transformations that his fee, which is healthy, seems a bargain, and 'thank you' becomes too small a word," wrote the woman of tomorrow.*

It is a quiet comfort to remember that, in the hype world of abhorrent exorbitance and odious disproportion, Kenneth remains proportionate.

---

* In truth, it was only when she finished writing this article that Gloria, happy at last, submitted to Kenneth's scissors for the first—and, as it turned out, the only time: She thought he cut her hair too short. She did, however, become a regular customer of one of Kenneth's colorists, whom she still goes to for streaks. And today, Gloria Steinem is as well known for her well-cut mane of streaked hair as for her feminist politics.

5

Maury Hopson:
Hair Artist/Hype Artist

If Kenneth is the Bentley of hair in the star super syndrome, a willowy Texan by the name of Maury Hopson is the Maserati—revving up at a thousand dollars a day. (Those who feel that a thousand dollars a day is a disproportionate reward for the combing of hair on human heads might consider that overtime and weekends further swell Hopson's coffers.)

Maury is a self-styled "free-lance hairdresser." Although today "free-lance" is just a fancy word for "unemployed," time was, a freelancer was a warrior, a soldier of fortune who would hire himself out to whoever would pay his price—have lance, will travel.

Maury has been traveling ever since the day Kenneth hired him fresh out of beauty school in Houston. Confronted almost immediately with one of those sticky situations that grow out of the hothouse world of celebrity hairdressing, the Maserati that is Maury shifted into second gear.

"When I first went to work at Kenneth's, I knew nothing of the hierarchy of New York society," Maury says with great sophistication today, "who was what or who or anything. And there I was, suddenly thrust into being kind of an overseer of Kenneth's room. I knew that the people who came in there were all very intertwined, I just didn't know any of the particulars. So I began reading *Women's Wear Daily* and 'Suzy.' I learned a lot from them.

"And I'm glad I did, because one day the salon was really buzzing—Slim Hayward was sitting in Kenneth's chair waiting for a cut, she had her feet in a tub for a pedicure and—you could've knocked me over with a feather—in walks Pamela Hayward. She *used* to be married to Randolph Churchill, and now she's married to Averell Harriman, but *then* she was married to Leland Hayward, and that doesn't even touch on all the powerful men she's been friendly with, like a Rothschild and Aly Khan and Gianni Agnelli, but I can't talk about any of *that*. Now *luckily* I remembered from 'Suzy' or someplace that Leland Hayward had left Slim Hayward to marry Pam—and it was Slim who'd introduced them! And there *I* am, combing the tangles out of Slim's hair as Pam is escorted through to the other end of Kenneth's room, with a towel over her head and a *schmata* on. Slim's thumbing through *Vogue* and doesn't even notice. And *I* just think—I don't care how civilized people are, if these two see each other, it can't be a good experience for either one of them. So, with everything I can muster—'cause I'm trying to maneuver and I don't even know if what I'm doing is correct, all I know is that the minute Slim looks up from her magazine she's going to spot Pam in the mirror, and, shit, it's all gonna hit the fan—I say to Slim, 'Excuse me, Mrs. Hayward, but I think you'd be more comfortable in there,' and I take her chair with her in it and swing it out the door, making sure Slim's back is to Pam, and I motion to the pedicure girl to follow. So I got Slim around the corner into another room. Then I collapsed.

"Slim just sat there looking at me, like, what the *fuck* is going on here, and I said, panting, 'I just thought you might be more comfortable in here, Mrs. Hayward,' and she said, *'Why?,'* and I said, gulping, 'Well, Mrs. Hayward, Mrs. Hayward just came in—I mean, Mrs. Pamela Hayward—and took a seat at the other end of the room.' And the look she gave me was just this, well, *click* of understanding: *'Bless* you, Maury, for sparing me that.' I was really just doing my job. I was protecting *both* of them, I was protecting Mrs. Hayward as well as Mrs. Hayward. I mean, Mrs. Hayward was a nice client, too. Apparently, Slim discussed the whole episode with Kenneth, and I must say it was quite a little gold star in my report card."

This Slim-Pam flim-flam was Maury's baptismal fire. He went on to become Kenneth's chief assistant. Then gradually Kenneth weaned clients to him and they became Maury's own. He was also sent on glamorous magazine assignments, and before long the boy from Texas was reading his own name in the magazines he used to pore over: "Half Moon Bay coiffures by Maury at Kenneth." This particular credit was for a pineapple hairdo he'd planted on Marisa Berenson's head. It was Maury's first *Vogue* trip. Diana Vreeland had dispatched a crew to photograph fashions on the "divinely beautiful beaches of Trinidad in front of all those pistachio and coral houses." Only there were no beaches to speak of in Trinidad, and the pistachio and coral houses had been torn down fifty years before. When the talented young fashion editor Caterine

Milinaire called Vreeland and said, "Listen, where did you see the beaches and the beautiful coral houses?," she answered, "Oh, but it all looked *so* divine from the air. I was coming back from Venezuela and we landed in Trinidad to refuel and I saw all these wonderful *colors.*" At which point, Milinaire switched the shoot to Antigua.

"So I got my name in *Vogue,*" Maury reminisces, "but then it was back to the salon, back to my regular bookings and my regular salary, which was poor."

Today Maury does not see private clients, whom he refers to as "civilians." He's available only to advertising agencies, film companies, cosmetics companies, fashion houses, and magazines.

He's the professional's professional; he works on models, actresses, film stars, rock stars, and other celebrities "upgrading," as he puts it, "their fashionable aspect." At Kenneth's, Maury took sows' ears and turned them into silk purses; now that the purses he works on are silk to begin with, he turns them into spun gold.

"I have to push further with my kind of client than a hairdresser does in a salon situation," he explains. "I have to bring them to a peak real quick. *I* don't have four weeks." (At a thousand dollars a day, no client has four weeks, either.)

"A free-lance hairdresser's work is easier," says Kenneth. "They do one client a day. I have to stand and please twelve or fifteen women a day. You know how free lance got started? Few hairdressers from salons were interested in doing magazine pages because all they got was credit. But then a *Vogue* editor had the bright idea of actually starting to *pay.*"

"When I left Kenneth's," Maury says, "there were exactly zero people doing what I do now. Then Ara Gallant and Alan Lewis Kleinberg and Suga and Hugh Harrison followed my lead. And now there are about five hundred of us—not only hairdressers but also makeup artists like Way Bandy* and Sandy Linter—who depend totally on free lance." (Picture this parade: five hundred soldiers of fortune all marching into

---

* Bandy is the author and illustrator of two best-selling books instructing people in how to play doctor to their own faces. Among the faces Bandy has prepared to meet the faces that they met are Catherine Deneuve, Barbra Streisand, Iman, Gloria Vanderbilt, Claire Bloom, Mick Jagger, and Harry Reasoner. "One day," Bandy recounts, "Barbara Walters and Harry Reasoner were being photographed together, I think for *Vogue,* and Harry Reasoner found out that I was doing Barbara's makeup, and insisted that I do *his* makeup, too. I hear he made a big scene about it behind the scenes. So I did him, too. But remember, this was right at the moment when all that rivalry was going on between them." Amusingly, Harry Reasoner's recent memoir is titled *Before the Colors Fade.*

the brave new world with scissors, powder puffs, and eyelash curlers.) "They don't *all* make the same kind of money I do," adds Maury, who is planning to purchase the Manhattan brownstone he lives in.

Here is how hairdressing works at this disproportionate level of recompense: Maury is booked through his agent, Armand St. Gelais, who is actually a booker, not an agent (nor a dessert), in the sense that he doesn't go out and find Maury work. "I've been with Armand since I began," Maury states. "He was the lover of Suga [the China-born Japanese hairdresser who was also once one of Kenneth's hand-picked assistants]. And he was writing a book, so he was home all day, and I needed somebody to answer the phone. I've only seen him in person eight times in ten years. He does my billing and sends the checks to my accountant, where all my real business is done, and I give him ten percent. I'm his original client. Me and Way Bandy. Needless to say, Armand St. Gelais makes a lot of money.

"Come to think of it," Maury adds, "I can't imagine *what* Armand is writing a book on." Odd that Maury doesn't see what could happen in the fullness of time. Armand's book might be about *him*—making Maury the man the booker double-booked.

Were Armand really writing a book on the making of Maury, he would have to devote a whole chapter to the heady feat that fueled Hopson's success.

"The thing I did that got me the most publicity," Maury reminisces, "was the famous Martha Mitchell makeover for the cover of *New York* magazine. Way Bandy did her makeup, Francesco Scavullo took the photo, and I did her hair. Her hair was really *quite* nice—smooth, silky, Renoir sort of hair—a real goldeny color—and it went about halfway down her back when it was let down. While I was rolling it on hot curlers, I told her she looked like Lana Turner, because I'm a mood synthesizer, too, you know what I mean. That's one of the things I'm paid for. Then, while Way was putting her mouth on [the mouth that the press had so mysogynistically hyped and that Bandy romantically describes as having been "beautiful, full, soft, wet, inviting"], I brushed her hair straight up in front and twisted it in back into a knot on top. Then I fastened a fall to the knot. Well, that definitely changed my career. I went on all the TV shows with Scavullo and Way to talk about what it was like to transform Martha Mitchell. And you want to know something, I think the kind of portraits Scavullo has been doing for the past few years—with me sometimes doing the hair—*and* his beauty books came out of Martha Mitchell, at least subliminally."

Although what they were doing, those creative three, was writing fiction, composing a fictitious form of human beauty, Maury describes Martha Mitchell as his first "realie." As comic as it sounds, a "realie," in free-lance hairdresser parlance, is a thousand-dollar-a-day term for a rather unreal humanoid, an individual rich or famous enough to be featured in the editorial section of a magazine, rather than a model in an ad. "The 'realies' I do are usually very, very famous or very, very social," Maury amplifies, "but they still don't know what they should look like. And when you *tell* them, they still only want to look like what's acceptable at their club. It scares them that they might look different from their neighbors—frankly, I think it all has to do with politics. So it takes real heavy-duty double muscle to get them to go along with what you want to do, because after their photo is taken they're going to be going right back to their clique or crowd. Now when you're dealing with models, *you* are their clique or crowd, so they trust you."

Maury is right to recognize that "realies" have to be careful to look neither too good nor too bad since their way of maintaining themselves in their social place is to look exactly like everybody else. But what Maury neglects to consider is that every model is working overtime to become a "realie," because that's where the *real* money and position lie.

Maury had been racing from rags to riches and "realies" for a number of years when one day the opportunity to do real royalty presented itself. His friend Bandy asked him to help prepare the world's reigning film star for a *Good Housekeeping* cover. The Maserati spun wildly into overdrive.

"As we were pulling into the driveway of the Warner estate in Virginia," Maury breathlessly recounts, "Way looked at me and I looked at Way and we said, 'Holy shit, *Elizabeth Taylor* lives here!' When we finally reached her, we found this lady who'd been . . . like . . . hangin' out on the farm—you know, with no public appearances necessary. Way made her up, then I did her hair. And we had a fabulous, fabulous day— five hours in the bathroom, just the three of us. And because of how well it turned out—I mean, she looked *great,* she *loved* it—I see her all the time. She just called me to do her for a *Bazaar* cover—'If they're gonna do a cover, honey, *you've* gotta do me.' You know, she's a friend on that kind of basis.

"And whenever Elizabeth comes to New York for a premiere or a party, she always books Way and me in advance. We meet her at her hotel and get her ready to go. She's taken me on trips with her and everything—to spas in Klosters. And the most fun thing is she cuts my hair. And you know, she noticed an interesting thing—that I always cross my hands in front of my crotch when I'm having my hair cut. I always tell her *I* should have been the movie star and *she* should have been the hairdresser, because she's such a *good* hairdresser. She cut Richard Burton's hair for most of his movies and plays." (*This* Queen Elizabeth likes running her fingers through her hairdresser's hair. Another— Queen Elizabeth II—raised her hairdresser to Honors in the 1964 New Year's List; his royal reward was membership in the Victorian Order.)

Maury is so adept at writing fiction when he dresses hair that he can't help dressing up stories about his escapades. He has given us a hyped and highly edited take on his first encounter with Elizabeth Taylor, because, in fact, when he and Way Bandy arrived at that Virginia farm, they were made to wait a long, long time. At last Elizabeth Taylor appeared at the head of the stairs, saying she'd had a rough night the night before. There were iron-gray oysters under her eyes; her face was swollen with booze. Their hearts plummeting, they sent out for supplies.

For two hours they applied quarts of yogurt to her face to bring it down so Bandy would have a face to work with. Her hair had been tinted by the local hairdresser in Virginia—the Middleburg hairdresser whom nobody in Middleburg ever went to—and by then it had nothing to do with human hair; it looked more like fur or a nylon area rug. Most of it had to be cut off.

Now the real work could begin. An entire face had to be painted on. The neck, which looked like a white watermelon, had to be painted out, and a new neck drawn in. At three in the afternoon Elizabeth Taylor said to the hungry and weary hairdresser and makeup artist who had had to get up at six to catch an early shuttle to Washington, "You boys must be hungry. There's a good drugstore in the village of Warrenton. Why don't you get yourselves some sandwiches."

When the Scavullo photo of Elizabeth Taylor graced the cover of *Good Housekeeping,* it looked slightly strange. Who was to know that Hopson and Bandy had performed a miracle, effected a makeover every bit as dramatic as Martha Mitchell's. At least now the reading public could tell that it was Elizabeth Taylor. And that must have pleased John Warner who, running for the Senate at the time and wanting his then wife to be in the public eye as much as possible, is said to have arranged for her to do the cover.

As the interlocking world of hype turns, yesterday's servant can be tomorrow's master. Maury Hopson felt deep satisfaction when he found himself in a position to send Kenneth a very important client.

"I remember it was a Friday night," he says. "I was going away for the weekend on a job I couldn't cancel, and Elizabeth was at the Waldorf and needed her hair done at the last minute for some campaign thing with Mr. Warner. So I called up Kenneth. He canceled his evening plans and took a cab right to the Waldorf and did her hair. They got on just fine. Elizabeth said they had a lovely time. Of course she kept him waiting and all that other stuff. I mean, she likes to tell hairdressers how to do everything. Except maybe Alexandre—her first allegiance has always been to *him,* she's always had this *incredible* relationship with him, even though they don't speak the same language. I mean, I don't think Alexandre can speak English, and Elizabeth does not speak French. But she loves the way he does her hair. Now in *my* opinion, Alexandre isn't *near* the hairdresser Kenneth is."

That Elizabeth Taylor enjoys perfect communication with a star super whose language she does not speak should be no more surprising to us than that Alexandre enjoys perfect communication with a superstar client whose language *he* does not speak. At their level of life, they could certainly afford a translator, but they don't need one. All they have to do is look into the mirror at each other's eyes. Alexandre's are saying, *Chérie, il n'y en a pas deux comme toi!* And Taylor's are replying, Darlin', you're the greatest, you make me feel like a trillion bucks.

Kenneth has something of course proportionate to say about Elizabeth Taylor. "I told her I thought she ought to cut her hair somewhat. She is a client that doesn't understand *me* at all. I'm much too ordinary for her—I don't know any other word to use."

Kenneth was looking at hair, not at Elizabeth Taylor. Although he's commanded the whole panoply of hype, he's stayed with his craft. The Maurys of the hairdressing world fraternize with their clients and "mood-synthesize" them. Kenneth won't do that. He insists on saying the same sensible things he said when he was a promising young haircutter in the last booth at Helena Rubinstein. He still prefers hair to hype.

HOW PLASTIC SURGEONS HARD-SELL US A BILL OF PLASTIC GOODS

Socialite Charlotte Harris is very frank about the "eye-job" she had. She decided to have her eyes done one March after a long, cold winter. "All my friends were away," she said. "Sally Scheftel was in Paris, Chessy Patcévitch was in Nassau. I wanted to get away, but I would not go without my husband and he could not leave. So I decided to have my eyes lifted."

—*Women's Wear Daily*

1

Plastic Promises

A too-long snow leopard was coming down the street. It was ostentatious, there was much too much of it; it all too obviously cost a million dollars.

The woman inside it was wearing a very important hairdo, teased and sprayed. It was such an unnatural amount of hair, so unnaturally thick, and so mahogany, that it might have been an expensive wig. She had on white pants and in her high high-heels she was walking slightly ahead of a very European entourage of five chattering people, each one narrow and elegant.

The observer did a double take when he recognized the face of the woman trapped in the snow leopard coat. Just a few days before, he had seen, reproduced in some newspaper, a still from one of her sixties movies.

Since he had such a recent frame of reference for her, her present appearance shocked him all the more. The wonderful mouth, of a sensuousness hard to mistake for any other, was gone; the lips were thinner. From the bridge of the nose down, there was just a pulled-looking mask. And the eyes—huge and wide apart—which remained unchanged, were now out of proportion to the rest of her face.

These were not the ruins of a great beauty, such as the gothic cathedral that Garbo is today. These were the shambles of a great beauty, of a woman who was as celebrated for her face as Garbo and Gene Tierney had been for theirs. It was this woman's face that had haunted everyone. It didn't have very much in it, it wasn't a particularly interesting face, but it was extraordinary—the sheer passionate shape of it.

In the street the observer studied the alarming transformation. The liquid foundation of her makeup had been laid on so thick it was practically opaque, and the thick coating of powder on top looked like confectioners' sugar. The effect was grotesque, almost as if the makeup had been smeared on by a Bette Davis or a Joan Crawford doing her harridan bit.

139

The face was a glazed, lifeless doll's face. And all this artificiality was supposed to look real—which was why it looked so unreal. Everything in her face that had had any character was gone.

How could such a woman, who could have been so beautiful in the full afternoon of her life, have been brought to her knees like this?

The observer knew. In order to provide her public with the ageless face they expected from her, she had undergone plastic surgery. On her old face she would never have slathered the makeup so unskillfully. And perhaps the overdressy snow leopard would not have looked so flamboyant if Sophia Loren's new face had not looked so fixed.

There is a hype epidemic of plastic surgery raging in the United States of Advertising. Too many people—ordinary people, average women *and* men—have been hard-sold a bill of plastic goods and made to feel that they have an obligation to themselves to have the surgery, that it is, though logic tells us otherwise, preventive medicine for the "disease" of growing old.

Through nature's changing course, the human body ages. Paracelsus, the sixteenth-century alchemist, brooded: "Metals may be preserved from rust, and wood may be protected against rot. Blood may be preserved a long time if the air is excluded. Egyptian mummies have kept their form for centuries without undergoing putrefaction. Animals awaken from their winter sleep, and flies, having become torpid from cold, become nimble again when they are warmed." But human flesh putrefies.

Paracelsus was writing in the Age of Reason, and long before our unreasonable age of promiscuous plastic surgery. For no longer is plastic surgery the prerogative of rich women, vain homosexuals, and aging film stars who, unable to find the grace to bear the melodrama of their fading youth, fight to keep young with a losing passion.

Every year now, more than a million sleeping would-be beauties from all walks of life lie anesthetized and dressed as chafers, probers, chippers, squeezers, scourers, carvers, and consummate chiselers go about their business. Alas, these sleeping would-be beauties' sleep is not the sleep of reason. Not when one considers the following new technique for removing forehead wrinkles—as described by a prominent plastic surgeon: "We make a flap across the top of the head and we literally skin the whole thing down just like an Indian, right down to the eyebrows. We see the muscle underneath the flap that's responsible for the wrinkling and we're able to attack it directly." Those split Blackglama pelts were at least dead when *they* were skinned.

As the poet Robert Lowell wrote, well before the *embourgeoisement* of cosmetic surgery, "Beauty is terrible, expensive, skillful."

Plastic surgery is the most lucrative surgical specialty in America, and not coincidentally the fastest growing. Young doctors, recent graduates of the Ponce de León School of Thought, are flocking to the field, alighting on crow's feet in orchards of Granny Smiths. In less than ten years the number of plastic surgeons certified by the American Board of Plastic Surgery, Inc., has grown from about a thousand to almost three thousand. However, anyone who has a license to practice medicine—any dermatologist, for instance; any ear, nose, and throat specialist—can call himself a plastic surgeon and legally perform plastic surgery. Of these Board-certified three thousand, a disproportionate number practice in Beverly Hills and Manhattan, those Babylons of hype. There more than anywhere else, plastic surgeons' knives are sure to fit precisely in the wounds that hype inflicts with its remorseless retailing of the image of the body beautiful.

We, having learned hype's lesson well—that beauty needn't be a gift of birth—seek to match ourselves to the pictures our culture gives us of corporeal perfectibility. Why should we, after all, adapt to our imperfections when we know that reality itself can be cut to fit our fantasies?

So we refuse to take ourselves at our own faces' value, even when those faces are "young and easy in the mercy of [Time's] means." Some of us can't even wait till our faces fall to have them lifted (at a cost of anywhere from two thousand to six thousand dollars, including surgeon's and anesthesiologist's fees and hospital charges). And as we age—for, this side of science fiction, nobody grows younger, *yet*—we come to hate our bodies too. "Old age," writes Simone de Beauvoir, "inspires more repugnance than death itself."

Repelled by the stranger we see when we look into the mirror, we can either, in all hospitality, invite him in and let him live in our body, or else slam the front door in his face—and then rush out the back door to the nearest plastic surgeon's waiting room. There, as we wait for our number to be called, we close our minds to the possibility of death, for with any operation our number might be up. Not even royalty, tax-sheltered by birth from the blows of life, is exempt. Queen Mother Frederika of Greece recently expired as her eyes were being lifted.

We try not to think about the chances of major complications occurring, though in 9 to 20 percent of plastic surgery cases they do occur, and include blood clots, hemorrhages under the skin, injury to facial nerves, permanent infections, abnormal scarring, and reactions to anesthesia, general or local. And we try not to think about the certainty of the pain we have chosen to punish ourselves with, just so the next time we lie about our age, our looks at least won't lie.

But isn't what the plastic surgeon shapes for us in his operating theater a tissue of lies—a lie in tissues, subcutaneous tissues, not to mention nerves and cells, blood vessels and veins, muscles and even organs?

Looked at in the light of reason, plastic surgery is our culture's most self-evident illustration of its belief in the pursuit of happiness, though certainly it entails more amendments to our constitution than were dreamt of by the signers of the Declaration of Independence—plastic surgery, in fact, could be seen as a declaration of dependence.

As metabolic and genetic cures are found for the diseases that blight our lives, as, one by one, the real problems of medicine are solved, we are left with the luxury of pursuing our cosmetic—that is, our fictional— problems, which are, however, real to those of us who can afford to devote our lives to our romantic fictions.

Like most readers of romance fiction, plastic surgery patients tend to be women. And small wonder, when a woman with gray hair and wrinkles is perceived as being old, while a man with gray hair and smile lines is perceived as being powerful and sexy.

But more and more men are requesting facial cosmetic surgery. Many plastic surgeons report that men account for as much as 20 percent of their practices. These are men not only from professions where their looks are as important as any talent they may possess—acting, newscasting, politics—but also from the groves of academe and the fields of medicine, law, merchant banking, advertising, big business, and, yes, even the clergy.

A more youthful appearance, they judge, will enable them to keep their jobs, hold their own against younger competition, and even hold younger women or, if they have what the pollsters call "other interests," younger men. (In the homosexual culture, with its pitiless rules, youth has always been the currency of intimacy—without it, forget it.)

Traditionally, cosmetic plastic surgery has concentrated on protruding ears, droopy lids (eyelid surgery was performed in tenth-century Arabia, without, we will shudder to recall, any anesthetic), bags beneath the eyes, sagging faces (face-lifts were performed in Europe and America in the early 1900's), noses (the first nose operations were performed in

India and Egypt about 600 B.C.), corrugated foreheads, and assorted un-sightly bumps.

But thanks to the introduction of the bikini in the fifties and later to the spread of nude beaches from Europe to America, far more than cor-rugated foreheads were a sight for the naked eye. Whereas in a past not too remote we would have been publicly humiliated had we dared to bare our bodies, today we feel humiliated if the bodies that we bare are bumpy. So growing numbers of women at younger and younger ages now request modifications and alterations of body parts once considered cosmetically untouchable. These body-contour operations begin in trans-fusions (whether or not we need them—the doctor often has the patient donate *in advance* a couple of units of blood) and result in transforma-tions that exact belief at the same time that they strain credulity.

2

Thomas Rees, MD:
Patrician Propagandist

One of the most celebrated agents of grace in the far-flung empire of the plastic art is, by public and professional consensus, Thomas D. Rees, M.D., F.A.C.S., age fifty-four, of Manhattan. Rees may fairly be described as the plastic surgeon's plastic surgeon, and not alone because he is said to have lifted the face of the world's richest and most fashionable plastic surgeon, Dr. Ivo Pitanguy of Rio de Janeiro.

Pitanguy—out of gratitude?—wrote the foreword to the second volume of Rees's plastic surgery textbook, describing it as "an endeavor that could come only from someone who is constantly pushed by an intimate sense of harmony, creativeness, and duty." Author Rees in the same volume rose like the George Jessel of plastic surgery to the occasion, praising Pitanguy as "a legend in his own lifetime . . . I am envious of Ivo's extraordinary energy, multifaceted personality, incredible skill, great charm, and considerable athletic prowess." (Pitanguy has a black belt in karate.)

Rees is the plastic surgeon's plastic surgeon because he has made himself a spokesman for the plastic surgeons who have gone before him and a carrier of their accumulated ingenuity. Early in his career, he took care to apprentice himself to the pioneering plastic surgeon Sir Archibald McIndoe at London's Queen Victoria Plastic and Jaw Center; Sir Archibald had been among the handful of British doctors who developed techniques to rehabilitate the grotesque casualties of the First World War.

Rees comes of pioneering stock himself. "His grandparents crossed America in wagon trains," begins one testimonial to him, "settling in Mormon Utah at the bidding of Brigham Young." But there is no Mormon mark to be seen on Rees. Or has the mark been removed by Pitanguy?

By his own admission, Rees has not been a pioneer; he's opened up no professional frontiers. Still, his *curriculum vitae* runs to fifteen pages: Clinical Professor of Surgery (Plastic), New York University; Chairman, Department of Plastic Surgery and Surgeon Director, Manhattan Eye, Ear, and Throat Hospital; President of the American Society for Aesthetic Plastic Surgery (1979–80); Thomas Jefferson Visiting Professor of Plastic Surgery at the University of Virginia, and so forth.

Rees's publications run to some 126 scholarly papers, including "Baggy Eyelids in Young Adults," "The Use of Inflatable Breast Implants," and "Question, Is There a Place for the Staple Gun in Plastic Surgery?"

Rees is licensed to practice shooting his staple gun in the following states of grace: New York, Connecticut, Florida, and California, all of which happen to contain their unfair share of those graduates of youth rich enough to have escaped being called "senior citizens."

The raised letterhead on his stationery reads "Plastic and Reconstructive Surgery." In a field so vulnerable to the charge of catering to the vanity of the rich and frivolous, one wants to know what the ratio is of cosmetic surgery (more profitable and better publicized) to reconstructive surgery (the reconstruction of birth, burn, and cancer disfigurements and deformities), which the doctor performs.

"That's a difficult question," Rees hedges. "I have a very hard time drawing the line between what may be considered reconstructive and what is cosmetic—incidentally, I prefer the word 'aesthetic.' [For the same transparent reason, no doubt, that Pitanguy prefers the title "professor" to that of "doctor": It sounds more dignified.]

"It's *all* really rehabilitative surgery. If I'm fixing a large hooked nose on a teenager who is in severe emotional distress because of that hook, in my view I am accomplishing almost the same thing as if I were repairing a harelip in a baby." ("When they start to give you the line about how cosmetic surgery is really therapeutic and da da da, I say oh, *bullshit*," Kenneth says, with characteristic candor. "I mean, it just drives me crazy.") "I have to admit, my practice in the city of New York is very heavily slanted toward aesthetic surgery, for the simple reason that that is where we are *at* in this society, that's where the patients are coming *from*. I maintain a deep interest in reconstructive surgery and I do as much of it as I possibly can, particularly in my African endeavors."

In 1955 Rees and Sir Archibald McIndoe, dislocating themselves from Queen Victoria's Jaw Center, visited East Africa, where they were so powerfully struck by the lack of available medical care that the next year they returned to found the Flying Doctors Service of East Africa. A quarter of a century later, their health-care and -education service based in Nairobi, with satellite centers in the rural areas of Kenya, Tanzania, and the Sudan, is still flying strong.

"It's a perfectly selfish motivation on my part—I'm enriching not only the lives of others but my own life, too," Rees says of his yearly service with the Flying Doctors. "It completely refreshes me—changes the tempo and the type of work I do. Fundamentally, what the Flying Doctors does is get me away from Park Avenue."

It has also given Rees some new ideas for his dinner wear. One of his most exalted patients reports bumping into her plastic surgeon at the fashionable Bistro restaurant in Beverly Hills. "He was busy operating," she says cynically. "Hobnobbing with Swifty and Mary Lazar and Billy and Audrey Wilder, and wearing, my *dear*, either a tiger-striped or a zebra-striped dinner jacket, I don't remember which."

The truth is that Rees may get a kick out of Kenya but that back on Park Avenue his reputation glows anew with a philanthropic phosphorescence. Should one be too far from Rees's office to see this emanating glow, one could always read his hype bulletins, such as the following breathy puff from Liz Smith's syndicated gossip column:

> I ran into the remarkable plastic surgeon **Dr. Tom Rees** at Hisae's West and he was looking awfully fit. He'd just returned from a stint in Kenya, where he helped form the Flying Doctors of East Africa 20 years ago. Rees goes there every winter to practice for charity. It is his greatest love and hobby. Now, back to those rich and beautiful women who flock to him up on 72d St. (I mean Dr. Tom makes them beautiful; I suppose God made them rich!)

Rees's Seventy-second Street office, styled, "Plastic Surgery Associates," occupies the first three floors of a converted double brownstone off Lexington Avenue. The doctor and his wife and children live above the shop, hang out above the shingle. As one enters the office, one passes two terraria placed where window boxes would normally be found. The artful displays under the plate glass of these terraria change with the seasons, the four seasons of life, just as nonplastic surgery patients change with *their* seasons and plastic surgery patients do not. One recent Halloween, the terraria featured three smug pumpkins, all with their eyes, noses, and mouths professionally incised—with sharper instruments, you can be sure, than you and I use when we cut out scary faces on *our* Halloween pumpkins.

"The plastic surgeon's room," Rees wrote in his textbook on plastic surgery, "should be comfortably decorated and aesthetically" (Note: *not* "cosmetically") "pleasing so that the patient can feel relaxed." In Rees's designer-decorated waiting room, the grays and beiges speak soft and low to the patient's high anxiety. At first glance, the seating seems to have been arranged at most peculiar angles; a second glance and we comprehend the ulterior design—that no two patients in this waiting room should ever have to look directly at each other!

The art on Rees's office walls is of the same bloodless, painless kitsch as those silly Halloween terraria—tie-dyed bongos and gazelles, declawed tigers, and other creatures of that kitschy ilk and stripe, all domesticated a step beyond even Walt Disney's wild animal taming.

Possibly there's a subterranean psychological motive behind Rees's selection of office art. A plastic surgeon can't afford to hang realism on his walls, representational pictures with normal-looking people in them. Patients might compare their own faces with these, interpreting the paintings as though they were fraught with cosmetic as well as aesthetic significance.

An arterial corridor leads from the waiting room of Plastic Surgery Associates to the consulting room, the treatment rooms, and, God willing, the recovery room. Dramatically positioned beyond the recovery room is Rees's *sanctum sanctorum,* whose open-aired casualness hints not in the least of the clandestine interviews that take place regularly there between those in pursuit of happiness and the man who can—and even may—perform, in Aldous Huxley's phrase, the "great task of happiness." The office looks out on a small pebbled garden, where a lone tree appears to be weathering well.

Leaning forward in his chair, the better to advertise his full head of close-cropped, carob-colored hair, dressed by New York's fashionable Pierre and Fred, the youthful-looking Rees speaks with scorn of how hype has invaded his profession.

"The most terrible aspect of the explosion of plastic surgery in this generation," he begins, "is all the public exposure it's been getting, be it in *Vogue* and *Harper's Bazaar, McCall's,* or even *The New York Times Magazine.* They all make plastic surgery sound like nirvana, like the pot of gold at the end of the rainbow, like some quick, frivolous way to beauty. I particularly abhor the wording that's come out of this, such as the little *'nips'* and *'tucks'* and *'snips'* and *'clips'* and the *'mini*-lifts.'

"So because patients have read about magical results in all these newspapers and magazines—*and* books—they come in assuming that the plastic surgeon can always just wave his wand and with his magic scalpel perform a miracle. Now even the most sensible patients, who would protest that they don't feel this way, do, in fact—at least subconsciously."

Rees's diagnosis is that hype has caused a grievous injury to his profession, and he holds out little hope for its rehabilitation. "What distresses me most," he complains, "is the way people now equate the performance of plastic surgery with fashion trends. The trouble is plastic surgery, because it's aimed at improving people's appearance, *can* be roughly lumped into any of the many services designed to do that, including the fashion and hair industries. That's why people see what Kenneth does and what I do as the same thing. I hate to admit it, but Kenneth *is* in a *similar* thing. But there is *no way* that the actual work we do can be compared. Naturally, women gossip about us to their hairdressers, because they realize that hairdressers see the scars behind their ears." ("I see it *all*," Kenneth acknowledges. "Behind. In front. Across. I know exactly how much work a client has had. And they know that I know. Now, there are those who will tell you, and there are those who won't say a word," says Kenneth from the inner sanctum of his salon, which was given such a decoratively durable face by Billy Baldwin that it has never had to be lifted. "I've seen too many people ruined by plastic surgery—people who had faces to start out with, beautiful faces or interesting faces, faces that were alive, lived in, that had a sense of reality to them. The euphemism is that after a face-lift they look 'rested.' Well, they don't to me. They look stressed—there's a stressed look about the eyes.")

Rees is a positioned patrician in his field; the blood on his surgeon's apron is blue. But just how does a plastic surgeon rise, become a star? How does he attract the caliber of patient that Rees has attracted?

What is it that drew the fabled society beauty Mrs. William S. Paley to Rees's quiet, deliberately tasteful consulting room?

What is it that drew New York fashion plate Nan Kempner?

What is it that drew the genial Johnny Carson to Rees some ten years ago for an eye-lift?

What is it that drew the sixty-eight-year-old TV game show producer Mark Goodson of Goodson-Todman fame?

And what is it that one week before the Reagan assassination attempt of March 30, 1981, drew Barbara Walters to Rees for an eye- and face-lift? The show must go on, and when the President was shot,

Walters, the world's top female broadcaster and one of the nation's most mercilessly scrutinized faces, was asked to go on the air. Unfortunately, her face was not yet entirely healed, although the stitches had been removed. Her celebrated cool deserting her, she pressed the panic button, summoning Rees and the makeup artist and hairdresser he recommends for postoperative plastic surgery camouflage. Barbara Walters did keep up career appearances—a scarf around her head hiding the more distinguishing signs of her plastic surgery—before what must surely have been the largest audience of her record-breaking career. But when she frowned with seriousness, how it must have hurt!

Rees is a man of epic reticence and at least overt probity when it comes to naming names, though at some level plastic surgeons, who carve and decorate the famous for a living, must all long to decorate themselves in public by way of those they've carved—and stride from their offices at high noon dangling all those fashionable scalps from their belts.

Pressed to divulge the names of at least some of those he's worked to make look "rested," Rees refuses, but Dr. Tom can't resist grandly tossing off the aside: "Just look in any good restaurant in New York around two o'clock. My work is on exhibit."

Shifting a bit, then leaning farther forward in his chair, Rees considers the question, "How does a plastic surgeon rise, become a star?"

"Plastic surgeons," he replies, "usually consider the stars to be those men who have contributed significantly to the growth of the field, men such as Sir Archibald McIndoe. As far as achieving so-called stardom in the eyes of the public—one way, which is anything *but* a service to the public, is to hire a press agent and get yourself some publicity, which unfortunately is being done at the present time in certain areas of the world, notably Los Angeles, New York, and some places in Europe and South America. It is, I am happy to say, a very tiny, a really insignificant number of plastic surgeons who employ press agents, but some of them do achieve a stardom in the press, which in most cases is poorly deserved. I personally have never sought this type of billing and I don't particularly relish it."

Just a minute, Dr. Tom. How can you continue to be so scornful of the popularization of your surgical specialty when you were one of the first plastic surgeons to be regularly featured in the magazines that "sell" plastic surgery to their readers—the ladies' magazines? You've gone on record as saying, "Every housewife in this country, whether she admits it or not, has thought about having a face-lift." You've also been quoted as saying that "plastic surgery is the ultimate form there is of improving the quality of life." Forgive me, but your promotable pronounciamentos are nothing other than aesthetic propaganda.

And what are we to make of your vaunted admiration for Pitanguy, a doctor whose every samba step in the fleshpots of the world is recorded by the press and who himself has been reported to be the subject of a samba?

Pitanguy's favorite dance hall is the gossip column. "To see Pitanguy sense the presence of a society photographer is to witness high-voltage circuitry crackle into action," writes Warren M. Hoge, *New York Times* Rio bureau chief. "Ivo never misses a party in Rio," Suzy reports. "Why should he? It gives him a chance to say hello to all his best customers. By the way, all the Brazilians keep saying that Sophia Loren is tucked away on the seventeenth floor of Rio's Marina Palace Hotel, but she has yet to set foot in public. Maybe her carnival costume isn't ready."

In your textbook, Doctor, you described Pitanguy as "a legend in his own lifetime," but you neglected to mention that it was Pitanguy who made himself a legend. And what becomes a legend most? In Rio, not so much a Blackglama coat, because it's rather warm down there, as a black belt in karate.

3

Howard Bellin, MD:
Bourgeois Barker

Howard T. Bellin, M.D., age forty-five, is, by public and professional consensus, the most widely publicized agent of grace in the far-flung empire of the plastic art. Although Bellin, like Rees, has both a university and a hospital affiliation (he professes plastic surgery at New York Medical College, and is Chief of Plastic Surgery at Cabrini Medical Center in the Bronx), his *curriculum vitae* is more a *curriculum dolce vita,* consisting chiefly of newspaper cuttings and gossip-column clips.

Like many other plastic surgeons, Bellin started out doing reconstructive plastic surgery. "My plastic surgical training was in head and neck cancer, hand surgery, birth defects, and burns," he explains, "but now I don't have time for anything but cosmetic surgery."

Bellin is licensed to practice shooting his staple gun in New York, New Jersey, Florida, and California, where he is considering spending one week a month in order to have, as he so awkwardly puts it, "a foot in both coasts."

Pondering the question "How does a plastic surgeon become a star?," he expostulates, "First of all, excellence! But *I* had a press agent.

"An old college friend," Bellin elaborates, "was working for this PR agency where one of the clients was a plastic surgeon who was getting lots of media attention, but because I was already getting *more* attention in the press than him, they wanted to drop him and take me on."*

---

* If this seems like nincompoopism, it pales beside the letter that Ethel Scull, the mom of Pop art, once received from Serge Obolensky Associates, Inc., Public Relations: "Dear Ethel, Congratulations! I was flabbergasted to read so much about you in the newspapers recently and it occurred to me that perhaps you could use Public Relations Consultants, such as Serge Obolensky Associates, to make you even more famous than you are."

Bellin had been functioning as a press agent for himself long before he was famous enough to attract a professional press agent. The son of the owner of a small department store in South Orange, New Jersey, he entered the great world by marrying Contessa Christina Paolozzi, daughter of an Italian father who bore a papal title, and of an American mother who is an heiress to the United Fruit Company fortune (no southern oranges but heap big bunches of southern bananas). "Marrying Christina was the best move I ever made," Bellin says today. "It got me listed in the *Libro D'Oro d'Italiano*."

Howard Bellin and Christina Paolozzi conjoined in holy matrimony determined to wow the world.

Like her husband, Christina Bellin had functioned as her own press agent before she was famous enough to attract a professional press agent—and then famous enough to become one herself. Her notoriety dates from a 1961 Richard Avedon photograph of her wearing, from the waist up, her birthday suit. Diana Vreeland, at that time fashion editor of *Harper's Bazaar* and a woman intent on wowing the world herself, calculated that were she to publish in her respectable magazine the first fashion photograph exhibiting frontal nudity, it would have an immediate shock effect.

If a woman has a classic body, however unclothed she may be, she is clothed in the perfection of her flesh. But since Christina Bellin's body, even when rendered by such an artificer as Avedon, was by no means perfect—the breasts, hips, and thighs, in fact, were not much more than average—she looked naked, not nude. And she appeared all the more naked because her face was the face of a fashionable person. Here, the photograph telegraphed, is a well-known person naked.

In promotional terms, the shock value of the photo worked like electricity. *Harper's Bazaar* got promoted—not only on the newsstands but in the press itself—as a bold, innovative magazine. Diana Vreeland got promoted, eventually to fashion editor of *Vogue* and from there to editor-in-chief, and after being fired in 1971 for having gotten stuck in the sixties look (she was seventy at the time, and said she wouldn't go out with anybody but teenagers) and filling the pages of the magazine with blue hair, pink noses, and violet lips, she was elevated to Special Consultant to the Costume Institute of the Metropolitan Museum of Art, where the only nudes are sculpture or oil paintings and the costumes decidedly not birthday suits. Avedon got promoted, eventually to the same museum, which in 1978 honored him with a fashion retrospective, and from there to the cover of *Newsweek*. And Christina Paolozzi got promoted, overnight, from a well-known person naked to a well-known naked person.

But hype is a full-time job. The Bellins could not afford to rest comfortably on Christina's naked haunches. There was Howard's career as a fashionable plastic surgeon to invent and, once it was invented, to promote. The couple began to entertain on a scale commensurate with their ambition. Howard cultivated a racy image, acquiring, successively, a Pantara, a Carrera, and a Porsche Turbo, then an Instrom helicopter (another flying doctor!), a Beechcraft King Air (chartered to corporations when Bellin wasn't using it), and, finally, the lease on Flushing Airport in Queens, where he operated a flying school he speedily renamed Bellin Aviation, a charter service, and a gas station. (Meanwhile, Pitanguy had a jet plane, several high-powered boats, and a private island.)

Bellin also acquired a brown belt in karate. "That's one step below a black belt," he says defensively, as if mindful of the higher honor that is Pitanguy's. "Actually," he adds, "what I have is a brown belt with black tips."

While Howard was busy earning his tips, Christina busied herself publicizing her philanthropy—Vietnamese war victims. (Bellin had philanthropic tendencies, too. During the Six Day War he flew to Israel to volunteer his medical services.) Then husband and wife conjointly— when it was still shocking to have, let alone espouse, let alone *broadcast,* a sexually open marriage—appeared on Barbara Walters's television show, *Not for Women Only,* to discuss theirs. Once again the shock value worked like electricity. (As for Barbara Walters, when her time to stop time came, she repaired, as we know, to the close-mouthed Rees rather than to the Bellin who had opened his big mouth on her show.)

For years the Bellins' "Greetings from Around the World" Christmas-card-cum-newsletters prompted friendly giggles from the upwardly mobile thousands they descended upon. Shamelessly illustrating one Bellin newsletter were snaps of Howard and Christina with perhaps the oldest creature on earth, a Galapagos Islands sea turtle, whose layered folds and wattled wrinkles would make even any preplastic surgery patient's face look "rested"; of Howard on the great central plain of Java—bare-chested—that is, wearing, from the waist up, *his* birthday suit; of Howard and Christina at "Christina's birthday party with Yul Brynner," who was as usual wearing his head nude; of Howard and Christina at the opening of the Metropolitan's Avedon retrospective, proprietarily positioned before Avedon's "Christina" as it held pendulous sway in the tabernacle of art where, a few years before, Andrew Wyeth's

Christina, "Christina's World," had reigned equally speciously. Directly beneath Christina's photographed nipples on the newsletter were printed Howard's plastic surgery office address and telephone number.

On the back of the newsletter, Christina summarized the year's events in an unrapid run-on sentence: "It was thrilling to find my nude was a show stopper on Nov. 13th I was Hon. Chairman of a benefit for the Churchill School at Studio 54 After two years at Columbia U. learning to write I had my 1st article published 'ROCK KEEPS YOU YOUNG' in New York magazine it was exciting being described in the Press as a journalist."

So why did people like the Bellins, who could invent, stage, and even perform their autobiographies, feel they needed professional help in the form of a hired PR super?

"It was a stupid thing to do," Bellin acknowledges. "My press agent was supposed to get me exposed in all those articles about plastic surgery in the fashion magazines, but all he ever did was publicize the fact that here was Howard Bellin, this prominent socialite plastic surgeon, with a press agent. Listen," he says, turning defensive again, tightening that brown belt with the black tips, "I can name you five plastic surgeons in New York right now who have full-time press agents. Richard Coburn, for one."

Curiously, shortly after Bellin fired his press agent, he was himself the agent, the unwitting engineer, of more publicity than any plastic surgeon has ever received, or been able to obtain.

The threat of litigation hangs over any plastic surgeon's head. The sky fell on Bellin's when a former patient, Mrs. Virginia O'Hare, charged that, in the course of performing an abdominoplasty on her, the doctor had relocated her navel two and a half inches off-center. "A centered belly button," she declared, "is a valuable, feminine attribute."* A Manhattan supreme court awarded her $854,219.61. All things considered, Bellin got off relatively easy—there are cases on record of dissatisfied patients murdering their plastic surgeons.

The story appeared in newspapers throughout the world, with the

---

* Though Mrs. O'Hare did not choose to mention it, it is also the most atavistic connection to human life we have. Nor did she mention that an off-center belly button would have rendered her unsculptable by such a perfectionist as Praxiteles (c250 B.C.), who refused to shape a female of the species unless her navel was positioned exactly midway between her genitals and breasts. Nor did she mention in her brief how even *The Arabian Nights* descants at length upon the navel, describing one luscious lady's as "carved so deep that it would have held an ounce of nutmeg butter." O'Hare did remind us, however, that "Cher made millions on her belly button."

New York Post viciously dubbing the plastic surgeon "Dr. Howard Belly Button Bellin."

Today Bellin still insists that he relocated O'Hare's navel only half an inch off-center, as though that changed the case: A half inch is still a Ptolemaic universe away from where nature placed the button. "The jury believed her and not me," he explains, "because they were reading all about me in all the papers, about my glamorous life-style. It was, forgive me, a somewhat lower-class jury, and they just decided they were going to sting the rich doctor. After she beat me, she went around New York trying to peddle a book on her famous belly button. I think two hundred thousand dollars was the asking price. Luckily, there were no voyeurs *that* needy."

While one might imagine that Bellin's practice would shrink from all the unfavorable publicity, the reverse is the shocking truth. The ten months following the belly button ballyhoo were the busiest in his plastic surgery career; he treated some seven hundred cases. Practice doesn't make perfect, but imperfect practice makes headlines, then profit. Had Bellin been an airline pilot who landed a 747 off-center, he would have been suspended; had he been a brain surgeon who misplaced a cerebellum, Bellin would have been sent to Bedlam.

The nuisance suit behind him, Bellin was cheered to be made a member of a coterie of very famous—suits. "I get my suits made in London, at Kilgour, French, and Stanbury," he recounts. "In their establishment, they have hanging on the wall the individual suit patterns of all the famous people who go there. When I first went in there for a fitting, twelve years ago, I was in *awe.* I thought I'd never be hung up there. To me, that seemed the epitome of stardom. Well, after the belly button episode, they hung *my* pattern on the wall. So the O'Hare malpractice suit accomplished something I wanted very badly. I'm right next to Prince Michael of Kent. On the other side of him is Her Royal Highness the Queen. They make her riding clothes there. So I'm two away from the Queen. Not bad. If you go in there, I'm in the back on the right." (May Bellin's London tailors be careful in *their* stitching and not sew a trouser fly two and a half inches off-center.)

That Christmas, Christina Bellin presented Howard with a red leather album as sumptuous as a first edition. On the cover, in letters of gold, was engraved the legend "The Belly Button Book." Inside, she had pasted all the belly-button cuttings, beginning with a photograph of herself on page one of the *New York Post,* captioned: "Countess Christina Paolozzi Bellin bares her 'Bellin button' for a good cause. She helped raise more than a million dollars in May 1979 at a star-studded fashion show for Israel Bonds at the Waldorf-Astoria. The countess showed her navel was in tip-top shape."

By the time Christina did her belly dance for Israel Bonds, she was a professional press agent. She pressed her husband into hiring one of her clients, a decorating firm, to put a face on his new Madison Avenue penthouse office. Howard Bellin enthuses that "the decorators were very responsive when I told them to use soft colors to make the place warm and human, as much like a familiar, expensive, nonmedical surrounding as possible. You'll notice I don't have any surgical instruments present, I don't have any hard metal objects around, and I don't have any 'before' and 'after' mugshots on my walls." The paintings in Bellin's waiting room are of "fun wild animals," including two hippopotamuses with exceedingly long eyelashes.

When the decorating was finished, Christina gave an office warming to show off all the shiny new appointments to her husband's patients. (One can imagine them all inspecting one another to see who'd got a better nose-job or eye-lift, staring to see if they could see any scars, creating opportunities to whisper so they could peek behind the ears. The Bellins, strategic hosts that they were, did not do a lot of cutting up of beef at this party.

A notoriety resting on gossip-column clips is a fragile thing. One of the most effective ways to translate career fragility into career solidity is, as we know, to write a hardcover book in one's field of expertise, with—since, remember, there's usually not a great deal of expertise outside the expertise—the help of a ghostwriter or quote-unquote coauthor.

Until recently, it was considered somewhat unprofessional for a plastic surgeon to write a book for the layman. One Manhattan doctor violated this unwritten ethic by publishing a determinedly popular book under the desperate title *Doctor, Make Me Beautiful.* Attacked by the profession for what is construed to be a form of advertising, he sent a letter excusing his actions to prominent Board-certified plastic surgeons. (Might it have begun, "Doctor, Forgive me"?)

Just a few years after the appearance of *Doctor, Make Me Beautiful,* medical professionals were granted the right to advertise directly—in newspapers and magazines. As a result there was no longer a stigma attached to doctors writing books. Plastic surgeons lost no time in boarding that particular gravy train and helping themselves to a large serving.

Even such a pillar of the plastic surgical establishment as Rees seriously entertained the idea of writing a so-called popular book. He went so far as to interview a number of coauthors, and he engaged Alan

U. Schwartz, a prominent literary and theatrical lawyer who numbers Truman Capote and Mel Brooks among his clients, to represent the project.

It goes without saying that Rees's book would not have divulged the names, addresses, and ages of any of the celebrities he's operated on; rather, it would have explained how good—how natural—it is to have plastic surgery. Yet Rees, a practiced shaper of images, was concerned that such a book could blemish his own image. The doctor didn't exactly fancy himself appearing on Merv Griffin with the talk-show catch of the day—some Vegas showgirl perhaps.

But whom *would* Rees expect to appear with him on the tube were he to be flogging a book on cutting, snipping, and stapling? Johnny Carson? Barbara Walters? Imagine how unreal it would be for them to have to countenance the existence—on their own talk shows—of their very own plastic surgeon.

Rees may bristle at the thought of appearing on TV. Bellin, however, grabs every talk-show opportunity, knowing that he blossoms beautifully on television. "Howard's reputation and his immense talent and the caliber of his surgery," one of Christina Bellin's last newsletters husband-hyped, "has drawn the attention of CBS-TV, NBC-TV, WNEW-TV, and WPIX-TV, and we all agree if he was not a surgeon, he would be a very dramatic and attractive actor."

"I did a face-lift on a housewife on the CBS *Morning News—national*," says Bellin, blooming. "The reporter, John Osborne, came into the operating room with his equipment and interviewed the patient before and after the surgery. And four weeks later, they had me back to do breasts and a body. I've been on all *three* networks nationally with plastic surgery. And I've done just about everything locally you can imagine. I did an hour-and-a-half special with Geraldo Rivera called *The American Search for Youth and Beauty.*

"And," Bellin beams, "I did two *America Alives*. Phyllis Diller was on one of them with me. She joked how in a school production of Cinderella, she once played *both* ugly sisters, but that since she's had plastic surgery she feels a lot better about herself." (Phyllis Diller! One can picture only too well the Rees of Plastic Surgery Associates recoiling from such a tacky television association.)

"And Robert Goulet was on the other *America Alive* with me. He admitted to having had his eyes done. Very badly, I might add. Then I did two breast augmentations on the local CBS *Evening News.* By the way, a salesman for the breast implants told me I did the second biggest number of breast augmentations in New York City last year—eighty-nine. And *Midday Live* ran a piece on me operating on a perfectly straight male advertising executive."

Whatever for? To make him crooked? We needn't laugh, because if in some appalling lapse Dr. Bellin were to make a patient crooked, he could always make him straight again. Bellin's recently published *Dr. Bellin's Beautiful You Book,* coauthored by Peter Steinberg, is not subtitled *More Than 150 Ways to Make Men and Women Beautiful Through Plastic Surgery* for nothing. (The party to hype its publication was held on Veterans Day, a woefully inappropriate time to commemorate elective wounding, at the Manhattan discotheque Xenon; at midnight Bellin's book party merged with Stan Dragoti's birthday party: Everything connects.)

Billed as a "reference book and consumer guide," *Dr. Bellin's Beautiful You Book* answers more questions than even the most recklessly determined plastic surgery addict would ask. And it comes fully equipped with a page-long introduction by Bellin's Tarter-faced, shaven-pated friend, Yul Brynner.

To peruse the doctor's operating table of grisly contents is to take a funhouse tour of a chamber of horrors. Strap yourself tight in your seat because, ladies and gents, heeeerrre's—

The Chemical Face Peel ("The doctor," Bellin writes, "mixes a caustic agent, trichloraecetic acid, with a number of other ingredients and paints the resulting solution over the entire area of the patient's face. Then he covers the face with a special adhesive tape, leaving slits for the eyes, nose and mouth. Two days later the tape is removed; and as the face now exhibits a gooey layer of dissolved skin, the doctor applies an antiseptic drying powder that turns the soupy mass into a large scab." Now you're ready to scare someone other than yourself in the amusement park. And they call plastic surgery *aesthetic*?!)

Enlarging the Chin When the Teeth Don't Fit (Wouldn't it be simpler to keep the chin and chisel the teeth—and then recap?)

Lowering the Voice ("Haven't you ever sat in a restaurant and wondered about the woman at the next table, 'How could anyone live with that voice?' " Bellin asks, raising his voice.)

Raising the Voice

Making a Dimple ("A dimple can be created" Bellin writes, "by making an incision inside the mouth, removing a certain amount of tissue in the area of the cheek, and then pulling the undersurface of the overlying skin in and fastening it with sutures. Hopefully, the external depression that ensues will now look something like a dimple.")

Removing a Dimple

Taller and Shorter ("Even though it seems incredible," Bellin barks, for the carnival ain't over yet, "it's actually possible to make somebody taller or shorter. However, the two procedures . . . involve pain, a prolonged recovery period, and the prospect for serious complications. So individuals must be highly motivated before seeking them out. Very tall people, for example, often feel awkward and self-conscious; while those who are extremely short, especially men, are quite likely to feel inferior and insecure." To be made shorter, one must submit to two operations and "be prepared to lose from 4 to 8 inches.")

Torn Ear Lobes ("The main risk," Bellin writes, "consists soley of the surgeon's failure to . . . put the ears back in exactly the right place." If they *are* misplaced, patient may proceed directly to freak show. It's no accident that payment for cosmetic surgery is demanded in advance.)

Cosmetic Surgery of the Future ("Eventually," writes Bellin, perhaps impulsively, certainly unduly optimistically, "we may be able to develop an electrical device that can be worn at night to enlarge the chin and cheek bones, or even to provide additional height. Redesigning the entire body could be done by feeding personalized contour information into a computer. Then the patient would be put to sleep and the computer would direct a programmed energy beam over his body to remove all unwanted fat. Then, if we also had the implant material, it could be injected wherever needed to finish off the reshaping. So everyone could have his own ideal body." And what we would have is half the population of the world awakening as Peter Beard clones and the other half as Cheryl Tiegs clones.)

The Unfavorable Result ("A few results are so poor that the patient loses faith in the surgeon's ability," Bellin writes, too brazenly for a doctor whose notoriety is based on an unfavorable result.)

The Celebrity Lift (Multiple Mini-Lifts) ("The operation goes like this," Bellin explains. "An entertainer or politician, someone in the public eye, comes in every three to six months and has a small face-lift in a series of three or four, and like Dorian Gray going the other way, he has a gradual rejuvenated appearance. I have never actually done this, but it's theoretically possible, so I put it in my book in case anyone out there wants it." Bellin the carnie barker might as well be braying: "Calling all mini-celebrities. Wanna be a major celebrity? Step right up. Come 'n' get it. Get your mini-lifts here, get your mini-lifts here. We'll pull your skin right back into place. That's the ticket. This is the show.")

4

Stitched Celebrities: Names—*and* Faces— Revealed

"Almost no respectable person hasn't had plastic surgery done at some point in their lives," enunciates Dr. Howard T. Bellin—a remark that should earn him an entry in the *Guinness Book of World Records* under "Most Vapid Generalization." What *is* true is that no celebrity today, respectable or disreputable, goes unscrutinized for the telltale signs of sudden youth. It is even truer that most celebrities will deny having put out thousands of their easily earned dollars to stay fixed in time so they can earn some more easily earned dollars.

A curious thing about hype is that some celebrities are so enamored of their own fixed images of themselves that they not only admit to but advertise their bloody operations. Cher speaks freely of her two breast uplifts. And the "Paganini of words"—Gore Vidal's pointed description of Truman Capote—has widely publicized *his* excursions in true blood into the netherworld of plastic surgery. The last word on Capote's latest looks (those of an old child) comes from makeup artist Way Bandy, something of an expert on plastic surgery since Rees and other noted plastic surgeons refer patients for postoperative makeup care to him.

Says Bandy, flashing the two-even canines of the capped, "Michael Hogan, in my opinion the best plastic surgeon in America—he's more *quietly* famous than Tom Rees—fixed Truman on his last time out. I just wish Truman had found him sooner, because the one thing you *never* see from Michael Hogan is that cosmetic look that Truman's face betrays. Truman's eyes are *not* Michael Hogan's!" (No, Way: They're Truman's.)

Bandy's own eyes are insistently unlined. He's a dermal illusion; at almost fifty, he glows with the epicene beauty that graces youth—and credits his extended youthfulness to Michael Hogan.

"Way was the first man to come out and admit to plastic surgery," says Bandy's good friend, free-lance hairdresser Maury Hopson. "But believe me, the publicity about his surgery has been far more extensive than the surgery." (Let's wait just a minute, Maury. The first disproportion is that anyone would have *any* elective surgery done; the second disproportion is that anyone would publicize having had it done; and the third disproportion is that someone in the cosmetics business would give credit not to makeup but to cutup.)

"Way's really had so few things modified," Hopson adds. "Just a couple of temporal lifts to tighten the eye area, and his nose—he had his nose done over. But that's all minor, just a slit here and there. People *think* that Way is the bionic makeup artist, that he has snaps up the back of his head—like, you pull it here and you snap it back, y'know. But Way is *naturally* handsome—he was a great beauty *before* he had any surgery. I didn't know him then, but I've seen pictures of him from before he went to Michael Hogan." (Yes, but those pictures you saw may have been retouched or even artfully reconstructed by some version of Peter Rogers Associates. If *you* don't realize that this is a real possibility, *we* do—by now.) "By the way, Scavullo photographed Michael with his wife and son, and they looked just marvelous." (Makeup by Bandy? Hair by Hopson? Photo by Scavullo. The whole hype package. Can it be that everybody is involved in the fabrication of everybody else? By now we don't have to ask this question. We know the answer.)

What is, as Alice says, curiouser and curiouser is that public figures far more public—and therefore, one would have thought, far more private—than Capote and Bandy have advertised the fact that they've had plastic surgery. Obviously, plastic surgeons use these show-and-tell cases to hype the surgery. Senator William Proxmire of Wisconsin, Chicago Mayor Jane Byrne, and former First Ladies Betty Ford and Rosalynn Carter have all publicly and unabashedly discussed their operations in unpleasant detail.

Despite all the repugnant revelations surrounding Watergate, who would ever have thought that the wife of a President of the United States would announce that she'd had a face-lift? One would never expect such a thing from the Queen of England, but then, it's hard to make any firm pronouncements even here, because we don't know what's going to happen if she starts looking worse than her horses.

When it comes to First Lady face-lifts, Betty Ford's is in a class by itself: a lesson in the school of aesthetic overkill. The surgeon simply went too far. Her appearance was so utterly different after the operation that it was difficult to believe that her mind and spirit wouldn't also be different as a consequence of her erased face.

Last year, in another one of those episodes that strain credulity while they exact belief, Betty Ford's Palm Springs plastic surgeon, Dr. M. R. Mazaheri, sued another Palm Springs plastic surgeon, Dr. Borko Djordjevic, for taking credit for Betty Ford's fixed face. Dr. Mazaheri's suit alleged that Dr. Djordjevic claimed to have "performed cosmetic surgery on Betty Ford . . . to correct damage done by Mazaheri"; also that a female patient died in Dr. Djordjevic's office and that the woman's husband maintained that his wife had originally sought care from Dr. Djordjevic "because he told her he operated on Betty Ford."

Dr. Djordjevic claimed that the legal action was a "publicity stunt" by Dr. Mazaheri, involving "professional jealousy."

Betty Ford refused to stick her face, forged either by Dr. Mazaheri or by Dr. Djordjevic, *or* Dr. Mazaheri *and* Dr. Djordjevic, into the fracas. "We're trying to stay out of it," said the former First Lady's secretary.

Curiouser and curiouser and curiouser in our looking-glass world—which is far more topsy-turvy than Alice's—a celebrity who hasn't yet submitted to the plastic surgeon's scalpel, Andy Warhol, raves about and recommends the virtues of plastic surgery.* As long ago as the early sixties, Warhol was painting his acrylic on canvas nose-job series: Before and After I, Before and After II, and Before and After III—each of the three dyptichs featuring a female face with a before hook nose and an after pug.

Recently, Warhol gave one of his old Factory retainers the present of plastic surgery for Christmas. The gift certificate was good for an eyelift at Plastic Surgery Associates. As it turned out, Rees had just done the Factory worker's mother for the third time, and she was able to reassure her nervous daughter that she wouldn't be in bad company; on her very first visit to Dr. Rees, she divulged, she'd seen Johnny Carson in the waiting room.

A couple of months ago Warhol met a plastic surgeon who offered

---

* Not to mention makeup. Warhol recently purchased a tube of Revlon lipstick at Bloomingdale's, confessing to his surprised companion, "My lips are starting to get smaller and I can't stand it." That night he put some of the lipstick on his hand and rubbed it on his cheeks in the elevator before going into a party. At the gathering, where everybody told him how well he looked because he had color, he turned to his companion and said, "You *see.*" Warhol also uses blush-on. Shortly after his happy discovery of cosmetics, he became a model.

to barter some of his work for some of Warhol's: "I'll do your face if you do my portrait." Both jobs would presumably be highly cosmeticized versions of the original. But at this, Warhol drew the line—he wasn't going to trade a thirty-thousand-dollar portrait for a five-thousand-dollar face-lift he could buy whenever he felt like it.

Truman Capote and Way Bandy and Betty Ford—all three so open about their operations—and Andy Warhol—so eager to have one—are the celebrity exceptions; most celebrities still insist on secrecy.

A few months ago the *New York Post* headlined "BABA'S FACE IS ALL HER OWN." "Barbara Walters hasn't had a face-lift," the newspaper's "Headliners" column began. " 'Who'd have the time?' she asked a *Ladies' Home Journal* interviewer . . . Revealing that after her TV specials, viewers ask 'where I got my face-lift,' Miss Walters, 50, said it wasn't surgery but 'great care' by makeup and lighting people that enhanced her looks. The interview concludes with Miss Walters—who admits she's 'not much of a feminist'—giving her recipe for chocolate macaroons. She claims they're better than Katharine Hepburn's brownies." It could be that Walters's cookie claim is as untrue as her plastic surgery disclaimer. As we already know, Baba has had her own macaroon lifted by Dr. Tom.

Plastic surgery may be the only subject still tabooed in the precincts of the rich and famous. In the most dramatic society scandal and one of the most hyped trials of modern times, in which Claus von Bülow stood accused of having twice tried to kill his heiress wife "Sunny," Mrs. von Bülow's maid of twenty years was cross-examined by the defense attorney about the face-lift her mistress had undergone (reputedly at the hands of Dr. David Ju). Although the maid had revealed in nearly three days on the stand all the sordid details of Mrs. von Bülow's eating habits, drinking addiction, and bowel movements, she stared at the defense attorney and told him: "I am not going to answer the question, because I swore to Mrs. von Bülow that I would never talk about it. I never even talked about it to the children."

Not only lady's maids but plastic surgeons themselves have gone to great lengths to camouflage, and on occasion actually hide, the fact that Ms. X, Mrs. Y, or Mr. Z has visited a plastic surgeon's office.

One amusing incident involved society columnist Suzy, whose syndicated column is thickly peopled with the very socialites and celebrities who sooner or later make that date with the plastic surgeon, one date they take care to keep. Invoking the name of the fashionable doctor who, in fact, is married to the editor-in-chief of a fashion magazine, *Vogue*, Suzy confides, "Bill Cahan saw me at a party and said to a mutual friend, '*I* don't want to tell her because it might make her nervous, but *you* tell her that *I* mentioned that I'd noticed she had a mole on the back of her neck and that maybe she should have it looked at.'

"*Well,* when I heard that, I called my dermatologist right up, Dr. Berman, but he was out of the country. So I thought, I'll call Tom Rees. I went right over to his office, and *my* dear, when *I* came in, they *spirited* me away, they hid me in a little room, and I said, '*Why* are you *doing* this? *I'm* not coming in here to have anything *done. Why* am I being *hidden*? I mean, I'm just having a *mole* removed from my neck.'

"And they said, 'No no no, it isn't that we think *you* don't want to be seen here, it's that *we* don't want our *patients* to see *you.* Because if *they* see *you,* they'll get nervous—they'll know *you* saw *them.* ' "

Ironically, this was probably the one time that those people in Rees's waiting room wanted neither to be seen by Suzy nor to make her column. After all, they were there to see about having their faces done so she could describe them in print as looking "fresh and rested."

Suzy is no stranger to plastic surgeons. Several years ago, when she was asked by *Ladies' Home Journal* to compile "Suzy's Secret Lists" for a cover story it was doing on her, she included, along with "Suzy's Dazzling Dozen—the World's Most Beautiful Women," "Suzy's Perfect Little Dinner for Ten," "Suzy's Beautiful People Restaurants," "Suzy's List of the Most Fashionable (and Exclusive) Resorts," and "Suzy's Snob Test,"

Suzy's List of Plastic Surgeons to the Beautiful People

1. Dr. David Ju
2. Dr. Thomas Rees
3. Dr. John Converse
4. Dr. Franklin Ashley
5. Dr. Ralph Millard
6. Dr. Ivo Pitanguy
7. Dr. Robin Beare
8. Dr. Jean Lintilhac

Note that, because she was going to a plastic surgeon for a mere mole excision and not for plastic surgery, Suzy didn't bother to go to Dr. Ju, number one on her list, she went to Doctor Number Two. Odds are that Rees, when he saw his name resident in *Town & Country,* for all his huffing about the co-opting of plastic surgery by fashion magazines—and all Suzy's puffing—didn't blow the house down. Doctor Number Three was, alas, dead, and doctors four through eight practice in Beverly Hills, Miami, Rio de Janeiro, London, and Paris, respectively.

Back in New York, Doctor Number Two did do some huffing and puffing when he received a rejection letter from Cheryl Tiegs. "Tom Rees," she says, "wrote me a long letter congratulating me on my perfectly symmetrical face and asking if he could use my picture in his slide shows and lectures all around the country. I wrote back good *God* no." Even though Rees had promised to clear Tiegs's name of the inference of plastic patienthood, she realized that she couldn't afford to be included in a plastic surgical context.

Gore Vidal shares the discomfort that most celebrities feel when the press places them in such a context. When he heard that Martin Amis, son of novelist Kingsley Amis—and a journalist who once declared to the *New York Times* his preference for covering "the most vulgar and lurid things I can find"—was planning to publish the rumor that the fifty-seven-year-old Vidal had had not only a face-lift but also an ass-lift, or a gluteasmaximusplasty as they say in the trade, Gore went wild, threatening to bring suit. Amis backed down.

Speaking of his enemies collectively, as the Roman emperor Caligula (for a time "Gore Vidal's Caligula") spoke of his when he wished that the Romans had a single neck so he could wring it, Vidal intones, "*They* are an ass, and if you *are* an ass, pain is bound to come your way, isn't it?" (Yes, Gore, but perhaps only from those who are preoccupied with that part of the anatomy.) "Amis was in *love* with the ass-lift allegation. I did admit to having my teeth capped," Vidal says, grinning toothsomely, "and of course, to the English with *their* notoriously bad teeth, capping is a sign of degeneracy."

5

From Flesh and Blood to
Frantic Franchising

What germ in the culture caused this disease that prevents us from growing old gracefully? Even so measured a creature as the English novelist and playwright Enid Bagnold caught the cultural germ. In her autobiography, the author of *National Velvet* and *The Chalk Garden* confessed that at the age of sixty-six she had had a face-lift performed by Sir Archibald McIndoe, Rees's esteemed mentor. After the operation Bagnold asked Sir Archibald how much skin she'd had taken off. "Enough to cover a handbag," he replied. She then asked if, should her symptoms reappear, she would need to have a touch-up. "Not for ten years," Sir Archibald told her, "and then you won't want it."

One would expect there to be a point at which all plastic surgeons would advise against further elective cutting. This is evidently not so.

"That's the strangest conversation I ever heard—I can't imagine Archie McIndoe saying to this English writer that she would not want the face-lift done *again*," Rees comments, the aesthetic propaganda machine beginning to gurgle. "I've operated on patients in their late seventies."

Bellin informs us in his book that "the benefits of the face-lift procedure last forever, but the aging and deterioration continue as before." In other words, the benefits of the face-lift procedure which last forever last until the patient needs another face-lift, which will last forever and a day.

Bellin is no more concerned than Rees is with his patients' age. "*My* oldest face-lift was eighty-five," he announces. "And I just did a breast uplift and implant on a seventy-six-year-old. I probably wouldn't have done it except I'd gone out with the woman's daughter, so, I mean, I knew the mother socially. I was *crazy* about the daughter! The mother

169

came to see me saying her boyfriend had just died and she wanted to get another guy—she *implied* with her body. I mean, why not? What difference did her age make if she wanted to use her body?"

"That is no country for old men," wrote Yeats. This is no country for old women, either. Old age is perceived as a social problem and experienced as a source of unhappiness. People persist in having cuts and alterations made in the text of their flesh because they see old age as the greater mutilation.

But the body can stand just so much mortification. "After about four face-lifts, after the skin has been pulled that many times," Bellin acknowledges, "a person begins to look unreal. That's what happened to the Duchess of Windsor."

When the duchess was in her late seventies, with many face-lifts behind her, she demanded one more. "Tighter!" she commanded her plastic surgeon, Dr. Robin Beare, "tighter!" Judging that at her age she might not be able to withstand the trauma of major surgery, Beare refused to lift her highness's face again. The duchess, long frozen in space and time as one of the world's canonical images of classic chic, had no aesthetic alternative but to repair to another surgeon—some say Pitanguy—for what Noel Coward so archly called "a little cosmetic refreshment." When she returned to Paris, her French women friends all cackled behind her back, *"Elle s'est encore fait tirer le museau."* (She's had her muzzle stretched again.) All in all, Wallis Warfield Simpson Windsor has undergone the greatest number of elective surgical invasions of the human face.

"The greatest number of face-lifts I've performed on one person is three," Bellin states. "On the other hand, I've only been in business twelve years." That's one every four years. Assuming that Bellin's patient is a plastic surgery addict who will return at the same rate, by the time Bellin retires at sixty-five (with a gold watch and a silver staple gun), she will have had eleven lifts—and will be declared the winner of the Duchess of Windsorplasty Prize.

Overlifted women are instantly recognizable—in the words of *School for Scandal,* "the connoisseur may see at once that the head's modern though the trunk's antique." Witness all those ladies at the Reagan Inaugural. They certainly hadn't started out in life looking alike, yet now, with their poor little overlifted faces and the ash-blond, cotton-candy hairdos that top them, they're interchangeable. Indeed, so interchangeable that last year the Best Dressed List gave a special citation to a coterie of Nancy Reagan's close friends for, in effect, parading around looking like one another.

The skin has been pulled so tight under their chins that there's no graceful transition between their faces and their necks. Their heads sit on their bodies like balloons on strings. Like jack-o'-lanterns on fence posts, or like the masks on sticks that partygoers hold before their faces, where only their own eyes peer through. In this context, the Reagan Inaugural was a masked ball, and Truman Capote's famous 1967 Black and White masked ball at the Plaza was a doubleheader.

If one of the cautions of plastic surgery is having it done too often, another is having it done inadvisedly. Aging actors often undergo elective lifts in order to grab parts and steal shows. As William Holden once said to his friend Peter Beard over a hot campfire and a long, cool drink on the shores of Lake Rudolf in northern Kenya, where they were on safari, "*Sure* I've had a face-lift. I had the pouches taken out from under my eyes. Plastic surgery is a fact of life in this business—it's a business of appearances. And I'm a businessman, and plastic surgery is a business reality. Shit, there's hardly a middle-aged male lead in Hollywood who hasn't gone under the knife."

But to live as an actor is to live in a world of reiterative surprise. When Robert Mitchum underwent facial surgery a couple of years ago, it was with the firm expectation that he would be professionally revivified. He could not have known that director Louis Malle had decided to give him first crack at playing the aging numbers runner in his film *Atlantic City*.

"I flew out to Hollywood to offer him the part," Malle says, adding carefully, "let's say that my meeting with Mitchum was slightly disappointing for reasons, let's just say, that have nothing to do with talent. Let's just say that Mitchum was only interested in playing younger men, young romantic leads, and not down-at-the-heels hoodlums like Lou." Let's just say that Malle's face fell when he saw that the face of his first-choice actor was no longer the craggy, lived-in one we all know as Robert Mitchum's but rather a lifted, creaseless clone of it.

Burt the unlifted Lancaster was chosen to play Lou, and so it was *his* career that was revivified. "Practically the same day I saw Mitchum in Los Angeles, I met with Burt," Malle continues. "In the beginning I was worried that Burt was carrying his past with him—especially since I was very interested at the time in Deborah Kerr for the role of Lou's girlfriend, Grace. Deborah wanted to do it and she would have been wonderful, but she was going to be on tour in Australia. Anyway, it would have been sort of weird to have Burt and Deborah on a beach twenty-five years later."

Malle is referring, of course, to the scene in *From Here to Eternity* where Lancaster and Kerr make love by a fiercely beating sea. Though they were dressed, the scene remains the sexiest in the history of American cinema. Perhaps a sixty-seven-year-old Burt Lancaster and a fifty-nine-year-old Deborah Kerr coupled on a grainy beach again would have violated their old—that is, their invincibly youthful—images for us. Their performance might have been experienced, very uncomfortably, as a prurient parody.

For his performance in *Atlantic City,* Burt Lancaster was nominated for an Academy Award for best actor. Although in the event he lost to Henry Fonda for *On Golden Pond,* he did win the Los Angeles Film Critics Association, the National Society of Film Critics, and the New York Film Critics Circle awards for best actor. *New York* magazine pronounced Lancaster's Lou "the best thing about the picture—dressed like an Italian cavalier in white suits, Lancaster looks at [Susan] Sarandon with his tired old eyes, and the movie's conceits almost seem like poetry."

Had Lancaster's eyes looked "rested," as Robert Mitchum's had, he would never have been given the opportunity to play the greatest part of his career by a director passionately committed to the human face. ("There's nothing more interesting than the human face," Malle has said. "I remember this incredibly long close-up of Ingrid Bergman's face in *Autumn Sonata.* Her face was like a map, like a landscape, it had all the stigmas of time. I could have watched her face forever.")

"Burt was difficult," Malle reminisces. "I mean, he wasn't extremely easy to deal with. He would become—Irish, very Irish. He'd start drinking around five o'clock, like a lot of people do, especially old people, like when the night falls. Not too much, but still, y'know . . . I'm sure he *was* a boozer. When you had dinner with him, he would drink, like, cocktails, the way they used to do—martinis. Night shooting with Burt was always a problem."

To live as an actor is to play a game of hide-and-seek with time. Take the case of the urchin actor, singer, and dancer Joel Grey, who early in his career had his nose reduced so it would be just as cute as the rest of his tiny self and he could get to play all the good juvenile leads.

What he didn't realize was that the day would come when the permanently fixed button nose would no longer fit the maturing face. In the long run, plastic surgery may have stunted Joel Grey's career. He may have succeeded only in immortalizing himself stuck in time at the age of ten. He looks too boyish to be taken seriously. We don't want them to be cute at fifty.

We do want them to be cute at twenty-five. If actors undergo elective surgery to hold on to the public's image of them, models undergo the surgery to be even cuter imitations of themselves than they already are. It seems a paradox that successful young models would desire plastic surgery; the words "successful," "young," and "model" spell self-sufficiency.

"Models," Bellin explains, "are always coming in with photographs of themselves. They never say, 'Look at *me*.' They say, 'Look at my photograph.' And then they point out whatever it is they want fixed—usually it's the nose, to get some shadow eliminated, but often it's the chin and cheekbones, too—all so they can photograph better." Since many plastic surgery patients bring to their first appointment pictures of noses, chins, or cheekbones they covet—torn out of *Glamour* or *Vogue*—the law of probability dictates that a percentage of these photographs must be of some of those model patients who came to Bellin for surgical retouching with their own torn-out tearsheets.

"The red-flag warning to a surgeon," says Rees, who at least recognizes a red flag when he sees one (Bellin is too busy waving it to recognize that it's red), "is a patient who comes in with a picture of Robert Redford and says, 'This is what I want to look like.' If they do that, you know you've got a bummer right away."

What, one wonders, would Rees have made of the distraught Jean Harris, had she, in the waning months of her doomed love affair with Dr. Herman Tarnower, sought Rees's services? Would that red flag have waved? In the infamous "Scarsdale Letter," Harris wrote, "I thought of going and borrowing five thousand dollars and going to a doctor to make me younger, then thought I might wind up uglier than before." Deranged as she was by jealousy and grief, she had marbles enough left to realize that plastic surgery was not the magic solvent for her woe.

For Rees, that red flag flaps when he's asked whether he would ever suggest plastic surgery to an acquaintance. "To suggest to an individual that his appearance should be improved is to point out a deficiency—which is to me totally unprofessional and just unthinkable," he says. Bellin, on the other hand, makes no bones about pointing out physical deficiencies to those he knows, including his own flesh and blood.

"I actually went up to my niece, Marissa," he boasts, "my only sister's only child, and said, 'Let's do your nose.' She said, 'So let's do it.' So I did it. And she's deliriously happy with it. We're all happy with it." One great big happy family without that great big Bellin nose.

If Bellin had had his way with Barbra Streisand, she would now be singing another tune and blowing another nose. "About ten years ago," he recounts, "I was at a very nice party with about eighty other well-known people. Across the crowded room I saw a quick flash of this *incredible* nose and I thought, 'Oh, my God, I've got to operate.' I was drawn to it, it was so bad. So I went across the room to suggest that I was, you know, a plastic surgeon. And it was Barbra Streisand, I *swear.*" Bellin wanted to cut off her nose despite her fame.

"My own nose," the self-regarding doctor observes, "is not a great nose by any means. But it doesn't bother me, because I grew up never realizing it was large. I'm starting to look a little tired under the eyes," he obsesses. "And I also don't like the lines that run from my nose to my mouth—these furrows in the side of my face here. I'm going to have them injected with collagen or some other experimental filler material. I'm going to get a freebie. Why not? This is a fraternity of sorts.

"I know *plenty* of plastic surgeons who've had plastic surgery. One of them was just operated on by his lover, who's also a plastic surgeon— in fact, they share a practice. Among other practices, I guess. Another prominent plastic surgeon has his hair dyed—his hair colorist, who came to me for tattoo removal, told me."

On the short list of plastic surgeons who have undergone plastic surgery themselves is Rees. He had an eye-lift a couple of years ago— performed, some say, by his colleague Dr. Cary Guy. The operation didn't stop Rees from performing his own operations. Shortly after his eye-lift, he was operating with the stitches still in his eyes. And we know that the famously vain Pitanguy (the "professor" straps on elevator shoes to appear in public) is said to have had his face lifted by Rees, who naturally denies having done it.

It's considered acceptable for plastic surgeons to repair to other plastic surgeons. But what's the rule when a plastic surgeon's family members turn to him for help?

"A doctor does *not* operate on his wife," Bellin pronounces, "or on any member of his immediate family. He can't afford to let anything nonmedical get in the way. I once saw a plastic surgeon kill his father-in-law! But I have to confess that I did operate on my wife. She didn't want to go through all the nonsense of making doctor's appointments and sched-uling surgery. So I did her in my office after hours."

Rees has also performed a face-lift on *his* wife, a former fashion and commercial model, whom he unfailingly refers to as "my beautiful wife" or "my wife who was and is beautiful." (Seven days after her operation, he took her with him to a medical convention, the stitches still in her face.) And Dr. Richard Coburn, who Bellin has told us employs a press agent, has also operated on his own wife.

Maury Hopson, a mere—albeit pretty fancily remunerated—free-lance hairdresser, draws the scissors shut at the notion of reconstructing *his* lover's image; he doesn't think it's right for him to cut "Jim's" hair. Yet Bellin and Rees cut their wives' faces, and Coburn cuts into his wife's breasts.

To many, beauty is a matter of life and death. To some, it is a matter even more important than life and death. A fashionable New York fashion editor, whose doctor had told her that under no circumstances should she have an eye-lift, since she had had open-heart surgery (which didn't defer her from cavorting nakedly later on—scars and all—in the Fire Island Pines) and the risk was just too great, naturally went right ahead and had it. Half an hour into the operation—one of her eyes had been started; the other had not even been touched—her heart stopped and her lungs filled up, and they wheeled her off to Intensive Care. The first thing she is said to have said when she revived enough to realize what had happened to her was that she wanted to have the second eye done as soon as possible. Her friends were all relieved to read in Liz Smith that "one of the best fashion editors around, **Carrie Donovan** of The Times mag, is out of danger in Baker Pavilion at New York Hospital. She suffered heart arrest while under anesthetic for a minor operation."

Meanwhile, a housewife who'd been reading, in her dentist's office perhaps, hype articles about the wonders of plastic surgery, perhaps in the fashion editor's own magazine, decided to lay her life on the line.

"She was," Bellin narrates, "a woman married to a man who owns a bakery. She came to me for an abdominoplasty, and she also asked me to fix some little thing on her nose while I was at it. As I was finishing her abdomen, I noticed that the anesthesiologist had somehow dislodged the endotracheal tube and my patient was blue. She was *gorked*. She'd had some kind of cardiac arrest. We zapped her with heart massage, then wheeled her into Intensive Care, not knowing whether she was going to make it.

"The next morning I went in to see how she was doing, and everything had worked out fine—no brain damage, not even any heart damage. I told her how lucky she was to be alive—I mean, everybody around her was dying, right? And you know the first thing she said? She was hooked up to the cardiac monitor, and she had a tube in her stomach and a catheter in her bladder, and she said, "That's terrific, but there's one thing I don't understand. Why didn't you do my nose?' Six or seven months later, I knocked off her nose."

The fashion editor, broadcaster of hype bulletins, is finally the active victim of her own hype. Farther down the ladder, the baker's wife, ideal receiver of hype bulletins, is hype's passive prey, as is—down, down, *down*—the mother of one of the child murder victims in Atlanta, who shocked the nation by confessing to having used the whole of her government stipend for a "tummy tuck."

All of the above—and untold millions more—have been hard-sold a bill of plastic goods by the superstaplers, the craftiest of whom take their own names and distribute them down, down, down. There's a name for such wholesale distribution: franchising.

It's one thing when franchising is done with ice cream, soft drinks, and hamburgers, quite another when it's done with human flesh.

The germinal moment of this kind of franchising came in 1978 when the Supreme Court eliminated sanctions against doctors soliciting patients, thus freeing the former to engage in aggressive, competitive advertising. In magazines and newspapers across the country, ads instantly appeared asking, "What can be done in an hour, costs less than a new designer dress, and makes you look and feel years younger?"

This type of hard sell promotes the new trend in franchising—one-day plastic surgery clinics or "boutiques." "In at 9, out at 5," the brochures read. "Surgical procedures performed in the office—Simple! Safe!!"

In ethical terms, the franchising of plastic surgery is—in a word—sick. We think of the doctor as the priest of our time. (Certainly the politician is not the priest. Nor is the priest the priest.) And there's something deeply disturbing about the priest mass-peddling his wares.

"Some of these doctors who advertise," Rees comments, "are highly qualified and good, others are dangerous, but how can the public evaluate them? On how clever their ad copy is?"

Rees, then, does not franchise. He keeps that apron of his, with all that blue blood on it, clean.

But Bellin franchises. One of those plastic surgery boutiques that advertise in the *New York Post* and the *New York Times* is his. "The Plastic Surgery Center of New York is mine," he announces proudly, waving his ad in the *Post:*

> The Plastic Surgery Center of New York. Our Penthouse facility is unique in all of New York, yet our rates are

totally affordable. Enter in the morning and leave after recovery the same day. No hospitalization is required ... Our Director is a Board Certified Plastic Surgeon, and the facility is unparalleled. So if you are considering elective plastic surgery of any type contact us first for a private consultation. After all, we are the Plastic Surgery Center of New York.

"We are"? As opposed to what? To "they are not"? That Bellin has not yet given his own name to his operation doesn't whiten the spots on his apron. The Center occupies the back rooms of his midtown office. "The word 'penthouse' really grabs 'em," Bellin says. "My copywriter and I together came up with *that* angle." According to Bellin, a high percentage of the roughly fifty calls a day his ad elicits are "people at the top of the income pyramid."

Now why would a prominent and already prosperous plastic surgeon franchise?

Bellin's reasons are the same all-American reasons that most franchisers would give if asked to justify the mass production of their product. "There are plenty of people with less to spend on plastic surgery than names like me charge in our regular practice," he says. "What I'm doing is making plastic surgery available to *everyone*. You might even say I'm performing a public service."

("If these plastic surgeons who advertise really wanted to be doing a public service," comments a former chairman of the Ethics Committee of the American Society of Plastic and Reconstructive Surgeons, "they'd be advertising scar corrections, tumor removal, or cleft lips.")

But sooner or later with franchising, corners are cut. And as always with hype, the product becomes cruder as it filters down by way of imitation.

"At my Plastic Surgery Center of New York facility, I have young plastic surgeons doing the surgery," Bellin explains. "I don't do any of it myself. That's why the fees are approximately two thirds of what my own fees are. But don't worry, I have ascertained in my mind that the guys doing the operations are all excellent surgeons, albeit not totally experienced, because you've got to go through a lot of years doing plastic surgery to pick up certain nuances.

"I'd like to branch out to every city in America. I can automatically get licenses to practice in forty states. I'll be the director of all the centers—put my stamp of quality on the operations, hire only the best guys to do them, and make sure they're done to my specifications. And the guys'll pay me such and such percent of their *gross* profit," Bellin concludes, hitting it, for once, right on the button.

Even at the level of hairdressing, more sense is shown: Kenneth never wanted to branch out beyond his New York salon, because, as he explains, "If a stylist comes in with a hangover and cuts off someone's ear, it's my salon and I want to be there."

For all we know, plastic surgeons might branch out to where the majority of Americans do their shopping, the malls and plazas. The franchisers could set up shop in every supermarket, between the Harlequin romances and the meat section—knowing, as they do, that whoever gets the position gets the sales; after all, they have to catch the shopper's eye before they can fix it. And then, for franchising purposes only, the butcher could be trained to trim a different kind of fat and pare a different kind of gristle.

And someone, you can bet, will come up with the idea of a plastic knife for a plastic surgeon, plastic being so much less expensive than stainless steel.

Plastic surgeons haven't really put their minds to all the possibilities.

REPRISE

She was in her late thirties—good-looking, rich. There was a slight bump on her beautiful long nose which no doctor would fix because no one could see it except her. But then the doctor who was doing her dermalmastopexy, not wanting to lose the bosom, said he'd do the nose. She instructed him not to make it any shorter, not to do anything to it except shave the bump.

Both operations were successful. The nose was perfect.

Two months later, admiring her new self in a shop window, she was hit by a cab and smashed right down on her face. And so the nose—her unset, ungelled new nose—was demolished.

When the doctors told her that to rebuild it they would have to use a piece of her hip bone as a graft, she refused—she wore tiny bikinis.

So they injected silicone into her nose instead. The nose rejected it; the fluid came running out of her nostrils.

Now the hip graft was a necessity.

After the operation, she asked the nurse for a mirror. She was refused it. The next day she asked again. Again she was refused.

But when the bandages came off, she sneaked into the bathroom to look at herself. In shock, she fell on the floor. On her nose. The nose was now like batter on her face.

The doctors informed her that it would be shorter when it was fully reconstructed. Today her nose points at the sky; one can see right up her nostrils. She's been to every doctor and none of them will touch it, because there's nothing left to work with.

She is a daily customer of New York's leading makeup artist. To distract attention from her nose, he heavily paints her eyes. But looking into the cruel mirror at herself, she remembers the beautiful, flirtatious creature she once was.

HYPE'S HIRED GUNS

BOBBY ZAREM, SWIFTY LAZAR,
HERB SCHMERTZ, JOSEPH E. LEVINE,
JOHN SPRINGER,
AND HOWARD J. RUBENSTEIN

AGENTS OF FACTS, FLACKERY, FAKERY, AND QUACKERY

It's in a publicity man's nature to be a liar. That's what I pay you for. I wouldn't have hired you if you weren't a liar.

—Clifford Odets, *The Sweet Smell of Success*

In the age of hype, images undergo plastic surgery just as faces and bodies do.

There's a term for those who perform plastic surgery on images, contouring and carving, reshaping and reconstructing them. And the term is as well known as any of the images *these* plastic surgeons inflate: PR man.

Traditionally, PR men do press for film stars, socialites, sports figures, and other types hungry for favorable publicity or, failing that, for any kind of publicity, even unkind publicity, as long as their names are spelled right—because, without publicity, how could they even begin to remain famous?

Today, when the need for the "right" image has permeated all occupations, even those sober citizens who once dismissed public relations—bureaucrats, board chairmen, doctors, college presidents, and, increasingly, lawyers, who rank below used-car salesmen in surveys on public confidence in professionals—deliver themselves up lickety-split, run, dash—*leap*—into the press agent's arms.

As a consequence, the PR man has acquired disproportionate power in our society.

1

This Line Is Busy

Let's suspend what remains of our disbelief and imagine for a moment that several press agents and a couple of fellow travelers in the "communications" business, having put all their clients on hold, are on a conference call.

Their business, after all, is to talk on the telephone—doesn't every photo of a PR man show him with a big fake smile on his face, a fat cigar in his mouth, and a phone growing out of each ear? Remember how vociferously adman Stan Dragoti, Cheryl Tiegs's ex-husband, objected to a *People* magazine photo of him on the telephone because it made him look like a "wheeler-dealer, someone who's on the phone all day creating hype out of nothing"? One PR man on the West Coast has a house with fourteen rooms and twenty-two phones, seven of which have twelve buttons each. His wife refers to their youngest child as "the phone" because her husband makes better love to the telephone—and much more often—than he does to her.

They're having a conference call about a pressing problem: the bad press public relations gets.

They may have done well with their clients—New York City, New York State, Mobil Oil, and so forth—but they haven't yet made a very convincing case with the public for public relations. PR, they realize, is a dirty word, and they're going to do their darndest to clean it up.

Remember maxim-monger Dragoti's dictum about the importance of being able to "separate gossip PR from meaningful PR"? Because now our promoters of public relations are going to do some "meaningful PR" for PR. In other words, launder the Oldspeak, hang it out on the line to dry, press it, and then wear it as Newspeak.

185

Maybe they'll even decide to change PR's name from Public Relations to, say, Pure Relativity.

In any case, they're preparing to spend a lot of time doing some very persistent pressing of the press on behalf of their mutual client, PR. They certainly don't have to sell *themselves* anymore. Their kind of persuader no longer wishes to remain hidden; almost the first thing any self-respecting PR man does today—having sucked from the tit of psycho-analysis the pop platitude that BEFORE I CAN HELP OTHERS, I MUST HELP MYSELF—is get himself gushed about in gossip columns, profiled in feature articles, and paraded onto talk shows.

Our six conference call communicants are, in alphabetical order:

Swifty Lazar, literary and show-biz agent dynamo—sells books, plays, short stories, television and movie scripts to publishers, theatrical producers, the networks, and movie companies; born Irving Paul Lazar in Stamford, Connecticut; known professionally as "Swifty" (nickname coined by client Humphrey Bogart, who had once acted in a Broadway play called *Swifty,* after Lazar lined up five movie deals for him in a single day); called Irving by friends; age seventy-seven; educated Fordham and Brooklyn Law night school; cue-ball bald, dapper, diminutive (wears size 5½ rust suede lifts); wears thick-rimmed black glasses, monogrammed underwear; manner regal; has morbid fear of germs (said to wash soap before using it); famous for getting clients record-breaking advances and percentages of the action (pioneered 60/40 and 75/25 paperback book splits); publicly accused by Random House co-founder Bennett Cerf of wrecking pricing structure of entire publishing industry; started out booking bands for mob-operated nightclubs in the Depression; practiced law in New York City till 1935 and with Music Corporation of America 1936–42; in the forties produced shows at the Copa; became agent; literary, political, and show-biz clients have included Irwin Shaw, Lauren Bacall, William Faulkner, Richard M. Nixon (memoirs), Ernest Hemingway, Ira Gershwin, Truman Capote, Clifford Odets, Neil Simon, Herman Wouk, John Huston, Edna Ferber, Art Buchwald, Noel Coward, Vladimir Nabokov, Moss Hart, David Merrick, Theodore H. White, Helen Gurley Brown, Elia Kazan, L. B. Mayer, Ben Hecht, Billy Wilder, George S. Kaufman, Cole Porter, Brendan Behan, George Axelrod, James Stewart (autobiography), Burt Reynolds (autobiography), Lillian Hellman, Maxwell Anderson, Ruth Gordon, Garson Kanin, Orson Welles, Deborah Kerr, Peter Viertel, Betty Comden, Adolph Green, Tony Curtis (novels), Arthur Rubinstein, Arthur Schlesinger, Jr.; properties represented include *Sound of Music* (first over-a-million movie sale), *The Thorn Birds* (represented publisher, Harper & Row, on film and paperback sale; secured for *Thorn Birds* author an unprecedented 5 percent from the first dollar of the movie receipts of the gross, not the profits, plus 10 percent of the profits); *The Brethren; My Fair Lady; Singing in the Rain; An American in Paris; Gigi; West Side Story;* Ian Fleming's *Thunderball* (received $600,000 fee for negotiating film sale); said to be richer than any of the writers he represents (does *not* represent himself—has engaged ICM superagent Lynn Nesbit to handle his memoirs); makes well over one million dollars a year in agent's commissions; collects art; drives Rolls-Royce; maintains offices in Beverly Hills, New York, London, Paris, and Rome; maintains wife twenty-five years his junior but claims marriage to the telephone, which costs him roughly sixty thousand dollars a year; putative phone instrument preference—Celebrity Phone with Touchamatic 16; Conference Call Code Identification—BOOKS.

Joseph E. Levine, showman, last of the big-time movie moguls; born on Billerica Street in slums of Boston; age seventy-eight; unschooled; short, stout, autocratic (once compared by Sean Connery to a four-star general); started out in retailing, switched to the restaurant business; became small-time film salesman peddling westerns in the northeast; became small-time theater owner; acquired moniker "The Boston Barnum"; wrote the book on promotion; famed for PR gimmicks and publicity stunts; owes success to low-level made-in-Rome spectacle-film *Hercules,* starring "Mr. Universe" Steve Reeves; bought it for $110,000, opened it in 627 theaters at the same time all across U.S., spent over one million dollars promoting it—TV and print saturation-advertising (including thirty-six "beefcake"—i.e., homosexual—magazines, fifty-foot billboards, and sky banners); distributed solid chocolate Hercules dolls graven in Steve Reeves's image to six hundred movie critics; gave away fifteen hundred Hercules bicycles in promotional contests; sold his company Avco Embassy Pictures for forty million dollars; has made, financed, bought, imported, co-produced, and/or distributed 495 films, including *Jack the Ripper, Hercules Unchained, Godzilla, Boccaccio '70, Two Women, Paisan, Open City, Bicycle Thief, Divorce—Italian Style, 8½, The Carpetbaggers, Harlow, Darling, The Graduate, The Producers, The Lion in Winter, Carnal Knowledge, Day of the Dolphin, A Bridge Too Far, Magic, Tattoo;* recently sold his collection (world's largest) of Andrew Wyeth paintings; currently CHAIRMAN, JOSEPH E. LEVINE PRESENTS, INC.; maintains Park Avenue office with facsimile of Billerica Street street-sign above door; no Hollywood office; putative phone instrument preference—Horizon 400; Conference Call Code Identification—MOVIES.

Howard J. Rubenstein, public-sector public relations powerhouse—representative of new species of PR man who exerts political and editorial influence and formulates public policy for union, labor, political, and corporate clients; Brooklyn-born; age fifty-one; educated University of Pennsylvania and St. John's Law; youthful-looking; favors blue serge suits with gold apple in lapel; walks softly and carries a big *shtick;* included several times on *New York* magazine's list of ten most powerful people in New York; started out assistant counsel judiciary committee U.S. House of Representatives; owes success to long-term connection with former New York Mayor Abraham Beame; became mayor's closest adviser (unsalaried); currently PRESIDENT, HOWARD J. RUBENSTEIN ASSOCIATES, INC.; has 125 PR accounts; clients have included President Carter, Rupert Murdoch, the Association for a Better New York, Rockefeller University, builder Harry Helmsley (Rubenstein once hired men to wear King Kong costumes to hype the Helmsley-owned Empire State Building), Tishman Realty, the Rent Stabilization Association, the Real Estate Board of New York, the ASPCA, McDonald's, Weight Watchers, the Group Health Insurance Plan, the Uniformed Sanitationmen's Association, Macy's, the New York Jets, the National Association of Letter Carriers, Channel Thirteen, Bus Stop Shelters, the Bee Gees (Rubenstein hyped a Bee Gees concert in Madison Square Garden, a Rubenstein client, then arranged reception for Bee Gees at Gracie Mansion, home of another Rubenstein client, with all proceeds going to PAL, the Police Athletic League, of which Rubenstein is a director), *Saturday Night Fever,* most of the twelve major teaching hospitals in New York City, the five major New York City municipal labor unions (sanitation, fire, housing police, correction officers, and teamsters), the Housing and Patrolmen's Benevolent Association, the Metropolitan Fair Rent Committee, the Associated Builders and Owners of New York, the New York Convention Center Corporation; Phoenix and Odyssey Houses; also advises numerous state senators, assemblymen, and city council members, usually gratis; employs staff of over forty, including urban affairs specialist; maintains glass and beige office with panoramic view of Central Park in building owned by one of his clients; decor consists of signed photos of Rubenstein with MacArthur, Truman, JFK, RFK, LBJ, HHH, Wagner, Lindsay, Beame, Eleanor Roosevelt, Rockefeller, Carey, and Carter; putative phone instrument preference—Teleconferencing System; Conference Call Code Identification—POLITICS.

Herb Schmertz, corporate image-maker—created new mode of corporate PR: controversial aggressive-defensive confrontational saturationblitzing; born Yonkers, New York; age fifty-three; educated Union College and Columbia Law; currently VICE PRESIDENT OF PUBLIC AFFAIRS, MOBIL OIL CORPORATION and DIRECTOR MOBIL OIL CORPORATION AND MOBIL CORPORATION, second largest corporation in America, with 207,700 employees and gross revenues of more than $63 billion;

well groomed, sleek; mastermind behind Mobil's masterpiece of PR status-theater; spends thirty Mobil millions a year underwriting quality TV (*Mobil Masterpiece Theatre*, "television's most honored series") and culture with a capital "k" (kept garden of Museum of Modern Art open at night—describes cultural underwriting as "one of the facts of this corporation's personality"), and advocacy advertising—places weekly ads in editorial form on "Op-Ed" page of *New York Times* (a recent one began: "To this day, there are people who believe some of the apocryphal stories told about the gasoline shortages of the 1970's.") and in ten other American newspapers, pushing Mobil's point of view on moral and political issues—describes "Op-Ed" propaganda as "pamphlets—we're engaged in the honorable and ancient art of pamphleteering, and the newspapers are a delivery system for our pamphlets"; places Mobil "A Fable for Now" commercials on commercial TV to sell Mobil's ideas; Schmertz described on TV by *New York Times* television critic John O'Connor as "one of the great promoters in the U.S. today—Herbie's a showman . . . the David Merrick, the Sol Hurok, the Barnum of the oil companies"; formerly general counsel for the Federal Mediation and Conciliation Service, New York City; adviser to Senator Edward M. Kennedy's 1980 presidential campaign; board member Radio Marti, station set up by Washington to beam propaganda at Cuba; heads PR staff of seventy-five; supervises Mobil "command center" where world media communications are monitored, then recorded on videotape and computer terminals; maintains office with heavy security in Manhattan's Mobil Building; author of the coauthored *Takeover*, a thriller about the oil industry, published by Simon and Schuster, which also published *The Truth About Energy* by Mobil Corporation, a promising new author; putative phone instrument preference—the Dimension System; Conference Call Code Identification—OIL.

John Springer, oldfangled show-biz PR type; born Rochester, New York; age sixty-seven; educated University of Toronto; sharp face, thinning white hair, mustache, slight build; wears silver-rimmed glasses; bland, discreet, evasive; a forty-year veteran of the PR business (RKO Radio Pictures, Twentieth-Century-Fox Films, Arthur Jacobs Public Relations); on his own since 1964—currently PRESIDENT, JOHN SPRINGER ASSOCIATES, INC.; known for sustaining long-term relationships with clients, who have included Marilyn Monroe, Judy Garland, Henry Fonda, Robert Preston, Warren Beatty, Bette Davis, Joan Crawford, Elizabeth Taylor, Richard Burton, Montgomery Clift, Ingrid Bergman, David Frost, Marlene Dietrich, Mike Nichols, Hal Prince, Peggy Lee, Tony Randall, Liv Ullmann, Mary Pickford, Regine; partner with Sybil Burton Christopher in the sixties discotheque "Arthur";

author of four film books—*All Talking! All Singing! All Dancing!, The Fondas, They Had Faces Then,* and *Forgotten Films to Remember;* producer-host of stage-screen shows starring Bette Davis, Myrna Loy, Sylvia Sidney, Joan Crawford, Rosalind Russell, Debbie Reynolds, Joanne Woodward, and Lana Turner at New York's Town Hall and on tour, U.S., Australia, Great Britain; owner of one of world's largest collections of movie stills; employs staff of six in New York, with associates in Hollywood, London, Paris, Rome, and Madrid; maintains cluttered Madison Avenue office lined with old theatrical posters; putative phone instrument preference—Early American Cradlephone; Conference Call Code Identification—OLDSTARS.

Bobby Zarem, newfangled show-biz PR type; born Savannah, Georgia—speaks with southern accent; age forty-six; educated Andover and Yale; round, rumpled, balding, nail-biting, joint-rolling analysand; wears safari jackets; started out at Rogers and Cowan Public Relations—handled Dyan Cannon, Cher, Cybill Shepherd, James Caan, Dustin Hoffman, Ann-Margret; on his own since 1975—currently PRESIDENT, ZAREM, INC.; has represented the films *Fort Apache, Loving Couples, Pumping Iron, The Four Seasons, The Seduction of Joe Tynan, The Ritz* (he took over The Four Seasons Restaurant with pool to hype movie comedy set in a gay bathhouse), *Tommy* (he rented the Fifty-seventh Street subway station and gave a black-tie dinner dance for seven hundred to hype rock movie), and *The Wiz,* plus Alan Alda, James Jones (posthumously published book), Peter Beard (African book), Diana Ross, the Bee Gees, the State Office for Motion Picture and Television Development, the restaurants Tavern on the Green and Maxwell's Plum, the Professional Karate Association; known for short-term relationships with clients; claims to be the Einstein of what *he* claims is "the most successful public relations campaign in history," the "I Love New York" campaign; christened "superflack" the same week by both *Time* and *Newsweek,* thereby realizing every press agent's dream to be the subject of twin stories in the two magazines; employs five people in two cluttered rooms five floors above Madison Avenue; office sports photo of *Pumping Iron* star Arnold Schwarzenegger inscribed to "Mr. Savannah of 1956"; uses Elaine's as nighttime office; spends seven hours a day on phone; putative phone instrument preference—Superfone 7800 with clock, calendar, stopwatch, alarm, sixty-four-number memory dialing, redial, hands-free dialing, and call transfer; Conference Call Code identification—NEWSTARS.

Notice that the names of our conference call communicants signify their calling. Indeed, so appropriate are their names to their task that the communicants might have invented them themselves. Springer, Zarem, Swifty, Schmertz, Joseph L. Levine, and Howard J. Rubenstein are all onomatopoetic. The first three names connote speedy motion; the fourth, Schmertz, suggesting *schmaltz* and *schmooze*—in fact, the whole *schmeer*—leaves just as little to the auditory imagination, and incidentally means "pain" in German; the fifty, Joseph E. Levine, sounds mogulish, and the sixth, Howard J. Rubenstein, markedly municipal.

Let's eavesdrop on their conference call. The best way to understand how disproportionate most PR is is to listen to its superstar promoters and hear the gobbledygook that is their speech.

Each communicant, interviewed separately for *Hype,* uttered each word herein ascribed to him. (When Lazar told his friend the actor Martin Gabel that someone had just been interviewing him about hype, Gabel, mishearing "hype" as "height," exclaimed, *"You,* Irving? *Height?"* Lazar without his elevator shoes is 5′2″, half an inch shorter than his client Truman Capote.)

And so, if one may borrow Joyce's method of a symphony of fragments—styles stridently struck against one another—to make a perfect harmony of hyperbole:

JOHN SPRINGER (OLDSTARS): You know, let's face it, "press agent" is a dirty word. The picture that most people have of a press agent is somebody sitting in a phone booth with the cigar and saying, "Hey, sweetheart, do I have a scoop for *you,* baby!" Well, that's the picture, and there is a certain breed of press agent that is that, but there's also ones that are very honest and honorable in their dealings both with the people they represent and the people they represent them to—the press. Now, the press trusts a person like *me,* who gives the information straight.

HOWARD J. RUBENSTEIN (POLITICS): Ya, it's a dirty word. When I went into this business, my friends were *aghast.* I was an honor graduate of the University of Pennsylvania, first in my class at St. John's Law School and all that—I'm an attorney, ya—admitted to the bar in '59— assistant counsel to the House Judiciary Committee, Congressman Cellar's committee—and then suddenly I end up as a press agent?! If you say "press agent," people think of—what was that motion picture where a very unethical press agent would peddle tips to columns? Press agents have been known to get very terrible publicity for *themselves* because of stupid, dishonest things they try to push, going after the superhype.

BOBBY ZAREM (NEWSTARS): Someone's been on the carpet and they're trying to lay it on me. Did I ever tell you about the yellow linoleum for

The Wiz, which I handled? Yellow brick road linoleum. We put it over the Brooklyn Bridge, over everywhere—we just laid it out wherever we went. Our initial order was for twenty-five miles. Just follow the yellow brick road—it goes from Munchkin Land to Emerald City.

HERB SCHMERTZ (OIL): When the attacks that are made against us are that aggressive, we have no choice—we have to become counterpunchers.

HOWARD J. RUBENSTEIN (POLITICS): When the SEC attacked Abe Beame—we were right in the middle of his second mayoral campaign—attacked him as not revealing all of the facts to the city—they accused him basically of a *crime*—we stayed up all night writing a counterattack, blasting back, calling the whole thing a political hatchet job. We felt that unless we did that brutal counterattack, it was all over. It was all over anyway, but at least we were able to reestablish a serious candidacy for him. He went down incredibly low with the SEC attack, and in a matter of a day or two he came back to near where his polling had been before, so without a doubt we salvaged his reputation. That's the kind of thing public relations does.

JOHN SPRINGER (OLDSTARS): *I* call myself a public relations representative but I'm also a press agent, I'm also a flack, I'm a publicity man, I'm a whatever-you-want-to-call-me. Those are the names they've given me, so that's what I've been doing. But I guess at this stage of the game, calling a press agent a flack is like calling a black person a nigger or *boy*.

BOBBY ZAREM (NEWSTARS): I've had migraines and pinched nerves for years over PR's bad image, and sore throats over PR's very bad word of mouth. A lot of so-called public relations in this day and age is just hype. I'm so sensitive to the word "hype" I really sometimes really want to shoot myself. I hate the word "hype." I detest the word "hype." I *loathe* the word "hype," you know, and that's how I feel. *I'm* not a hype artist. I have a built-in intelligence, a sensitivity, an instinct and what-not that makes me damn good at what I do, that's all. And what I do is *not* hype. Because hype is not hard work, it's not *honest* work. Hype *means* "falsely built . . . bombast . . . *slanted* bombast." That's the book definition of hype, which I took one night on *The Tomorrow Show* when I was faced with this same identical problem. Tom Snyder grilled me on this subject for half an hour, then he brought out two others in the public relations industry, people who actually *practice* hype. One of them has a license plate that reads HYPE and he held it up to the camera. Now, that's not straight communicating—which is what *I* do. I am a public relations *representative*. I don't pretend to create a product. Hell, the product is already created and I just represent it like it is—I make an effort to let it be known, you know. I have never in my life not told a journalist the truth filmwise—I have never lied about the quality of a movie I'm handling. I don't even exaggerate or false-lead people. The problem relative to me insofar as working in this business is that basically *I* am in the profession of just communicating information, informative information, in an intelligent and communicative way, in hopes that the person with whom I'm communicating can relate to what I'm talking about and digest it and respond to it. And I really do mean this.

SWIFTY LAZAR (BOOKS): I would like to elevate myself but, frankly, the term "pitchman" is the more precise allocation of what I do. I try to interest people in a property and then I employ the arousal of competition for it.

HERB SCHMERTZ (OIL): We want to make people see our point of view so they can respect us. We don't necessarily want them to love us. It's our sense that we have made an enormous achievement when we've gotten them to at least consider our point of view.

JOSEPH E. LEVINE (MOVIES): It scares the shit out of me. The trouble with our business now is we don't sell ourselves right. Nobody goes out hustling anymore—very few the way I did. Producers are their own greatest press agents, you know. When I made *Magic*—I don't want to talk about myself—I visited twenty-eight cities in the United States. Sure. Myself. I was a little too old for that shit but I did it, I went on talk shows in every town. We got all that free time—if you added up the time, we got millions of dollars. *Magic* did fabulous. We got seven hundred fifty thousand for Home Box Office. Five years ago they only paid fifty thousand. Five years from now you'll get five million first-run Home Box—or ten million, or twenty million. For one movie, yeah, sure, that's what it's coming to.

SWIFTY LAZAR (BOOKS): Any movie today has a potential to do a hundred million dollars. This is an age of communication. There's just a greater frame of reference—paintings sell for more, new painters get more, new sculptors come along and get more, a theatrical piece opens up and becomes, you know, a two-hundred-twenty-five-thousand-dollar-a-week success if it's *sold* right. Bantam Books got sold to Gianni Agnelli of Fiat, who paid about sixty million I think it was, fifty plus ten maybe. People said he could never cost-justify that. He then sold *half* his interest four years or three years later for fifty million, so he now owns for nothing a half. So a good salesman is someone who has his own convictions about what he's selling, he thinks it's really worth its weight, that's the first thing. And maybe the second thing is he's got to have the discerning eye for the best product. Ya, and he's got to be willing to work at it. A lot of hard work is always attached to selling. And there's a great deal of pride attached there. And you work as hard as *I* do, then the law of averages is with you—if you have at least ten irons in the fire, one of them has got to get hot; if you try to sell five hundred things in the course of a week, you're bound to sell five anyway. I sell maybe two hundred fifty books a year. And I get more publicity than my clients get and *they* have to write the books.

JOSEPH E. LEVINE (MOVIES): Shit, the secret of sales success is multiple saturation. Like I always said, a *little* advertising is a dangerous thing. The heavier the advertising barrage, the more money you *save*. Hit every market simultaneously when introducing your product. And remember, selling the public isn't enough, the industry's also gotta be sold.

BOBBY ZAREM (NEWSTARS): I don't look at myself as someone who's selling. I'm not selling *myself* or my *own* product. I get a flat fee out of something over a period of one or three years. I feel I'm part of *building* something in the long-term continuity—for prosperity, I mean posterity.

JOSEPH E. LEVINE (MOVIES): *I* built a helluva lot of people—made them stars. Sophia Loren—I won her the Academy Award for *Two Women,* promoted the shit out of her *within* the industry, and she didn't even mention me in her book. And don't forget Dustin Hoffman in *The Graduate.* I made a helluva lot of directors, too. I hired Mike Nichols the first one—won him an Oscar for best director, *The Graduate.* I hired Mel Brooks the first one—on *The Producers.* Yeah, it was his first picture, he couldn't get his mug in anybody's office. I was going to call it *Springtime for Hitler,* but the Jewish groups would have hated me for that, so I called it *The Producers.* Now I'm sorry I didn't use my original title.

JOHN SPRINGER (OLDSTARS): When I started my own company, I had Hank Fonda, Robert Preston, Richard Burton, Hal Prince, Warren Beatty, who was just this kid who I saw had great potential—I mean, *I* had him before *Splendor in the Grass*—and Paul Newman and Joanne Woodward I *thought* I had. I didn't realize they had a long-term contract with another public relations company, which said it was going to sue me. Paul wanted to fight it and I said no, I didn't want to start my business with a court case—being accused of stealing another office's clients. So I lost Joanne and Paul, but then within two weeks I had Elizabeth Taylor and Mike Nichols, so I had a real good start. Of those people, for the time being I'm on a hiatus situation with Richard and Warren where I still, y'know, officially represent them, but I'm not billing them at this particular point and won't get actively involved with them again until they need a publicity image.

HERB SCHMERTZ (OIL): Image is something that we simply don't think about. It's not a consideration. Image is a euphemism for "trying to get people to love you," and that's not our motivation at all. What we're trying to do is participate in the marketplace of ideas by giving the public a wider spectrum of news, opinions, and thoughts.

SWIFTY LAZAR (BOOKS): Listen, pal, to use the most simplistic of verbiage, you get a shovel. You get a shovel and a pick and a poke and you sell more than anybody else.

HOWARD J. RUBENSTEIN (POLITICS): I pick out the area where a client needs me the most and then I personally take over from my staff. For example, with McDonald's.

JOSEPH E. LEVINE (MOVIES): Let me tell you about The Four Seasons. By the way, it's right up the street from my office. My office used to look out on the Madison Avenue side and all I saw was the ass of some fuckin' building, so there was another office right here and we took the wall out, my desk was *there* and we moved the desk *here* so I could get this beautiful view at night, you know—every night there's the most beautiful sunset you can imagine here. Anyway, the Four Seasons charged you five-fifty for six *beautiful* big shrimp, terrific. Now they charge you ninefifty and they've cut it down to four shrimp. How dare they offer me four shrimp! I rebelled, I said I don't mind you raising the price if you give me back the six shrimps. I've been around, you know. I've tasted of almost everything on earth.

HOWARD J. RUBENSTEIN (POLITICS): I represent McDonald's now for about eight years. I helped them solve their community relations problem, when the local communities were actively attacking them at most of their new locations in New York because the perception of a fast-food operation is very negative. When they announced they were going to go into an elite upper-crust neighborhood, Lexington Avenue at Sixty-sixth Street, the local neighbors mobilized instantly—eleven thousand people signed a petition in opposition and delivered it to Mayor Beame. McDonald's hired me in the middle of the confrontation, at a time when two or three editorials had already run in the *New York Times* saying they didn't belong in the neighborhood. So I stepped into the battle, met with the neighborhood people, then flew out to Chicago for a meeting with McDonald's top brass where the first thing I told them was to give up, to surrender the site. Then I helped them negotiate *out* of the situation, *but*, as a result of losing this one location, they cooled down the very antagonistic atmosphere around them, and *then* they were able to go in and build forty or fifty or more McDonald's in locations throughout the city using the tactics I suggested—going in and talking to the community in advance, explaining what they will do in a civic way, what kind of help they will give community and religious groups, the employment opportunities and tax advantages. So a new pattern was set, and today they're in not one major confrontation. They're in good neighborhoods, too. I decided to get into the McDonald's thing myself because I have a particular background of negotiation as a conciliator.

SWIFTY LAZAR (BOOKS): The point is that the fact is that what is important is that you turn it around. Because there is always potentially a very heavy situation.

JOHN SPRINGER (OLDSTARS): After Sybil and Richard Burton broke up, I represented Richard Burton and Elizabeth Taylor—*and* Sybil Burton Christopher and Jordan Christopher—*and* Debbie Reynolds, and there was no problem with any of them that I was representing the others, and there was no conflict.

HERB SCHMERTZ (OIL): We are making progress. Hostility is an emotion, and an emotion gets in the way of judgment-making. We try to provide information to the public so that they can use the information to make judgments.

BOBBY ZAREM (NEWSTARS): There's one of my other phones. Will y'all shoot me if I go away? I mean, can you hold a teeny weeny—I mean a half a minute?

JOSEPH E. LEVINE (MOVIES): *Eight and a Half!* I made that film with Fellini, who was as phony as a glass eye as far as I was concerned. I would never make another deal with him again, I didn't like the way he operated. *Eight and a Half* was a co-production deal—Columbia Pictures took the whole world except Italy and the United States and Canada, *I* took the United States and Canada, and a man by the name of . . . what was his name, a Milanese, an Italian . . . took Italy. Rizzoli! Angelo Rizzoli. I remembered the name. I can remember things that happened to me sixty-eight years ago when I was seven, and six. I remember when my father died. I don't remember *him,* I remember the *day* he died. I remember seeing his box in what we called the parlor. I did a helluva job with *Eight and a Half.* Made a profit on it, too, which was unusual for an art film—you better believe it! I had like a *hundred* screenings in New York. I showed it to every egghead professor school that I could find and it became what *I* call a cocktail picture: "Have you seen *Eight and a Half?"*—you know. I don't think half of them understood it. I remember watching it with Fellini in the Festival Theatre, a theater that *I* built for my own pictures. "Federico," I says, "what the hell does *that* mean?" and he says, "*I* don't know." Now I don't know whether he was putting me on or not, but *I* wasn't putting *him* on, and I think a lot of that shit he just put it in there, like he does now. And the eggheads ate it up. Every egghead found something *different*—like looking at a painting. Now it's become a picture you teach from, a fuckin' *classic*. It won the Academy Award, you know, in '63. That Fellini was selfish, too. Never mentioned *me*, never mentioned the poor bastard Rizzoli who put up the money, made it possible, *never* mentioned his name, got up there—they almost had to yank him off the fuckin' podium. I gave the picture, the original print, yeah, to the Museum of Modern Art.

HERB SCHMERTZ (OIL): We think this institution is worthwhile to support in our society, and we are doing everything we can to help strengthen it so that society can be a better place for all of us.

BOBBY ZAREM (NEWSTARS): I'm in constant touch with everybody.

JOSEPH E. LEVINE (MOVIES): Yeah, I did okay on *Eight and a Half.* Want to hear about a big bust?

JOHN SPRINGER (OLDSTARS): And then Elizabeth married John Warner, and I flew over to Vienna, made the original personal announcement of their engagement from there, got the pictures taken, and got it all out on the wires.

JOSEPH E. LEVINE (MOVIES): I co-produced a picture in England called *Jack the Ripper,* admittedly a piece of shit. I made a distribution deal with Paramount Pictures, and we opened it in like seven hundred theaters, six hundred ninety to be exact, because, always remember, the secret of sales success is multiple saturation, and it dropped dead in every theater. In *spite* of a mammoth campaign. Because the public didn't want to see it. They smelled it out even before the reviews. Before the public got wise to us, if you spent enough money on a picture—on radio, TV, newspapers, magazines, because, remember, the heavier the advertising barrage, the more money you'd wind up *saving*—people would at least come the first couple of days, but now they don't even do that. Or maybe one lousy movie wouldn't sell, but two lousy movies on a double bill could always be a box-office smash.

SWIFTY LAZAR (BOOKS): A movie which is very good will be twice as good at the box office with a star, whereas a bad movie with several stars will be of no help whatsoever.

JOSEPH E. LEVINE (MOVIES): Today you can beat the shit out of a picture—drums, parades—and the public still won't come. You can't get away with hokum now the way you used to. Unless it's a piece of hokum that they *want.* What do they want? Today we don't know what the hell they want.

SWIFTY LAZAR (BOOKS): *They* know what they want.

HOWARD J. RUBENSTEIN (POLITICS): What people want from a PR man, whether they admit it or not, is fame and fortune and *power.* Because notoriety, being well known, often leads to power. They first would like the people that know them to think well of them, primarily: maybe their competitors, maybe their enemies, it doesn't have to be your friend—your friend thinks well of you. But even your friend, reading about you, hearing about you, seeing the accolades and all, will think a little differently of you. I just had a personal experience—for a number of years I've been getting a lot of publicity: I was in the ten most powerful men in New York in *New York* magazine two or three times—I was on the cover, they did a cartoon, 1974 I guess, and the *New York Times* did a split-page feature on me, half a page with a picture, plus two or three profiles on me, and the *New York Post* did a half a page profile—and what I found is that even my friends react a little bit differently after all that was in. It was interesting, the reaction. Ya, a little more carefully, it was a riot. So first you want the people that you know to think *differently* of you—not even *better,* not even well, necessarily, just differently. To some of them you want the appearance of power and they should quake and quiver.

HERB SCHMERTZ (OIL): Power is something that we simply don't think about.

HOWARD J. RUBENSTEIN (POLITICS): We tell the client how to tell his story as powerfully as he can. The first thing we do is advise him on what his and/or the corporate action should be; secondly, we determine whether that action should be projected or not; and, thirdly, we do the actual legwork of projection. Like introduce clients to reporters and opinion-makers, arrange for feature articles and talk shows—sometimes we have to help clients with the anecdotes. For instance, I got a profile on Stigwood into *Fortune,* which helped bring him along as a nationwide figure.

JOSEPH E. LEVINE (MOVIES): Ever see the *Fortune* thing on *me?* It was a good story.

HOWARD J. RUBENSTEIN (POLITICS): We also set up exclusives, major stories—major *breaks.* Did you happen to see the cover of *New York* magazine—"The Men Who Own New York"? Helmsley, Durst, Trump, Lawrence, Rudin, Lefrak, Fisher. All described as the last of the great new-time real-estate entrepreneurs—the men who own and manage most of the space New Yorkers live and work in. Now, I have seven or eight of my clients featured in that article. Fisher is mine, I represent them—they own the building my offices are in. Trump is mine, I handle *them*. Durst is mine. I handle Rudin, Rudin is mine. Helmsley is mine. Lefrak is not mine. So I have most of the article. The reporter, Nick Pileggi, and I worked on it together. We know each other fairly well—a brilliant guy, very straight—so one day he said, *he* said, "Nobody knows very much about the real-estate industry and the people who own it," and I said, "You're right," and he said, "Maybe I should do something on that," and I said, "You're right, and here are the people you want to do." So then I put the cover together with him. I would say that he arrived at his point of view on his own but in close discussion with me. And it's probably the best PR break that the real-estate industry has ever had. Spectacular, spectacular.

BOBBY ZAREM (NEWSTARS): Can I put you on hold? Yeah, they're going to be casting in the next couple of weeks relative to that film.

HOWARD J. RUBENSTEIN (POLITICS): But the most successful technique I use is the press conference. We plan the theory, write the material, brief the client, and then the client conducts the conference. We must run three hundred press conferences a year—sometimes in one day we'll run three or four—and most of our news conferences are covered, and covered very well. I have a personal relationship with hundreds of newsmen and reporters, and if I went through my entire staff and figured out the reporters and writers they know, it would run into the thousands, at virtually every level of the media. I find the press conference the best way to really make a dent on the public—you go right across the board and flood an area, through radio, television, and print, all at the same time.

JOSEPH E. LEVINE (MOVIES): Hit every market *simultaneously* when introducing your product.

BOBBY ZAREM (NEWSTARS): *Newsweek* was doing a cover story on a movie I was handling, *Pumping Iron*, with really great tender care—right from the beginning I had a real feeling about how to handle it, and I'm someone who acts out on every single instinct. And then *Time* called and wanted to do a story on *me*. How do you handle it, how do you *handle* it? I mean, it's everybody's lifelong fantasy to be in *Time* magazine, because its inherent audience nationwide is sufficiently huge and its importance to the rest of the media because the media as a body read each *other*. So I called *Newsweek* to tell them *Time* had called me and what should I do, and they said *they* wanted to do a story on me now, too. So I called *Time* to tell them that now *Newsweek* was also doing me, and they said fine, they still wanted to do me, they wanted to do me more than *ever*. Then *Newsweek* heard that *Time* was rushing me into that week's issue, so they crashed *their* story on me to come out the same week—so I touched both bases. And in the end my movie didn't get the *Newsweek* cover; I guess they just decided to give *me* the big push instead of my client. You wanna know something? I remember when I was eleven years old and visiting New York from Savannah, Georgia. My parents always took me to the Starlight Roof of the Waldorf-Astoria and we always got seated right near the door, and whenever I saw a movie star or an entertainer come in, I would go right up to them and speak extemporaneously and they would give me their autograph and I would get a real rush. I would jump up and down—I mean, *literally*.

JOSEPH E. LEVINE (MOVIES): My *first* important break was in *Life* magazine, the Christmas edition, where they talked about the up-and-coming Boston Barnum—*me*! Then some guy from *The New Yorker* came to interview me and *he* said, I'll never forget it—about *Hercules*—"You mean to tell me people actually liked this picture?" He wanted to say "piece of shit," but he didn't 'cause he was from *The New Yorker*. Well, that was years ago—everything was a cocktail party, everything was a party for the press. You know, I took an eighty-six-page ad once. That was one of the small ones. I always said a *little* advertising is a dangerous thing. So then I took a ninety-nine-page ad—in *Variety*. And I took it four times. For my product, sixty Joseph E. Levine pictures. My company was growing up and I wanted everybody to know about it. Avco Embassy, yeah. A smart little company that was on its way to the moon, yeah. *Springtime for Hitler. Lion in Winter.* Mike Nichols, best director. Poor Mike can't make a picture now.

JOHN SPRINGER (OLDSTARS): Mike I still officially represent but I am on a hiatus situation with him now because he wants to keep a very low profile. At the point where he wants to let his publicity profile *be,* then I will go back working with him again.

JOSEPH E. LEVINE (MOVIES): Remember when we appeared on the *Today Show*—me and Rosalie, my wife, who has always worked closely with me? I move about, you know—all kinds of ways. I think we had an hour uncut with Hugh Downs. He's a very nice man. He's still hustling.

SWIFTY LAZAR (BOOKS): I almost always never fail. I don't care who their other agent is, they always give *me* their book. Because I get them better deals—higher percentages of paperback royalties and gross amounts of monies—and I have more massive best sellers on the famous *New York Times* best-seller list—and that's the matter of record and fact. That's why in this life every good writer has two agents, their own and Irving Lazar. John Huston has another agent, an agent who has a big literary school, but he came to *me*—he and myself go back a long way. Or I came to *him,* I said, "Why don't you do a book with *me?*" and he said, "Okay, see if you can cook something up for *me.*" So I acquired the representation of John Huston's book. I felt personally it was a hit potential, and I got him what he needed.

JOHN SPRINGER (OLDSTARS): Well, ya, money, but I understand that it is also part of many PR people's jobs to line up girls or boys, or if someone really wants to know where to get a fix you get it for them. I not only don't do that but I've never been asked to do it. I wouldn't if I *were* asked but I never *have* been asked. Once or twice it came up when I was with RKO Pictures, and I just said that's not my bag, I'm not into that. I don't know what other PR people's ethics are, but I know mine. I mean, if Henry Rogers, the board chairman of Rogers and Cowan, which is a very old-line entertainment public relations firm, feels he can now tell intimate secrets about people he represented years ago—he wrote that book, y'know, *Walking the Tightrope: The Private Confessions of a Public Relations Man*—well, that's his bag. But unfortunately, I would say that he's not only hurt himself, he's got a lot of people thinking, "Oh, Jesus, Henry Rogers is a comparatively well-respected press agent, and now here he is, telling all, so maybe I shouldn't trust John Springer or Pat Newcomb or, y'know, a couple of other press agents who are considered honorable and honest and decent." So it's bad for *me,* too, when somebody like him gives PR a bad name. *I've* been offered plenty of money to talk about my clients, too. But I don't care how long Judy Garland and Marilyn Monroe are dead—they *trusted* me. Besides, what would people think of me if I started talking about my clients?

HOWARD J. RUBENSTEIN (POLITICS): If I wanted to make a raw grasp for money, I probably could earn a good deal writing a gossip-type book—*Behind Politics with Howard J. Rubenstein* or *Inside Politics with Howard J. Rubenstein*—but I just absolutely would never do that. Right now I'm in a position of great trust. My clients talk to me as if it were a lawyer-client relationship, they tell me anything and everything. I would have to go out of my business if I decided to write the inside story of my client relationships. To put that on paper and hold it out for the world to see and ridicule the client is a disgrace in my mind, a *very* unethical thing to do. You have to have some ethics.

BOBBY ZAREM (NEWSTARS): Me, I've proven myself in this community. I have single-handedly fuckin'-A saved the city of New York, economically, spiritually, and every other which way. The "I Love New York" campaign. I'm not looking for credit, but almost anybody who knows anything knows it was me. Yeah, the ad agency Wells, Rich, Greene did come up with the specific slogan and I guess the idea of a sixty-second commercial of ten different Broadway shows verbalizing or singing "I Love New York." But I'm the one who handled the public relations, which were *enormous*. The day before Stan Dragoti's commercial even got started, I gave a luncheon at Tavern on the Green—the owner, Warner LeRoy, is a client of mine—and I got everyone from Diana Ross to Paulette Goddard and Frank Langella and Yul Brynner to the goddam governor and mayor of New York to come, and the picture of all of them together got printed in every paper in the world. And that photo single-handedly lined up every conceivable audience as a potential market. And then Wells, Rich, Greene, who are really people who didn't have New York at heart, used *my* campaign to get *themselves* other clients! God, I can't *stand* people who take credit for someone *else's* idea! Anyhow, the effect of my campaign for "I Love New York" was just incredible. There was a story on its success in the *Washington Star* three days before the Senate Banking Committee voted to lend the money to New York, and I was sent word from one of the committee members saying it was my promo launch that made everybody feel that the city was taking the steps necessary toward self-help. So I was instrumental in the voting to lend the city the money. *I* had New York at heart. And I saved the state and taxpayers millions of dollars. I'm not looking for credit, but almost anybody who knows anything knows it was me.

HOWARD J. RUBENSTEIN (POLITICS): I helped found the Association for a Better New York, Lew Rudin's group—a group of businessmen who meet every Wednesday for breakfast, for ten years now. We have political forums, and the last time out, all the presidential candidates came to speak to us—Reagan came, Kennedy, Bush, Anderson. But what I'm even prouder of having my hand in is the New York Marathon. I handle all the publicity for that. When I first came into the Marathon six or seven years ago now, it had twenty-four runners, and when it would hold a news conference, maybe one reporter from an FM station would show up. And then Lew Rudin—the Rudin family is one of the four or five sponsors of the Marathon, and I represent them in their real estate— Lew called me and said, "You gotta do something." So together we planned the five-borough Marathon, taking it *out* of Central Park, and then we started a real hype on it—we got the five borough presidents and the mayor to shoot the starting gun off, Mayor Beame at the time, and now Mayor Koch is deeply involved.

Today the Marathon is probably New York's major event, with fourteen thousand entrants—we have to turn away *another* fourteen thousand. We get literally fifty million dollars' worth of free time and space, for New York City basically, on the Marathon. It's an astonishing international performance—crowds of millions along the route, millions of people watching. It's hit page one every year of the *Times* and *Daily News* for as long as it's been big, which is as long as *I've* been in it. I take a very minor fee, because I really enjoy it and I'm very proud of the bottom line that I've achieved there.

SWIFTY LAZAR (BOOKS): I'm a short-distance sprinter. Generally I work very quickly. I don't like to negotiate. I like to make the best deal I can in the shortest amount of time, get it over with, then go on *fast* to something else. I don't believe any good salesman lingers. You give a little and take a lot, but you convince the other fellow he's getting a fair deal, and once you get your price, you grab the cash and catch the next train out of town. That's the theory. And that's the title of my book, the autobiography I'm writing that I've been offered a million dollars for: *Grab the Money and Run for the Train.* That's Swifty, Swifty the agile agent. The whole idea is to be in as many places as you can and see as many people as you can, and out of it, if you go to the right places at the right times, will come—something. And that's a fact.

JOSEPH E. LEVINE (MOVIES): Well, at one time, while President Kennedy was President, they used to publish a list of the ten people in the United States who got the most publicity. I was Number Five or Six. So when I went to a dinner party at President Kennedy's brother-in-law Steve Smith's house, a supper party to be exact, and the President was there, he says to me, "For *God's* sakes, Joe"—he really said "for christsake," but let's leave it "for God's sakes"—he says, "That's *all* I ever *read* about is Joe Levine, Joe Levine, Joe Levine"—you know, because he was a great reader of *Variety.* Sure that's an entertainment rag, but even Presidents have to have good sources!

SWIFTY LAZAR (BOOKS): I would never take a book which knocked the Kennedys, *never,* because I liked, admired, Jack Kennedy, admired Bobby, and I like the family. I once talked to them about that, and they said, "Oh, we're not *that* sensitive, Irving, you know," but *I* am, about *that.* Probably the biggest book that could bring the largest audience to the purchase of a single copy would be a book by Mrs. Kennedy, Jackie

Onassis Kennedy. I just wouldn't want to be associated with a book that *knocked* the Kennedys—or knocked Leland Hayward or Dick Rodgers or Moss Hart or George S. Kaufman or Maxwell Anderson or Neil Simon or Ira Gershwin or George Gershwin or, if you take a higher level of a life-span, Vladimir Nabokov or Hemingway, because they were all clients of mine and they were friends. Ya, there were giants in those days, but there were others who were *not* giants but were bankable on a little lesser level—can't think of their names. You know something, someone told me they just heard *me* described as a giant, a condensed giant to be exact, but I'm very suspicious of the source.

JOHN SPRINGER (OLDSTARS): Once upon a time there was a star I was representing, and Earl Wilson called and said he had a very derogatory story about this star from a very reliable source, and one thing, I don't lie. Oh, maybe before I started my own company about twenty years ago—before that, y'know, I was with RKO and Twentieth-Century-Fox, but I shouldn't be talking about myself, it's not proper—maybe back then I had to lie to the extent of saying so-and-so is really very nice when I knew he was a bastard, or so-and-so is just a brilliant actress when I knew she couldn't act her way out of a paper bag, but my rules to myself, and I haven't had to break them yet, thank *God,* are that I would only represent people that I liked as people and respected as talents, and projects that I believed in. So I didn't say to Earl Wilson, "That's not *true,*" I said, "Well, Earl, I'm gonna leave it up to you. All I can tell you, and I'm gonna level with you, is that if you use that story, it'll hurt this star very badly." And he said, "John, I'm a newspaper man." But in this particular instance he didn't use the dirt, so the next time there was important news about this star, I gave Earl the scoop. But once upon a time if you said to Hedda or Kilgallen or Winchell, y'know, that something would hurt a person very badly, *boy*!, it would be *headlines* the next day. The more they could hurt someone, the better they liked it.

HERB SCHMERTZ (OIL): Our intention is always to set the record straight. We have a major obligation to correct inaccurate information or fill in the gaps when the information is inadequate, so that the public can be fully informed. As I said, and I repeat, we don't want them to *love* us.

BOBBY ZAREM (NEWSTARS): They like me, they trust me—I have a mutual credibility thing going with the press and not everybody does. My credibility is hopefully unquestionable. One night at a premiere I got all these photographers from the *Post,* the *News,* AP, UPI, to wait forty minutes in a snowstorm for Bianca Jagger to show—she'd promised me she would, and *I'd* promised *them.* So the next morning I sent each of them a very, very exquisite Gucci wallet with their initials on it for waiting. I guess that's what they mean by "the Zarem Touch." Last night we had a real *hot* screening. The air conditioning broke down and, I mean, I just went really crazy. I saw people *fanning* themselves. One of the most important critics in this country was sitting there fanning herself and I thought, "Oh, this enormously great movie is just gonna die and *I'm* gonna die," and then I heard today that she liked it so I bounced all the way back up. I feel very high.

HOWARD J. RUBENSTEIN (POLITICS): Sure everybody likes it when it's hot. Even Wall Street—they sell the sizzle as well as the meat. The *appearance* of where a company is going is crucial. It may have tremendous assets, good earnings, good earning *power,* but it feels that it's missing something in the marketplace if it can't convey that feeling of glamour and growth and progress.

BOBBY ZAREM (NEWSTARS): Excuse me one second. Hello, hi, how are you? Will y'all wait another weeny second? Do you know what your extension is? Okay. I'll have to get back to you.

SWIFTY LAZAR (BOOKS): Listen, unless it's long distance, don't call me.

Every word of the conference call we've just eavesdropped on was uttered by our six PR communicants, though not to one another. Had the call actually taken place, they would all certainly have taped it. And later, playing it back, they would have listened to their vapid generalizations, glib oversimplifications, circumlocutions, distortions, distinguished incoherence, rodomontades, and inflated presentations of self—listened to, but, of course, not heard.

Were there to be a follow-up conference call concerning the still low and sorry image of PR—call it public relations, call it pure relativity, call it flacking—the following would doubtless transpire:

A. Schmertz would underwrite a seven-part dramatization on PBS: *Six Superflacks Who Shook the World*—Parts One and Two on Schmertz, and Parts Three, Four, Five, Six, and Seven on Zarem, Lazar, Levine, Springer, and Rubenstein, respectively.

B. Zarem would orchestrate an earthshaking party for PR in the swaying elevators of the World Trade Center (having first cleared the location with Rubenstein, who represents the rival Empire State Building).

C. Springer, sprinting off hiatus, would talk Warren Beatty, Richard Burton, and Mike Nichols, as well as Liv Ullmann and Elizabeth Taylor, into making personal appearances at the Zarem "Event."

D. Levine would finance, produce, and distribute the movie made from the footage of the party: *Atlas Holding Up the World Trade Center*. He would then take a ninety-nine page ad in a beefcake magazine.

E. Rubenstein would take the case of PR to President Ronald Reagan and come away with a tax abatement on the profits from the movie.

F. Lazar would sell the book, *The Making of the Movie*, by his client Theodore H. White.

G. Rubenstein would persuade three of his real-estate clients to endow two chairs in public relations, a chaise longue at Princeton and a stool at Bryn Mawr; Erich Segal would be installed in the stool and Joyce Carol Oates in the chaise.

H. Schmertz/Mobil would build a library to house the whole incunabula of PR, from press releases to taped conference calls: a living memorial to the only value we have today—celebrity.

Shortly before the conference-call-that-never-took-place, three worldly wise men of hype actually did get together to give their own good names—three of the best names in hype, in fact—some good PR. In a single episode, covering a mere five hours, they succeeded only in proving that PR, however adeptly coordinated, can never be given a good name.

Here, just as in the preceding pasquinade, no names are changed, for again there are no innocents to protect.

The date: August 6. The place: Sixty-third Street, off Park—Halston's town house.

Behind its corten-steel and reflective bronze glass façade, a birthday party for one of the world's most famous living artists is progressing: It's fifty years tonight since Andy Warhol first drew breath.

The partygoers are the interchangeable young men and women who help maintain the Aura of Andy—the assembly-line workers at his famous Factory—with some of Halston's gang of gossips—assorted seamstresses, models, and sexually congenial camp followers—thrown in.

Andy, in old denims and a faded blazer, easily eclipses everyone. His celebrity poison penetrates the atmosphere. Life with Andy, the party people realize, is simply more exciting, more full of possibility and adventure, than any of them had dreamed possible.

In the low light of Halston's dove-gray, double-story, sepulchrally sumptuous party room, at least a dozen photographers are positioned, waiting for the promised payoff.

At midnight Steve Rubell, owner and impresario of Studio 54, the most notorious disco in the Western world, appears on the second-floor balcony holding a simple wicker basket.

Inside the basket nest a thousand crisp one-dollar bills.

Birthday-boy Andy is positioned directly below.

On a signal from Halston to the photographers, flashbulbs pop promiscuously and Rubell royally dumps the bucks.

On Andy's head.

The greenbacks flutter, fall, as "thick as autumn leaves that strow the brooks/In Vallombrosa." Andy throws his head back, the better to drink in this green shower. As the leaves stream down, he stoops to conquer, running his fluttering fingers through the smackeroos mounting up around him; picks some of them up and washes his face with their moist moment. For the photographers.

To some this may seem an act of stunning and complete crudity. To the denizens of the underworld of PR, whose values are those of the Vale of Vallombrosa, it is an act of stunning and complete cunning: Warhol's career, watered so disproportionately by a paltry one thousand dollar bills, will go on growing—the crop will be in the multimillions; through the mechanism of the flashbulbs, Rubell's business operation will be flatteringly spotlit in the press; and as for Halston, can the unveiling of his fall couture collection be far behind? The three wise men of hype will all harvest from the party far more than they sowed. Rubell put up a thousand singles, Halson put up his sepulchral place, and Warhol put up his birthday, and they will all benefit—well, disproportionately: disproportionately well.

The party abruptly ends. Palpable with purpose, it has had none of the gaiety of a gathering celebrating a friend's birthday, a friend's being.

In point of fact, this fiftieth birthday of Warhol's was only his forty-ninth, but characteristically he understood that a half-century would be so much more promotable. Unlike most people, he didn't mind adding a year to his age. After all, it was for the best of causes: PR.

2

We've Been Trying to Reach You

All six of the participants in our conference call are in the very lucrative business of communication—as Bobby Zarem defined, it, "the profession of just communicating information, informative information, in an intelligent and communicative way, in hopes that the person with whom I'm communicating can relate to what I'm talking about and digest it and respond to it."

Now wait just a minute. Communicate? Communicative? "What we've got here," as a character in *Cool Hand Luke* says, "is a failure to communicate." For communication, by definition, can occur only when the listener can understand the meaning of what is said.

So let's look at it all again. It's not what our PR communicants say that they're paid so disproportionately for, but rather, how they don't say it, how skillful they are in using jargon to talk around, above, beyond, and behind an issue. At the point where they manipulatively confound their listeners into accepting their hype, they win the title "Superflack."

Our PR communicants are all curiously unlettered men. Asked to state his criterion for a good memoir, Swifty Lazar—a *literary* agent, believe it or not—replied after a short pause: "Having an ingredient in the life-span so distinguished and unique that it creates envy or a vicarious way of life in the public that's insatiable in its desire to read the achievements of those who've done it." He then added for the record that "the American public today is one of the greatest reading publics in the history of book absorption."

Such men debase the very currency of communication: language or—to use, in Lazar's risible phrase, "the most simplistic of verbiage"—words.

They debase it at some cost, too. For the hyping up of language has the same consequence as the inflation of money: It makes the coin worth less. Our six communicants talk not turkey but Barnum & Bailey three-ring-circus talk. The very work they're engaged in out there under the big top—bartering, bargaining, selling, promoting—indecently encourages exaggeration.

To exaggerate is often to falsify. And our prime-time communicators are addicted to exaggerated speech. (Bombast *is* like drug addiction—word abusers need a stronger and stronger fix to get a kick from the hype hypodermic.) Jean-Luc Godard once said, referring to the number of frames passing, that cinema is the truth twenty-four times a second. PR is a flickering lie twenty-four times a second.

We depend upon the rich resources of language to chart our place in the scheme of things, but listening to these PR communicants ballyhoo everything at the tops of their voices, we lose all critical orientation. How are we to discriminate between one hype and another? As bad money can drive out good, in Gresham's Law, so, too, can false language drive out true.

All hype is based on worn-out words, on a handful of fatuous superlatives that collapse under the least intellectual pressure. Every hype adjective, every hype sentence, may as well have an exclamation mark. "Remarkable!" "Profound!" "Superb!" "Sublime!" "Magnificent!" "Exceptional!" "August!" ("Some of the most august people with whom I work go to Elaine's," says Bobby Zarem. "August"?) Soon, anything less than "incomparably great!" or "uniquely grand!" will have to be interpreted as a put-down.

As this cheapening of the language intensifies, our standard of speech goes down—down, down, down—as the twentieth century draws to its close. But without a Hemingway to fight the sponginess and false expansion of language ("I distrust big words," he said), without a John O'Hara to puncture the soft underbelly of language ("I never use an adjective or an adverb," he boasted), without such regulators of words as these, how can the culture possibly maintain a language?

Perhaps it's too late to go back to speaking plain, to speaking—as Emerson wrote—straightforward American narrative. We've been pushed out of the good garden of simple language, most cruelly by those whose work it is to know better: our critics. They, certainly, should be above ballyhooing; *their* prose, at least, should stay close to earth, tethered to the ground.

But criticism, as it's practiced today, with few exceptions, is a form of hype. Too many critics indulge in high-flown, superheated language.

Too many of them are too kind to the work they're given to evaluate. The chief art critic of the *New York Times*, John Russell, for example, is exceedingly civil, if not sweet, to *everybody*. But when criticism is uniformly benevolent, standards cannot be maintained any more than they can be when criticism is uniformly malevolent. The theater critic of *New York* magazine, John Simon, for instance, is persistently venomous, but he very cleverly turned his own contrariness into something that's become an establishment feature itself.

If both Russell and Simon subvert the purpose of criticism, which is to try out some kind of truth-telling down the middle, it is Clive Barnes, the former dance and theater critic of the *New York Times* and the current dance and theater critic of the *New York Post*, who is the cautionary tale of how the corrupt use of language can transform a critic into a flack. In effect, what Clive Barnes does is PR: He praises—indeed, raves about—absolutely everything. (This may be what the *Post*, which battens on theatrical advertising, requires of its theater critic, but it is not what the theater-going public requires.)

Critics today mostly gush—daily, biweekly, monthly, quadrennially. Gushing is a gratifying activity, no doubt, but it is not an intellectually edifying one. The fact is many of our critics are merely reviewers. And there's a significant distinction between criticism and reviewing. The chief function—the obligation—of reviewing is to impart information on a fairly simpleminded level: what happens and what is it like to read this book, or see this film or play. Criticism, on the other hand, has little to do with whether or not the critic "adored" a book or film or play (in any event, the true critic would know that the word "adore" should be reserved for a deity); it is an inspection of the work in relation to larger issues.

If most of our critics are reviewers and most of our reviewers are flacks, then it's flacks who are setting standards today. But no matter how insistently they push their laundered images, these promoters of public relations are first and finally the downgraders of public discourse.

The all-American model Cheryl Tiegs and adman-husband Stan Dragoti advertising their happy marriage. "I never get tired of looking at him," she told *People* magazine. The near future would remove both Cheryl's smile and Dragoti's wedding ring. ▲

Tiegs, having taken her eyes off Dragoti, marries photographer, adventurer, and socialite Peter Beard. A few months earlier, she'd become the corporate bride of Sears, Roebuck, signing the most lucrative merchandising contract yet offered a celebrity. ▲

Tiegs, having slipped on a jersey from her Sears signature line, puts her eyes back on Dragoti, who here manfully directs his former wife for a Sears television commercial. ▲

Tiegs glows as she signs her "signature" name to a record-breaking five-year contract with Cover Girl Cosmetics at the Hotel Pierre. ▶

Concerned ecologist Tiegs with Nobel Laureate Dr. Norman Borlaug during her television special on overpopulation in Africa. "Too many people, too large animals, too little space, Cheryl," Dr. Borlaug has just explained. ▲

Concerned conservationist Peter Beard ◄

Beard's mill being moved to its new site. The mill would become a celebrity itself, a lodestar for the rich and famous. ▲

Wide World Photos

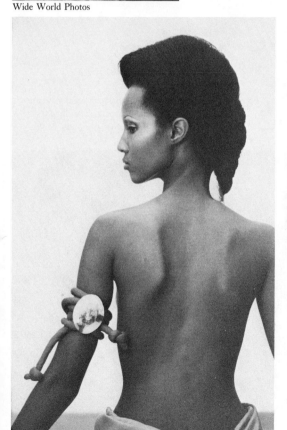

The rich and famous Candice Bergen, a former companion of Beard's, displaying the nose that Beard had to be "careful not to nuzzle too hard" ▲

Iman, the world's number one black model, whom Beard "discovered" in Kenya. Awed by his first glimpse of her, he broke into Swahili: *"None mana-muki maridadi kapisa!"* ▲

Bianca Jagger personifying her nickname "Vampira" ◄

Mick Jagger and Bianca en route to Beard's mill. The camera shot when it saw the whites of his eyes. ▼

Society columnist Suzy purring for Blackglama mink. Over the years, dozens of celebrities, ranging from Liza Minnelli to Lillian Hellman, have appeared in the ad that both confers and confirms legendhood. Hellman's appearance proved that big legends need more than little foxes to keep them warm. The ad campaign made Blackglama the star among furs and resuscitated the mink industry. ◄

Diana Vreeland, long-lived doyenne of the fashion world. Some mistook her here for Richard Boone. ►

Adman Peter Rogers, who selects the "Legends" for Blackglama legendhood, getting into the act with actress Angela Lansbury ▶

Kenneth, the world's most unflamboyant hairdresser ▲

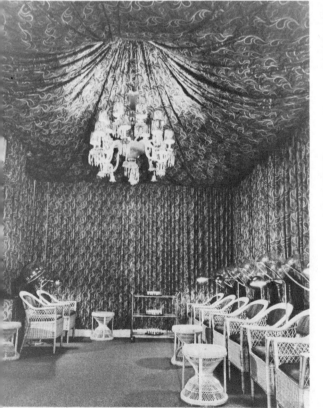

The drying room at Kenneth's, the world's most flamboyant beauty parlor ◀

First Lady Jacqueline Kennedy, Kenneth's most celebrated client, at a 1963 state dinner at the White House. The bouffant hairstyle that Kenneth created for her became a national landmark. To the eyes of the eighties, her hair looks stiffer than the starched shirts she was entertaining that night. ◄

Maury Hopson, the peripatetic thousand-dollar-a-day "free-lance hairdresser," with one of his show-biz clients, Raquel Welch. ►

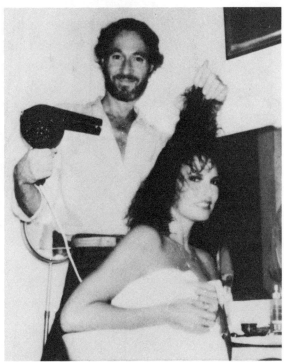

Plastic surgeon Dr. Howard "Belly Button" Bellin in front of his Cessna 310 at Flushing Airport, where he operates a flying school ▲

Dr. Bellin operating. "I've got two breast augmentations on Broadway," he boasts. "One in *Nine* and one in *Cats.*" ▲

Dr. Thomas D. Rees, the plastic surgeon's plastic surgeon ◄

Mrs. Bellin is the former Contessa Christina Paolozzi. Richard Avedon's famous photograph of her in *Harper's Bazaar* was the first frontal nude ever to appear in a fashion magazine. ▶

DR. and MRS. HOWARD BELLIN

First Lady Betty Ford before and after an extreme face-lift. One Palm Springs plastic surgeon sued another for taking credit for her fixed face. ▲

Andy Warhol, who is eager to have his first face-lift, with Truman Capote, a plastic surgery veteran. ◄

Joseph E. Levine presents Sophia Loren. ▶

Herb Schmertz, Mobil Oil's corporate image-maker, who is as smooth as the silk in his custom-made shirts ▲

Wide World Photos

United Press International

"Swifty" Lazar, the world's best-positioned literary agent ▲

Bob Lichtman

Seasoned press agent John Springer, who numbers Elizabeth Taylor, Warren Beatty, and Mike Nichols among his clients ▲

James Hamilton

PR man Bobby Zarem in an uncharacteristic moment: off the phone ◀

Columnist Suzy, premier referee
of the social game, links arms with
an old beau and his current wife. ▶

Elaine posing under the marquee of her restaurant, the
place where public people go to be private in public ▲

Elaine with President Carter's son,
Jack. The fists forming here were
once used to rough up Norman
Mailer's girlfriend. ◀

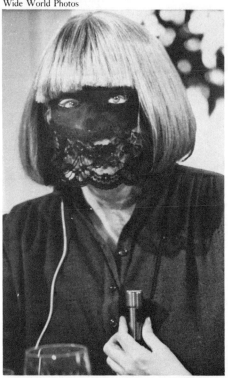

Mimi Sheraton, the *New York Times* food and restaurant critic, appearing on television wigged and masked. She resorts to disguises to keep restaurants from recognizing her. ◄

Sheraton undisguised. This is the mouth that's launched a thousand restaurants—and beached at least as many. ▲

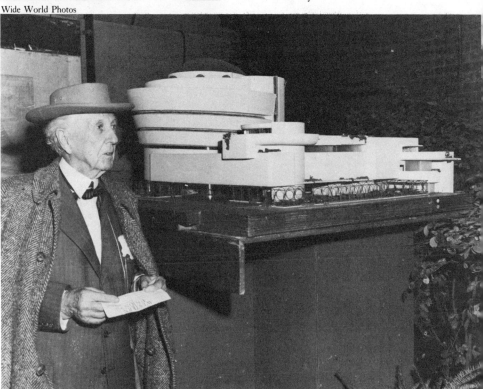

Frank Lloyd Wright, world-renowned architect and self-mythologizer, presenting himself along with his model for the Guggenheim Museum ▲

Philip Johnson, the most famous living architect and the leading promoter of modern architecture and architects, promulgating ▲

Johnson with an influential friend. "I sometimes lie down on Madison Avenue to look up at his A. T. & T. Building," Jackie gushed to the *New York Times.* ▲

I. M. Pei, preeminent corporate architect ▲

Peter Eisenman, the most cerebral architect of his generation, caught in the act of thought ▼

Richard Meier, whose persona is as elegant and controlled as his impeccably abstract buildings ▲

Vincent Scully (*right*), Yale professor and architectural mythmaker, and Robert Stern, the architect-teacher-historian considered likely to succeed Philip Johnson as the leading spokesman for American architecture ▲

Jaquelin Robertson (*right*), dean of the University of Virginia architecture school, determining the fate of shape with Michael Graves, the architect of the moment ◄

Famed heart surgeon Dr. Denton A. Cooley with famous actor Donald Sutherland at Cooley's Texas Heart Institute in Houston. The surgeon would soon play a bit part in the actor's film and the actor would soon become a bit of a surgeon in the surgeon's operating theater. ▶

Texas Heart Institute

© Mafuta Mingi Productions, Inc., 1982

Dennis Rayaon, the seven-year-old boy from the Philippines who was selected to receive free heart surgery by Dr. Cooley. The operation was in aid of a documentary about the doctor that begins, "This is the story of a great heart surgeon and a little boy." ▲

© Mafuta Mingi Productions, Inc., 1982

Cooley, the great heart surgeon, comforting Dennis, the little boy ▶

Romance novelist extraordinaire Barbara Cartland, the world's best-selling author, snapped at Heathrow Airport en route to New York to promote three new perfumes named after three of her three hundred novels ▲

A dressy photograph of Cartland, retouched to sell ritzy romances—and perfume on the side ▲

Diana Trilling, cultural critic and moral judge ▲

PART

V

THREE REFEREES:
WOMEN WHO
RULE THE GAME

If Cheryl Tiegs's apple pie is really cheesecake, if Lana Turner's peach melba is really dried apricot, if the Duchess of Windsor's smooth-skinned grape is really wrinkled raisin, if the spun-sugar confection that was Jacqueline Kennedy's hair was really a thin gruel, if critics are really no more than flacks, and if flacks are no less than the downgraders of public discourse, then we badly need some referees.

For referees apply the rules that order every competitive game.

Including hype.

The players in hype, like boxers, hit below the belt and get hit below the belt; like baseball players, hit a home run or get struck out; like tennis players, ace or are aced; and like football players, make a touchdown or fumble.

The referees sit in judgment, sometimes on the sidelines, sometimes in the middle of the action. They arbitrate technicalities, rule on infractions, impose penalties—they know the score.

As in any competition, in hype there are good referees and bad.

1

SUZY

Syndicated
Gossip Columnist:
The Last Word
on What Happened
Last Night and
the First Word
on What's Going to
Happen Tomorrow

I have to look down my nose at some of these climbers and the way they climb. It's just so obvious. There's no subtlety, there's no diplomacy worked anywhere, there's no timing on their climbing, they're just getting hysterical, they're just . . . *crazed,* they're desperados, they really are, and of course the first one they come to is *me* to tell the world what they're doing.

—SUZY, in conversation

Gossip is to hype what copulation is to conception—and there's nothing immaculate about it.

It's no longer the decorous and polished art once practiced by Boswell, Walpole, Pepys, Addison and Steele, Saint-Simon, Proust, and Virginia Woolf. That indolent gossip of the tea table, coffeehouse, and billiard room has disappeared along with gas lamps, horse-drawn carriages, and the grand tour.

Thanks to today's license to billboard the secret side of public lives, gossip is more aggressive than ever in making and breaking reputations, careers, marriages, even governments. While all of us indulge in it privately and idly, there are many who practice it publicly and professionally. These days the business of minding other people's business is practically an industry.

And certainly a competition. Never before have there been so many gossip columnists in America. Once upon a time, it was only Walter Winchell ("How long ago and far away you seem . . . /As fragile as a whisper in the dark"), Hedda Hopper, Louella "My first exclusive for tonight is" Parsons, Leonard Lyons, Ed Sullivan, Cholly Knickerbocker, and Dorothy Kilgallen who dished up tidbits, sweet or sour, mostly about film stars, royalty, and high society.

Today, treating us to whole groaning tables—course upon course of gossip for every possible reader's consumption—are such columnists as Eugenia Sheppard, Earl Wilson, James Brady, Rona Barrett, Marilyn Beck, Jody Jacobs, Bob Colacello, George Christy, Herb Caen, Irv Kupcinet, Maxine Mesinger, Diana McLellan, Taki, and Liz Smith, in addition to such newspapers and magazines as *People*, *Us*, *New York* with its "Intelligencer" column, *Time* with its "People" column, *Newsweek* with its "Newsmakers" column, the *Star*, *Palm Beach Daily News*, *National Enquirer* ("for people with inquiring minds," as the ads say), *Women's Wear Daily* and *W*, *American Lawyer*, and even the *New York Times* with its "Notes on People" column, recently renamed—to dispel the notion that the *Times* gossips, too—"New York Day by Day."

The raw material for this cornucopia of columns has expanded from the upper regions of stardom down, down, down to include businessmen, publishers, athletes, pop musicians, cosmetics tycoons, fashion designers, record company executives, gay liberationists, porn stars, hairdressers, plastic surgeons, coroners, and gossip columnists themselves.

Garnishing this already overrich gossip feast in recent years has been a glaze of confessional autobiographies, matricidal and patricidal biographies, book-length advertisements for selves, tell-all diaries, and telltale memoirs.

Also morning, noon, night, and late-night talk shows—many of them featuring a gossip columnist dressed unsensationally for the cameras as a "personality journalist" or "investigative reporter." One harrumphs remembering that Mike Wallace once described Maxine Cheshire as an "investigative society columnist."

Naturally, with all this food set before us, we overeat. If we get an unhealthy amount of pleasure from a gossip-column item about a celebrity's rise, we get an unholy amount of pleasure from an item about his—hers, too, because in gossip there's sexual equality—decline and fall. *Or* destruction, for to the seven deadly sins there should be added an eighth: gossip at its most vicious.

Gossip at its most delicious has been served up to approximately twenty-five million readers five days a week for the past twenty-five years by a 5′ 3½″ Texas-born, California-educated columnist with wide blue eyes, a helmet of copper curls, a gash of pouty lip, and a rich embarrassment of bosom, named Aileen Elder Mehle. Her nom de plume, Suzy, has passed into the language as generically as has Dom Perignon or, for that matter, aspirin.

But unlike champagne when *it's* been around for a long time, Suzy's effervescence has never gone flat. Thanks to her novelist's instinct for the way reality can be presented, her columns amount to a *mis en scène* about a *mis en scène:* the *soirées de gala* (be they charity affairs, movie premieres, Broadway openings, small private dinners, or extravagant masked balls), tempestuous love affairs, dangerous liaisons, magnificent obsessions, capricious feuds, and scatological scandals of the rich, the worldly, and the privileged wicked.

Yet for all Suzy's fizzy lightheartedness, she is a shrewd and deft referee of the social game. Arbiter, editor, and censor, she chooses among names—names that for the most part can be recognized quickly by her readers—starting with kings and queens and going all the way down to clowns, to make a tapestry of social prominence: an American Court Circular, as it were.

Suzy's judgments are the only next-day postmortems that matter. She alone can bring back to life the most important corpses of the night-before's party.

Men, women, and even children from all walks of life—from all stations of life, upstairs to downstairs—follow her column. For those upstairs, the pleasure of reading Suzy lies in verifying that their world is in place; for those downstairs, that that world is still worthy of their snobbish ideals—for there is still no appeal like snob appeal. But for those climbing from downstairs to upstairs, pausing on the landing to read her as they, above all, must, there is pleasure only when they find their own names flashing in their faces. As Clare Boothe Luce once said, "People don't know whether they are alive, married, or dead until they see it in Suzy's column."

Suzy herself leads a life so glamorous she could be in her own column (and *has* been—see page 70). After all, how many gossip columnists have been romantically linked with the likes of Walter Wanger, John Ringling North, and Aristotle Onassis? And how many gossip columnists have been described by the notoriously press-hating Frank Sinatra as "articulate, witty, charming, groovy, and incredibly bright and funny"? But then, how many gossip columnists have had romances with Frank Sinatra?

Suzy's own escalator ride upstairs began down south. A gay divorcée, Aileen Elder Mehle started out writing a social column in the *Miami News* for a lark. Not wanting to use her own name (in the naïve belief that Society would slam its standoffish door in her face), she borrowed—because it was snappy, saucy, and close at hand—the name of her fiancé's six-year-old daughter, Suzy.

When she divorced him two years later, she returned his name, resuming her first husband's name, Mehle, but did not return this second husband's daughter's first name.

It was as Suzy that she was hired in 1957 by the *New York Mirror*. When the paper closed in 1963, she was taken aboard the *New York Journal-American* to fill the slot of Cholly Knickerbocker, the society-columnist trade name owned by the Hearst Corporation; overnight the column underwent a sex change, for the new by-line read Suzy Knickerbocker—and soon it would read just plain (glamorous) Suzy. When the *Journal-American* sank, Suzy scuttled to safety at the *New York World-Journal Tribune;* and when *it* went under in 1967, she surfaced at the Chicago Tribune–New York News Syndicate, whose flagship paper is the *New York Daily News,* America's largest-selling general-interest daily. Clearly, Suzy is a survivor.

Her readers all swam after her to the *News.* By now she was far and away the most widely read society columnist in the country. From the moment she first set sail in Miami, she sent out rollicking waves of pleasure to every reader of her column. Everyone saw that here was something new in social reporting, something breezy, good-humored, and funny—"Oh hahahahaha" is one of Suzy's favorite punchlines—something witty but not bitchy, naughty but never mean. "I give the people I write about a kick in the pants with a diamond-buckle shoe," she once laughed.

Even President Kennedy had laughed when Suzy wrote that his suits were rumpled. Later he told her editor, "Tell Suzy I had my pants pressed." And that, ladies and gentlemen, is how Suzy achieved the distinction of calling the first and perhaps only presidential pants press conference in American history—Oh hahahahaha.

Suzy's flag-waving fan club is flourishing. She recently received a thank-you note from General Alexander Haig saying how gratifying it was to be in such a prestigious, highly regarded column as hers. (She had described him as "handsome . . . his smile as bright as the medals he wore when he was the head of Nato.") Truman Capote says, "She is one of only two or three columnists who ever wrote well. She makes each of her columns a little short story with a moral commentary at the end." And in affectionate homage, her friend William F. Buckley, Jr., wrote a parody Suzy column when he and Suzy were sailing the Caribbean on the good ship *Sealestial*, which he later incorporated in his book *Atlantic High*.

Another reader sent Suzy—as a playful joke—a parody of her column headlined "The Sock Murders," in which ten socialites are murdered by ten different sorts of socks. The column opens with Mica Ertegun, wife of the head of Atlantic Records, being found behind the Castelbajac counter at Bloomingdale's strangled with a silk stocking.

Black-stockinged nuns also number themselves among Suzy's devoted readers. One of them wrote in to say she reads the column out loud every day at breakfast and that the sisters all giggle and call *her* "Sister Suzy."

And there's a thirteen-year-old girl somewhere out there who has saved—she claims—"every single Suzy column that's ever been written in my entire lifetime." The complete library.

Just the other day the following letter arrived at the *Daily News*:

Suzy dear,

I'm a very old gaffer, 3 months from achieving, if I make it, nonagenarian status. I derive, so far as I know, only one benefit from my great age and senior citizenship. Once every 6 weeks I drive in my 1970 Dodge from the village I live in to a larger village 10 miles south where a barber cuts what remains of my hair for $2.50; the regular price is $3.00. Next to the barbership is a drugstore that sells the NEWS. My delight on these excursions is to purchase a copy and read your jottings. I love to know all about the beautiful people. I am stimulated. Inspirited! Sinatra, Bo Derek, of whom I had never heard until today, Beverly Sills, Walter Annenberg, whose late father, I suspect, owned the racing paper, Mrs. Vincent Astor, with whom I once had tea, toast, and duck eggs at the St. Regis. She grabbed the check, said her husband owned the joint. I devour it all, voraciously. I wish the drugstore in our village sold the NEWS. I could relish you every day. I am trying, at this late date, to write my life story. I don't suppose Swifty Lazar who you say is a literary agent would be interested. There would be so little, I suspect, that would interest a fellow known as "Swifty." I've lived in the same house more than 52 years; with the same woman for 53. Anyway, keep on top of it, keep buzzing, keep hot.

This voice from a little house on the prairie might just be the voice of America. And to think that Suzy actually hears from such a person!

Socialites, nuns, teenage girls, very old gaffers, and incipient sock murderers all tune in to Suzy because, in addition to being so terribly entertaining, she regularly delivers salty social scoops.

It was Suzy who broke the stories about the successive Henry Ford marital breakups. It was Suzy who heralded that improbable marriage of art and medicine, Picasso's ex-mistress Françoise Gilot to Dr. Jonas Salk. It was Suzy who predicted the inconceivable union of Greek shipping tycoon Stavros Niarchos and the late Tina Onassis, former wife of Aristotle Onassis and sister of Niarchos's first wife, whom he had supposedly beaten up. After Suzy's prediction came true and the couple was married, she was read as the oracle.

And even though Suzy's beat is hardly Hollywood, the three red-hot front-page movie stories of the last while have been hers: the marriage of Fred Astaire to jockey Robyn Smith, the marriage of Cary Grant to Barbara Harrison, and the breakup of Elizabeth Taylor and husband Number Seven, the junior senator from Virginia. Back in the sixties, when Louella Parsons was dying, the Hearst people had asked Suzy, who was then on the *Journal-American*, if she wanted to take over Parsons's column; and when Hedda Hopper died in 1966, the New York head of the Chicago Tribune–New York News Syndicate that handled Hopper had asked Suzy to take over *her* column, with all the syndication. Both jobs were based in California. Suzy turned them down because, as she said (but did not sing), "I love New York." (Today she adds, "There's no glamour in Hollywood anymore anyway. Lazar says they all sleep in their jeans and live in phone booths, and it's true, they do.")

In the Louis XV Revival sitting room of her Upper East Side brownstone duplex, as a breeze blows through the big windows, ruffling the skirts of the voluminous cloths that cover several round tables—skirts that she will lift up before long to expose goodies from the grateful—Aileen Elder Mehle, premier referee of the social game, recently gave the inside scoop on when Suzy says, when Suzy doesn't say, how Suzy says, why Suzy says, what Suzy says, and where Suzy goes to say it.

Social Game-Play: First of all, does Suzy ever regret not putting her real name on her column?

Suzy's Ruling: Listen, people who've known me for a hundred years can't say **Aileen Mehle** correctly. They're still calling me Eileen or Elaine or Ellen. Most of the time it's Eileen. Almost every European I know calls me Eileen. I rely on the men that are around to correct—like a husband or somebody I'm going out with. Once in a while, when I can't stand eight Eileens in a row, *I* correct. A lot of people call me **Suzy**. I don't mind that at all. Aileen and Suzy are interchangeable almost.

Review of Suzy's Ruling: One wonders whether Mary Ann Evans minded when people, remembering that she used the male pseudonym George Eliot, called her George.

Social Game-Play: Gossip, tittle-tattle, scandalmongering about the personal and private affairs of others—feeding on and fueling as it does secrecy, snobbery, bitchery, treachery, and envy—has, like PR, always enjoyed a bad name. Does Suzy believe that gossip's age-old reputation for dangerous triviality is justified?

Suzy's Ruling: Not at all. I've sat around tables with so-called intellectuals and all *they* do is gossip. I mean, I get some of my best gossip from intellectuals, *so*-called intellectuals. God, the whole *world* is a network, a hotbed, of gossip. Of *course.* Gossip is just talking about other people anyhow. It's all we do, it's all *any*body does—and I mean every doctor, every lawyer, every banker. It all goes back to people. We're talking about practically all there is in the world. What else *is* there?

The front pages of almost all our newspapers are filled with gossip. Not to mention the sports pages and business pages. Every time somebody's fiscal misdeeds are discussed, much of that is gossip. *The New*

York Times Magazine turned into one big gossip page there for a while. They run big stories on the **De la Rentas** and on **Gloria Vanderbilt,** and what is all that but gossip, just a long . . . piece . . . of gossip. Of *course* it is, and they needn't put their noses up in the air—not that they do. Maybe they don't at all.

There used to be a person on the *Times* whose job was to read the **Suzy** column. He came over to me at a party and told me that he'd been assigned to read the first edition of the *News* every day and pick up from my column anything the *Times* could use. So whenever I'd write about a big up-and-coming party, the *Times* would go right into action—they would call up and say, "We see you're giving a party and we'd like to be invited." And the hostess would say, "We're not having the press—it's a *private* party." And the *Times* would say, "But isn't Suzy going to be there?" I mean, can you imagine?

Social Game-Play: Gossip today is bolder and, therefore, potentially more gangrenous than ever. Has Suzy ever abused her considerable power?

Suzy's Ruling: To begin with, the power is in the page. *My* power exists only as long as I have my column. I'd be crazy to feel that **Aileen Mehle** has the power. Without my column, I'd be just like a president out of office. Any columnist who doesn't have a column anymore is "out of office." Now, a lot of other columnists don't understand that. Anybody who has a little typewriter, a little pen, thinks *they* have the power. Those little chits get very full of themselves, like ticks puffed up on blood. They get drunk with a little tiny bit of power. They don't know how to handle it.

They're all birds of a feather anyway—a bunch of low-life, no-talent broads. I think they're trashy and they have a trashy style. They like to pretend that we go to the same parties. I have been asked many times over the years to appear on programs with other columnists and I have never done it. I do not consider myself in the same league. I look at myself in a different way from the way I look at *them.* We are just not in the same world. I'm sorry. True or false, that's the way I perceive myself, and that's the way I shall continue to perceive myself.

Anyway, as we know very well, anybody who has the printed word at his fingertips does have a weapon. It's easy to hit somebody hard with a typewriter and still stay well within the laws of libel. I don't use my column as a weapon. I have no wish to destroy, and besides, I think that, rather than destroying *them,* it would destroy *me,* it would make *me* worse than *they* are. I do think it's perfectly all right to criticize a person who's been rude—for instance, I criticized **Madame Marcos** roundly for coming into the Metropolitan Museum and letting her bodyguards push and shove people around. I feel that I have the right as a, let's say, observer of the scene to state my opinions. And I do have them, and I *definitely* have a point of view, which my column reflects. It's easy to be saccharine, to make your column all molasses and no sulphur, to say sweet and precious and adorable things about everyone. It makes for popularity. And a lousy column. Maybe what *I* do is flick people on the wrist. But I don't stick in the knife. And I pull that needle out in a hurry. And rub the wound afterwards.

Social Game-Play: Most gossip columnists make mistakes. Some make nothing but mistakes, and end up squandering column space issuing retractions. Has Suzy, despite her reputation for impeccable accuracy, ever been inaccurate?

Suzy's Ruling: No one can possibly bat a thousand. Not when you're writing day in, day out, day in, day out. Every now and then you have got to make a mistake. But the mistakes in my column have been few and minor. Being totally credible is the only thing that makes you last, that gives you the reputation of, well, "If it's in **Suzy's** column, you know it must be true, it must be."

The majority of mistakes in my column have been typesetters' errors. They've had **Billy Baldwin** in lavender caftans, for godsake. They've had **Mary Lea Fairbanks** getting thin on a diet of meat and **George Plimpton.***

And they've had one of **Lord Harlech**'s daughters carrying on at a party of **Cecil Beaton**'s with a diamond-butterfly clip holding her fly together. The instant I saw *that* in the paper, I called my publisher. I said, "This is big trouble, you've got it all garbled, and I'm not going to take the rap for it. I'm going to retract and I'm going to say just what happened, that the printers left out a line." So, *that* fast, I got in a retraction. And the next day I was at a dinner at the French Consulate on Fifth Avenue and on my way to my table, a hand reached out and grabbed me, and the man said, "I'm **Roswell Gilpatric** and *you're* a *very* good *girl.*" He told me that the Harlechs had called him all the way from South Africa to

---

* Since Plimpton, a professional amateur, who once charged two thousand dollars to appear at a Washington party, as well as the founder of the *Paris Review*, a very little magazine, is long, lean, and lanky, it wouldn't be hard to slim on him.

complain that they'd read that their daughter was doing—well, what she wasn't doing at all. They're bad enough, those kids, they're bad *enough,* but the diamond clip in the fly was *crazy.* And Ros Gilpatric said, "And before I even had a chance to call you about it, you had a retraction in the paper, running at the head of your column, not the way other columnists do it, where they put it in such infinitesimal type you miss it."

But the biggest mistake of my career—and this one I made all by myself—was when I announced that **Katharine Graham,** the owner of the *Washington Post,* was going to marry **Edward Heath,** who was then the British prime minister. How do you like that for a biggie?

My scoop had come from what both I *and* my editor at the *Daily News* considered an unimpeachable source, a big *big* newspaper type. So we went with the story, and it made headlines every single place in this here world.

That same day Kay Graham called me and said, "Aileen, there's no truth whatsoever to the rumor. I do know Edward Heath but we're no more than acquaintances. Who told you? **Walter Annenberg?** I *know* Walter Annenberg told you, he's always hated me."

"No no no Kay, no no no! He did *not,*" I told her. "Kay, I'm *sick* about this, it makes me feel *terrible.* Not only for *you* but for *me*—I don't like being wrong. Let me retract it. Let me make it right for everyone."

"No," Kay said. "Just let it stand." And then said something I'll never forget. Now remember, this was before the *Washington Post*'s Watergate exposé made her a household word. "Aileen," she said, "you made me a *star.* My picture is on the front page of every paper in England and it's being picked up all over the world." So I saw that in a sense she was genuinely loving it all.

A few years after this, I was having lunch with Kay and her family out in the country, and they were all saying how much they hated publicity, *hated* it. And I said, "You can't escape it, Kay." And she said, "Ugh, I know, but the *less* I get the better I like it." And the kid in the family, the little one that's now gone into producing—**Steve Graham**—said to me, "*I* love it. I *love* publicity. *Please,* Aileen, every time you get a chance, put *my* name in your column 'cause I'm *crazy* abut publicity and I *want* to be in there *all* the time."

Review of Suzy's Ruling: The rumored Graham-Heath merger was a ridiculo-trans-Atlantico-socio-sexual-politico mismatch anyway, because, as everybody knew perfectly well, Edward Heath was the very oddest gentleman one could ever meet. So if this is the most serious mistake Suzy has made in her long career, she's batting way above average.

Social Game-Play: Gossip columnists make mistakes in part because they rely too heavily on press releases. To what extent does Suzy depend on press agents' handouts?

Suzy's Ruling: Most press agents don't even know how to spell. They don't get any dates right, and they get the rest of their information all wrong. If I'm going to use any part of what they give me, I have to make at least five phone calls: "You didn't say *when* this was, you didn't say *where* this was, you've got 'Ann' spelled wrong—are you *positive* there isn't an 'e' in 'Ann'?" By the time I'm finished with them, I don't want their bloody item, which wasn't very good to begin with. *I'm* the one who has to make it interesting. You see, it's like—suppose you're given a little dance to do and it's a terrible little dance, but it's the only dance you have—well, then, you better get out there and kick your legs and twirl for all you're worth.

Press releases that come from other kinds of agents are more likely to be *accurate.* **Sue Mengers,** the ICM talent agent, once told me that **Gore Vidal** had fallen asleep at his own Beverly Hills party, and I printed that. Later I got a little note from Gore saying "Darling One, I do not fall asleep at my own parties." It was a sweet note. *Nevertheless.* I told Sue Mengers that Gore insisted he hadn't dozed off, and she said that he certainly had, that he'd just closed his eyes and was completely out.

Review of Suzy's Ruling: Here we have another of those instances in life where the person who was awake is more accurate than the person who was asleep, even though the person who was asleep may have awakened believing his nightmare that he'd been awake at his own party.

Social Game-Play: The Suzy column is, among other things, a vehicle to social prominence for some. As Suzy herself has said, "No one hates publicity, just unflattering publicity." Almost everybody would like to be featured in her column. Has anyone ever tried to bribe Suzy? *Can* Suzy be bribed?

Suzy's Ruling: *Never.* I have cases of Dom Perignon and kilo tins of caviar under every table and in every closet. I have no place left to put them. But those aren't bribes, they're just what people send me for presents. And I can't *stand* it. I mean, who drinks champagne around *here?* When people first started sending me things, I asked my editor on the *Mirror,* **Mr. Neville,** if I shouldn't send all the stuff back. And he said,

"Of *course* not, you'll hurt their feelings." And I said, "I understand they're not allowed to accept *any* professional tokens of appreciation at the *New York Times*." And he said, "It's not like you're getting anything anyhow. They're not giving you diamond bracelets."

If anyone ever actually offered me money—you know, cash under the table—I don't know *what* I'd do to them. Oh, wait a minute, I do know what I'd do, because I did it. A lady I had mentioned in a column sent me a check for a thousand dollars—just like that—with a note saying, "Dear **Suzy,** I don't know what to buy you as a present because I know you have everything, so I'm just sending you this as a little token. Please buy something lovely for yourself." I tore that check into a thousand pieces and mailed it back to her with a note saying, "You're a darling, but I don't do this sort of thing."

Review of Suzy's Ruling: For Suzy there is a big difference between accepting a magnum of champagne from a pleased benefit-committee chairwoman whose charity she's cheered (Suzy's is the largest private collection of champagne in the Silk Stocking District) and accepting a four-figure check from a thirsty social climber. Anyway, were Suzy to break a champagne bottle into a thousand pieces and mail it back, more than the donor's feelings might be hurt when she opened her morning mail.

Social Game-Play: Suzy refuses to take bribes. It is, however, a fact that in 1972 the late Charles Revson, who so shamelessly sought a social image, nominated Aileen Mehle to the board of Revlon, the nation's largest over-the-counter retailer of cosmetics. There were those who saw a possible conflict of interest in the society columnist's acceptance of the social climber's bounty.

Suzy's Ruling: Now let's get into the truth of the matter. **Charles Revson** and I indeed were friends. I did socialize with him, not all the time but from time to time. I was on his yacht, as were many others. But I wrote Charles Revson's name very seldom in my column, unlike **Eugenia Sheppard** who wrote it until it was *nauseating.* The moment, the *instant,* Charles Revson said to me, "I have been searching and searching and searching for a woman to put on the board of Revlon and all of a sudden I thought to myself, '**Aileen Mehle** would be fantastic,'" from that moment on I stopped writing his name. I just thought, well, look here, I'm not going to be criticized for any conflict of interest. They'd all *leap* on me—I *know* them. They'd say I was on that board so I could publicize Charles Revson, when the reason I was put on it was that he'd sized me up as being able to offer him something in the way of the company. In fact, I think I got along with him better than anybody else—of my sex, let's say. My God, I write **Estée Lauder**'s name a hundred times more than I ever wrote Charles Revson's. And now I don't write his successor **Michel Bergerac**'s name.

At the annual stockholders' meeting a woman stood up—**Wilma Soss,** the corporate gadfly—and said, "I'm sick and tried of reading about Estée Lauder. **Suzy,** you've got to take Mr. Bergerac out into the world, you have *got* to take him out to dinners—he *has* to be noticed." Michel said, "Well, Miss Soss, I'm not here for that, I'm here to run a company." "No," she said, "I think you should get out. Suzy, you have to take Mr. Bergerac out." Now I almost went through the floor, since my position should be—and it *is,* indeed it is—that I would bend over backwards *not* to mention Michel, which he knows—and he bends over backwards not to *be* mentioned.

At that same stockholders' meeting, another woman got up, another one of those gadflies, and said to Michel, "There are seventeen members of the board and you only have one woman." And Michel said, "Yes, but *what* a woman." And the whole room burst into applause. I was so . . . *undone.*

And as for being the only woman, *New York* magazine used to do a feature on the ten most powerful men in New York. And not only was I the only woman on it, but I got a lot more votes than many of the men. There were ten lists and I was on three of them, including **Bill Buckley**'s and **Elaine**'s. They didn't ask for women. Well, they got this one.

I'm not a braggart, by the way. In fact, it took me a long time to be able to say what I'm saying right now, but I knew if *I* didn't, nobody else would, so I had to get around to, you know, talking about myself. I don't have an agent out there trying to say, well, she's popular with the readers or something.

I went to Paris when Revlon opened an office there in this simply ravishing house, and I had dinner with ninety-eight men. That's right, ninety-eight men and one woman—the heads of all the departments of Revlon from all over the world and *me.* I felt wonderful. I said to Michel, "We've got to take my picture. For my mother." So I stood up in the middle of this restaurant in the Bois and had my picture taken with all ninety-eight.

What exactly do I *do* on the Revlon board? I do just what any board member does. I run the company. We meet once a month, and I vote on every move that the company makes. I'm on the stock-options committee, and that is two additional meetings a year. All board meetings are more or less the same—you take up new business and discuss new ventures and listen to the auditing of the company and hear about new products and vote either yes or no on various things. You also decide who's going to be promoted, how much money all the officers are going to make, how long Michel is going to be employed—you *run* a company.

Of *course* I use Revlon products. I use them because they're very fine products—shampoos, soaps, skin lotions, cleansing creams, lipsticks, blush-ons, mascaras. I always say at every board meeting that I get sent complimentary cosmetics by everybody *except* Revlon—which makes them all scream and laugh.

Review of Suzy's Ruling: Suzy the society columnist has conquered the barons of industry. Her sixteen fellow board members probably think how nice it is to have a nonsubversive woman aboard who is also pretty and smart. Men look into women's eyes—to paraphrase Virginia Woolf—to see themselves mirrored twice their size. Suzy may have perfected feminine wiles (imagining her with the ninety-eight department heads, one thinks of Cheryl Tiegs blowing kisses to the chairman and president of Sears at that stockholders' meeting), but she is no mere accessory. She is a better board choice than, say, some female Nobel Prize-winning chemist, because she imparts to Revlon products the glamour of the world she referees. It's fortunate that Revlon doesn't send Suzy cosmetic freebies, since they might wind up in her closets and under her tables with the champagne, caviar, and other complementary compliments.

Social Game-Play: Most reporters' work is subject to the excising blue pencil of an editor. But Suzy's not only a reporter, she's also an editor. She edits before she even begins to type her column—she edits parties, she edits people. Has any big public name so offended her that she blue-penciled it forever from her column?

Suzy's Ruling: *Well.* There's a very highly placed state official with walnut hair whose name you will never see in my column again. I won't even say it now. I wrote the story of his breakup with his heiress girl-friend of five years, and it made the front page of the *Daily News.* I'd bent over backwards to make it nice. Then **Rocky Converse** [widow of Gary Cooper and, more recently, of Dr. John M. Converse, Number Three on "Suzy's List of Plastic Surgeons to the Beautiful People"] told me she'd seen this highly placed state official with walnut hair, who shall remain nameless, at a cocktail party and that when she happened to mention my name, he said "I never want to hear Suzy's name again!"

And after all I had done for him! When I think of all the times I knew his girlfriend wasn't interested in him anymore and was about to give him the gate—the old over and out—and didn't write it . . . He could be on my *lap* now and I wouldn't mention him in my column.

The other night I was at Carnegie Hall's ninetieth birthday party. I'd been placed at a table that included my fellow Revlon director **Ezra Zilkha** and his wife, **Cecile,** and **Jerry Zipkin** and the president of Merrill Lynch, **Bill Schreyer,** and his wife. And I was sitting quite contentedly when whom should I see working her way toward me— she must have had a map with pins in it and the maneuvers all worked out—but this highly placed state official's new bride, whom I cannot stand. I can't stand her because I can't stand her, do you know what I mean?

Now, there are a lot of people I write about that I know push. I even have some friends who do that, but that's okay, that's all right, they're all trying to make their way in the world. What I disapprove of is *un*believably un*attractively tacky* pushing.

So suddenly the new bride of this highly placed state official is sitting down at *my* table. I turned my back to her immediately, *immediately,* and began talking to Ezra Zilkha, whereupon *she* turned to Cecile Zilkha and Jerry Zipkin and asked them, "Is **Suzy** nice?" Cecile said, "Oh, *very.* If she doesn't like somebody, she won't write anything mean about them, she'll just never mention their name." Which I thought was a *riot,* since not mentioning *their* names would be the worst punishment. I always hated having them in my column anyway—they just pulled it right down. So then she said to Cecile, "Present Suzy to me"—which is very Greek-ish. And Jerry Zipkin, who knew how I felt about her, who *certainly* knew, because I had gone through a whole tirade against her while she was moving herself around the room, table-hopping all over the place, pushing so loudly you could actually hear her— Jerry whispered no to Cecile, who quickly changed the subject. Of course, I didn't hear any of this till afterwards, because I had my back to her.

Review of Suzy's Ruling: Some might see it as reckless and disproportionate for a gossip columnist to dismiss a governor—albeit one who Jimmy Breslin wrote "appears to get most of his philosophy from *Women's Wear Daily*" and who, though he occupied the top floor of the Empire State, was still climbing, along with his bride, who owned her own empire of real estate. But Suzy has ascended beyond the state level. She's been at the federal level for some time now. As we shall soon see,

Presidents, both current and former, have entertained her, and she in turn has been charming about *them* in her column. For example, in two columns chronicling "an evening with the Richard M. Nixons" at their new New Jersey house, she described the former President's "vigor, vitality and life-force" as "stupendous"—adding that "even his enemies grant his magnetism, if not his charisma"—and Mrs. Nixon's hospitality as "matchless."

As Suzy calls it, even in the best circles—where the movement, she knows, is not so much circular as vertical—it's how you climb—in a word, your climbing style—that spells social success.

Social Game-Play: On the whole, Suzy has to maintain her long-term personal and professional connection to the rich and powerful. But she is first of all a reporter, and for a reporter to remain powerful she must beat other journalists to the first edition. So what does she do when she has to report something slightly unpleasant about a friend?

Suzy's Ruling: Well, take the performance that **Gloria Vanderbilt** put on in front of about three hundred people in the Starlight Roof of the Waldorf, at a Bonds for Israel dinner honoring **Warren Hirsh,** who was then the head of Murjani International, which markets Gloria Vanderbilt jeans. Now, I didn't want to hurt her. That was the first thing I thought of, because I *like* Gloria Vanderbilt and I like her very much. But I was torn, knowing that if *I* didn't write the story, somebody else would get it, it was just too hot—it was a big, juicy story. So I had to find a way to present it that would not make her look like a horse's ass. Now *she* may think I'm a rat for writing what I did write, but a less kindly person than I—someone who didn't *know* Gloria, let's say—would have just run with the facts.

Gloria was seated on the dais. The master of ceremonies at the dinner was **Marvin Traub,** the head of Bloomingdale's. While he was speaking, giving his *spiel* about Hirsh, Gloria wandered over to the microphone, interrupted him, and gave a speech herself about Hirsh, just nattering on and on and on. Then she went over to Hirsh and kissed him on the face and cheeks. Then she went back to her place on the dais and sat down. Later, while Marvin Traub was giving his closing *spiel,* she went over and took the microphone away from him again and chanted, "*I* was a child of the Depression. One day when I was driving along in our gray Rolls-*Roy* with my aunt **Gertrude,** a *lady* selling apples *on* the corner stopped me and said, 'Oh, *help* me, little Gloria.' " Then she went back to her seat, fell off her chair, picked herself up off the floor, and walked out. The whole room absolutely buzzed.

Then back she comes. *Back*. **Alan King,** the stand-up comedian, now had the mike, and as he saw her come back in he said, *"Here* comes **Madame Pagliacci."** She was dressed in one of those white frocks of hers with a high, black-ruffled collar, and with that dead-black hair and that dead-white skin of hers, she did look like Madame Pagliacci. She went over and grabbed the mike away from him and said, mentioning her former husband, who had recently directed Alan King in *Just Tell Me What You Want,* **"Sidney Lumet** is a very good friend of mine—very good. *I* think stand-up comedians are hostile. So don't you be hostile to *me,* Alan King, or *I* will tell Sidney Lumet and *he* will never work with *you* again." Then she left—for good.

Now I thought to myself, *what* am I going to do? I swear to God I don't want to hurt Gloria, but I can't let this story go by, because if I do, I'm not a newspaper woman. There were all these people there and *they* are going to talk, and then I'm going to read it in somebody's else's column, and I'm going to have to say to myself, *"Damn* you, Aileen, for being nonprofessional." So my problem was not whether to write it, but how to write it.

After a bit of thought I decided to start the column out saying, "You can't take the spotlight away from **Gloria Vanderbilt,** so don't even try." And end it with "Glo-Glo went back to her seat again, seemingly unaware that she was the star of the show. Maybe they should always invite her. Because that night they raised $1.6 million for Israel Bonds." Now I didn't have to write it that way, I could have told it exactly like it was. I could have told about the audience reaction: Is she drugged? Is she drunk? What's come over this crazy woman? Instead, I made her a *star* who upstaged everybody. After the column appeared, I got a divine letter from Alan King saying, "Thank you, thank you. I have never seen such blatant kindness—whether I work for Sidney Lumet ever again or not."

Review of Suzy's Ruling: Suzy saw an old friend, in effect, washing her dirty linen in public and took the sting out of the stink that Gloria Vanderbilt created by printing a sanitary scoop. With every ingenuity at her command, she found a way to protect one of her pets. When friends behave tastelessly, Suzy can be counted on to record the display tastefully. (She really is, as she once quipped about herself, "the champion of the over-privileged," the world's poor-little-rich girls. "I remember," Suzy says, **"Brooke Astor** once said to me, 'Please never mention my jewelry, I'm a woman alone!' and I said, 'Never, *never!'* ") Tastefully, but also quite tastily. And in this highly skilled balancing act that she performs, Suzy will maintain the allegiance of both her friends and her readers.

Social Game-Play: Suzy has been around—and also made—powerful people in her years of social refereeing. Does there ever come a time in powerful people's lives when they are no longer impressed by being around other powerful people?

Suzy's Ruling: The first time I went to the White House for dinner, when the **Fords** were there, I was seated at **Mrs. Ford**'s table. My placement was fantastic. I was between **Cary Grant** and **Van Cliburn.** **Harold Wilson,** who was the guest of honor, and **James Callaghan,** his foreign secretary, were also at my table. And **Beverly Sills** sang and, *typically,* **President Ford** referred to her as Beverly Stills. During dinner, Van Cliburn whispered to me, "Everyone is so *grand* at this table. I'm so impressed. I'd love to have their autographs but I'm too embarrassed to ask." I said, "Well, *I'm* not—give me your menu," and that darling said, "First *you* sign it, Aileen." And after I signed **"Suzy,"** I passed Van's menu to Cary. Oh, and **Happy Rockefeller** was on the other side of Cary—that was when **Nelson** was Vice President and alive. And everybody was tickled pink to sign it.

And then Callaghan and Wilson passed *their* menus around for everybody to autograph. Callaghan loaned us his fountain pen to use, which he said he treasured—he'd probably signed documents of state with it. And he said something great like, "Everybody's so great at this table I can't stand it."

The next time the Fords invited me to dinner at the White House, I was seated at President Ford's table. And this time the guest of honor was the **Shah of Iran.** You must remember there were only eight people at that table, and *I* thought *that* was pretty snappy for *me* to be seated *there*. I was between Secretary of the Treasury **Donald Rumsfeld** and **Henry Ford.** And **Ann-Margret,** who was the entertainment that night, was also at my table. I'd bet **Bobby Zarem,** who was coming in after dinner—he used to handle her—twenty dollars that President Ford was going to mess up her name, but all during dinner he got it right, and afterwards he stood up and introduced her correctly as Ann-Margret, and I figured I was going to lose the bet. But later he said, "Thank you, Margret-Ann." So I got my money from Bobby Zarem. Oh, Bobby's been to the White House a *lot*. He was there a lot when **Carter** was President. Oh, I don't mean for state dinners, but he went for receptions and teas.

Betsy Bloomingdale was also at my table—oh, and the **Shabanou.**

I was very snappily placed because the **Kissingers** were seated someplace way over *there*. And all those Washington columnists were absolutely green, *green*, because there I was, and there *they* were, sort of hanging suspended on the outside, or coming in after dinner with their little press cards and pencils.

Review of Suzy's Ruling: At that first White House dinner, only Suzy would not have felt like a hick handing the menu around in such a down-home, chicken-lickin' manner. It's something that only the most popular girl in the class could have gotten away with. Suzy dares to be ingenuous—after all, it's the behavior Americans are known the world over for—because she understands that we all live in the rush of connections to power, that the people at her table were as gratified to be grouped together as they would be, later on, to be assembled together in her column. In passing that menu around, Suzy became the tour director of the group's celebrityhood. (Today the momentous menu is probably positioned on the wall over Van Cliburn's majestically grand piano.)

Fortunately, President Ford didn't have to introduce any of the other guests at his table. If he had so much trouble with such a simple Anglo-Saxon name as Ann-Margret and such a monosyllable as Sills, he would have been sure to tangle his tongue on Bletsy Boomingdale, and as for the Shabanou—if the President had thought to sidestep the difficulty by introducing her as Empress Farah Diba, she could easily have come out of his mouth as Fawcett Farrah.

As for Suzy, she didn't need a press card—she never does. She didn't even need a little pencil—she could always have borrowed a feather quill from the then-proud occupant of the Peacock Throne, the Shahanshah, King of Kings, Defender of the Faith, and descendant of **Darius the Great.**

Social Game-Play: The Carters brought peanut people with them to the White House. The Reagans have brought a commodity that Suzy herself trades in—glamour. The gossip is that Suzy has Reagan White House clout.

Suzy's Ruling: Well, at the Republican National Convention, in Detroit's Joe Louis Arena, I sat in **Nancy Reagan**'s own private sky booth, Number Nineteen. In fact, I was with the **Reagans** every minute of the convention. Nancy Reagan is my friend—she's warm and real and kind—and I like her very much. I like *him* very much, too. I couldn't like them better. And I know they like *me* because they've made it very, very clear that they do. And I love *them*. I like them *tremendously* and I always have. I've known them a long time.

Nancy and I were "Legendary Women of America" in Birmingham together in 1973, along with **Lee Annenberg, Betsy Bloomingdale, Helen Hayes,** and **Lady Bird Johnson.** On our way to the Birmingham Civic Center where the gala was being held, Nancy, Betsy and I scrunched way down in our gowns in the backseat of our limousine so we could get a better view of our names, which were revolving in lights on top of one of the tallest towers in Birmingham. We were thrilled because it was like being up on a marquee. We told the driver to wait while we watched our names going around and around and around. Nancy kept saying, "I can't believe it, I can't believe it." I remember she laughed. A pretty laugh. I love to hear that pretty laugh of hers. A *beautiful* little laugh, beautiful—half bird song, half silver bells.

Review of Suzy's Ruling: When journalists began attacking Nancy Reagan for spending a disproportionate amount of her time and her cronies' tax-deductible money extensively redecorating the White House, her friend of long standing—and scrunching down—wrote several columns boosting the First Lady's efforts.

> At least this First Lady has a sense of beauty and of history. . . . It is not for **Rosalynn Carter** to comment on the White House china ordered by **Nancy Reagan,** who is trying her best to make the White House beautiful and well-equipped, and at not one cent of cost to the taxpayers. If she sets her table with a patchwork effect in Plains with a different plate at each place, that is Rosalynn Carter's problem. She should also take a few lessons in butting out from **Betty Ford** who, though outspoken, has always been charming and gracious and who had the good sense not to turn green in the Blue Room.

Grateful to the nation's leading society columnist for her understanding that the beautification of the White House, that symbol of American power, is the First Lady's first mission, Nancy Reagan wrote Suzy in a flowing schoolgirl script a note so sweet it makes a Barbara Cartland heroine seem sour by comparison:

Dear One,

Thank you for the pat on the back which I really needed at this time. To read some of those columns you'd think I was knocking myself out for myself instead of the people. It's *their* house, not mine, and I'm just trying to maintain it. Anyway, I love you and thank you.

Nancy

Like birds of a feather, "Legendary Women of America" in Birmingham stick together.

Social Game-Play: As the *bon ton* commentator of our age, Suzy has been feted not only at the White House but everywhere glorious and grand. Where does she most like to hang out for plain and simple pleasure?

Suzy's Ruling: I love Elaine's. I think it's cozy and fun, and everywhere you look there's a *name*—I mean, you're falling all over them. Everybody *means* something, as a political figure or a show-biz figure or even a society figure if you want to come to that. There's an air of excitement about Elaine's.

Review of Suzy's Ruling: Since entertainment is Suzy's work, it's not surprising that Elaine's is what Suzy does for entertainment. There she can supervise her own star-studded column. And there she can be even more of a referee than Elaine, who merely decides which celebrities get to sit in the celebrity section of her restaurant. It's Suzy—when she selects from Elaine's celebrity section certain names for her column—who referees who will be nationally syndicated.

Social Game-Play: One of the hype bulletins about Suzy reads that she's the only gossip columnist who doesn't tattle tales outside her work. Suzy is a gossip columnist, but is she a gossip?

Suzy's Ruling: When people start gossiping and I'm there, of course I gossip. But I gossip discreetly—and with discrimination. I know exactly what I'm saying and to whom I'm saying it. I know how much I can trust the person who's hearing it, whether it's a hundred percent—and there are about two of those—or whether it's eighty-five percent or forty percent.

Review of Suzy's Ruling: However attuned Suzy's antennae are to the truly trustworthy, she has here in these pages been gossiping 100 percent to a readership of more than two.

2

ELAINE
Sweet-and-Sour Proprietor of the Restaurant Where Public People Go to Be Private in Public

Elaine, New York's restaurateuse to the famous, gets them all. Through her portals lately have passed such as **Marcello Mastroianni,** who stopped off on his way to Rome via Mexico with a gang of Mexican and Italian bosom buddies. All the regulars keep checking in, such as **Woody Allen,** who wears little caps and cuts his hair short, **Mia Farrow,** who is never without Woody, **Liza Minnelli** with her husband, **Mark Gero,** and **Robert DeNiro, Alan King** with beard, **Linda Evans** and **Joan Collins** doing a tête-à-tête (things are that bad?), **Ron Howard, Henry Winkler, Penny Marshall** and **Cindy Adams** (next to the coffee pot) and, next to them, **Warren Beatty, Robert Evans, Diane Keaton** and **Jack Nicholson.** Enough? Not quite.

Rudolf Nureyev in a cossack hat comes in and sits with **Franco Zeffirelli. Nastassia Kinski** comes in with her daddy, **Klaus Kinski.** Scattered are **Norman** and **Norris Mailer, China Machado, Nan** and **Gay Talese, Cher, Sandy Dennis, Karen Black,** the last three with their "Come Back to the 5 and Dime, Jimmy Dean, Jimmy Dean" director, **Robert Altman,** French rock singer **Silvie Vartan** and designer **Sonia Rykiel.** Enough? Not really.

Barbra Streisand walks in with **Jon Peters,** goes to a table for two at the end of the restaurant, eats and walks out without really anyone recognizing them. **Lauren Bacall,** in Halston's beige silk pajamas and Fortunoff pearls, comes in with **Harry Guardino** and a gang. **Christina Onassis** was at the table at the window with a party of 12. Right next door were producer **Richard Zanuck** and **David Brown** and **Mrs. (Helen Gurley) Brown** and actor **Roy Scheider** with his wife. Seated at a little square table were **Sally Fields** and her gang. In another part of the room were spooky movie director **Brian de Palma** with his actress wife, **Nancy Allen,** and **Sissy Spacek. Rod Stewart,** the bleached blond rocker, and his wife, **Alana,** were at the table by the Venetian mural. Then **Diana Ross** walked in in a little black dress and a sable coat, and necks started craning. Enough? Maybe not. But it will have to do until Elaine gets some names in the place.

—Suzy, the *New York Daily News*

How can a former 357-pound chalunka from Queens, who brags that she "graduated high school, barely," become not only an editor but *the* editor—the social editor—of the literati? How can a former night cosmetician at a pharmacy on Broadway, whose job was selling paint and powder to prostitutes, become famous selling food and drinks to models, producers, admen, socialites, intellectuals, writers, agents, politicians, film stars, celebrity athletes, nobility, royalty, and hungry voyeurs of all of the above? Is it possible that someone who used to read the *Daily News* underneath her desk at school now makes the *Daily News* almost daily?

Yes! Because she makes news nightly. So how did this chalunka chomp to the top?

Press!! She plunked down ten grand for an ordinary-looking neighborhood saloon, inconveniently located on Manhattan's Second Avenue at Eighty-eighth Street, and turned it into a salon for, mostly, the media people who create the myth of where-it's-at: journalists, editors, screenwriters (Frank Perry had Carrie Snodgress make a frenzied entry there in *Diary of a Mad Housewife,* with a waiter whispering *coraggio* to her; and Woody Allen had a meal there in *Manhattan*), Broadway playwrights, novelists (Renata Adler revved up the place in *Speedboat*), gossip columnists ("I think everybody who goes there is honestly, subliminally, hoping to write or be written about," observes Liz Smith), and flacks— all of them talking scripts, package deals, soft-cover, front money. The proprietor cashed writers' checks, even knowing they would bounce. She kept her restaurant open late, knowing that creative writers, always in a state of either euphoria or depression, keep erratic hours, and that journalists *never* sleep—they're always up looking for a story. She framed their photos and hung their autographed book jackets on her walls, knowing that writers who kept bouncing checks at erratic hours would keep coming back to see if she'd bounced their book jackets. She once offered to lend a press agent money so he could go into business for himself; Bobby Zarem didn't accept her offer, although he did go into business for himself, and now after business hours he does business with her other favorites at one of her favored tables—and the next morning they all appear in the *Daily News*. So who *is* this broad? What's this joint called?

Elaine is the dame, and the dive is Elaine's.

For twenty years Elaine Kaufman has kept her trattoria trendy in a town where restaurants have the life-span of goldfish. Her mouthy manipulation of the media paid off—as even a *schnorrer* from Peoria who never "graduated high school" could pick up from a speedy reading of the following collage of hype bulletins:

"Elaine's is bigger than the fuckin' Algonquin in its fuckin' heyday. It's the fuckin' be-all and end-all." (Bobby Zarem) *** "Manhattan's literary wet nurse." (Gael Greene) *** "A place where a writer could go to nurse a block, or watch the competition goof off, a Toots Shor's for the quality lit set." (Thomas Thompson) *** "Elaine gives us a sense of community." (David Halberstam) *** "A sort of verbal disco for grownups . . . gossip about money and power . . ." (Michael Arlen) *** "Elaine *writes* that restaurant the way a good writer writes a book—every detail accounted for." (Bruce Jay Friedman) *** "Elaine's mix is compellingly chic." (*Women's Wear Daily*) *** "Remember the night Leonard Bernstein and Dietrich Fischer-Dieskau began playing and singing . . . the night Gloria Steinem brought Gianni Agnelli . . . the night George Plimpton stood on his hands . . . the night Elaine chased paparrazo Ron Galella down the street, brandishing a garbage-can lid . . . the night Elaine roughed up Norman Mailer's girl . . . the night Mailer and Jerry Leiber went through the wall . . ." *** "Henry Ford and his wife had to wait half an hour for their table. 'She's just a middle-class Italian,' says Elaine." *** "Elaine is a patroness of the arts." *** "Elaine is internationally known, recognized on the streets of London and Paris." *** "Arthur M. Schlesinger, Jr., according to Calvin Trillin, is working on a two-volume history of Elaine's." (Anatole Broyard, the *New York Times*) *** "Elaine is a rare and beautiful gift of nature." (*Esquire*)

And this is just a taste of the hype bulletins about Elaine and Elaine's that we've been consuming lo these many years.

About ten years ago, around about eleven at night, a prosperous-looking, conservatively dressed middle-aged couple—he was wearing a Brooks Brothers jacket and Gucci loafers; she was wearing a pale linen suit and sensible shoes—were cooling their heels at the noisy bar at Elaine's, sipping their second Manhattans and waiting for a table. They'd made a reservation for 10:15.

For three quarters of an hour, they'd been watching one mangy-looking bearded caricature of a bohemian after another slouch in and parade past them to empty tables along the wall of the long room, nodding to friends and acquaintances en route. After her third Manhattan the woman walked over to the owner, who was at her post by the cash register at the end of the bar, totting up bills, and said, "Excuse me but . . ."

"Yes," the owner said, glancing up for a second.

"My companion and I have been standing here for almost an hour now. I know you don't know who I am or anything, but I'm a rather important person. I happen to be the president of Red Cross Shoes."

There was a long pause. Then Elaine looked up from her bills again and growled, "So what? Your shoes are full of shit and so are you."

The woman then did the only sensible thing: She turned on her heel and with her companion left the restaurant.

Restaurant? That was the president of Red Cross Shoes' first mistake. Elaine's is less a public restaurant than a semiprivate club.

We know how we get out—through the front door.

But how do we get in?

Well, it's a mostly male club, as a glance at the photographs of club members on the walls will tell us. And a mostly macho male club. "Elaine discouraged the gay set by the simple expedient of refusing to seat two tables of men side by side," *New York* magazine reported in the pre-Stonewall sixties. "They're a thankless lot," says Elaine in the post-Stonewall eighties. Such a homophobic remark seems odd coming from someone who learned the restaurant business in Greenwich Village. But then, Elaine didn't welcome working girls at Elaine's, either, unless they arrived with writers.

Elaine is a one-woman committee on admissions. She proposes, seconds, writes all the letters of recommendation, elects—and blackballs—candidates.

The membership dues at Elaine's consist of members being in attendance, which itself consists of much more than their just being there—they must chat up Elaine and hype the restaurant in any publication they have access to. Charter members pay their dues nightly; others, at least weekly.

Club privileges and prerogatives consist of their being shown to a good table right away, getting to talk to Elaine herself at their good table, and getting to order for their now-groaning table special dishes that do not appear on the menu.

Most clubs have an occasional open house. Elaine's has open house every night. The public at large is invited in to ogle from their troglodyte tables in the back the celebrated club members celebrating each other and Elaine, the master of seating segregation—one of the most effective instruments for social control ever devised. Everybody gets his money's worth: The celebrities have the thrill of being observed as they perform status theater; the chalunkas have the thrill of gawking at them; and Elaine cleans up.

But Elaine's is a club where members, even if they pay their dues on time and perform at all the open houses, can never be quite certain of their membership. Some members have entered the premises to find Elaine staring at them with the stigmatizing glare of nonrecognition; overnight they'd become anonymous, thanks to some offense they had evidently committed which they could only guess at and might never know.

They feel terrible—they *care* what Elaine thinks of them, these critics and intellectuals who determine what the rest of us think. And they know that they're going to feel worse, that Elaine will give them psychological indigestion by putting them at an unsavory table. They can't stand the thought of being ostracized.

Over the years very few club members have ostracized themselves, despite many provocations from Elaine. But in 1975 Elaine's long-time waiter, maître d', and, for three years, her 35 percent silent partner, Nicola Spagnolo, resigned and—even more treacherously—opened a rival restaurant called—of all things—Nicola's, six short blocks away, seditiously staffing it with Elaine's third chef, one of her dishwashers, and a couple of her waiters. (In 1978 another partner of Elaine's, Elio Guaitolini, would defect and open Parma on Third Avenue, and in 1982—inevitably—Elio's, on Second Avenue, just four short blocks from Elaine's.)

In the wake of Nicola's departure, several club members tendered their resignations and became habitués of Nicola's. They felt right at home there—the decor was a close clone of Elaine's: blue-and-white checked tablecloths, green floor covering, autographed book jackets and authors' photos framed and showcased behind glass.

Then came the necessary first puff of inflation: *Women's Wear Daily,* after its editor-in-chief Michael Coady had a fight with Elaine, labeled Nicola's "the IN place to go." Soon it was packed with celebrities, preppies, stockbrokers, and models.

Elaine didn't take Nicola's defection sitting down, and a much-publicized—some say much-hyped—dogfight broke out between the two.

Interviewed separately for *Hype*, the now thinner Elaine (she'd lost 207 pounds of aggravation in less than two years) took the Fifth Amendment. But the former 35 percent silent partner, Nicola, sounded off 100 percent.

ELAINE: To what do I owe my success? Well, y'know, I went slow. I didn't grow to be twenty-one years of age overnight. Also I can deal with original minds—some people can't. . . . Am I kind of a paid professional hostess? Nah. Sometimes where I seat customers just depends on whether *I* want to talk to them, because then I put them where I can reach them, which is near the bar, so when I'm free, I can sit down and, y'know, talk. . . . I'm gonna lecture again this season at the New School for Social Research. Nah, I don't know what on. They'll just tell me what they want me to talk about and I'll talk about it. It's very simple—give me a minute on anything and, like, I'll just, I mean, like, I'll go. . . . The worst mistake I ever made? Putting my name on the place! Because it makes it too personal. I wasn't, y'know, looking to be Elaine's. I just was looking to make a small restaurant. Which is what this is. Basically. With terrific food. The best food on this end of the island—like our ad says. . . .

Am I *what*—a traitor to my class? Do I treat BBQs as an underclass? Nah. Every customer is part of my family, my extended family. I'm the Big Mama of them all. Yeah. I mean, I'm a mother as well as a motherfucker. And a mother gets a separation anxiety when she doesn't have her family around all the time, right? I don't like transients, I like regulars. So if Jackie Onassis comes in, I help her out—she's, like, family. I get her a seat out of the way, because even if you're a face like Jackie Onassis that's known in the press, I still think you have a right to sit with your friends, and, y'know, say what you want without somebody hanging over you eavesdropping or, like, lip-reading your lips.

Y'know something, stardom doesn't really mean anything here. I mean, Alan King was in last night, it was his wife's birthday, and we had a whole bunch of people here, and he was walking back and forth, saying hello to this one, hello to that one, kidding with Ali MacGraw, fooling around, y'know, because they'd just done a picture together. And that's just the way Elaine's is. Nobody's on. On the contrary. The mainstay are very hardworking people. They're not nine-to-fivers—the people who come in here work *until* the project is finished. And the people who might be too intimidated to come in here may not have a desire to achieve or work. I mean, somebody who works a straight job who is not willing to give any more than what is necessary to his job is certainly going to feel uncomfortable here. . . .

Which press agent handles the Elaine's account? *Jesus Christ!* I've never in my life had a press agent! I know some do—ya, individuals. Ya, I know who they are. They know I know. They pay some guy to push them in the press. I feel sorry for them. I mean, what does publicity have to do with success? My preoccupation is to get the food out with the greatest quality. I mean, I'm in the food business, right? We serve two hundred dinners a night here and they're *all* choice. I try to keep the food down to a pure form. It's really the food here gives me the greatest satisfaction. Ya, the rest is a by-product.

NICOLA: Every successful guy has a good wife behind. I was the fucking wife of Elaine. Don't get me wrong, I never fucked Elaine. . . . Putting people together at tables at Elaine's it was *my* idea. I says, let's get a big table. So we call it the Club Table—the fourth table when you come in. I put people to that table because I know they're gonna meet somebody on their status, some of their *friends*. You have the same kind of people, they discuss the same thing all the time—you know, all the time it's the job, Hollywood. We get so successful, so *packed* we get our doors stormed with people.

But like I always says, a chalunka is always a chalunka. Chalunka is a word I invent. It's, you know, a BBQ, a *schmuck*. I don't mind serving people with class, but when I got a chalunka, my stomach it goes like this. In this business you cannot mix the silk with the rags. As a matter of fact, if I'm gonna open up another restaurant, I'm gonna call him a chalunka. But a celebrity, that's a *celebrity*. The crew makes the port, the port . . . doesn't . . . The harbor doesn't make the . . . The sailor doesn't make the harbor, the harbor makes the harbor or whatever. It's an old saying, very old—*Il marinaio non fa il porto, il porto fa il marinaio.* The clientele it makes the place. When Jacqueline Kennedy came the first time to Elaine's, I recognize her right away. I says, "That is Jacqueline Kennedy," because I got one thing—I know faces. And it was the day before she made the announcement she was gonna marry Onassis. She was there with the lord, the English lord—Harlech. They were going together. She says, "Either you marry me or else I'm gonna marry the other guy," and the English guy then he says, "No, I don't wanna marry you." So she turn around and she marry Onassis. . . . Does Elaine have a PR man? Sure. Zarem. She says to me, "He's so good, he's so dedicated, he work so hard." I don't know if she pays him money. If you don't do it for money, you do it for something else. . . . You know, when I opened up my place, Elaine she blackball people when she knew they was coming here. "You go to Nicola," she says, "*go* to Nicola, don't come to *me*." One girl she made a mistake and she go to Elaine's by mistake in one of my T-shirts that says "Nicola's," and Elaine she call her a whore and throws her out. If you go there with my matches even, forget it. But I don't *give* a shit, because I know my potential.

* * *

"I know my potential" is a phrase that Nicola may have picked up one night at Bobby Zarem's table at Elaine's—indeed, it's a phrase not hard to overhear *every* night at practically *every* table at Elaine's.

Curiously, Elaine speaks in an even more obscure American dialect than Nicola does. One would have thought that through osmosis alone, having spent twenty years talking primarily to writers in a restaurant dripping with book jackets, she would have picked up some feeling for how an honest sentence flows in English.

Like a flower child spouting all the wishwash of sixties sentiment, Elaine claims she's just feeding her extended family. She won't own up to being in the hype business, to running a restaurant that sells clannishness and exclusion to a poisonous degree. "We don't keep people out," she maintains. "That's *their* fantasy." It is, however, a fantasy she caters to and licenses her favored writer-customers to retail in the press.

Sounding as though she's had as many sessions with Veblen's disciples as she's had with Freud's, Elaine self-servingly recasts her caste system of stars as a caste system of achievement. She has the nerve to say that nobody who doesn't, in fact, *over*achieve is entitled to enjoy her restaurant. So now it's an oligarchy of overachievers.

One would think, to hear Elaine talk, that Elaine's is a kind of after-hours Guggenheim Foundation, smacking of good fellowship and scrumptious fare, rather than a place where the habits of pleasure become the tools of business. "At Elaine's the chief emotion is envy," says Gore Vidal. "When you enter that room, you can cut the envy with a knife. Luckily," he adds, "I have a knife."

Elaine has reminded us that the ads for Elaine's say "the best food on this end of the island." But for those savvy enough to read between the lines, the doors of Elaine's say—along with AMERICAN EXPRESS—GOOD TABLES TO RICH AND FAMOUS ONLY.

Into this haven of hype one snowy January evening waddled a dumpy-looking, middle-aged female of indeterminate social station.

She was shown to a table in the back—next to a swinging kitchen door—just as she would be on each of the five other occasions over the next two months when she shuffled into Elaine's.

Although her table was consuming a disproportionate amount of steamed mussels, squid salad, baked clams, fettucine Alfredo, veal scaloppine piccata, calf's liver Veneziana, scampi Livornese, cheesecake, and zabaglione, nobody working at Elaine's paid disproportionate—or even, in fact, proportionate—attention to her.

But then, nobody working at Elaine's, especially Elaine, knew who the dumpy-looking, middle-aged female was.

Then, one feisty Friday during the last week of February, there appeared on the restaurant page of the all-important *New York Times* a review of Elaine's by the *Times* food and restaurant critic, Mimi Sheraton. The review ran in part as follows:

> If you enjoy watching writers eat steaks, chops and some basic Italian trimmings, you may find a visit to Elaine's worthwhile. Should you be lucky enough to be given a table within staring distance of these charter customers, and if you recognize them from dust-jacket photographs, you may hardly notice the brusque service and the careless and indifferently prepared food . . .
>
> Each time we have had them, the mussels were plump but sandy and swimming in a broth that could easily have been pure salt water. The squid and shrimp in the salad were stale and cottony on at least four visits. Baked clams arrived not more than eight minutes after they were ordered. Judging by their dryness and scorched crust of crumbs, they had been reheated, not cooked, to order . . .
>
> The soupy fettucine Alfredo and doughy tortellini [were] both ruined by a dismal grade of waxy Romano-type cheese . . . The overcooked, totally unsalted linguine gained nothing from its so-called sauce of chopped clams . . .
>
> It is hard to understand how chicken Parmigiana could become as poor as the version served here, inedible under a cheese topping that tasted downright soapy. Calf's liver Veneziana, soured with what tasted like distilled white vinegar, was just as bad and scampi Livornese had been so overcooked that the meat could not be pried from the shell. Moist and fresh red snapper, inexplicably topped with slices of apple, could be considered a good main course, if the apples are brushed aside . . .
>
> Desserts such as floury cheesecake and an improbably orangy and grainy zabaglione made me wonder whether any regulars had ever tried them and still remained regulars. One hopes that the dilapidated women's washroom, with missing tiles and blistered plaster, is not an indication of the management's level of respect for the customers.

3

MIMI SHERATON

New York Times
Food and
Restaurant Critic:
The Gourmand's
Guardian Against Hype

What is food to one, is to others bitter poison.

—LUCRETIUS

"If only" are perhaps the two saddest words in the whole English language. If only Elaine, a careerist who built that solid career of hers on wooing writers, coddling critics, and face-recognizing name customers, had been able to identify food critic Mimi Sheraton on any of the six occasions when Sheraton was on the premises carefully researching her review so that when it appeared she wouldn't have to eat her words! If only . . .

Then perhaps Elaine, opening her *New York Times* that frantic Friday, wouldn't have found herself reading an obit notice for Elaine's in Mimi Sheraton's restaurant column, and gone on to suffer such *tsoris* that she couldn't even eat the night-before's leftovers. Her friend Noel Behn, author of *The Brink's Job*, tried to console her. "The hell with it," he told her. "That review's not going to stop anybody coming here. Why don't you blow it up and stick it in the window!" But Elaine was inconsolable. Gay Talese, another of the writers coddled by Elaine, elaborates: "For a while she went around saying, 'What does Mimi Sheraton know about food anyway!,' but she still couldn't get over the review, because she takes such pride in her food."

The thin-skinned Elaine, reacting badly to the acid Mimi Sheraton used in her critical image-peeling and idol-dissolving, must have had a painful moment when she asked herself the question, "How could I have missed coddling that critic?"

To coddle a critic, Elaine, you start by recognizing one.

But how *can* a restauranteuse recognize a restaurant critic whose working strategy is to eat incognito?

The first step toward recognizing Mimi Sheraton, Elaine, is to pay no attention whatsoever to anybody walking into Elaine's carrying a *New York Times* open to the Friday restaurant review.

The second step in pinning the face on the incognito critic is to do some research of your own. Try to get into the back reaches of those restaurants where there are photographs of Mimi Sheraton tacked up above the kitchen sinks. "At least that's what people have told me," Sheraton says. "I've never actually seen my picture in a restaurant, but then, in order to get into the kitchen I would have to say who I am."

But even if you succeed, Elaine, in pushing your curious face into the kitchen of one of the restaurants where Mimi Sheraton's face hangs in state over the sudsy sink, the odds are you'll have a bit of trouble distinguishing human features: Sheraton's photo, used no doubt as a dart board by disgruntled chefs and angry waiters, is probably quite badly gashed.

So here's a wiser wile for you: Dispatch an undercover waiter to infiltrate the wig department at Macy's and get the dope on the season's wig line. Mimi Sheraton has a large collection of wigs to aid and abet the anonymity she seeks when she visits restaurants in the line of duty. "I've been in restaurants where I'm *positive* there were pictures of me up and haven't been recognized," she says with the deepest satisfaction.

To recognize Mimi Sheraton if you're ignorant of what her face and hair look like, be on the lookout for women like yourself who've graduated from diminutiveness. Mimi Sheraton, as the whole overfed world might suspect, is plump. She didn't have much choice. Eating is her job. She has to eat out every night, whether she feels like it or not; she has to taste slowly, letting the food touch all parts of her mouth and tongue—then judge every bite, review every single mouthful. The process entails chewing an awful lot of food she doesn't really want to chew, or even swallow. In fact, the only difference between Mimi Sheraton and a Strasbourg goose is that the former lives in Manhattan.

On the other hand, sighting a fat food critic might not do you much good, Elaine, because Mimi Sheraton came back from a recent sabbatical having laboriously lost forty of her professional pounds on the broiled fish and yolkless omelets and rose-hip tea of a fat farm. Of course, since Sheraton is partial to disguises, she might just cover herself in layers of her old special-size muu-muus and stuff them with a sofa's worth of goose-feather pillows to trip up the restaurateuse whose eyes are peeled for a *trim* critic.

A surer way to recognize Mimi Sheraton, Elaine, is by the company she keeps. She always has a husband in tow when she goes out to feed. "My *present* husband," Sheraton amplifies. "An Italian who imports silver and china and fancy cookware, mostly from France."

So, Elaine, while your intelligence agent is at Macy's checking out the wig line, he should also infiltrate the cookery department to see which products mostly from France are currently being distributed by an Italian married to a wigged-out food critic, because it's possible that that gentleman over there with the copper skillet sticking out of his pants pocket is Mimi Sheraton's husband.

An even surer way to recognize Sheraton, the dumpy-looking broad in the flowered muu-muu with the Macy's wig without the *New York Times* and with the husband with the copper skillet sticking out of his pants pocket, is to keep a lookout for the rest of the company she keeps. So if there's a young man in the party wearing a Columbia sweatshirt and carrying a cookbook open to a page on the preparation of gelatin, the woman with him may be Mimi, his mother.

"He has a good, natural palate," Sheraton says proudly of her son, a recent Columbia graduate. "The other night we went out to a fancy French restaurant, and for dessert I had a soufflé crêpe with sort of a lemon *bavaroise* filling, and my son had a bite and said, 'Mother, it has hardly any taste—there's not enough lemon, there's too much gelatin, and it's much too stiff.' And you know, he was absolutely right. I was thrilled, because for a long time he had a very limited range in what he would eat—hamburgers and *no* vegetables except corn and mashed potatoes. But now he loves to go to Lutèce with us, or Grenouille, or Chantilly, or the Palm. He only likes to go if it's good. He doesn't like to take a chance. Unless," she adds, remembering Elaine's, "he figures it's going to be fun.

"We took him to France with us last year, when we did our tour of the three-star restaurants, and he was not swept away by the fact that they were three-star restaurants. If he didn't like the meal, he said so. And I think that's very healthy, because when the food at those lavish restaurants is bad, many of the customers think it's they who've failed the restaurant, that the food is *supposed* to taste that way and there's something wrong with *them*."

But Mimi Sheraton's son may be too busy these days to ritually accompany mater and pater—he's probably at Columbia Journalism School learning how to be a famous reporter so he can get a better table when he goes back to Elaine's than he got when he went there with his mom.

Okay now, Elaine, scan the tables for—in addition to a husband and a son—four fat friends (if they're Mimi's tasting companions, they're fat): a veritable squadron of Strasbourg geese transplanted to Manhattan's Upper East Side.

"I'm out almost every night on the job," Sheraton says, "so if our friends want to see us, they have to come eat out with us. I usually take along three of them. It doesn't matter if they don't know about food, except that people who aren't interested in food generally find it very boring to go out to dinner with us. I have some friends I almost never see anymore because they just don't like to spend a whole evening talking food. I mean, I really have to pay attention to what I'm doing, I can't be so social that I forget what I'm eating. It's really work. In fact, the real reason I take friends along is so I can taste *their* food." If only (sad words) you had known enough to telescope in on the gaggle whose geese were nibbling each other's feed, Elaine!

"Of course," Sheraton adds, "we're not the only diners in New

York who exchange pieces of this and that. Only, *they* do it slyly, we do it systematically—although we try to be relatively discreet about our back-and-forth tasting. On my first visit to a restaurant—and I go at least three times before I write about it, and often as many as eight times, and I've even been twelve times in some cases, but four to six visits is normal—my friends are quite free to order whatever they want, but after that, I narrow down their choices, and by the last visit I'm telling them what to eat, because there are certain dishes I need to taste again—I mean, if something was terrible once, I have to make sure it's terrible again before I write it.

"Good restaurants are generally consistent; that's one of the tests—consistency. Or if I like something and my husband, let's say, says 'yech,' I'll take another taste, but nobody's opinion ever matters except mine. What I write is what *I* think. I'm no more interested in taking a survey than a drama critic would be—I mean, can you imagine him going up and down the aisles saying to the audience, 'What do you think of the play?,' before writing his review? Mimi Sheraton stands and falls on her own opinion."

But you're still trying to identify Mimi Sheraton, Elaine. So what should you do next? Well, you should know she's the woman not taking notes at table. She may be the only not one scribbling at Elaine's, because over there are the flacks and gossip columnists, all busy taking notes, and there's the ogling audience making note of what will surely be the staple of their next day's dinner: "Guess who I saw at Elaine's last night? Look, it's in 'Suzy,' too."

"To take notes," Sheraton explains, "would be a dead giveaway. What I do instead is get the menu. Sometimes I take it myself, and other times I have my secretary at the *Times* ask the restaurant to send it along way before I go there. Anyway, I have it to jot down notes on the minute I get home from the experience."

Hey, Elaine, over there! Mimi Sheraton is the one with her ear cocked, the one listening to everybody else's conversation.

Sheraton admits to being an eavesdropper. "Like most women," she says, "I can listen to six conversations at once." The last of the six times she visited Elaine's, a couple of hours, in fact, before she went home and, fresh from the experience, made notes on the menu for Elaine's obit notice, she overheard a really scrumptious tidbit.

Elaine had seated Sheraton that night in the second room next to two dowdy middle-aged ladies. Sheraton heard one of them complain to the other that the cheese topping on her Chicken Parmigiana "tastes just like soap." Her companion took a bite and exclaimed, "Ugh! Mimi Sheraton should taste *this*!" Mimi Sheraton freeze-framed in the middle of a mouthful of dry baked clams and ordered one of the four friends at her table to order the Chicken Parmigiana, which quickly made a cameo appearance.

But you may not find her that way, either, Elaine, since everybody else's ears at Elaine's are cocked, too, positively aching for hard-core celebrity gossip.

Pssst, Elaine, that's Mimi Sheraton over there, with the one-of-a-kind egg timer. Only, you won't be able to recognize her—and if you can't recognize her, you won't be able to coddle her—because the egg timer is in her head.

"I try to time the intervals between courses," Sheraton explains. "I watch to see how long customers are kept waiting between their appetizer and main course. I'm interested in what kind of service everybody else is getting, too, but obviously I can only keep tabs on this at the few tables I can see up-close. I also like to see how everybody else's food *looks,* how it's presented.

"And I love to see what kinds of combinations people order. One of the most bizarre combinations I ever saw was at Sammy's, Sammy's Rumanian Jewish Restaurant—or is it Jewish Rumanian?—on the Lower East Side, near Delancey Street—where the food is excellent in a lusty kind of way. I gave Sammy's three stars. You ought to try the mush steak with a bowl of mashed potatoes with greeven cracklings and chicken fat—there's a maple syrup pitcher of chicken fat on every table—or with kasha varnishkes. I once saw a guy at Sammy's eating chopped liver with chicken fat and onions and a dessert, and drinking, alternately, a glass of white wine and an eggcream—I mean, he had the whole business going at the same time!"

Elaine, if only—if only!—you would zoom-lens in on the woman whose index finger is doing a disco dance, testing the heat of the plate. Mimi Sheraton knows that the minute customers give their orders, in restaurants all across America, completely frozen entrées—actual blocks of ice—get shoved into radar ranges, and a few minutes later, plates are placed on tables burning hot, the food on them semi-icy. She understands that when waiters caution us to "be careful of the plate, it's very hot," we should translate that warning as: "If you think the *plate* is dangerous, just wait till you taste the frozen food." Sheraton is painfully aware that the test can be not so much taste as touch. One needs all five senses—not to mention a roll of Tums—to be a food critic.

If only, Elaine, you knew enough to cater to the woman jabbing her fork into that french fry! That's Mimi Sheraton, who knows that there are very few restaurants in New York where one can get a french fry that isn't frozen. "It makes no sense for a restaurant to have somebody just peeling potatoes," she explains, "and a potato-peeling machine like the army has is expensive and impractical unless you have an enormous volume of potatoes on hand, which you can't because they're perishable. But there are ways to get around the problem now, since there are so many different stages of conveniencing for potatoes.

"It goes without saying that the more convenienced they are, the worse they are. Already-peeled potatoes are going to be a little better than prefrozen or precooked—or dehydrated, for that matter, which are hideous. So that's why I poke potatoes—to see if they're real french fries. But what I *really* like is mashed potatoes. Which are unbelievably hard to get these days.

"A few years ago I was in Hamburg, Germany, a city that I think is vastly underrated for its food, and I went into a nice old restaurant and ordered the special of the day, calf's liver, and as is the custom in the country, it was served with applesauce and mashed potatoes, and when I tasted the mashed potatoes I almost cried. Because I realized that in no restaurant in years had I had mashed potatoes that tasted real. That Hamburg place had made its own mashed potatoes. And they were heaven—I almost forgot about the liver. But in *this* country, mashed potatoes have no status. Nobody in America bothers to make real mashed potatoes anymore because there's no status in good home cooking.

"One of the things that Kansas City, for example, used to have going for it was that you used to not be able to get fancy French food there. *Now* what you can't get there anymore are fried gizzards and fried chicken and ribs and chili dogs and barbecue and real mashed potatoes— all their own dishes that they used to make so well. Today the restaurants in Kansas City give you high-priced, mediocre, snobby French food and lousy American regional food. Because what could be more unchic than mashed potatoes? Or more delicious! Lots of butter and salt and pepper and maybe a little bit of nutmeg.

"Most Americans don't even know how to *boil* potatoes. The Germans know. And the Scandinavians. Boil them, peeled or unpeeled, in plenty of well-salted water, and when they're done, put them back in the dry pot and shake them over the heat to dry them out until the outside looks floury. And whatever you do, don't overheat them—you don't want them wet and soggy. To begin with, get the right kind of potato:

new potatoes if you want them waxy and firm, and old potatoes if you want them white, soft, and absorbent for gravy.

"What interests me most about food is finding out what a product is all about, knowing where it's from—what the difference is, for example, between a Florida orange and a California orange. It may take more California oranges to produce a glass of juice—plus the oranges are harder to squeeze—but that juice will have a more intense orange flavor than Florida juice. Do you know what the difference between a California lemon and a Florida lemon is? California lemons are tart, oval, and thick-skinned, while Florida lemons are sweet, round, and thin-skinned. And what about the difference between a Long Island tomato and a New Jersey tomato?" (Now, Mimi, let's just think that one over. The tomato from New Jersey has a terrible accent, and the tomato from Long Island suns itself on Asparagus Beach in Amagansett.) "Long Island tomatoes receive more water and are heavier, but they have less firmness and flavor than the meaty tomatoes grown in New Jersey. They're softer, but not in a nice way—in a pulpy way. They're just not as good.

"Let's face it, food grown in one location is going to be different— better or worse in terms of color, texture, shape, aroma—from food grown in another. Because of climate—temperature and wind—and the chemical composition of soil and water. 'The geography of quality,' I call it. I mean, *show* me a peach as good as a Georgia peach, or a lobster as good as a Maine lobster. And how about Carolina rice, Long Island ducks, Atlantic salmon, and Idaho potatoes? I once met a spice importer who could tell just by looking at a bay leaf whether it'd been grown on the sunny side of a hill in Turkey or on the shady side of a hill in California, and which year's crop it was from."

Now, Elaine, should you *still* be stalking Mimi Sheraton, you'd better keep your eye on A. M. Rosenthal, executive editor of the *New York Times,* to see if, when he looks up from flossing the sand out of his teeth, courtesy of one of your clams, his jaw tightens while the skin around his eyes crinkles. He might have spotted one of the horses in his writing stable.

"One of the nights I visited Elaine's," Sheraton confides, "Mr. Rosenthal was there. We weren't in the same room." (No, Elaine, they weren't—you'd recognized the publishing titan and placed him at high table.) "Two of the six times I was there, they put me in the little room on the right, and the rest of the times way in the back. Mr. Rosenthal spotted me, but he didn't give me away. At a lot of restaurants I'm recognized by a customer, someone I know, who goes and tells the restaurateur—to be a hero. So I always made sure I got to Elaine's at seven, when hardly anybody was there yet, so I wouldn't have to walk the gauntlet and be recognized."

Take another look around, Elaine—come on now, which table harbors the food critic? Maybe it's the one where there's billing but no cooing, one of the few tables in your restaurant where no seduction of any kind appears to be taking place. Restaurants—not just yours—traditionally pulse with lovers' talk; too often, more goes on there than in bedrooms. All of us have sat in restaurants and over candles and wine played the game of courtly love.

"I try very hard not to confuse the stimuli," Sheraton says. "When I was fifteen, a boy named Danny gave me a frozen Milky Way to neck with him, and I became aware of the seductive powers of food. I'll never forget the sudden sweetness of the melting chocolate, crisp caramel, and cocoa-cream nougat—Danny and that Milky Way were one. Ever since then, I've kept food and sex separate."

Elaine, you should give your eyes a rest and let your ears do the work. Listen for the suggestive words a food critic might be apt to utter: "hard," "sticky-sweet," "soggy," "stale," "fishy," "tender," "throbbing," "rubbery," "slow," "disappointing," "oversoft," "overthick," "tiny," "lusty," "slippery," "oily," "sinewy," "creamy," "juicy," "sinful," "limp," "pickled," "meager," "careless," "beefy," "badly burned," "washed out," "gummy," "lacks salt."

Not that Mimi Sheraton is your average reckless adjectivalist, Elaine. It's just that the vocabulary of the food critic is, as she admits, "disastrously limited. It drives me crazy," she says. "Take the word 'delicious.' I try to avoid it, but sometimes, if something *is* delicious, it's better to write 'delicious' than something like, 'it was like dawn coming up over the Atlantic.'" (What could possibly be so delicious, Mimi Sheraton, that you *would* compare it to dawn coming up over the Atlantic? One of Danny's frozen Milky Ways? One of Sammy's Rumanian Jewish mush steaks?)

The problem, Elaine, is that many of the words a mushy food critic might use are the same ones that all those cooing or feuding lovers are whispering to each other about the meaning of their meaningful relationships.

Okay already, you still haven't found her? Go stand by the ladies' room. The woman coming out with the recombed wig and a pained expression on her face is Mimi Sheraton. "That ladies' room is *really* disgusting," Sheraton reports. "I sent my husband into the men's room and he said that wasn't so bad."

What? You *missed* her? You have one last chance, Elaine. Look for comic-strip food balloons above a wigged-out head—pictures of what one tough customer fantasizes eating when she gets home. Look! She's dreaming of the chicken sandwich she's going to make herself back in her Greenwich Village brownstone. "I do like sandwiches," Sheraton says, "though I *might* make myself a hamburger or a steak."

But first she's going to drop by Sammy's Rumanian Jewish or Jewish Rumanian Restaurant—she can never get the combination right—for a real old-fashioned eggcream. "Eggcreams at Sammy's," she sighs. "Customers make their own. On every table there's a blue-glass seltzer bottle and a container of milk and a bottle of Fox's U-Bet chocolate syrup. I'll tell you how to make an eggcream. Pour U-Bet in the bottom of your glass, add some milk—the proportions are very personal—and then shoot it up with seltzer so there's a big head of foam on top. There's a right color with an eggcream. And don't stir it up too much or you'll lose the bubbles. And drink it within fifty seconds or it'll go flat." It goes without saying that just before Mimi makes that chicken sandwich, she's going to go into her very own—very clean—powder room and take her wig off.

Elaine, it's all over—she's gone home. But for next time, remember to look for the bewigged frump who's no chalunka, dressed in four padded muu-muus, accompanied by three fat friends, a son with a Columbia sweatshirt on and an eye toward journalism, and a husband with warming drawers and a copper pot in his pants, whom you've placed with the lower orders, two hectares away from A. M. Rosenthal but only a quarter of a centimeter from the ladies' room.

And if you still can't spot the *New York Times* food and restaurant critic, the surefire way to identify her is to know that she's the one who—no matter how badly you seat her, no matter how badly you treat her, no matter how badly you feed her—is going to keep coming back till she's eaten enough raw material to write one of the most egregious reviews of your life.

And Elaine, let the *tsoris* simmer and—bon appétit!

As we know, Elaine never did recognize Mimi Sheraton. Nor did she recognize her own restaurant when she read Mimi Sheraton's bad review. In Elaine's book, critics who bad-mouth her good food are bad critics.

Yet the Mimi Sheraton who blew the whistle on Elaine's is not only a good critic but a taste potentate as well. Whatever Sheraton says reverberates all along the food chain. Her words carry the imprimatur of that monolithic structure the *New York Times*. Thanks in part to the paper's reputation, we believe in the open-mindedness of Sheraton's judgments and evaluations, to the point where sometimes we forget that food reviewing is based on the most personal of tastes.

Fairness is Mimi Sheraton's warranty as a critic. She doesn't just take potshots at restaurants. She may have a big mouth—and certainly she has a big broadcast area—but she uses them well: to warn the public against indiscriminately sucking the hype popsicles manufactured by the industry that present-day eating has become. (Last year American restaurants, of which there are a statistically mind-boggling sixty thousand in New York City alone, took in seventy-five billion dollars.)

Although in Europe today one cannot get anywhere through cuisine, nouvelle or *ancienne*—socially speaking, gastronomy has little value—in the United States in the last ten years it has become a tremendous trump card, a shortcut to social success. Even in a time of recession, the American middle class is willing to spend a great deal of money cultivating the cultivated habits that will serve to distinguish them from the "catastrophic public."

These days, to be knowing about food and wine—to know, for instance, that nouvelle cuisine is slowly but surely on the way out, that gravlax with mustard dill puts even Scotch salmon to shame, that certain vintages of several *crus bourgeois* can be most favorably compared to some of the *grands crus*, that once champagne is out of the refrigerator, one shouldn't put it back unless one wants to kill it, that *brut absolut* is the only drinkable champagne—is to create a place for oneself in the charmed circle of stylistic discrimination. For the cycle of taste that spins on clothes and cars and boats and pools and clubs and houses now rotates on food as well—food and all its hype spin-offs.

These spin-offs include health foods, natural foods, diet foods, kitchen utensils, cooking schools, cookbooks (a statistically mind-boggling five hundred were published in America last year, leading Mimi Sheraton to quip that "if there is a single winning cookbook title of the eighties, it is likely to be *The Salt-Free, Fat-Free, Quick, Natural, Easy, Economical, Traditional, Gourmet Diet Cookbook*"), food magazines, food editors, food decorators (free-lance food stylists who fashion food for food photographers to shoot for shelter magazines), and restaurant consultants.

There are also food superstars, beginning, of course, with Julia Child. (In 1960 she made an omelet on the air, and that fertilized egg grew fancy feathers in the form of a long-lived TV series, *The French*

Chef. With her background in advertising and PR, the jovial Child was supremely well equipped to popularize French cooking, which was already on its way thanks to Jacqueline Kennedy's installation of a French chef, René Verdon, in the White House.) And ending perhaps with Craig Claiborne's sick-making exercise in bad taste—his describing on the front page of the *New York Times* his four-thousand-dollar, thirty-one dish, nine-wine *grande bouffe* in Paris at a time when old people were reduced to eating dog food.

And finally, there are the food reviewers, who on the whole fill their columns with hysterical hype prose: "stunned," "shattered," "transported" by "sinfully delicious, positively celestial"— —flapjacks!

It would certainly be in keeping with the tenor of the times to call a useful and reasonable critic such as Mimi Sheraton a guardian angel. But Sheraton is a guardian mortal, one of the few proportionate people in a multibillion-dollar industry. Her critical acid efficiently dissolves much of the hype we are often fraudulently force-fed about food. She realizes that food is first of all a physical necessity and that what most people do anyway is guzzle and gorge 2 or 3 square meals a day if they're lucky, 365 days a year if they're luckier, for 70 years if they really luck out, and that it's only those in the market for a cultural self-image who can afford to make a fine art out of eating.

Eating as an art form is not an invention of our time. It has a solidly discernible tradition going back to the reign of French *cuisineur* Antonin Carême, the son of a poor Parisian mason. By the time Carême died in 1833—"burnt up by the coals of his ovens and the flame of his genius," in the words of the decadent writer Laurent Tailhade—he had fulfilled his ambition "to raise his profession to the status of an art," raising it, in fact, almost to the state of architecture.

In 1815 Carême published his celebrated *Patissier Pittoresque,* which consisted of 125 plates—engravings, not dishes—of food he had sculpted in the shape of towers, rotundas, belvederes, hermitages, and pavilions. The originals of these plates have long since been demolished; in fact, they were instantly deconstructed—that is, bolted down—by such of Carême's patrons as the Tsar, the Prince Regent, Talleyrand, and the Barons de Rothschild, all of them practicing not just the art of eating but the eating of art.

Mimi Sheraton, mercifully, is no arty food critic. In the age of hype, where menus are often floridly, and even luridly, overwritten ("Aphrodisiacs from the Sea: Oysters, Sushi, Clams, Caviar, Ceviche, Smoked Salmon"—"Erotic Entrées: Chateaubriand, Angel Hair Pasta with Ratatouille, Hearts of Palm and Olive Salad"—"Sweets for the Sweet: Sugar Glazed Grapes, Fresh Strawberries Piped with Whipped Cream" —"Love Potion: Tulips of Champagne"—all concocted by cooks invariably trained in "Continental cuisine" in Swiss hotel-schools), Mimi Sheraton calls a spud a spud, mashed potatoes mashed potatoes, small potatoes small potatoes, truffles truffles. (Trufflettes, imitation black truffles made in Maryland for Gourm-E-Co Imports, she describes as being "more similar in color and texture to a handball that had soaked in water for two months" than to real truffles.)

Sheraton distinguishes for us the difference between one food product and another, one dish and another, and one restaurant and another. She gave "21," despite its double-digit name, one star out of a possible four. She also gave the largest-grossing restaurant in the world, Windows on the World, despite its gluttonously global name, one wee star. And she gave Tavern on the Green, the pastoral promise of its place name notwithstanding, no stars—just a mediocre "fair."

To La Coupole, the Manhattan clone of the brasserie on Paris' processional Boulevard Montparnasse, whose launching was a model of spendthrift PR, Sheraton gave the sledgehammer blow of "poor," writing, in her characteristically tangy style that calls a spud a spud and a dud a dud:

> After a steady stream of publicity that has drawn a huge, amusingly costumed crowd, La Coupole is turning out badly prepared food that is a perfect match for the inept service. . . . A line of guests often backs up at the door, crowding those already seated at uncomfortable tables near the checkroom, where low clothespoles keep coats resting on the floor. . . . Red velvet banquettes are too low for comfort and tables skid on the slippery tile floor; many are in the paths of chilling drafts. Each table seems to have three waiters who rarely communicate, so diners are asked the same questions several times, and no one knows who gets what when food is delivered. Meanwhile, busboys pour water into glasses of Perrier, remove clean silver, leaving the soiled, and take away condiments before the food is finished. . . . The expensive steaks, gigot and rack of lamb were tough, gray and much like steam-table meats. Calf's liver had the mushy interior that results from freezing, and all fish was stale, overcooked and tasteless.

Chilling as the drafts may have been for the restaurant critic, the winds whipped up by her review and blowing toward La Coupole were positively iceberg-cold; after just two months in operation, the restaurant was rumored to be up for sale.

But it was for Regine's that Sheraton reserved her most delicious distaste. "In seven years of reviewing," her piece began, "I have never come across service and food that have been so consistently poor as that found at Regine's, the well-known Park Avenue discotheque and restaurant. Regine's would be considered beneath serious criticism were it not such a highly visible restaurant garnering much publicity from its fashionable clientele and from its former connections with the talented French chef Michel Guérard, who used to be the consultant to this New York branch of Regine's Paris original."

Sheraton found the staff overbearing, pretentious, rude, and inefficient, the captain unshaven, the mussels spoiled, the salmon stale, the duck-liver pâté and mussel soup metallic-flavored, the shrimp in avocado iodine-flavored, the minted cream on the strawberries toothpaste-flavored, and the strawberries themselves unripe. "In the course of four recent visits, during which all appetizers and desserts and most of the main courses were tried," she concluded, "I did not find a single dish worth recommending." This review represents Sheraton's finest, most unforgiving moment.

Regine, though, didn't hang her red head in shame; the Queen of the Night raised it regally, and reaching into the coffers of her considerable kingdom, took a full-page ad right opposite Sheraton's space in the *Times* to announce a culinary award Regine's had won.

But Mimi Sheraton goes beyond the parochial—marking, as she has, the difference between one fast-food franchise and another. Her comments have been known to send the fast-food industry spinning. She roasted the Kentucky Fried stores around New York; then clearly unpersuaded by *Time*'s hype cover story on Big Mac, "The Burger That Conquered the Country," she went on to grill McDonald's:

> The food is irremediably horrible, with no saving grace whatever. . . . The meat is ground, kneaded, and extruded by heavy machinery that compacts it so that the texture is somewhat like that of baloney sausage, and it becomes rubbery when cooked. Once cooked, the burger is insulated in a soggy bun, topped with pickle slices that seem recycled, or dehydrated onion flakes, or shredded lettuce that is more like wet

confetti, and one or another of the disgusting sauces. All is wrapped in paper, then closed in a sturdy, airtight box, "cooked to inventory" as they say in the trade, and set aside until ordered. Potatoes may be crisp, but they have no taste. The shakes (significantly not called *milk* shakes) are like aerated Kaopectate.

Sheraton informed us also that McDonald's food is more expensive, less tasty, and less nutritional than its competitors'.

Mimi Sheraton is a commendable guardian against hype because she's kept her independent mind. Despite her surname, she is no relation to the hotel chain. She did not come by her transfiguring obsession with food through marrying a man named Sheraton any more, say, than Elizabeth Taylor Hilton Wilding Todd Fisher Burton Burton Warner came by *her* transfiguring obsession with food—and husbands and hotels—through marrying a man named Hilton.

Sheraton is one of the few positioned food writers who is not tainted by commercial association. James Beard has represented, and been remunerated by, a host of food companies: Nestlé, Restaurant Associates, Planters peanut oil, Green Giant, and Pillsbury, among others. And Pierre Franey, Craig Claiborne's sometime cookbook coauthor, is executive chef of Howard Johnson's. They've most of them, these impartial cookery critics, cashed in on their credentials somewhere along the food line. In contrast, Mimi Sheraton is an incorruptible presence on the restaurant and food-reviewing scene. However limited the aspect of the culture which she examines may be, her work happens to illustrate Matthew Arnold's definition of criticism: "a disinterested endeavor to learn and propagate the best that is known."

It's the best that has been grown and cooked that Mimi Sheraton learned, and propagates. As a girl growing up in Brooklyn, she went to school in her mother's kitchen—indeed, she did her homework at the big kitchen table, the scent of good home cooking in her nostrils.

In 1978 she wrote *From My Mother's Kitchen*. Another cookbook, yes; but an honest one. It's also an honest homage to her mother, celebrating, without excessive sentimentality, matrilineal wisdom as well as culinary skill. The book, informed by Sheraton's conviction that food is an emotional necessity, too, nourishing the bonds of families, communities, and cultures, makes up an agreeable organic whole.

"There were some things my mother made that were terrible," she reminisces fondly. "I did not include those recipes in my book because why perpetuate them. It's best that they died with her. She had one chicken dish that was inedible. She made it every Friday night, too. The rest of the family ate it, but what did *they* know! She would take the chicken that she'd used to make the soup—and on Friday night there was always soup—and she'd cover it with salt and pepper and garlic and paprika, and then she would roast it. *Roast a boiled* chicken! 'Brown it in the oven' was her phrase. What she did was make balsa wood out of it. I couldn't swallow it, it was so dry. I would eat the appetizer, and the soup was good and usually had noodles in it, and I would have dessert.

"But on the whole my mother was a great old-fashioned natural cook. She had a repertory of Polish-Rumanian-Austro-Hungarian Jewish specialties, and *her* mother, my grandmother, was an even better cook, a wonderful baker. But then, she didn't do anything *but* cook, all day long every day. It's hard to imagine how I could have avoided my profession. When I told my mother that I was going to write *From My Mother's Kitchen* and that that meant I was going to have to cook with her, and that *that* meant she was going to have to measure with me—she rarely measured; once I asked her how long it took to make her cinnamon coffee cake and she answered "the longer the better"—she insisted that I would drive her crazy and she offered to pay me not to write the book. I said, 'How much?' and she said 'Fifty dollars!' That display of maternal confidence in my earning power really got to me. She thought she could buy me off with fifty bucks. Less than touching."

Mimi's mother evidently had little or no idea of the good money a hard worker like her daughter had been making all those years—first, as a food consultant preparing material on food for gallery exhibits, then as a free-lance journalist researching and writing magazine and newspaper articles about food and its preparation, and, since 1976, as the food and restaurant critic for the *New York Times*.

Upon easing herself into the critic's chair, Mimi Sheraton constructed a critical code. Some of Sheraton's Rules of Tongue and Regulations for Reviewing are:

Rule #1 As food and restaurant critic for the *Times*, Mimi Sheraton goes to great lengths, as we know, to avoid being recognized. To begin with, she never makes a reservation in her own name. (There *are* restaurant critics who announce themselves before their arrival.) That way, even if the restaurateur recognizes her when she walks in, at least he hasn't known in advance that she was coming. "And the better they know me," she says stoutly, "the more times I go before writing the review. And the more I order dishes that have already been prepared. I mean, what can they do to a pâté when they see it's me? What they *might* do is cut off the first slice if it's dried out and give me the second. But they *can* do a lot with reception and service. The smartest restaurateurs when they recognize me play it very cool. André Soltner of Lutèce says *'Bonjour, Madame,'* and Madame Masson of Grenouille might just say *'Bonjour.'* But other restaurateurs hang around the table and hover over me as I chew. They make me feel just like Alexehante in that Colombian coffee commercial, where a guy with a big white hat on drinks the coffee and everyone stands around looking terrified, and then slowly he smiles and ah! the sun shines and the music plays and the children laugh and dance—presumably, if Alexehante didn't smile, the kids would starve."

Rule #2 Mimi Sheraton, when she knows for sure that she's going to be recognized at a restaurant, asks her guests to arrive before she does and get a table. "And I *take* the table that my friends were given," she declaims. "Restaurants often want to move us to a better table when they see it's me, but I don't let them because, really, there should be no bad tables in a restaurant. The customer should not be made to feel that a table is a label. I realize that if the restaurant knows a customer, whether it's a famous person or just a regular, it's almost impossible not to show a little favoritism and give him a slightly better table and a slightly warmer hello than they give a total stranger. But the service should definitely be the same for everyone. And most importantly, the food should be equally good."

Rule #3 Mimi Sheraton rates a place by its food. "Some really overwhelming aspect of the decor or service which negatively influences the food—such as poor ventilation or lighting and lack of cleanliness and friendliness—might tip the balance when I'm trying to make up my mind about stars," she says. "Also, the current style in decorating makes for very noisy restaurants. A lot of them are trying for a pub look—Ye Olde Taverne, A Touch of Olde Englande—or an Art Deco look. As a result they have too many hard surfaces and not enough draperies, carpets, tablecloths, upholstery, and acoustical ceilings, all the things that absorb sound. Metal ceilings are very popular now—pressed tin—and the noise bounces around like crazy, ruining the meal. You can't even hear the people you're with. New York has become very decor-conscious in the way that San Francisco always was. More and more, the setting is the thing. People are going out to dinner for a theatrical experience; they've chosen their clothes as costumes, and they want a set. I think of the whole social experience of eating out today as Living Theater. None of which has any bearing on how good the food is, unfortunately."

Rule #4 Mimi Sheraton ranks restaurants by stars: None = Poor to Fair; * = Good; ** = Very Good; *** = Excellent; **** = Extraordinary. She bases her ratings on her "reaction to food and price in relation to comparable establishments."

Rule #5 Mimi Sheraton alone chooses which restaurants to review and rate. "My editors give me free rein," she insists. "I ask them to make sure my description of a restaurant suits the star rating I've given it. And if it doesn't, then I fix the writing, not the rating." Last year Mimi Sheraton proved her independence from the gastronomic preferences of her employers by knocking extra hard a theater-district steakhouse close in more ways than one to the *New York Times*, frequented as the restaurant is by Sheraton's bosses, A. M. Rosenthal and Arthur Gelb. Defiantly, she stuck a thumb in part-owner Sidney Zion's eye, writing that Zion, a former *Times* reporter, "holds forth with all the writers and Broadway personalities who are his friends and who make up his clientele. Unfortunately, he confuses the role of mine host with that of mine guest." Coolly, she judged that only some of the food at Broadway Joe's was edible.

Since Mimi Sheraton's prevailing concern is with standards, we must ask what *her* standard of evaluation is for the small slice of the culture she scrutinizes. What is it that gives Sheraton the confidence to dispense "the acid that dissolves images and idols"—in her case, restaurants and culinary reputations?

"It takes a long time to learn how to eat professionally," she says. "I'm fifty-five, and for years I've been traveling all over the world doing fieldwork, getting to know the originals of all the dishes. I've studied cooking in many places, including the Cordon Bleu in Paris, and with private teachers in New York and Bangkok and Istanbul and Beirut. A food critic has to have a standard of comparison. I remember S. J. Perelman was once visiting a friend of his in Florida and overheard a woman in the local supermarket saying that the rye bread there was wonderful; he said he was tempted to go up to her and ask, 'Wonderful compared to what? And that's the question: *compared to what?*

"In this country, people are seduced into cooking and ordering food for which they have no standard of comparison. For instance, where would they have tasted bouillabaisse before, that Provençale soup stew of fish and shellfish that's served with a hefty, garlic-perfumed *rouille* sauce, unless they'd been to France? It's important to know what a dish *should* taste like, and for a food critic it's also essential to know how it's prepared. A critic absolutely has to know how to sear meat properly. He can't get away with not knowing how to keep a sauce from breaking down, or how to fillet fish or knead dough. Of course, he also has to know all the tricks and shortcuts." Because in the age of hype there *are* no comparative standards—spin-off people simply go on connecting nothing with nothing—it is good to see a critic paying studious attention to the details of her task.

So Sheraton has her own standards. But we all have standards we could, periphrastically, call our own. The question arises: *Is* there a standard in taste? Is any one palate, whether cultivated or inborn, nurtured or natured, finer than any other?

"I think there *is* such a thing as an objective standard in taste," Sheraton says. "Tastes differ, of course. Take my mother. She didn't cook French food. She cooked Jewish food, which is sort of soul food for me. It's what I grew up on, though so-called Jewish cooking is really the cooking of all the countries in which Jews have ever lived. But I think if you know food, you know it wherever you taste it. Good cooking is good cooking. Frying is frying, broiling is broiling. Not everything has to be new and attention-getting. The *seasoning* can be a change.

"Also, people who know food will agree at a certain level, the way two people who really know and understand art might have an argument as to which is Picasso's—or Rembrandt's—best painting or best period, but they would not argue about his fundamental greatness as an artist. If they do, one is a jerk. Now, one person may prefer Grenouille and another *may* prefer Lutèce—I gave them the same rating, four stars for extraordinary—but I don't think they would dispute their both being fine restaurants. But if they were comparing Lutèce to Tavern on the Green, let's say . . ."

Like many other critics of the contemporary world, Sheraton sees everywhere about her a decline and fall in quality. "Each generation has lower standards than the one preceding it," she maintains. "There used to be fewer convenience foods available, so people had to cook from scratch more. The ingredients they used were natural, and the flavors were clearer and purer. Nobody knew about most of the artificial flavors and essences we have today. The science of food chemistry had not advanced, if that is the word, to its present level.

"There was also greater variety in produce. A hundred years ago there were literally thousands of different kinds of apples in America, and now even the few that are left are getting worse. And chickens! It's very hard to get a chicken with real flavor, because they've all been fed chemical formulas in indoor factories."

As Sheraton speaks, one remembers with fondness how the ethologist Robert Ardrey, author of *The Territorial Imperative* and a man whose work was connecting human and animal life, used to joke half-seriously to friends that the reason he became an expatriate in Italy was that he couldn't get good chickens in America. When chickens were cooped up, they lost their behavior, he said, and when they lost their behavior, they lost their taste; the reason Italian chickens tasted so good was that the Italians let them lead chicken lives, pecking around the barnyard and scratching in the dirt.

As Mimi Sheraton calls it, it is clearly—as Cyril Connolly once so finely phrased it—"closing time in the gardens of the West."

"There is simply less good food around now," Sheraton goes on, "in spite of all the stuff being written about food. And partially *because* of all the stuff being written about food. A lot of food writing takes people's eyes off the ball. All that purple prose about all those complicated dishes never once takes into account the basic quality of the ingredients. I'm not very happy with *any* food magazine. They all celebrate food, they're never critical, and I just don't like noncritical food writing. As I said, I think it's responsible for a lot of bad food."

Nor does Sheraton have any use for careless, predigested food *talk*. "It's become chic to talk food," she says. "People talk food the way they talk art, the way they used to talk poetry, masticate T. S. Eliot—without the knowledge. There are an awful lot of people affecting a knowledge of food and as a consequence eating things they don't really want to. I don't think anybody ought to eat what he doesn't like. If someone prefers McDonald's burgers, then that's what he should eat. Everybody ought to know his own taste." (Sheraton's Rule of Tongue #6: Know your own taste, and—whatever other food critics may say—*trust* your own taste. And suit your own taste—after all, you eat to please yourself.)

Trusting one's own taste can have its pitfalls. State Trooper Gene Kleinsmith of Carmel, New York, was brought to trial on a charge of theft of services from the Blue Marlin Restaurant in Montauk, Long Island, where he had refused to pay a dinner check for his party of four. The defense's argument was that the state trooper was innocent because the food was guilty; the prosecution's argument, that the food was innocent and that, in any case, most of it had been eaten. Selections from the testimony of State Trooper Kleinsmith:

> The filet mignon was supposed to be medium-rare, and it was so well done that it was emaciated. It was unreal. [The attorney for the defense queried, "Was there any notation in the arrest report concerning the status of the steak?"] The clams casino were ladled with onions. . . . One of the girls in my party ordered the stuffed flounder, and I tasted her order. The fish itself wasn't bad, but it tasted like the stuffing itself was straight flour, like pancake mix. I couldn't have eaten it. . . . The scallops I can only describe as feeling like rubber balls. I ate them. They cost $8.35 and I was lucky if I got a dozen. . . .The Caesar salad was okay. . . . I cannot recall any problem with the bouillabaisse, but my friend says his bouillabaisse had no fish in it, it was just tomato soup and celery. . . . I will never return to this establishment. . . .

The jury of six filed off under the vigilant eye of the court bailiff, who was also the town dog warden. After an hour's deliberation, the verdict, later overturned on appeal, was announced: FOOD INNOCENT, STATE TROOPER GUILTY. Shortly after the trial, Kleinsmith, who had by now been dismissed from the state police for unrelated reasons, served the restaurant's proprietor with a libel suit seeking damages of approximately $1.6 million.

Although the state trooper's testimony reads like a parody of one of Mimi Sheraton's reviews, we can see for ourselves that a new food critic has been born—and one only too happy to pronounce on the quality of bouillabaisse, a dish that Sheraton says Americans cannot properly evaluate without having sampled it in France. We also see that, like any food critic—and these days every diner is a fussy free-lance food critic—the state trooper made a point of tasting the dishes of everybody at his table.

This slice of Americana serves to show how seriously people can take their daily bread when they're overpaying for it in a restaurant. The state trooper, our guardian against crime, wouldn't put his money where his mouth had been, and wound up paying for his palate's purity. Our sad state trooper sat—unemployed—on the lowermost rung of the food critic's ladder.

From the topmost rung swing out the skilled inspectors of the *Guide Michelin,* whose annual evaluations and reevaluations have been gastronomically codifying all of France for some eighty-three years now.

"During the twenties and thirties," A. J. Liebling aptly wrote, "the proportion of French restaurants that called themselves '*auberges*' and '*relais*' increased, keeping pace with the motorization of the French gullet. They depended for their subsistence on Sunday and holiday drivers, who might never come over the road again, and the *Guide Michelin*, the organ of a manufacturer of automobile tires, ominously began to be the arbiter of where to dine—a depressing example of the subordination of art to business."

French chefs have killed themselves—and worms have eaten them, but not for love—when one of their Michelin stars was rubbed out. In the American culinary firmament, can Mimi Sheraton's stars mean death? We know they can mean new life.

"I think my review is very important to a restaurant," she says, "but I don't believe I can close a restaurant. I can *make* a restaurant, or, let's say, a good review in the *New York Times* can do a lot to make a restaurant. But a restaurant can slough off after getting a good review. Several things can happen—they can get complacent, they can get cocky even, they can overbook and start packing too many people in. So I constantly reevaluate. It's up to the restaurant to hold on to the stars I've given it.

"I demoted Claude's on Eighty-first Street from three stars to one, and I reduced Mortimer's from a two-star rating to a fair." ("Middle-aged preppies with tired stomachs can count on bland, soft, minimally decent food to see them through lunch and dinner at this attractive, convivial pub-tavern on Lexington Avenue," Sheraton's review began.) "And the languidly trendy Le Relais I knocked from two stars to poor—boy, if there was ever a restaurant spoiled by success, that's it—because the noise is compounded by indifferent service, and although the prices would seem moderate if the food were good, at its best it's only passable. And there are one or two other restaurants that are due."

In the eyes of at least one restaurant, Mimi Sheraton went too far—went too far, that is, in not going too far enough. Sparks Steakhouse on East Forty-sixth Street, sparked—*ignited*, rather—by rage, served her not a juicy steak but a dry, rather stark summons announcing that it was suing her for libel. "They didn't like it," she explains, "that I gave them one star. Which means pretty good. It means *good*, in fact. And their food was . . . pretty good."

But as we know, fair words butter no parsnips. Incensed by its single star, Sparks had burst into litigious combustion, reacting as though

Sheraton had stated—shades of our sad state trooper—that her steak was so well done it was "emaciated." What insidious connection there exists between New York State steaks and juicy libel suits demands further investigation.

One recent gastronomic scandal was not only "further investigated" but shamelessly publicized. *Time, Newsweek, The New Yorker*, the *New York Times, New York* magazine, *The Village Voice*, the *Los Angeles Herald-Examiner*, the *Detroit Free Press*, the *Times* of London, the *Guardian*, and *L'Express* all devoted a disproportionate amount of time and space to this tornado in a teacup, until there was practically nobody alive and munching who did not know, *A*, who a chef called "Otto" really was, and, *B*, that it was Mimi Sheraton, our guardian against hype, who, ripping off his pseudonymous disguise, had revealed the true identity of the man masquerading as a master chef.

This kitchen-sink drama has four acts, a climax, an anticlimax, and a denouement.

ACT ONE

John McPhee, a *New Yorker* staff writer and one of the most esteemed journalists in America, publishes in *The New Yorker*—yes, *The New Yorker*, perhaps the most esteemed magazine in America—a fifty-page Profile, "Brigade de Cuisine," chronicling the zesty excellence of a chef so retiring that he made McPhee promise that neither the location of his restaurant—"Just say it's somewhere within a hundred miles of New York City," the shy chef advised the receptive reporter—nor his identity be revealed—"Just call me 'Otto' in the piece"—explaining that he wanted to go on in blissful obscurity, he didn't want a whole lot of people flocking to his place—"the quality would go down the drain"—and anyway he couldn't accommodate more than fifty energetic eaters at a time. (Now wait just a minute. Doesn't everybody want name recognition? If ours is a culture where the oil that lubricates the engine is *named* "Name Recognition," then isn't disguising himself the most iconoclastic pose a cook can strike? "I'm convinced," Sheraton says, "that if Otto truly was not interested—at some level—in publicity, he wouldn't have given McPhee the story.")

In *The New Yorker* piece, McPhee, whose style is usually nothing if not measured, milks the language of culinary superlatives to describe Otto's cooking. Readers' lips smack, their gums water, their tongues loll, and their stomachs growl as they read "golden," "crunchy," "crisp," "fresh," "ultrachocolate," and so on.

ACT TWO

In the piece, Otto takes advantage of his disguise—the way writers and critics sometimes do of pseudonyms—to knock some of New York's most expensive restaurants. The most expensive, Lutèce, he hits below the belt, saying he suspects that the turbot, Lutèce's *turbot de Dieppe poché*, is frozen, which is the worst rap one can lay on a fish short of saying it's spoiled. Lutèce's *chef-propriétaire*, André Soltner, demands an apology and a correction from *The New Yorker*—yes, *The New Yorker*, which, thanks to its rigorous checking department, seldom has to print retractions. Soltner waves the bills from his fish supplier in editor William Shawn's face—bills that prove that the turbot Lutèce serves is so fresh it practically flaps to its death on the customer's plate. "To allow an anonymous source to hide behind the great prestige of *The New Yorker* is irresponsible," the restaurateur lectures the editor.

ACT THREE

Scenes and subplots ensue. In Manhattan, the hype center of the world, the hackles of every food and restaurant critic worth his or her boiling tongue and profit-making palate are raised. Each sets out to discover the identity of Otto and the location of his restaurant, which, made famous just yesterday, is by today positively fabled for its "golden"/ "crunchy"/"fresh"/"ultrachocolate" cuisine. Someone quips that a war criminal would be safer in the vicinity of New York City than a chef who had been so lavishly complimented. Indeed, the critics are put out that they, connoisseurs and taste-makers nonpareil, aren't already favored habitués of Otto's, not to say enraged that a non-food-fraternity member, McPhee, beat them to the scoop. "In the world of culinary journalism," *Time* would hype-bulletin, "the great Otto flap caused almost as much consternation as the 1926 disappearance of Agatha Christie did in London."

ACT FOUR

Climax

Meanwhile, offstage, Mimi Sheraton puts on the figurative garments of Agatha Christie's Belgian detective, Hercule Poirot, to track

Otto down. Since she's so good at disguising her own identity, she's bound to be good at ferreting out those who try to disguise theirs. Sheraton has an idea worthy of Poirot himself when she deduces that, since politicians always know interesting, out-of-the-way spots to eat, she should query politicians in the small New Jersey town where McPhee lives about the whereabouts of Otto's. Thus is she able to close in on the Bull Head Inn in Shohola, Pennsylvania, and unmask Otto as Allen Lieb.

Anticlimax

The food is execrable. Whereas "golden"/"crunchy"/"crisp"/ "fresh"/"ultrachocolate" were the adjectives that oozed from McPhee's fountain pen, "bland"/"cloyingly sweet"/"truly awful"/"soggy"/ "dank and musty"/"heavy"/"watery"/"tough"/"almost raw"/"bordered on inedible" are the words that leap from Sheraton's Remington. ("I believe McPhee sincerely thought Otto's food was good," Sheraton comments today. "I also believe that what McPhee wrote about Otto's working so hard and caring so much was true. It is perfectly possible to be hardworking and sincere and to use honest, good ingredients and still be a lousy cook—the same way a painter can grind his own colors and stretch his own canvas and not compromise on anything and work from morning till night and still be a lousy painter.")

Denouement

Aspiring eaters-out all across America jam the wires of the Bull Head Inn, booking weeks in advance for the opportunity of arbitrating between McPhee and Sheraton, between *The New Yorker* and the *New York Times*. Is Otto's food really that good? Is Otto's food really that bad? They will make up their *own* minds. The beleaguered Lieb, hounded by a baying pack of biters, tasters, and chewers, gives up. Hype's latest victim, he puts the Bull Head Inn up for sale.

When the curtain came down on this tornado in a teacup, the applause was for Mimi's craftiness, not for Otto's craft. In blowing the whistle on Lieb, Sheraton used her idol-dissolving acid to protect both the eating public and the reading public. Mimi *is* our guardian against food hype— just as proportionately as Kenneth is our guardian against hair hype.

But let's step back a minute. Surely Mimi was also thinking of herself: "Me! Me!" She was working overtime for that scoop. She just *had* to sit on top of John McPhee.

"The minute he heard through the grapevine that I'd found out who Otto was, he called me and asked me not to run the story," Sheraton recounts, and the question of censorship stirs this little tiny teacup. "He said if I ran the story, it would be a breach of trust. *Whose* trust? That was my question. *I* never promised anybody I wouldn't tell who Otto was."

With Mimi Sheraton on top of John McPhee, the *New York Times* was on top of *The New Yorker*. And Sheraton was sitting—fully employed—on the topmost rung of the food critic's ladder.

Let's face it, Mimi Sheraton broke several of her own rules—Sheraton's Rules of Tongue and Regulations for Reviewing—to get that scoop. Although she usually goes to restaurants no fewer than three times and sometimes as many as twelve before writing her review, she went to the Bull Head only once. And with two tasting companions instead of her usual gaggle of four, which means that she wasn't able to nibble at the usual multiplicity offered by everybody else's dishes.

Sheraton concedes that "it's possible Otto had an off night." Nevertheless, she holds fast to the position she took in her bullheaded review, that "while it is true that one cannot make a definitive evaluation of any restaurant on the basis of a single meal, it is equally true that there is a minimal level of quality below which a great and experienced cook cannot sink even on his worst day."

"*Unless . . .*" Sheraton shrugs her shoulders. "There's a theory that when McPhee found out I'd tracked Otto down, he called to warn him I was on my way, and that Otto then *deliberately* gave me garbage because he didn't *want* a good review. Well, you never know." She shrugs again. "If he wanted a bad review, he got it."

Shrug though she might, Sheraton's Otto scoop amounts to a feat of investigative reporting of the sort that, were her name not mud with Elaine, might have won her a prized front table at Elaine's. She would be seated instantly, positioned up front beside winners of the now-smeared Pulitzer Prize, those Pulitzer poop-scoopers whom Elaine nightly courts, coddles, and cuddles.

And who knows, Mimi might even have been offered Elaine's Saturday Night Special (not Friday's fish fingers), which Elaine herself would prepare for her and her alone: a filet of turbot flown in from France unfrozen—that is, fresh. And served hot, on the house.

BUILDING BUILDINGS, BUILDING REPUTATIONS: WHICH COMES FIRST?

Architects are by nature spellbinders. If they cannot sell a suggestible individual or even a skeptical building committee something far more elaborate than they need, they will fall back upon selling them snake oil. Christ performed the miracle of turning water into wine, but architects daily perform the miracle of turning money into stone—the more money the more stone. Think of how Richard Morris Hunt gloriously bamboozled a nice young man named George Vanderbilt, who is said to have asked for a simple shooting box, into letting him build Biltmore House, the greatest country house ever built in North America. Think of McKim persuading J. P. Morgan to let him build the Morgan Library in the ancient Greek fashion of marble blocks laid without mortar.

—BRENDAN GILL

If referees rule the game and supers superintend the players, looking after the metaphoric bricks and mortar, architects use real bricks and mortar to build their own superstardom.

1

The Daisy Chain
of American Architecture

Architecture is public relations reified. It is itself part front, part façade. A building may be proportionate; the message its architecture broadcasts is often not. And however straight the edifice, the reality behind its symbolism, behind the building's contained association, can be crooked.

"You can trust *us*," the grand home offices of the giant insurance companies of America's Gilded Age announced. Their architecture pronounced, "*We* are absolutely stable. *We'll* pay off." The confidence of the premium payer was thus assured, at whatever cost.

In the halcyon days of American capitalism, banks could go broke—did go broke, in fact, the money going out the back door in some cases. However, having been built in slavish imitation of Greek and Roman temples, they *looked* indestructible. With the establishment of the Federal Deposit Insurance Corporation, banks no longer had to bewitch people into believing in the impregnability of the banking structure. Thus the glittering glass palaces of today, whose job is to lure us in so we'll take money out—money we have to borrow at 15 percent.

Architecture is also advertising, sometimes false advertising. Cass Gilbert's Woolworth Building, built in 1913 on the common man's nickels and dimes, is no five-and-ten-cent store. At the time, it was the tallest building in the world, all 792 feet of it sheathed in ivory-colored terra-cotta. A gothic "cathedral of commerce," the building was both a conspicuous symbol of F. W. Woolworth's success and a thirteen-million-dollar guarantee of the quality of the ten-cent product.

William Van Alen's 1930 Chrysler Building, sitting on a big base and rising up, up, up into the sky like some jazz-age mountain, like a diamond as big as the Ritz, lent its luster to each individual Chrysler, just as

Ernest Flagg's 1908 Singer Tower sang the simple efficiency of Singer sewing machines.

Just as, today, Edward Larrabee Barnes's IBM Building prints out in granite boldface IBM, while a block down on Madison Avenue Philip Johnson's 150-million-dollar A. T. & T. superscraper, of the Chippendale top and Renaissance base, telegraphs the immutability of the largest corporation in the world. Around the corner on Fifth Avenue, Der Scutt's Trump Tower trumpets Trump, the fair-haired scion of a Brooklyn real estate mogul.

In constructing these hype-bulletin buildings, architects are fashioning façades for corporations to hide behind—façades that pretend they have nothing to conceal. But as far back as the Gilded Age, architects were being called upon to provide what has been described as a "meretricious legitimacy to the brigands who had plundered their way upward onto a mountainpeak composed of money, ignorance, suspicion, and social unease."

Architects have traditionally leapt to do the rich man's bidding, because, in the process of serving *his* ends, they are also able to build monuments to themselves, "monuments," in Yeats's proud phrase, "to [their] own magnificence."

Architectural monuments are endlessly imitated, for in the hype process, taste filters down. In the nineteenth century, when architectural line drawings were routinely reproduced in magazines and house-pattern books, a style would spread in a matter of months across the whole of the United States. There are Venetian Gothic towers, Richardsonian fortresses, and Newport cottages all over America. McKim, Mead & White's shingle-style houses caught on especially rapidly, and architects everywhere pirated them.

Today we have mass architectural plagiarism, thanks to the plethora of shelter magazines—not to mention *Vogue*, *The New York Times Magazine*, *Life*, *Time*, and *Newsweek*, which all regularly publish architecture, *Architectural Record*'s annual Houses of the Year issue, sold on newsstands and targeted for nest-building newlyweds, and *Architectural Digest*, the ultimate hype bulletin because it manages to attract the rich and the socially insecure all over the world.

Much of eastern Long Island is defaced by imitations of Charles Gwathmey houses, which themselves resemble neo-Cubist sculptures. Some of the original Gwathmeys are happily enough married to their surroundings, but the hype product inevitably becomes cruder as it filters down by way of imitation. And the West Coast is dotted with copies of

Charles Moore's fanciful wood-sided versions of architectural vernacular. So the inexact cloning goes.

There's a wild story that our most famous living architect, Philip Johnson, appearing some years ago on St. Louis television, held up the model of a building he was designing and that, before it even went into construction, an architect who was watching the TV show put up an almost identical building—he just lifted it off the air.

Philip Johnson is famous for more than just his architecture. Well known for having in effect designed his own life, he is the only architect today who has face recognition.

Neither a great draftsman nor a mathematical genius, Johnson is an architect of taste with a working knowledge of history and how to use it. But more to the point, he is a master of hype.

At the age of seventy-seven he can look back with considerable satisfaction on a yeasty career as a historian, critic, curator, connoisseur, catalyst, platform lecturer, art collector, talent spotter, and trend setter. Singlehandedly, Johnson has cornered the architectural market, and he continues to operate in it in all his multiple capacities.

Born rich but not famous, Johnson must have decided at an early age that he would die very famous indeed and, if less rich, to hell with the cost. After graduating from Harvard in 1927, the driven young Philip consumed modernism in Europe in one rapacious bite. Returning to America, he proceeded methodically to force-feed modern architecture to his countrymen. In 1931 he founded a department of architecture at the then fledgling Museum of Modern Art, an institution that he had helped bring into being. (For fifty years this remained the only department of architecture in an American museum, and as its long-time director, Johnson, who paid his own salary, was in an ideal position both to propagate his aesthetic beliefs and to further his own career.)

In 1932 Johnson and the architectural historian Henry-Russell Hitchcock organized at the Museum of Modern Art what would amount to the biggest architectural hype ever, the revolutionary show "Modern Architecture: International Exhibit," which featured, through models, photographs, and plans, several of the works of Frank Lloyd Wright, Walter Gropius, Le Corbusier, J.J.P. Oud, Raymond Hood, and Mies van der Rohe. The show traveled throughout the United States for three years, establishing the International Style as the only architectural taste that counted for at least the next half century.

Seeing that the show, in true hype fashion, must go on, Johnson and

Hitchcock recycled it as a book, *The International Style: Architecture Since 1922.* Thus was modern architecture engineered.

Johnson, in another bid for international acclaim, became a disciple of Mies van der Rohe. He wrote the definitive book on Mies, emulated him in his own work, and in 1958 got him the commission of an architect's lifetime, the Seagram Building; for all of the above he was sardonically dubbed "Mies van der Johnson." Later, Johnson would do a complete about-face, denouncing the International Style as "boring, totally lacking in richness, totally wrong," and, true to his own maxim that "you cannot not know history," he would begin designing buildings in a more classical vein. Cynics like to say that Philip Johnson runs with the tide, blows with the wind. That's not quite accurate. Like Churchill, he sees—and seizes—the moment; at the same time, by lending it his authority and power, he helps to create it.

Influential as an architectural historian, Johnson didn't become an architect until he was practically middle-aged. One of the first things he designed after completing architecture school at Harvard in 1943 was a façade for his own life, a building to house, if not contain, his ambition: his own house, the Glass House in New Canaan, Connecticut, which remains his best-known work. A palace for an emperor in his new architectural clothes, the Glass House has been hyped as the quintessential modernist building of the twentieth century. "I think it's one of the most important buildings in America," the celebrated architectural historian Vincent Scully has written. "A real archetype—a fundamental piece of architecture, like a life-support pod."

Truly grand in concept—after all, to live in an architecture of all glass was what everybody had been talking about for fifty to seventy-five years—Johnson's house is, in fact, the only mid-twentieth-century modernist estate. It is also the only building of this generation to be accepted by the National Trust for Historic Preservation. It seems that people who throw stones *can* live in glass houses.

Over the years Johnson has erected on the property a brick guest house, an art gallery, a sculpture gallery, a study-cum-library, and a folly with a pond below, from which a water jet once ejaculated one hundred twenty feet in the air. It was in the Glass House, at the elaborate lunches and dinners that Johnson hosted throughout the fifties and sixties, that the Avant-Garde first met the Establishment. Jasper Johns, Merce Cunningham, and Andy Warhol could be found commingling with such earlier cultural avatars as George Balanchine, Lincoln Kirstein, Mrs. Bliss Parkinson, and Edward M. M. Warburg.

The architect Eero Saarinen and his bride, Aline, spent their wedding night in the romantic, heavily curtained interior of Johnson's guest house, and years later, in 1975, the Englishman John Russell, who would one day succeed Hilton Kramer as chief art critic of the *New York Times*, and the art *vulgarisatrice* Rosamond Bernier were yoked there.*

The Glass House in Johnson's country retreat. During the week he lives in New York, in a Fifth Avenue apartment building whose limestone façade he designed; it is not considered to be among his architectural triumphs. The building's phony mansard is inexcusable by any standard, and the classical moldings, instead of marrying the adjacent building—a 1911 McKim, Mead & White apartment house from which they were carried over—simply call attention to the new building as being imcompatible with the Metropolitan Museum neighborhood. The only possible explanation for Johnson's living inside such an eye-sore is that that way, he doesn't have to look at it.

Recently, Johnson gave architectural stature to a residential building he did not design—the forty-eight-story condominium tower being erected above the Museum of Modern Art—on whose board he still sits—by announcing his decision to move into it. "I took an apartment in the tower being built over the museum," he grandly informed the *New York Times*, "so I can see the A. T. & T., the Seagram's and all the other buildings I designed."

Philip Johnson epitomizes the architect as a hearty, party-going, self-appreciating personality.† He is a man equally at home in the worlds of art—he has long been one of the most astute collectors of contemporary art, especially of Abstract Expressionist paintings—and high so-

* Recalling her wedding day recently for *Town & Country* magazine, Bernier, who has forged a career lecturing to the blue-haired circuit on the wonders of what used to be known a very long time ago as modern art, gurgled (a stream rivaling Suzy's in the spouting of famous names): "The wedding was on a warm day in May at Philip Johnson's 'glass house' in Connecticut. Philip was the mother and father of the bride—he loves ceremony, and planned every detail down to which kind and how many canapés per tray. Aaron Copeland gave me away. Felicia Montealegre was my matron of honor, and her (and Leonard Bernstein's) daughter Nina was the flower girl. Lenny's gift was a composition he'd written just for the occasion. Irene (Worth) read Millamant's famous speech to Mirabell from Congreve's *The Way of the World*. . . . Stephen Spender's gift was an album of his poems, copied out in his own hand. Dick Avedon's was a portrait of the bride and groom. And most of our friends were there, from Geraldine Stutz to Jasper Johns, the greatest living painter. . . ."

† In 1966 Johnson went so far as to review *Philip Johnson Architecture: 1949–65* for *Architectural Forum*. To his credit, he reviewed himself with some critical distance. This is a brilliant book, he said in effect, but there *are* flaws. The review was a witty essay in controlled candor. "It is a pleasure for the historians to have a book on Johnson's work," he concluded.

ciety—he's the guest every hostess dreams of snaring. Jacqueline Onassis, whose dinner guest Johnson has been on many occasions, trilled to
the *Times*, of her friend's A. T. & T. Building, "I sometimes lie down on
Madison Avenue to look up at it."*

As the architect for A. T. & T. and other mammoth corporations,
Johnson is the only artist-type architect who has proved himself to be a
commercially acceptable commodity. In the late sixties and early seventies, he had experienced a decline—he was out of fashion with critics,
students, and clients alike—but then in 1967 he found his present partner, the much younger John Burgee, and began a new life as a corporate
architect, making real money for the first time.

Rich, famous, and powerful, Philip Johnson is the commanding figure on the American architectural scene, which is made up of a dozen or
so architects who spend a good deal of their time buoying one another
up. Johnson buoys them all up. He sets a standard, gives a scene of exhil-
aration to the profession. His mode of address and exhortation has been
fruitful for the younger generation of architects.

Indeed, the milieu in which one is most likely to see the architectural young is around Philip Johnson, usually at lunch, one or two at a
time. For although Johnson regularly lunches with his partner Burgee
and has been known to lunch with such members of the architectural establishment as Kevin Roche, Gordon Bunshaft, Edward Larrabee Barnes
(Johnson once called the preternaturally youthful-looking Barnes "a
sheep in sheep's clothing" and occasionally refers to him as "Eddie-Boy
Barnes, America's favorite aw-shucks architect"), he prefers to lunch
with the up-and-coming. The daisies in the chain must all be methodically
cultivated.

Architecture is a patronage game. And significantly, patronage in
its longest-lasting form doesn't come from clients, it comes from other
architects. As in all buddy systems—for instance, law, where it's important to go to work for the right firm or clerk for the right Supreme Court
justice—in architecture one must connect as close to the top as one can.
A generation ago, a stream of major architects—Robert Venturi, Cesar
Pelli, Kevin Roche, Gunnar Birkerts, and Harry Weese—emerged from
Eero Saarinen's office. Today in the small, egotistical, competitive profession of architecture, it is strategically important not to *work* for Philip
Johnson but to be patronized—to be flattered—by him: to be invited for

---

* Since one doesn't know whether Mrs. Onassis lies down for her friends in private, one
finds it slightly hard to believe that she would lie down for a building in public.

the weekend meal at the Glass House, to be asked to lunch at the Four Seasons Restaurant.

In the offices of any of today's promising younger architects the phone is likely to ring with what amounts to an invitation to court. "It's Philip," the voice says. "What's going on? Let's have lunch next week."

On the appointed day the younger architect will collect Johnson at his offices (Frank Stella paintings, Mies van der Rohe chairs) on the thirty-seventh floor of the thirty-eight-story building he collaborated on with Mies, the Seagram Building. At 12:30 sharp, they will descend to the ground-floor Four Seasons, which Johnson designed himself, down to the metal chain-link curtains that are in constant ripple. (Earlier that morning the Four Seasons will have called upstairs: "Mr. Johnson, are you going to be using your table today?" It helps to design your own restaurant.)

Johnson's is the corner table in the Grill Room—the table diagonally opposite the entrance. From there, like a captain on the bridge or a king on his throne, he can command the view.

Johnson will offer his lunch guest a drink. *His* drink. The ingredients are on the table when he arrives. He'll mix Americanos for two—a splash of soda into equal parts Campari and sweet vermouth. Ice is waiting in the glasses.

He will then advise his guest as to what's good on the menu. When it's time for dessert, he invariably recommends the Black Forest chocolate cake. "It's sinful," he'll say, for he is always dieting. But he will encourage his guest to order it, and when it comes, he'll help himself to a generous portion.

At 1:45 sharp, Philip Johnson will get up—lunch is over. On his way out of the restaurant, he'll pause to chat at one or two tables. (During lunch some of the patrons have clearly considered stopping by Johnson's table. Good friends have done so, as well as some people just trying to get ahead. The powerful who are not Johnson's friends have merely nodded from their own fastnesses.)

Johnson's lunch guest might well be one of the following younger architects:

Richard Meier. Age fifty. Called Richard by those who know him. The most internationally known of the younger group. A pioneer in the revival of the high-art International Style modernism of the twenties.

Meier's Saltzman House in East Hampton, Smith House in Darien, and Douglas House in Harbor Springs, Michigan, were at the cutting edge of architectural design in the sixties and seventies: austere white objects of complex geometrics and intersecting planes meticulously placed in the landscape but having, nonetheless, a kind of sleek marine look, as of white-painted aluminum ships. Rumored not to permit work of his to be published in a professional magazine unless he's guaranteed the cover. Was instrumental in the production and publication of a book that reestablished architecture as an art: *Five Architects: Eisenman, Graves, Gwathmey, Hejduk, Meier* (1972); Philip Johnson wrote the postscript to the second edition (1974). Designed Frank Stella's Soho loft; maintains close connection to the art world.

Robert A. M. Stern. Age forty-four. Called Bob. The youngest of the group, and the most protean: He writes, theorizes, proselytizes, polemicizes, designs, and teaches (at Columbia University, where he is a full professor of architecture feared for his acerbic tongue and caustic criticism). Was youngest president of the Architectural League of New York. Author of *New Directions in American Architecture* (1969, revised 1977), which isolated the split between traditional modern practitioners, such as Kevin Roche, Paul Rudolph, and Philip Johnson, and the younger architects challenging their position, such as Robert Venturi and Charles Moore. In his work, Stern has moved toward traditional architectural sources, which, however ironic it may seem, is a revolutionary position in architecture today. Best known for his houses on Martha's Vineyard and in eastern Long Island resorts, and is beginning to do work on a larger and more public scale, such as at the University of Virginia. The "discoverer"—and in his early work a disciple—of Venturi. Stern published a major section of Venturi's landmark post-modern *Complexity and Contradiction in Architecture* (1966) in the Yale architectural journal *Perspecta,* which he was editing and which Philip Johnson has generously supported since its inception in 1951. Also introduced Venturi to the art historian Vincent Scully. Like Johnson a patron of the young, Stern did two catalogues and exhibitions of the work of forty architects under the age of forty: one when he himself was twenty-nine, the other when he was thirty-nine. Johnson gave Stern a surprise fortieth birthday party, with forty guests, in a private dining room at the Four Seasons; it amounted to a gathering of the clan and represented the coming of age of the youngest of the group.

Peter Eisenman. Age fifty-one. Called many things: Peter, Petey, and, jokingly, Dr. Eisenman (an allusion to his Ph.D. in architecture from

Cambridge University). Eisenman in turn calls Philip Johnson "Dr. Johnson," as he vies for the role of Johnson's Boswell. The true intellectual of the group. Known for a handful of cerebral, highly esoteric house designs. An architectural entrepreneur. In 1967 he founded the Institute for Architecture and Urban Studies in New York, the intellectual center of architectural activity in the United States and the place where architects from all over the world come to sniff the breeze. The father of two architectural publications of note, *Oppositions* and *Skyline*. The latter, under the editorship of pioneering architectural journalist Suzanne Stephens, has become the liveliest journal about the profession: a cross between *New York* magazine and *The New York Review of Books*. After fifteen years of teaching, writing, polemicizing, and doing very little building, Eisenman recently went into private practice with his seeming exact opposite, Jaquelin Robertson.

Jaquelin Robertson. Age fifty. Jaquie to his mother and wife, Jaq to everyone else. Son of a Foreign Service officer from Virginia and of an heiress to a tobacco fortune. Educated at St. Mark's, Yale, Oxford (he was a Rhodes Scholar in politics, philosophy, and economics), and Yale Architecture—with Stern the most broadly educated of the group. Has spent most of his professional life in the area where architecture and politics come together. Director of Mayor Lindsay's Office of Midtown Planning and Development, then president of the Planning and Design Group at Arlen Realty and Development Corporation, then—as part of the firm of Llewelyn-Davies International—consultant to the Shah of Iran on his aborted five-billion-dollar new town in Tehran. Has designed only two houses. Currently dean of the University of Virginia School of Architecture in Charlottesville (considers Jefferson's design for the University of Virginia "the most brilliant complex of buildings on this continent") and partner of Peter Eisenman, whom he met during their postgraduate days in England. Once said to architect Frank Israel, who is neither married nor rich, "To make it as an architect you've either got to have money or marry it."

Charles Gwathmey. Age forty-five. Called Charlie by all. The most prolific—and the most financially successful—of the group, with a long string of houses and small commercial buildings to his credit, including Pearl's restaurant, boutiques for John Weitz, and hairdressing salons for Vidal Sassoon. His simple, clean, strongly geometric compositions have become a kind of paradigm of modern architecture, especially his beach houses, which have been both copied and cloned. Philip Johnson wrote the introduction to a book of Gwathmey's work.

Michael Graves. Age forty-eight. Native of Indianapolis. Called Michael. The architect of the moment, if not of the hour, if not of the age. Thinks of himself as the Michelangelo of his generation because of his capacity to draw exquisitely and paint murals, as well as design buildings. His drawings sell. The character of his work underwent a substantial transformation five years ago, shifting from a complex white cubism similar to Richard Meier's to a highly figural personal interpretation of classical humanism, somewhat art deco in character. A professor of architecture at Princeton. Recently chosen to design an extension of the Whitney Museum of American Art on Madison Avenue (Philip Johnson, who didn't want the job himself, was the Whitney's consultant). The building that put Graves on the architectural map—indeed, it's the most adventurous and controversial building of recent years—is the richly colored post-modern office building in Portland, Oregon (Johnson was the judge of a limited competition for the commission). A frequent talk-show guest. Once said to a colleague about another architect's pretentiously scribbled signature: "A signature is like Frank Lloyd Wright's cape. You have to earn the right to wear it."

Stanley Tigerman. Age fifty-three. Based in Chicago. His architecture is brash and rambunctious, like the man himself—sometimes witty, sometimes vulgar. Designed a brightly colored library for the blind. Recently built a house in the form of an erect penis, with two wings resembling flattened-out testicles; it's known as the Daisy House. The first of the group to publish his autobiography (*Versus*, 1982). The only one of the group to become an architect by first apprenticing in architects' offices. Later went to Yale to get his architect's pedigree. Befriended there by Paul Rudolph, who bent the rules for Tigerman so he could get a bachelor of architecture degree in one year instead of the normal four.

Frank Gehry. At fifty-five the oldest of the group. Canadian by birth. A Philip Johnson "discovery." Was a commercial architect in Santa Monica who did shopping centers but liked to hang around with artists. Made a mid-career change and became an architect of artistic importance by doing studios and small houses for artists. (Most architects do it the other way around, starting with small artistic houses and working their way up to big commercial jobs.) Famously tore apart a conventional old Santa Monica house and transformed it into something that looks to the average person as if it were—well, a building still under construction. Fascinated by conceptual architecture. Gehry's style is studied slap-dash—timber, chain link, and sheet metal. He's an architectural collagist.

Vincent Scully. Age sixty-three. Not an architect but a historian—the preeminent American architectural historian and critic of his generation. Trumbull Professor of History of Art at Yale. Known for his "charismatic" lectures. Has not only brilliantly assessed American architecture, which is his principal subject, but has made fresh interpretations of Greek and other non-Western architectures. Subject of a *New Yorker* Profile. Interviewed in *Interview* magazine by Jodie Foster. Built a house for himself in Woodbridge, Connecticut, which was important in the early fifties as an example of the influence of Marcel Breuer and Philip Johnson. Scully's favor is sought by every architect, preferably in writing. Wrote the introduction to a book of Stern's work published in England and the introduction to a book of Graves's work. The author of celebrated books on Louis Kahn, the Shingle Style (a term Scully coined), and modern architecture.

Odds are that one or another of the above, cloaked in his own extra-special architectural persona, would be Philip Johnson's lunch guest any day of the working week.

But one breezy Tuesday, Johnson was at his corner table in the Grill Room of the Four Seasons, mixing Americanos for two, and *not* talking to any of his favorite lunch guests. This combination *enfant terrible-éminence grise* was talking about them.

Philip Johnson Loves Them, Philip Johnson Loves Them Not

INTERVIEWER: Today nobody can imagine any architect creating the kind of synoptic vision of world order—man conquering the elements, et cetera, et cetera—that Frank Lloyd Wright not only created but embodied. He had an impassioned conviction about architecture, and he was attempting to make an impression on society that would alter the nature of society. He was *the* great mythological American architect. Like Whitman, he both sang the song of himself and sang the song of America. He had the nerve, the brass, and the sheer masculine force to assume the posture of being representative of the best of American life. He was so emblematic that Ayn Rand used him, melodramatically, as the model for Howard Roark in *The Fountainhead.* Gary Cooper played him in the 1949 film. But this isn't the movies—today we don't want to conquer the elements, we just want to live with them. Or *does* Wright's brave-new-world myth of architecture still hold in certain architectural circles?
PHILIP JOHNSON: No, of course not. It's like Shakespeare or any other great man—each generation has its own "take" on that kind of a character. There isn't *any* take on Wright now. He's in between takes. See, we hate Papa Mies—that's easy. But Grandpapa Wright we haven't really got a telescopic view on yet. There's a tendency today to find the whole Wright thing slightly ridiculous. Our architectural tastes are not "aw, shucksy," they're not middle-western Whitmanian idealism, nonsensical mile-high buildings—with the result that there's no focus on Wright's design. The man did change the whole course of architecture all by himself. It was he, don't forget, who made walls, roofs, wainscoting, and floors all independent elements of design. Unfortunately, I once said—I made the terrible mistake of saying it in a lecture—that Wright was the

greatest architect of the nineteenth century. Somebody told him and he was furious.*

INTERVIEWER: But what *about* the myth of the architect as someone who can change the world through architecture?

PHILIP JOHNSON: That's just Mrs. Rand's joke, Ayn Rand's joke.

INTERVIEWER: Wright didn't see Rand's joke, did he? He believed the myth.

PHILIP JOHNSON: Sure. So did I. So did the whole Modern Movement. Today we have our hands full just trying to save architecture, save what's left of Park Avenue, but back then we were out to save the world, rout all the philistines. *That's* what went when the Modern Movement dissolved: the belief that architecture would lead people to a better way of life—Corbusier's phrase, "If you have enough glass walls, you become free." He actually believed that you couldn't live a moral life or even a good life if you weren't surrounded by glass walls. The Modern Movement disintegrated because architects' morale changed from salvation through architecture to survivalism-is-all-we-'ve-got-left, damn-lucky-to-have-a-job.

INTERVIEWER: No architect has pure, idealistic goals anymore?

PHILIP JOHNSON: Oh, all the old people still do. But *I* think that that belief system is long since finished, the descendant of that you-can-do-good-by-having-social-housing-done-by-teamwork Gropius ideal, the architecture-as-a-weapon-of-social-reform thing—that's the one *I* hate. I don't mind Wright. Move the capital to the middle of the country, he said. Let's design a real capital. Not only said it, he designed one practically. A great park and building complex at the Golden Triangle—you know, where the Monongahela and Susquehanna become the Ohio. Oh, he was a great man. Magnificent. He was our greatest architect next to Richardson. *[Henry Hobson Richardson, the nineteenth-century architect, was an early American graduate of the École des Beaux Arts; his interpretation of the Romanesque style was so definitive that it is now known as the Richardsonian-Romanesque: heavy arches, massive masonry walls, low-slung massing of a building, little use of the classical orders. Richardson's was to become the dominant style of American architecture of the 1880s and '90s, as well as the first American architectural style to be influential in Europe. Richardson built Trinity Church in Boston, the Marshall Field warehouse in Chicago, and a double house for Henry Adams and Secretary of State John Hay in Washington, D.C., facing Lafayette Square, where the Hay-Adams*

---

* "He is a highbrow," Wright, retaliating, said of Johnson. "A highbrow is a man educated beyond his capacity."

Hotel stands today.] Jefferson was our most famous, but he was a politician, not a professional architect.

INTERVIEWER: In terms of how architectural reputations are made, is there a difference between the time of Richardson, the time of McKim, Mead and White, and our time? Back then, the *very* old boys' network really counted, didn't it? McKim and White got started working in the drafting room of Richardson. And often one got one's first job through a family connection. Billy Delano *[William Adams Delano, a distinguished twentieth-century "gentleman architect," now dead]* roomed at Yale with a Vanderbilt, and they were spending the summer just after graduation on the Vanderbilts' yacht, which was moored in Venice next to the yacht of a man named Walters, and Mr. Walters had heard that J. Pierpont Morgan and McKim had had terrible fights over the building of the Morgan Library and he reasoned that maybe if he asked this young fella if he'd like to design his museum, he could take charge of him and he wouldn't give him a hard time. So Walters gave this enormous commission to Billy Delano—the Walters Art Gallery in Baltimore. And at that time, as Delano himself said, he hadn't so much as designed a doghouse. So he started at the age of twenty-three with the Walters Art Gallery, but it was through the Vanderbilt connection. And he knew a Vanderbilt because he went to Yale and was a Delano.

PHILIP JOHNSON: That's right. They all did it the same way Billy Delano did—social connections. It was *fashionable* to work in Richardson's office in the early eighties. It's a business world now. You work for developers. That's where the power line is today, not with the mayor or the President or the pope. It's a venture-capital world. You work for serious businessmen who look you over: Can you produce . . . let's see your shop . . . what engineers do you use . . . who's the man who's gonna be on *my* job, 'cause if you've got six projects going, *you're* not gonna be spending all your time on mine and I wanna know who *is*. They have every right to know. You have to become kind of a businessman yourself.

The amusing way I got most of *my* jobs is all Gerry Hines, a big real-estate developer in Houston. We've gotten, I think, six tall skyscrapers from him. It was an accident, because he had a partner called Brochstein who had a furniture shop—he did all the cabinet work in my early houses—and he thought I was just great. So he said to Gerry Hines, "Why don't you get Philip Johnson to do you a building?" and Gerry said, "Who the hell is Philip Johnson?" "Oh, he's an architect," Brochstein said. So Hines said, "*All* right, send him down." And the chemistry was right. But it wasn't just *me*, it was my partner John Burgee *and* me, you see, because I never was in the big time before John Burgee joined me. Oh no, I was nothing. Just a simple farm boy. You see, he's capable, clear-headed, and a very good designer. And *that's* the combination: Johnson and Burgee. We're Hines's biggest architects now, and other people say, "Well, if Gerry Hines like them, they must be good." Hines introduced us to Liedtke, the chairman of Pennzoil, and we designed *their* corporate headquarters, the pure-modern, all-glass, monolithic as in quote unquote Pennzoil Place Building in Houston.

So one of the important ways you get jobs is by accident. I did a house once, my own house, the Glass House, and people visited it, and one of them was Dayton of Dayton and Hudson, the great department-store chain. He came in and said, "Well, will you do *me* a house? I love this house." I said sorry. Sometimes you turn down the damndest things. So he went back to Minneapolis and became a partner in I.D.S., Investors Diversified Services, which is a horrible company that built our biggest building—ours, theirs, it's the biggest building in the northwest. A nondescript building. I was the architect. What's famous is the courtyard in glass. "The Crystal Court," they call it—"the living room of the city." It was the first of the great interior atriums. The whole room's covered with clusters of glass cubes piling asymmetrically to a hundred-foot-high apex, a *crazy* high point. Damned if it isn't the most important downtown urban complex of its period.

But how they picked us is the interesting thing. I.D.S. had a list of five *genius* architects. By accident they came to us first. They were scared, they didn't know *what* to do. They talked to us for ten minutes and we turned them down, because they wanted us just to do the façade and we don't *do* façades. So they said could they come back and I said sure, come back at three o'clock. They came back and so I says, "Have you seen any of the other genius architects as in quote unquote on your list?" They said, "We don't want to see any other architects." So you see, it *wasn't* a competition, it wasn't even social, it was absolutely accident. The man Dayton that liked my Glass House had talked to somebody at I.D.S. lower down that'd talked to somebody way lower down and then the guy that picked us was way, *way* down the line. Same with A. T. and T.

INTERVIEWER: It can't be accident, it has to be Philip Johnson. How *do* you take a conventional project like an office building and stamp it so that it's a Philip Johnson? In other words, how do you introduce architecture into it, Philip Johnson architecture?

PHILIP JOHNSON: I don't know. Didn't know I did. Didn't know I ever did design a "Philip Johnson Building." You know, consistency is one thing I've never been accused of. Well, I don't like the buildings I see around me, so naturally I try to do something else, something individual, not-to-be-copied. Everyone said the A. T. and T. Building was going to be a real clinker, and you know something, it looks pretty good. All my women friends keep telling me to hurry up and finish it so they can get around the corner more easily to Kenneth's to get their hair done.

INTERVIEWER: Architects are famous for doing drawings that don't become buildings. You're famous for going into presentations with clients without any drawings and getting to do the buildings.

PHILIP JOHNSON: That's right, I have *never* used drawings. At A. T. and T. we had no drawings. I'm not interested in presentation.* Apparently, Kevin Roche Dinkeloo *[Kevin Roche and the late John Dinkeloo were heirs to the office of Eero Saarinen. The firm blends the slickness of the corporate world with historical architectural recall. Among its buildings: the Ford Foundation and the additions to the Metropolitan Museum of Art. In 1982 Kevin Roche won the Pritzker Prize, the equivalent of the Nobel Prize in architecture, which Philip Johnson had been the first recipient of two years before]* have two projectors—fade in and fade out—and nine screens. *We* don't even use slides.

INTERVIEWER: What *do* you do? Just talk?

PHILIP JOHNSON: That's all. So I lose jobs that way.

INTERVIEWER: Aren't you being too self-deprecating? You're the only architect who can get away with not putting on a show, with just talking. You can sell your work on the sheer force of your personality, as well as on the assumption that the prospective client knows what you've done in the past.

PHILIP JOHNSON: It does seem to me that my work is well known. Frank Lloyd Wright once said to a client, "You know my phone number. Call me when you've put fifty thousand in my account in the National Trust Company and I'll be yours." A job that Mies got from him, by the way. So *not* bothering to make the fancy presentation doesn't always work.

It doesn't always work for *me*. In the fifties I went into the competition for the air traffic controllers' towers that are all over the country now—federal towers—and I said, "Well, I think you all know my work. Now what I'd do if I got the job, I'd take the slip form thing, this wonderful dimension, and put through these cylinders like this if it's all right." Pei got the job.

INTERVIEWER: Those slender towers of concrete that flare at the top.

---

* Johnson has subsidized the publication (that is, paid the designers' fees and agreed to take no royalties) of two expensive books showcasing his work. He uses these books in his presentations.

Very elegant. Very repetitive. But *you* never repeat yourself, you never do the same thing twice.

PHILIP JOHNSON: You have to be a little adventurous in this world. Why would anybody go to the architect of *that* building and get another one just like *that* building? They *know* they won't with *me*. We know what Skidmore's gonna give us. *[Skidmore, Owings & Merrill, the premier corporate architectural firm with more than a thousand architects on its payroll, commercialized the epochal ideas of Mies van der Rohe. During the fifties and sixties, it was known as the "Three Blind Mies," meaning it couldn't see the poetry for the steel and glass, the concrete, and the aluminum. Frank Lloyd Wright ridiculed the firm as "Skiddings, Own-More, and Sterile."]* But if you come to Philip Johnson, you don't know *what* you're gonna get, but it's gonna be damned exciting.

INTERVIEWER: The Reverend Dr. Robert H. Schuller, the television evangelist, was so excited that he commissioned you to build him a church in Southern California higher than Notre Dame and with ten thousand windows—the Crystal Cathedral.

PHILIP JOHNSON: As in quote unquote. Interesting about that. He came to me because on a plane his wife picked up a copy of *Vogue* and read my name in a piece about this landscape project I designed in Fort Worth, and that same week *he* saw my name in another magazine that said I was this very exciting architect. And so he called the telephone book, asked for Philip Johnson in Fort Worth. But then he ran into somebody who told him my office was in New York, so then he called the New York telephone book and he came. And it was wonderful. He's *really* interested in architecture. "God is in the details, Philip," he says. I mean, heavens—an eighteen-million-dollar church! That's a lot of dollars per square soul.

INTERVIEWER: You get clients like that because you're a name, a name glamorous enough to be featured in *Vogue*. They don't necessarily know anything about the kind of work you do. How do you convince them that they should have something unique?

PHILIP JOHNSON: I don't sell. I never sell, that *I* know of.* I'm *for* sale. I'm a whore. I'm a practicing architect. I work for money for whoever commissions a building from me.

---

* "No matter what Philip says," remarks another architect, "I've been in his office when *Vogue* and some of the shelter magazines have called, and he treats all those little girls with their trivial questions as though they were Blanchette Rockefeller, so they'll call him again. Of course, he does give good quotes."

INTERVIEWER: There are many styles of selling. You're clearly attentive to all sorts of details relating to the presentation of self. God's in the details, Philip—remember. You dress beautifully. Robert Stern described you in print as a clotheshorse.

PHILIP JOHNSON: Bob Stern, of course, is describing himself. He was a slob, you see. Oh ya, and then he got married to a Gimbel and got into the chips, and he said to himself, "Philip Johnson is a clotheshorse, it must have something to do with success, *I'll* be a clotheshorse, too." This is my interpretation. People always describe themselves when they're talking about somebody else.

INTERVIEWER: So does an architect's personal appearance advertise his work, the way a movie star's does, or not? Are architects supposed to be stylish, idiosyncratic, and dramatic?

PHILIP JOHNSON: No. No. Absolutely not.

INTERVIEWER: What about Richard Meier? *He* has an aura. He just seems to float miles above the grit of everyday life—his silver hair, his silver Mercedes, the blue-white shirts. He's an artifact. His detailed design of himself must attract clients.

PHILIP JOHNSON: He hasn't attracted many. Oh no, he hasn't had much work to speak of. Yet he's the most deliberate of all the younger architects. And his work *is* awfully good. And he's very tall and very, very handsome, and *I* enjoy him enormously. I'd rather have lunch, let's say, with him than any living architect.

To me the ideal architects are Mies, Corbusier, and Wright—*they're* the three. Wright, of course, had his own way of self-projection. The purple cape. The purple hair. The hair was not really purple but blue, and the cape wasn't exactly purple, either—these things get exaggerated. But the other two were working on their work. That's *all* they did. Mies and Corbusier didn't give one damn about anything else. They might have thought they did, but they didn't. Even Wright didn't really care as much as he thought he cared, and his flamboyance wasn't really to the jugular of success as Stern's is.

I resent people thinking *I'm* that way, but I suppose they're right, that I'm a success because I work at that as the aim, whereas any artist worth his salt should work at art, and not the way Warhol does and Stern does, for success as a thing in itself. It's like money—plenty of people work for money. Like the Skidmore firm. It's such a big firm, what else would you work there for? You gotta keep the firm running, increase profits over last year. Now that I *don't* do, I never had to—money doesn't occur to me. Success I *thought* didn't occur to me as such, but when I analyze Stern's singleminded devotion to success, I wonder. I don't know. It's a question.

INTERVIEWER: What precisely are the ingredients in Robert Stern's success?

PHILIP JOHNSON: *Chutzpah.* He's a shit. You can call it arrogance if you want to be nice about it. And of course he got that style from Frank Lloyd Wright. But it's better to be honest arrogance than false humility. I'm very fond of Stern, because he's so intelligent. He wants to be the Philip Johnson of his generation.

INTERVIEWER: Does Philip Johnson think that Robert Stern has succeeded in his arrogant ambition to be the Philip Johnson of his generation.

PHILIP JOHNSON: Well, I wouldn't be another person if I said yes. You see, you can't expect Papa to say that the son is going to be as good. If he did, he wouldn't have enough *amour propre* to be his own success, would he? It's all very well to be interested in the kids, but do you *really* want them to be good? Does the father *really* want his son to rival his abilities? Wright didn't want *anyone* to come after him. It would be the end of architecture. He didn't want anyone to come before him, either. He wanted to be the only architect that had ever lived.* He actually said that Michelangelo created the greatest mistake of any architect in history by building St. Peter's dome. And Mies was the same way. And so was Corbusier.

INTERVIEWER: What precisely are the ingredients in Philip Johnson's great success?

PHILIP JOHNSON: Very much the same as Stern's—*chutzpah. I'm* a shit, too, you know. I'm not very good at human relations. I don't have a whole lot of friends. Mostly enemies. And quite naturally when you get to my status you have to have them—what would you do without them? But as for Stern, I'm not as bright as he is, anywhere *near.* That man can absolutely think rings around *me,* and his historical acumen and knowledge are second to none. I think he's the best architectural historian living, who can write. *[The most distinguished and prolific architectural historian living is Henry-Russell Hitchcock. However, he cannot write.]* Stern is a *marvelous* writer.

INTERVIEWER: Was it you who introduced him to Gerald Hines?

* "Once, after her husband had agreed on the witness stand that he was the world's greatest architect," according to *Look* magazine, "Mrs. Wright protested, 'Frank, you should be more modest.' 'You forget, Ölgivanna,' he replied quickly, 'I was under oath.'"

PHILIP JOHNSON: Ya, sure. Oh ya. I also introduced Gwathmey to Hines. And Charles Moore to Hines. *[The peripatetic Moore, once dean of the Yale School of Architecture, is the master of architectural vernacular; in the mid-sixties he designed the shingle-clad Sea Ranch condominium north of San Francisco, which redefined the character of resort architecture for his generation. He had his own face carved on the Doric wall of the huge downtown plaza he recently designed in New Orleans.]* And they've all done houses for Hines, who's a genuine patron of architects—he picks the very best. Only Gwathmey flunked out. He submitted plans for Hines's house in Martha's Vineyard that didn't get by the local design controls, and Stern took over. I just think that Stern is the *brightest* son-of-a-bitch. My lunch list would be Stern, *then* Meier. But for different reasons. Stern hates Meier, by the way.

INTERVIEWER: But he sings Meier's praises.

PHILIP JOHNSON: Guilt. Guilt. Stern *used* to say bad things about Meier, till *I* said, "Look, you damn fool, you're an architect, you don't talk that way about your fellow architects." The only way you can talk down architects if you *are* one yourself is the way Frank Lloyd Wright did with Saarinen. *[The late Eero Saarinen, Finnish-born and Yale-educated, led the break with Miesian Modernism in favor of a return to symbolically expressive architecture, as in his TWA Terminal at Kennedy Airport, which all but soars, and his Ingalls Hockey Rink at Yale, which is a paean to men on ice.]* Wright was five times Saarinen's age, he was the grand old man, and to him Saarinen was a stupid, unable architect—well, *that* didn't bother anybody. Anyway, Stern took my advice. Oh, he does. And now he's *generous* about his competitors, because he undersands that to talk down a competitor hurts yourself, not the competitor. I also taught him that architects must not publicly criticize other architects in print.

INTERVIEWER: You knocked Wallace Harrison in the *New York* Profile of you. *[Harrison, who died in 1982, was a mediocre, stylistically confused architect, but a good organizer, and a peacemaker in complex situations, such as orchestrating and bowdlerizing Le Corbusier's scheme for the United Nations.]*

PHILIP JOHNSON: Did I? Did I really? Oh, *shit.* Well, you see, it shows through. And I *liked* Wally. Of course, I tend to like people when they're no longer competitors. I'm much better friends with Bunshaft now that he isn't practicing. He doesn't admire *me,* because I was a shit. But I admire *him.* I really do. Oh, I was nasty about him. I'd say, "Well, if you want to do a lousy building, why don't you go to Bunshaft?" *Unnecessary.* Sheer jealousy. That's why I don't want Stern to make that mistake. Bunshaft was building every building in New York.

INTERVIEWER: Do you feel competitive with I. M. Pei, who's certainly not out to pasture? How, having done dozens of just decent, corporate-type buildings, has he gotten to be so revered? What's *his* secret?

PHILIP JOHNSON: He's one hell of a swell guy. A straight shooter. And if you call him the best salesman, it's either an insult or it isn't. His sales appeal is in his clarity of decisive intelligence, and you just sell a few people like Mr. Paul Mellon and you got yourself a reputation. Of course he doesn't publish the way I do. And he *has* done a lot of buildings that are sort of also-ran—you wouldn't ever notice them on the skyline. But I'm very fond of him, we're good friends—hell, I'm the one who got him introduced to Zeckendorf. He just practices differently from the way *I* practice. I do *all* the designing—but I mean *all* of it, including the window mullions and the screws—and he doesn't. He assigns it to Cobb *[Henry N. Cobb, the soft-spoken, cultivated Pei senior partner, is also chairman of the department of architecture at Harvard's Graduate School of Design; a native New Englander, he prefers to live in New York and commute to Cambridge. It was he who largely designed Boston's ninety-five-story John Hancock Tower, the world's fifth tallest building, with its mysteriously falling double-paned glass windows]* or Freed *[The German-born James Ingo Freed, an associate partner of Pei],* or to one of the other partners right from the beginning. He runs his firm the way a lawyer would, not the way an artist does, and it's a way of running a practice which is absolutely legitimate. Pei said, "I want to be the Skidmore, Owings and Merrill of my generation." He said that in my presence. And that's fine. I mean, if that's what he wants to do. I'd give him a job of *that* kind anytime.

INTERVIEWER: But Pei's done some artistic buildings, too. It's curious that they're all so highly praised. One of his most recent, the East Building of the National Gallery of Art in Washington, looks like a shopping center—the only thing missing is Santa at Christmas. The rooms where the art is displayed are hard to get to. They're also irregularly shaped and seem secondary in importance to the lobby. How did all the favorable publicity it received get generated?

PHILIP JOHNSON: Publicity has its own momentum. The East Building was written about in *Time, Newsweek, Life*—right across the board—all the newspapers, all the art magazines, and all the architecture magazines.* Plus, don't forget, the building was opened on national television.

---

* When Paul Rudolph's Art and Architecture Building at Yale was completed in February 1964, it was featured prominently in every architectural magazine simultaneously. But Rudolph is no longer famous today. As he says himself, wryly, "I'm still dynamite in

But it all started with Ada Louise the year before. *[Ada Louise Huxtable, pioneer preservationist and Pulitzer Prize-winning architecture critic for the* New York Times, *reigned as master of the alliterative putdown until she was elevated to the* Times *editorial board; she retired from the paper in 1982.]* She wrote that Pei is the greatest American architect and that this building proves it. When it was *done*, she wasn't so sure. But by then she was aboard, on the bandwagon. Critics can't back down.

INTERVIEWER: A point of information. You said she praised the building a year *before* it went up. You mean she went down to Washington to look at the drawings?

PHILIP JOHNSON: Nooo, *they* came up. Mr. Paul Mellon *[Chairman of the board of trustees of the National Gallery of Art]* and Mr. Carter Brown *[Director of the National Gallery of Art]* brought the models—the size of this room—up to New York to show her at a grand dinner in the Grenouille. Always helps. Of course, Ada Louise *would* like the building because it's a competent modern job done with exquisite detail and wonderful technique, and in the model you couldn't tell—should we call them—the problems. And Pei *is* the world's best salesman, he is absolutely marvelous. Just ask Jackie Kennedy. She was looking for an architect for the Kennedy Library in Boston—this was in 1965—and I was one of the ones she considered. She also went to see Kahn, Rudolph, and Pei. And she chose Pei because he had elegant manners, and beautiful flowers in his office, and the most *elegant* office of all the so-called artistic architects.

INTERVIEWER: You haven't yet indicated what *you* think of the East Building.

PHILIP JOHNSON: Well, again, of *all* people, *I'm* not gonna talk about Pei, because, A, I do museums myself; B, I lost the job—Paul Mellon was looking around; and C, as I said, I like Pei. It's just that there *are* . . . Let's put it this way, I wouldn't have done it that way. As for the public's favorable assessment of it, well, the critics went on and on, because they were just so glad it didn't look like the House of Representatives Building or one of those boring new Senate office buildings, and of course the critics set the tone for everything.

INTERVIEWER: Some people say *you* set the tone for much that is

---

Singapore." This fall from fame has much to do with the character of the man. Rudolph is a country boy, the son of a Baptist minister. He's shy and decidedly unstylish—he still sports the hairstyle of the fifties, the crewcut. And his artistic style is similarly rigid and set.

happening in architecture now, that you are the father and mother of many architectural sons. Now that Peter Eisenman has gone into private practice, do you see him as being out to kill the elder of the tribe—namely *you*?

PHILIP JOHNSON: Well, *I* fell in love with another architect, Mies van der Rohe, and later I revolted against him.

INTERVIEWER: Do you think that Eisenman's identification with the Institute for Architecture and Urban Studies is going to work for or against him, now that he wants to be commercially successful and practice architecture in a big way?

PHILIP JOHNSON: He's the brightest man in the country. My lunch list would be Eisenman, *then* Stern, *then* Meier.

INTERVIEWER: Another preferred lunch guest? *Another* brightest man in the country?

PHILIP JOHNSON: Eisenman's is an entirely different intelligence from Stern's. They're the *two* brightest people on the horizon. It *is* all very surprising that Eisenman and Robertson have gone into partnership together.

INTERVIEWER: From your experience with corporate clients, would you say that Eisenman will have to overcome his image as an intellectual in order to make it big in big business?

PHILIP JOHNSON: That's easy enough—send Robertson. Eisenman wouldn't appeal to an executive of Pan Am; Robertson would—he speaks easily and authoritatively, and he has a wonderful voice, *la voix d'or,* oh ya. But actually, Eisenman wouldn't hurt. He thinks he's an intellectual like the Italians, Tafuri *[Manfredo Tafuri, the leading Italian intellectual and theorist of architecture, whose writings are said by some to be as imcomprehensible in his native Italian as they are in their English translations]* and Rossi *[Aldo Rossi, the architect's architect, whose spare and very abstract use of classicism is a major influence in architecture today]* and those boys, and what he *is* is a terrific manager. I mean, you can't start a school like the Institute without a penny and work it for fifteen years and still be *around*, and still be *inventive*, without . . .

INTERVIEWER: Eisenman seems to function as a kind of impresario of the avant-garde.

PHILIP JOHNSON: Ahhh. Exactly. He's perhaps like that man in the dance, who do I mean, Diaghilev. He plays with all of us crazy people. He's wonderful with the crazies. He said, "Leave the crazies to me." He doesn't know how revealing that statement is about his own genius.

INTERVIEWER: Why? Is he also crazy?

PHILIP JOHNSON: Like a fox. He's got a terrific sense of how to *use* crazies and how to get them to work together—Koolhaas *[Rem Koolhaas, a young Dutch architect and former filmmaker and scriptwriter, writes wittily but as an architect has so far produced mostly beautiful drawings; he is the author of* Delirious New York: A Retrospective Manifesto for Manhattan, *a study of the metropolis as a phenomenon]*, Krier *[Leon Krier, a Luxembourg-born architect who lives in England, a Marxist turned classicist, and a strong influence on Michael Graves]*, Rossi, most of the Europeans of today, Frank Gehry. Eisenman can showcase *them* and still have a show of Wally Harrison and have a show of me—the oldies, you see. Eisenman's so broadminded, and so clever at getting the whole ball of wax together, that there's only one place in New York where architecture happens—at the Institute. He certainly did surprise us all by wanting to become a commercial architect. One more thing on his belt. He's so good at everything else that why shouldn't he be successful at that, too? Well, it's the Philip Johnson problem, you know—want to do everything well. Heavens, I've got seven over-a-hundred-million-dollar buildings. That's a lot of buildings, and the fees aren't bad.

INTERVIEWER: But doesn't it strike you as ironic that this man who loves crazies should choose for his architectural partner the solid and sane Jaquelin Robertson?

PHILIP JOHNSON: That's not so hard. Robertson's the essence of WASP political respectability. He's a Virginia gentleman's son—he will send you a Virginia smoked ham, which I can't eat. He's the real thing, political in the sense of WASP-getting-ahead-in-the-State-Department, correct-tie point of view. It sounds bad, but it needn't *be* bad. He has a genuine interest in political accomplishment. He'd like to be mayor of New York or President of the United States and reform the way the world *looks*. I was the one who persuaded him to become an architect. He was at Yale, starting architecture, and he asked me should he do that or should he go on to Oxford and study political science, and I said, "Look, we need people like you in architecture—he was very good at it—"so why don't you decide to become an architect?" Later he went into the city under Lindsay and did extremely well, but then Lindsay sort of drifted off into dogoodism. Then Robertson got into the big world through the job in Iran, and of course we know what happened to that, so he's had bad luck. But I don't think the thing's in yet—the judgment—on Robertson. He's very able. Very acute. What is going to happen to his actual design capabilities is a question mark.

Somebody like Gwathmey, who was at Yale the same time as Robertson and Stern, really got down and went to work. He put his nose to the grindstone *at once*—he's the success-boy type of the kind who'll get work and get it done. He's very sound; he does even, good-quality work, and I've always given more jobs to Gwathmey than I've given the others.

INTERVIEWER: Have you also patronized, in the oldest sense of the word, Frank Gehry?

PHILIP JOHNSON: I'm a great friend of Frank, but Frank is a great friend of everybody. He's one of the most attractive personalities on the *scene.* I've seen some work of his, mostly on paper, that I think is very interesting. When he gets into full scale, sometimes it isn't.

INTERVIEWER: And Michael Graves? He was virtually unknown ten years ago, and now all of a sudden he's the architect of the moment, his name is on the lips of architecture students and cultural types —he's a media darling. Is his current status well founded? And will his reputation just keep growing?

PHILIP JOHNSON: No one's reputation keeps going.

INTERVIEWER: *Your* reputation's kept going.

PHILIP JOHNSON: Mmmmmmmm. But I never had one of those. See, I was never taken up by the young gurus as in quote unquote. Not at anytime in my life. I never became a Kahn Pied Piper. *[Louis Kahn, whose mystical orations held a generation of students and young architects spellbound even before his major archaizing buildings began to refresh the waning modernism of the late sixties and early seventies.]* I never became a Michael Graves. Today three quarters of the students' work at the architecture schools is straight Michael Graves. I think that's because he has a take that is so very, very clear and so attractive. Plus he draws beautifully. But that's all quite different from building buildings, so we shall see. Now he's just *built* a building, the Portland Building in Oregon. I was on the building jury that chose him, so I guess *that* helped. But the judgment isn't in yet on whether he's a clear *consistent* producer of buildings.

Then there's Stanley Tigerman. He is the most delicious of all the revolters, and very, very *funny.* Now again, he's done *some* interesting buildings—an all-black house that looks like a silhouette: pure form, no shadows or edges. But we don't know yet about Tigerman, we just don't know. He organized that competition, a second *Chicago Tribune* Competition. *[The first, sponsored by Colonel McCormick to produce for the* Tribune *the world's greatest office building, was an international competition that attracted the leading revolutionaries of European modernism, including Adolf Loos and Walter Gropius. Eliel Saarinen, Eero's father, won second prize with an early modern design that was a haunting free interpretation of* *the Gothic; it was this competition that brought him from Finland to America, where he remained, building, among other things, the Cranbrook School that produced such architects and designers as Charles Eames, Harry Weese, and his own son, Eero, who went on to study at Yale. The* Chicago Tribune *Competition was won by the then unknown New York architect Raymond Hood, who went on to become the preeminent skyscraper architect of the twenties and thirties—the American Radiator Building, the McGraw-Hill Building, the Daily News Building (built for McCormick's cousin, Joseph Medill Patterson), and Rockefeller Center—and the leading spokesman for the concept of the tall building as an advertising symbol. Hood was brought in on the* Tribune *project by John Mead Howells, son of the novelist William Dean Howells.]* Tigerman called it "Late Entries for the *Chicago Tribune* Tower Competition." I guess he wanted to counteract the influence of Mies who had kind of a hammerlock hold on Chicago architecture. He wanted to see what the Competition would bring out *now* in designs, from *his* friends, all the kids. And, of course, I welcomed this exhibition very much. I went out to lecture on it, but I couldn't—the results were not good, I didn't like *any* of them. Stern's may be the best. So what I did was talk on the 1922 Competition. They were not overwhelmed with delight.*

INTERVIEWER: Tigerman, Eisenman, Robertson, Stern, Gwathmey, Gehry, Graves, Meier—does this list cover the up-and-coming architects?

PHILIP JOHNSON: You've got them all. No secrets.

INTERVIEWER: All of them seem to have presented themselves as well as their work to the world, tailored their personas to fit their ambition and, one would strongly suspect, their desire for fame, and then organized their opportunities accordingly. How did an architect like Robert Venturi manage to become so famous without having consciously tried to?

PHILIP JOHNSON: As a theoretician. He's not famous as an architect. In fact, I think he does rather bad buildings. The stage in Hartford, the addition to the Allen Art Museum at Oberlin College—they're bad buildings, ya, *oh* ya. Oh *yes*. Of course, it depends on who you talk to. Bob Stern, who's his inventor, thinks he's marvelous. I resent a little bit that arrogance of Stern's. He didn't discover Venturi. Venturi was perfectly

---

* One architect who was present has a different "take," as Johnson might say, on the occasion: "It was typical Johnson. He won everyone's good humor—told everyone they were terrible, but didn't hurt anyone's feelings, and then lectured on something they were all academically interested in."

able to discover himself.* He came by that book, the Venturi book on complexity and contradictions. And *really* the discoverer of Venturi is Arthur Drexler, my successor as head of the department of architecture at the Museum of Modern Art. He sweated editorial blood for years, because Venturi can't write. That book was a pile of junk, and to put it into any format at all took a Drexler. Drexler's a beautiful writer. He's just crazy—like everybody else.

INTERVIEWER: Clearly, architecture books are not just for writing and reading, they're hype tools. It's understood that Louis Kahn wouldn't have become "establishment" at the late age he did if Vincent Scully hadn't written that book about him in 1962. After it was published, Kahn was given a retrospective at the Museum of Modern Art and became a luminary, attracting large commissions.

PHILIP JOHNSON: Large commissions? You mean the capital at Bangladesh? Well, Lou Kahn and I were friends, and he *was* very influential. But he was not modern, you see. He was mystical. "We are born out of light." "Material is spent light." "In the beginning lies eternity." "I ask the brick what it wants to be, and it said it wanted to be an arch." His Beaux-Arts training, and the symmetry, and the circles, and the layering around them, and the window behind, were all fascinating, and La Jolla *is* great, the Salk Institute at La Jolla, but Kahn's was a minor talent—it didn't influence the world. And it won't stand the test of time.

INTERVIEWER: A minor talent? Isn't that just Philip Johnson killing off his competition retroactively? It's a fact that Kahn was the only threat you had in your generation—he commanded greater respect from both students and other architects. So today you state that Scully overrated him.

PHILIP JOHNSON: Scully overrates everybody. I think it's one of his charms. When he built his own house, he copied my Glass House, but he never gave me the full PR treatment. He gave Corbusier the full treatment. Then he did Kahn. *Then* he did Venturi. And now *Rossi.* Well,

---

* The fifty-seven-year-old Venturi, feeling perhaps that he's controversial and needs to smooth a few feathers among those who give out work, now has a PR super: Letitia Baldrige, Jacqueline Kennedy's social secretary when she was in the White House. When Philip Johnson recently came upon a press kit from "Tish" Baldrige hyping the Venturi firm on her PR stationery, he phoned an architect friend: "Did you know that Bob Venturi has a press agent?" The friend said, "I don't believe it." Johnson promptly sent him—and several other architects as well—a copy of the press release. In truth, Johnson was shocked. Tish Baldrige says: "I think they were very smart to hire a public relations firm to make people aware of them. After all, they're in Philadelphia."

they can't *all* be gods. But Scully is by nature an Irish elfin enthusiast—a type that I happen to love, so it's all right with me. But whether it's good for the subject or not in the long run, I don't know.

INTERVIEWER: You see Scully as a kind of publicist, then?

PHILIP JOHNSON: Nothing wrong with that. Less a historian and more a publicist, yes. Naturally, I can't be *too* enthusiastic about him because he's not *too* enthusiastic about *me*. In his foreword to the collection of my writings that Stern and Eisenman put together *[Philip Johnson Writings: Foreword by Vincent Scully, Introduction by Peter Eisenman, Commentary by Robert A. M. Stern, New York, Oxford University Press, 1979]*, Scully says, after all, Johnson's going to be known for his books, not his works. I can hardly complain. Only, I'm an artist. And artists are verrry sensitive. Scully's greatest fault is that he isn't overenthusiastic about *me*. Isn't that terrible? I mean, it's so personal and ridiculous. I don't mind admitting that actually I'm very partial to critics that like me. I don't find anybody that's any different. We're all human, we're *all* human. Goldberger *[Paul Goldberger, Ada Louise Huxtable's successor as architecture critic for the* New York Times, *is the single most powerful voice in the field. He writes clearly, enthusiastically, and persuasively about architecture. Balding and bearded, he looks older than he is—a mere thirty-two. Some say he owes his meteoric rise to his cultivation of Vincent Scully, whose student he was at Yale. It is a fact that his close friendship with Johnson, Stern, and Meier has not held him back—or them, for that matter. Goldberger's climb up the ladder of influence at the* Times *can be charted by the chain of his own residential moves—from a modest brownstone on West Sixty-ninth Street to the fashionable Des Artistes to the even more fashionable Dakota to a seven-room co-op in the equally fashionable San Remo]* feels that since he's a critic he can't write an article without saying something bad about even something that's good. . . .

For all Philip Johnson's tending of each petal of the daisy chain, for all his manifest generosity and self-deprecating charm, he has just been doing a hatchet job on his competitors—young and old, alive and dead.

Since, in Johnson's view, a good critic is someone who praises the work in question wholeheartedly, Philip Johnson can be termed his competitors' worst critic. But since he likes his own work so much, he can also be termed his own best critic. Such is the huff of hype—the huff and the puff that will blow your house up.

PART

VII

OPERATION HYPE

HEART SURGEON DR. DENTON COOLEY

I think it is improper to sell cigarettes in hospitals.

—DR. DENTON COOLEY to *Women's Wear Daily*

For an architect, the cardinal sin is designing an unsound building. For a cardinal, the cardinal sin is sin. For a doctor, the cardinal sin is breaking the 2,400-year-old Hippocratic Oath, which begins with the words, "I swear by Apollo Physician, by Asclepius, by Health, by Panacea, and by all the gods and goddesses, making them my witnesses," and goes on to demand that a physician "follow that system or regimen which, according to my ability and judgment, I consider for the benefit of my patients, and abstain from whatever is deleterious and mischievous."

1

Waiting for Mailer
with an Open Heart

Early one midsummer morning in 1969—it was already bright and hot and was going to be, as Texans say, one of those days when chickens lay fried eggs—free-lance journalist Harry Minetree, at NASA headquarters an hour south of Houston, encountered Norman Mailer, who was there researching his book about the space program, *Of a Fire on the Moon.*

Minetree lost no time telling Mailer about the book *he* was working on, a biography of Dr. Denton A. Cooley, the heart surgeon's heart surgeon, a man once described as practicing "moon-shot medicine." Indeed, Minetree went on to explain, the doctor not only had the lowest mortality rates on the world's riskiest heart operations, but he had also perfected many of his colleagues' operating procedures; and just a few months after Dr. Christiaan Barnard performed the first human heart transplant in December 1968, Cooley was performing three transplants—back to back, in seventy-two hours.

Minetree also mentioned that Cooley had operated on *him,* replacing the weakened portion of his aorta with eight inches of Dupont Dacron tubing. Would Mailer, by any chance, be interested in meeting Cooley and watching him operate?

As if a challenge to his manhood had been laid on him, Mailer replied, "You're goddam right I'll come up and watch him operate!"

Back in Houston, Minetree told Cooley that he had just run into Mailer at NASA.

"Mailer?" Cooley asked, needing to be told who that was.

In reply, Minetree handed Cooley that week's issue of *Life* magazine with Mailer's mug on the cover. Opening to the story, the doctor gasped in awe when he read that Norman Mailer, a *writer,* had gotten a four-hundred-thousand-dollar advance from a publisher to write a book about the moon. (Five years later, Cooley would read, now in *wordless* awe, that Little, Brown had given Mailer a four-million-dollar advance for a three-part novel, one part of which would take place in the present, one part on a spaceship in the far future, and one part in the reign of Pharaoh Ramses IX—all told from the point of view of a six-year-old boy.)

His interest piqued, Cooley pressed Minetree for some additional details about this Mailer. "How tall is he?" the 6′5″ Cooley asked.

"He's just a little fella," Minetree replied. "Five-six, five-seven."

"How," Cooley puzzled, "can someone that short get such big money for something he hasn't done yet?"

Cooley then told Minetree to go ahead and invite Mailer to watch him operate at three o'clock the next afternoon. "I'll be running a short schedule," the doctor added. "He'll be observing me with the last patient of the day."

Minetree dialed Mailer, and Cooley himself got on the line to give directions: "You come on into the doctors' reserved parking lot back of the Medical Center—that's on Fannin Street—and if they give you any trouble, just tell them you're Dr. Mailer, the brain surgeon from Brooklyn Heights." Cooley laughed—he had just read in *Life* that Mailer lived in Brooklyn Heights; Mailer laughed; and Minetree smiled—he liked his friends to get along.

But the next afternoon at three o'clock, Mailer was not there.

"Where the hell *is* he?" Cooley muttered.

Every few minutes Minetree was sent to check the parking lot for Mailer's car; and every few minutes he reported back to the operating room with the most up-to-date news of Mailer's absence.

On the operating table lay the prone patient, the last patient of Cooley's day, a middle-aged Caucasian in need of a change of heart—that is, a mitral valve replacement, wherein the diseased valve, located between the left ventricle and the left atrium, was to be replaced with an artificial one made of silastic and titanium. "I've done more MVRs than the entire cardiovascular surgical staff at Mayo's," Cooley was fond of saying.

In the middle of one of these MVR operations, the doctor had turned to his biographer, Minetree, and said, "You know, you've watched me do so many of these things, maybe you'd like to do one yourself. How'd you like to finish *this* one?" And Minetree had grinned, feeling squeamish.

Now Cooley decided not to wait for Mailer before proceeding with the preliminaries, confident that the writer would arrive by the time the virtuoso work began. On went his surgeon's blue-green gown and his rubber gloves; the wraparound sash was tied as he stepped up to the table.

There he was presented with the glittering knife. With sure, unthinking hands, he made a midventral incision; then, switching to a bone saw, he cut the sternum open. Working with a Bovie electric needle now, he cauterized the bleeders in the tissue and the two pieces of bone. Then he rubbed beeswax on the surface of the sternum, sealing the marrow into the bone. All as he had done a thousand, thousand times.

"Where the *hell* is Norman Mailer?" Cooley cussed as he cranked open the sternum with a retractor and the patient's chest opened wide.

But because the famous writer was late, the open heart would have to wait.

The delay meant that Cooley would now have to relieve the pressure of the ribs on the patient's vertebrae. So he loosened the retractor, closing the chest, and put wet sterile towels over both the incision and the retractor so all the viscera wouldn't dry out under the hot surgical lights while he—and his patient—waited for the author of *The Naked and the Dead.*

Finally, Cooley decided to operate without, he sneered, "the *brain* surgeon from Brooklyn Heights." Chances were the half-hour's delay hadn't made for extra risk in terms of the surgery itself, though of course the doctor knew it wasn't wise to keep a patient under anesthesia any longer than absolutely necessary.

Cooley strode over to the table with the rangy gait of the athlete he once was, cranked open the patient's chest, cut into the rosy pink pericardial sac around the beleaguered heart, attached the heart-lung machine, and clamped the aorta. The patient's heart stopped, and simultaneously the machine took over for the heart and lungs.

Certain of victory, Cooley plunged deep into the left atrium to the strains of the Rolling Stones; a couple of years earlier, he had had a tape-deck built into one of his heart-lung machines.

Mailer arrived just as Cooley was finishing up, and settled himself into the surgeon's box seat overlooking OR One. There wasn't much left to see. The artificial mitral valve was in; the heart and pericardium had been sewn up; the patient had been taken off the heart-lung machine, and the heart itself started with electric paddles; the retractor had been removed, and the instruments counted to make sure that none of them had been left inside.

Cooley was perfunctorily sewing up the sternum with heavy needles and stainless-steel wire—twisting and cutting the wire as he went through bone. He had only to stitch up the skin and put in the drain, and that would be that.

When Cooley entered his cubicle, he found Mailer sitting there quailing. Though all the writer had witnessed was the bloodless curtain call, he was white as a sheet. He apologized weakly for being late.

Then Cooley, the 6'5" heart doctor, and Mailer, the 5'6" or 5'7" writer with the four-hundred-thousand-dollar book advance, just sat for a while sizing each other up.

Cooley was the embodiment of everything that Mailer admired in this life: He was a good athlete, and he had a fine mind as well as a winning personality.

Cooley was taken with Mailer, too. After all, he had once quipped that though one might never guess it from the company he kept, he really preferred "the mentally alert to the socially elite." So there they were together on that surpassingly hot afternoon, sitting in Cooley's cubicle fanned by the zephyrs of each other's adulation.

Still, Cooley was disappointed that Mailer hadn't seen him do his stuff, but there was always tomorrow. Told that the writer had to return to New York that evening, the doctor called down to the photo lab in the basement of the hospital to summon a photographer. When Manfred Gygli, the head of Medical Photography at the hospital, arrived, breathless, with his Hasselblad, Cooley adjusted his coat and led Mailer out into the hall where they posed triumphantly in front of the heart-lung machine.

Then, slapping Mailer on the back in the geniality of their photographed friendship, Cooley invited him to tour the intensive-care unit. "I want you to see my day's work," he smiled.

All Cooley's patients—he had operated on only seven that day, but some days he operated on as many as thirty—were now in the ICU. Though the operations themselves had been virtually bloodless—for Cooley took great pains to make everything neat and clean—the ICU was a horror show, with patients lined up on dead-white pallets; with heart monitors bleeping, respirators wheezing, and life-support systems pumping passionately; with nurses running back and forth watching for signals, and alarms going off here and there. As one by one their new hearts began to function, Cooley's patients faltered awake into a real nightmare, many of them gagging on the plastic tubes stuck down their throats.

Now Mailer, having missed what had been beautiful operations, masterpieces of precision, was suddenly led from a quiet, empty, bland hallway into the violent aftermath of heart surgery, with Cooley saying genially, "Well, you know, here's my day's work." Mailer gritted his teeth, but the panorama confronting him made him realize that Cooley was a creature of harder, finer mettle than other men. Indeed, Mailer was forced to conclude that Cooley was in his own way a sort of saint.

The writer thought that he might even risk mentioning to the doctor the conclusion to which he had just come.

"A saint?" Cooley laughed. "Well, I remember some pretty savvy writer saying, 'I don't mind being reverenced and greeted and honored; I don't even mind being sainted in moderation, as long as I'm not expected to be saintly as well.' " And leaning down from his great height, Cooley put his arm around Mailer and said good-bye.

Minetree escorted the writer to his dark brown rented Chevy parked in the doctors' reserved lot. Mailer, secure behind the wheel, leaned his head out the window and said to Minetree, "Boy, that Cooley is *really* a handsome son-of-a-bitch. If he hadn't been a heart surgeon, he could have been a movie star. So tell me, is he gettin' any?"

"*Well*," Minetree replied, "I don't know. He spends a lot of time operating."

"Anyway," Mailer said, revealing his third greatest obsession in life, which, after movie stars and sex, is politics, "I'll bet you a hundred bucks he's a right-winger."

When Minetree reported all of Mailer's comments to Cooley, the doctor's face just lit up.

2

Letting Donald Sutherland
Leave a Patient in Stitches

One winter afternoon in 1980, the heart-preoccupied film director Richard Pearce (*Hearts and Minds* and *Heartland*) made a pilgrimage to Houston's Texas Heart Institute, a medical facility so dedicated to Dr. Denton A. Cooley that there is a bronze bust of him in the foyer.

Passing the bust, Pearce failed to genuflect, nonetheless recalling that Cooley was the world's best and most abidingly busy heart surgeon. In the past thirty-five years, Cooley had performed more than eighty-five thousand heart operations. Just the year before, he had generated some fifty million dollars in revenue for the hospital, of which nearly two million went to him. Cooley was also one of Houston's shrewdest real-estate investors; the doctor's diversified portfolio included 12 percent of Houston's Grand Hotel, 13 percent of the Houston Hilton, a piece of three Houston banks, and pieces of sixty-five other ventures; *Forbes* magazine conservatively estimated Cooley's holdings to be worth twelve million dollars on the books and thirty million at market, and his net worth to be around forty million.

In his battered briefcase Pearce was carrying an original screenplay by the pace-preoccupied screenwriter James Salter (*Downhill Racer*) for a film that was to star Donald Sutherland, the Hawkeye of Robert Altman's *M*A*S*H*, as a pioneering heart surgeon who defies medical authorities and implants the first artificial heart in a human being. The real-life model for Sutherland's starring role was widely assumed to be the superstar heart surgeon Dr. Denton Cooley, who had consented to be an official consultant to the film, thus diversifying his portfolio even more. Cooley, along with his wife, was also scheduled to make a brief appearance in the film, playing a medical associate of Sutherland's Dr. Thomas Vrain.

The very night he arrived in Houston, Pearce accompanied Cooley as he made his rounds. The director watched carefully as the surgeon processed the thirty-odd patients he would be operating on the next day, greeting and reassuring each, and quickly moving on. When Cooley observed how absorbed Pearce had become in his performance, he invited the director to watch him perform actual surgery. When Pearce observed how absorbed Cooley was in his absorption of Cooley, he asked if he could bring along a friend: Could Donald Sutherland also spend a day in the operating theater with Cooley before playing him on the screen? Cooley readily agreed.

A week later, Donald Sutherland arrived in Houston, in time to dine with Pearce and Cooley at Cooley's estate in the exclusive River Oaks section of town. It was an early dinner, for the performing heart surgeon Cooley's day always began at 6:00 A.M.

Pearce was soon to discover that he could judge the prognosis for recovery of Cooley's operative patients from where each had been positioned on the doctor's daily schedule. "It's children first," Pearce explains, "since those are the most delicate operations and the doctor has to be his freshest. The rest of the morning and the afternoon, he does people who are relatively well, but if you're scheduled for very late in the day or for the evening, it means there's a good chance you're going to die. Because those are the kind of patients that throw Cooley's whole day off. I went to one of those evening operations and watched a woman die."

Pearce will never forget that grim occasion. One of Cooley's residents was operating. When the patient was on the brink of brain death, an anesthesiologist motioned to Pearce. "Watch this," he said. Having glanced at the patient's name tag, the anesthesiologist called, "*Peggy! Peggy!*" The EGG jumped—her brain waves were responding, a hair's distance from death, to her name. "It was incredible," Pearce recalls.

The next morning at six, Pearce and Sutherland met Cooley at the Texas Heart Institute. "First of all," Pearce, explains, "Cooley and Sutherland are about the same height and build, so they got on very well. They were obviously awed by each other. Cooley showed Donald and me how to scrub up and dress in surgical clothes. The entire operating room had to wait till we were all properly scrubbed. But there's never an operation where Cooley doesn't keep a patient waiting. He's always late. Like a movie star."

But on that morning, there were two movie stars in the operating room. And there would be two heart surgeons.

Cooley walked over to the operating table and looked down at his first patient of the day, a six-month-old child. She had already been prepared for surgery; her chest was open, the tubing all in place.

"Her chest cavity was half the size of an envelope," Pearce reports. "Her heart was the size of a bird's heart. No—the size of a thumb." Cooley pronounced the patient ready to go on bypass, turning to explain operating procedures to Sutherland and Pearce. As they were about to learn, a heart operation is as highly choreographed as a dance; one erratic pirouette can throw off the whole *corps de ballet.*

Sutherland was instructed to stand opposite Cooley and place his gloved hands, as surgeons must, on the sterilized operating table. Pearce was cartwheeling around the room taking photographs for the art director of his film. (*Life* magazine would later try to buy the negatives from him.)

Meanwhile, the infant's heart was beating only very slightly. "Give me your hand," Cooley said suddenly to Sutherland. The actor gave the doctor his gloved hand. The doctor took it and put it in the infant's chest, then lifted the heart right out of the chest cavity and put that tiny heart in the actor's hand. *Now* when Sutherland played Cooley in the film, he would know literally what it felt like to feel a heart beating in his hand.

"Sutherland went white as a hospital sheet," Pearce remembers. Cooley remained calm.

"Cooley's fingers are extraordinary to watch," Pearce comments. "His whole genius is speed. This operation used to take six hours, now it's twenty minutes. Cooley is mass production. The man has a kind of conveyor belt of broken people looking for miracles. He takes the worst patients, ones that everybody else has said are inoperable. They come to him in droves—thirty a day on a conveyor belt. Operating is very repetitive for Cooley because he's got it down to rote, so to keep it alive and exciting he likes an audience. He even tells jokes.

"In the middle of an uncomplicated procedure—I mean, if it's just sewing a valve in or punching a hole in a ventricle, things he can do blindfolded—he'll start telling a story. Or to get a conversation rolling he might ask, 'Have you read *Serpentine* by Tommy Thompson?' "*

A heart was not the whole world Sutherland held in his hand that day. "I wasn't there when Donald started one of Cooley's patients' hearts with the electric-shock paddles—or when he did the sutures on another patient," Pearce says of the actor whose most recent film had been *Eye of*

---

* The author whom Cooley hypes during operations is the author who hyped Cooley's operations. Thomas Thompson, in addition to writing *Serpentine*—and *Blood and Money* and *Celebrity*—wrote *Hearts*, an account, the breathless jacket copy goes, "of the daily struggles of Mike DeBakey and Denton Cooley as astonishing as a coronary artery bypass operation."

the Needle. "But Cooley wasn't in the operating room for that one, either. His residents do the sewing up."

Cooley and Sutherland, at the end of a double day's duty (they had both been both doctoring and performing), posed with their director, Pearce, for a publicity photo.

A few weeks later, Cooley and his wife flew to Toronto, where the scene they were to appear in in the film was being shot. One night in a hotel bar, Cooley happened to overhear Pearce and Dr. Robert Jarvik, who had designed and built the artificial heart used in the film, talking—naturally—about the film. When Jarvik turned to Pearce and said, "Now tell me, what's this movie *really* all about?," with Texas swagger Dr. Denton A. Cooley announced, "It's about me."

Well, yes and no. The hero of Pearce's film disobeys a medical ruling to implant an artificial heart into the chest of a dying young woman. Cooley was sure as hell going to compete with his own screen persona. In typical Texas-bandit fashion, he bent some rules of medical ethics in his race to be Number One.

While Jarvik, thirty-seven-year-old surgeon and biomechanic at the University of Utah Medical Center* and a former carpenter and jeweler, was waiting for the Food and Drug Administration to approve his artificial heart for human experimentation, Cooley went ahead and implanted *his* artificial heart in a retired bus driver from the Netherlands without even bothering to submit an application to the FDA for permission to use the experimental device. After the patient's heart had failed to restart following bypass surgery and no human heart was available for a transplant, Cooley operated in the hope of keeping him alive until a human donor could be found. (*Life* was right there in Cooley's operating room, exclusively monitoring the life-and-death situation. In its September 1981 issue it was able to hype-bulletin: "The Artificial Heart Is Here.") The bus driver survived fifty-four hours with the plastic implant, then received a donor heart; eight days later he died.

Though Cooley maintained that he had acted under life-or-death exceptions to federal rules, FDA officials insisted that he had acted without legally required prior approval of the device. That the FDA had had to learn of Cooley's operation through the press says just about all that can be said.

* Jarvik was later to develop the Jarvik-7 artificial heart that was implanted in Dr. Barney Clark. Worldwide publicity surrounding the operation led Twentieth Century-Fox to schedule Pearce's film for a wide, saturation release. According to *Variety*, "Topical considerations pumped new life" into the film.

3

Practicing Philanthropy
for Public Television

After seeing an early screening of Pearce's film *Threshold*, Cooley phoned Sutherland and complained, "You made me one dull son-of-a-bitch."

To Minetree he was more candid about his feelings. "The movie is a piece of shit," he pronounced. (Perhaps what Cooley, supersurgeon that he is, really minded about Pearce's fine film was that he had been but a bit player, a spear carrier.)

Minetree had an idea: "How about my writing and directing a documentary about you operating on a charity patient?"

Cooley was pleased. He would be the star of his own show and be doing some highly publicized philanthropy at the same time.

So Minetree began scouring Cooley's overflowing file of requests from heartsick people who couldn't afford the doctor's fee; he was searching, of course, for the most heartrending case. "I want there to be a big difference between Cooley and the patient," Minetree spells out. "Cooley is six feet five inches tall, so I needed someone little—like a kid. Cooley weighs one-eighty, so I wanted a kid who weighed around thirty-five. Cooley's fair-haired, so I wanted a dark-skinned kid, a dark *Caucasian* kid."

In the end, Minetree hypecast a seven-year-old boy from a poor family in the Philippines. "His parents had sent along a picture of him," he explains, "so I knew he was a cute little bugger." The youngster had been diagnosed as having a Tetralogy of Fallot, a four-lesion congenital heart defect. His parents' letter began, "Please give our boy a chance to live a normal life."

"I lucked out on two counts," Minetree says. "Number one, that's Cooley's favorite operation—he once said he couldn't think of anything more fun that he could do with his clothes on than perform a total correction of a Tetralogy of Fallot. And number two, the national sport in the Philippines is basketball, and Cooley was All Southwest Conference at the University of Texas, so there would be the basketball bond between them."

Cooley had agreed to perform the operation without charge; nevertheless, the hospital bill, which is separate from the surgical fee, would be considerable. So Minetree, whose documentary was being funded by Texas oilman John Mecom, Jr., arranged to have that expense picked up.

Minetree then flew to Manila to film the boy, Dennis Rayoan, as he struggled to accomplish the most commonplace activities of daily life— opening doors, walking, climbing stairs. The moment Minetree saw Dennis's five-year-old sister, he decided to include her in the trip to Houston, knowing she would add to the documentary's pull on the audience's heartstrings. "She was a little china doll," he says. "She called me Papa Harry." Minetree had arranged with Juan Cruz, Jr., the chairman of the board of both Philippine Airways and the opulent Manila Hotel, where General MacArthur had had his wartime headquarters, to donate executive-class plane tickets for the Rayoan family's flight.

As they were boarding the plane, a cameraman on Minetree's crew heard one of the Rayoans' relatives whisper urgently to Dennis's father, "When you get to America, don't come back. Life is better there."

Two days later, in the "cath lab" of the Texas Heart Institute, the Tetralogy of Fallot diagnosis was confirmed, and Dennis's operation was scheduled for first thing the next morning.

The documentary begins, "This is the story of a great heart surgeon and a little boy." The scene is Cooley's operating room, where two cameras had been positioned, one fixed in the surgical lights, the other in the dome overlooking the theater.

Humming *Wie Mir Bist Du Schoen* as he cut decisively into Dennis's chest, Cooley saw that it would be ill-advised to do the Tetralogy of Fallot that he'd been looking forward to performing with the two cameras trained on him. Technically, he could do the operation; he could, in Minetree's chilling words, "get Dennis off the table"—that is, get him out of the operating room alive.

But Dennis would not be able to live very long after the operation because of what Cooley now saw was an undersized left ventricle, which could not handle the normal blood flow that a total correction would result in. He determined that when the ventricle matured, in about a year, he would perform the Tetralogy of Fallot—again, free of charge.

For now, he would perform a Blalock-Taussig Procedure. Coincidentally, Dr. Alfred Blalock, who invented the operation in 1944, had been Cooley's mentor at Johns Hopkins Medical School, and Cooley himself had assisted on the first Blalock-Taussig Procedure, now more commonly known as "the blue-baby operation."

Dennis's lips and fingernails had been blue all his life, because very little oxygenated blood could get into his system. They turned pink the moment Cooley rerouted the unoxygenated arterial blood back to the boy's lungs. "Isn't that great?" Minetree exclaims. "My film's in color. A Tetralogy of Fallot would have been more dramatic, but there's more color in a Blalock-Taussig."

When Dennis came out of anesthesia and looked down at his fingers through his transparent oxygen mask and saw that his nail beds were now pink, according to Minetree, "he looked up at his father and mother and said, 'American blood.' Later the kid asked his father, I kid you not, if the American blood would make him tall like Dr. Cooley. And you want to know something wild," Minetree continues, "Cooley was excited, too. He was so hyped-up that the day after he operated on Dennis, he set another record—forty-eight successful heart operations in one day!"

But Minetree couldn't film that record-breaking day, because his documentary had ended the evening before, with a shot of Cooley emerging from the hospital late at night, wending his way home under the starlit dome of the Texas sky.

Cooley's work for the documentary was done, but Minetree's was not; he still had to find a sponsor to "pick up the advertising for the show." Since the tubing that Cooley had used as a shunt on Dennis as well as the plastic graft that he had implanted in Minetree's aorta fifteen years before were both Dupont products, Minetree approached the public affairs director of Dupont. (He was receptive to the idea.)

The documentary needed a narrator as well as a sponsor. Although in the end John Huston was chosen, Minetree's first thought was Burt Reynolds, who had just formed a film company partnership with Minetree's backer, John Mecom, Jr. But Minetree decided that Reynolds might well upstage Cooley. His second thought was George C. Scott "because," Minetree patiently explains, "he starred in a marvelous movie called *Hospital*. Or I might ask Willie Nelson, because he's got a big heart." While mulling over these last two possibilities, Minetree contacted Walter Cronkite, who wouldn't commit himself to narrate but mentioned in passing that he'd gone to the same high school in Houston as Cooley and that his father had shared an office with Cooley's father, a dentist.

Like Cronkite, Cooley had gone farther than his father, and now he was going even further. For the documentary of Cooley operating phil-anthropically on a Filipino would be the doctor's longest-lasting opera-tion hype: It would not only be shown to a large public-television audience, but it could also be rerun.

Publicity stunts such as these tarnish the whole medical profession. It was entirely unethical of Dr. Cooley both to have held up an operation and to have allowed a nonmedical man to hold up a heart, and it was in ques-tionable taste for him as a doctor to have participated in a documentary that, however good it was that a boy's life was prolonged in the process, amounts to an advertisement for himself—but then, in the past, Dr. Cooley has pleaded guilty to eight counts of "publicity" before his local medical society.

"Denton Cooley is a great man, a *wonderful* man, so exhilarating, beatific—he's like a gospel," Donald Sutherland was quoted as saying. The actor then went on to justify his own unethical actions in the operat-ing room with the weak excuse: "Reach is very important when you're doing a movie like *Threshold.* You've got to look authentic."

Are we to conclude from Sutherland's remark that had he been signed to play a murderer, he would have researched the role by snuffing somebody's life out? Or that, had he been cast as a necrophiliac, he would have rented a corpse and practiced on it?

Had Norman Mailer, an author who enjoys "acting out" his work almost as much as he enjoys acting in major movies, been researching a novel that had a heart surgeon as its protagonist, and been offered the op-portunity to assist in a heart operation, we know that he would have ada-mantly refused. But we also know that his refusal would not have been prompted so much by ethical considerations as by sheer squeamishness.

Of course Donald Sutherland would not murder—or copulate with a corpse—for the purpose of film research. Yet he did stitch up a patient, and cup in his sterilized but untrained hands an infant's heart.

And Dr. Cooley, of the famously trained hands—and, one is forced to speculate, untutored heart—allowed those infamously untrained hands of Sutherland's to hold that childish heart.

THE COMPLEAT
KIT AND CABOODLE

BARBARA CARTLAND:
TOUGH MUTTON DRESSED
AS TENDER LAMB
AND MARKETED AS ROMANTIC MUSH

Close your eyes and think of England.

—BARBARA CARTLAND,
  advice on how to keep your man happy

Dr. Denton Cooley has spent the whole of his professional life repairing broken hearts. But hearts can be famished as well as faulty. And so romance novelists exist to feed them fantasies.

For both the heart surgeon and the romance novelist, the heart is always in a state of extremity: To the doctor, it may be an aortic aneurysm wrapped with wire mesh; to the writer, a valentine pierced by the arrow of love. For both, it is a source of plenty—plenty of money.

The heart of the preeminent romance novelist of our time palpitates not alone for love. She understands the throbbing connection between love and money.

She is English, ancient, and aristocratic, which are the last three adjectives we associate with hype. In fact, the hype about the English, the ancient, and the aristocratic is that they don't have to crudely merchandise themselves; they are, by definition, on an honorable and elevated level of civility.

This aristocratic English ancient, however, explodes the stereotype about lineage, nationality, and age ever so blithely, for Barbara Cartland is the happy hyper.

1
Trials and Tribulations

Were the *Guinness Book of World Records,* the world's most hyped treasury of trivia, accepting new categories, a slot under "The Phenomena of Disproportion" would be filled by an eighty-one-year-old Englishwoman named Barbara Cartland, who already takes up three of the book's well-thumbed entries. In 1975 Cartland broke the world writing record by putting out twenty-three books in a single year; and though in 1976 she fell three books behind her own record, she came back to triumphantly outdistance herself by writing twenty-four in 1979. In 1980 *Guinness* proclaimed her, already the world's most prolific author, the world's best-selling author as well.

Barbara Cartland's third entry in the *Guinness Book of World Records* is for occupying more space in *Who's Who* than any other woman; she takes up three times as much room as the British prime minister. Indeed, the only man with a longer *Who's Who* entry than Barbara Cartland was her late great and grand friend, Earl Mountbatten of Burma, the last viceroy of India and great-uncle and grand godfather to the Prince of Wales, in whose system of multifarious consanguinity Barbara Cartland herself now has a place. For through her daughter Raine's second marriage, to Lady Diana's father, Earl Spencer, Barbara Cartland is quasi-consanguineously the fairy-tale stepgrandmother of the Princess of Wales and the fairy-tale stepgreatgrandmother of the issue thereof: William Arthur Philip Louis, more popularly known as Prince William of Wales.

Were the *Guinness Book of World Records* accepting new categories, the slots under "Stepgreatgrandmother of Future British Monarch" and "Person Most Tenuously Connected to Ruling Royal House" would also be filled by an eighty-one-year-old Englishwoman named Barbara Cartland.

The reason this incorrigible *Guinness* record-breaker takes up so many lines in *Who's Who* is that she assiduously lists *all* of her three hundred paperback romantic novels.

Among those whose titles employ that persistent word "love": *Bitter Winds of Love, Love Is an Eagle, Love Is the Enemy, Love Me Forever, Love Is Mine, Love Forbidden, The Price Is Love, The Coin of Love, Where Is Love?, The Thief of Love, Love Under Fire, The Fire of Love, The Drums of Love, Vote for Love, Messenger of Love, The Wings of Love, Love in the Clouds, Love in the Moon, Little White Doves of Love, The Perfection of Love, Love in the Dark, A Touch of Love, Rhapsody of Love, The Love Pirate, Punished with Love, The Slaves of Love, The Wild Cry of Love, Lies for Love, The Vibration of Love, The Mask of Love, The Karma of Love, The Dawn of Love, Love Leaves at Midnight, Love at Forty, Conquered by Love, Who Can Deny Love?, An Arrow of Love, Love Is Innocent, A Song of Love, Love is Contraband, Love to the Rescue, Love in Hiding, The Treasure Is Love, Love Is Dangerous, Love on the Run, The Prisoner of Love, Love Holds the Cards, The Magic of Love, Love, Lords and Lady-Birds, Love Locked In, Love Climbs In, Lessons in Love, Look Listen and Love, Never Laugh at Love, The Tears of Love, Love in Pity, Moments of Love, Lucky in Love, No Time for Love, The Problems of Love, The Twists and Turns of Love, Love Has His Way, The Explosion of Love, The Ghost Who Fell in Love, The Devil in Love, The Race for Love, Flowers for the God of Love, Love and the Loathsome Leopard,* and *Love for Sale.*

Among the Barbara Cartland titles with noble titles in them: *Dollars for the Duke, The Duke and the Preacher's Daughter, The Prince and the Pekingese, The Duchess Disappeared, The Odious Duke, The Disgraceful Duke, The Wicked Marquis, The Marquess Who Hated Women, A Kiss for the King, The Elusive Earl, The Taming of Lady Lorinda, A Princess in Distress, The Cruel Count,* and *Lord Ravenscar's Revenge.* And among the Barbara Cartland titles with the promise of painful problems in them: *A Virgin in Mayfair, A Virgin in Paris, Kneel for Mercy,* and *Sweet Punishment.*

These romance pills for hungry hearts and lazy minds have been swallowed by hundreds of millions of readers, most of them between the age of twenty-six and forty-five, and many of them to be found in the United States of Advertising. According to Barbara Cartland's biographer, the pseudonymous Henry Cloud, a recent survey showed that while 39 percent of American women had never read a book in their lives, 18 percent of American women had read at last one Barbara Cartland novel.

For success as prodigious as Barbara Cartland's, there must be a tried-and-true formula. Here is the basic scenario for a Barbara Cartland historical romance, invariably set in the nineteenth-century: *Penniless, well-bred, fresh-faced VIRGIN meets and falls in love with tall, virile, devilishly HANDSOME and above all NOBLE stranger in EXOTIC setting. Though the couple do nothing more carnal than kiss, there are dangerous rapids on the river ROMANCE. But TRUE LOVE triumphs in the end. With MARRIAGE bells ringing, the novel closes on chambermaids drawing the curtains and turning down the sheets on the bridal bed.* "Then love carried them on the waves of ecstasy into the starlit sky, and they knew that nothing mattered except that as man and woman they were one now and through all eternity."

Another ingredient in the Barbara Cartland formula: Her novels are dressed uniformly. They all wear the same romantic tea gown of a jacket cover, styled by Cartland's friend, the artist Francis Marshall.

Barbara Cartland's formula works because it is psychologically accurate. Her books address—and satisfy—women's deepest, most untutored romantic fantasies—ridiculous as this may seem in a time when there are as few virgins left as there are dukes, and when women have justly been insisting that they have the same right to declarative passion as men do.

Some time ago, when Barbara Cartland's publishers suggested that she redesign her romances, modernizing them to exploit the current cultural obsession with sex, she resisted. Her feminine intuition told her there were lusty bucks to be made from blushing virgins. "The pendulum will swing as it always does," she predicted on the front page of *The Times* of London, in an article she titled—hopefully, against the highest possible odds—"A Virginity Boom?"

Having cornered the market on virginity in novel after novel, Cartland would now market it with a vengeance. In 1974, when she was seventy-three, she persuaded Bantam Books to buy 150 Barbara Cartland romantic novels for dissemination in America, for Barbara Cartland, virgin territory. A year later, having arranged for saturation magazine coverage and a priceless Cartland segment on *60 Minutes*, Bantam was releasing one Barbara Cartland virgin every week. The publisher had laid odds that the public couldn't read just one, and Bantam was right: Mass serial addiction ensued.*

The nucleus of Barbara Cartland's fantasy factory is a rather elabo-

* This is generally true of the romance fiction market. The *New York Times* recently reported that, the economic recession notwithstanding, readers were spending up to forty dollars a month in variety and bookstores and supermarkets or on mail orders catching up with their heroines. Brand-name romances now account for roughly 40 percent of all mass-market paperbacks sold in the United States.

rate physical plant, a romantically refurbished English manor house set in a vision of classic pastoral—four hundred acres of verdant parkland just twenty miles outside London. It is on a pink sofa in her library there that she writes the short paragraphs—taking care to limit them all to three lines, knowing that if they are any longer, her readers will nod—that make up her short, supersuccessful books. In fact, she does not *write* the paragraphs, she dictates them—rat-a-tat: six thousand to seven thousand words talked and taped between one and four every afternoon. On the seventh day of dictation, a forty-five-thousand-word Barbara Cartland is born full-blown.

Barbara Cartland provides the raw material—Barbara Cartland's Romantic Thoughts and Feelings—but the writing factory has workers contributing to the production of the consumer product. Employed—or indentured—on the assembly line are: an eighty-four-year-old lady's maid who brings her eighty-one-year-old mistress vitamins, honey, and a hot water bottle every morning and who also helps Cartland put her pearls on; a butler; a chef; a chauffeur who, according to Cartland's authorized biography, *Crusader in Pink*, not only collects from the county library the books she needs to research her romances but collects them in her trademark car, a white Rolls-Royce, which Cartland's résumé, a document that competes in length with the shortness of her novels and that will henceforth be referred to as "Barbara's Brag Sheet," tells us is the first white Rolls-Royce ever made.

There are also: a literary secretary; four full-time and six part-time general secretaries; a retired classics master who corrects Cartland's grammar; a professional manuscript typist; and finally, closer to home, Cartland's two sons, the elder of whom acts as her business manager, overseeing his mother's deals and contracts through a corporation called not Cartland Productions but, appropriately enough for someone whose epic vocation is promoting her productions, Cartland Promotions.

Barbara Cartland: prodigious, prolific, and *persistent*. She's worked long and hard to get where she's still going today. Well born though she was, when Bertie her father fell on Flanders' field, her mother Polly had to pick and package Pershore plums and sell them to her London chums. Young Barbara, rather than perform the genteel employments permitted distressed gentlefolk—cleaning jewelry; dusting rare china and furniture for family friends; walking, clipping, and washing dogs—chose to bring bacon home by selling her own plums—gossip plums—to the *Daily Express* at five shillings a plum.

Before long, Cartland had observed and absorbed enough about society to piece together a novel. She titled it, pertinently, *Jigsaw*. Knowing instinctively how to promote her person in the press, she billed the book as "Mayfair with the lid off": society girl tells society's story from the inside out. *Jigsaw* went into six printings, was translated into five languages, and at the age of twenty-four, Barbara Cartland was no longer just the daughter of a Pershore plum packager.

Presented at Court, she curtsied to their Majesties in a gown given her by an unknown designer named Norman Hartnell, clothed in his own early promise (he was to become *Sir* Norman Hartnell, the royal dress designer), in exchange for *her* promise to bring her society friends to his atelier to shop. A year later Cartland crowned Hartnell's dress with a hat, opening a smart hat shop of her own, and, by naming it "Barbara," took another sure step toward where she's still stepping today. (Later, Cartland would go into other garments, starting London's first Quick Cleaners.)

Then, piecing her own jigsaw together, she wrote a paragraph or two about the hat shop she'd just capped with her name, and placed the item in a London gossip column. It began: "Sixteen hours a day, society shopkeeper finds work agrees with her." Presumably, the other eight hours of her day went to designing the schema whereby she would one day take up three entries in the *Guinness Book of World Records* and, had it been accepting new categories when she became both the stepgreat-grandmother of a future British monarch and the person most tenuously connected to a ruling royal house, would have taken up five.

Among Cartland's major strategies for self-promotion was one that her *Daily Express* employer, Lord Beaverbrook, had recommended as the prerequisite for public success. He told her gravely to adopt a platform—much like a politician—so she would have a ready set of beliefs the public could identify her by and thus become "even better known to everyone." Cartland mounted a public platform at once, preaching FEMININE POTENTIAL THROUGH PROGRESSIVE SELF-ESTEEM. (Half a century later, she could be found still standing on that platform, writing a weekly column earnestly titled "All I Want to Do Is to Help You.")

Cartland did not need a Beaverbrook to tell her that philanthropy was a fail-safe strategy for announcing public self-significance. In one of her columns she had written that "charity has become a ladder with which to climb the social tree." She was already climbing it through a series of socially acceptable charity events which she coordinated, climaxing in her 1930 production and promotion of the first pageant since the Great War: "Britain and Her Industries."

Cartland had prevailed upon some of her grand friends to parade about the Royal Albert Hall costumed as British industries. Lady Ashley, in black tights, and with a black oilcloth train, was COAL; Lady Scarsdale, who fortunately did not live to see her noble name become the title of an ignoble diet book and murder scandal, was WOOL; and Cartland herself, in a massive dress, which she shared with three attendants and which showed an ocean liner lit up in every porthole, was THE WHITE STAR LINE. After the parade, according to Barbara's Brag Sheet, the Prince of Wales congratulated her on her good works.

So, well before the activity was even called "public relations," Cartland was actively practicing it. She continued to promote Norman Hartnell, and also took on a West End dressmaker as a client. She brought her fashionable friends to shop there, then packaged their shopping sprees as gossip plums for the *Daily Mail*, the *Bystander*, the *Tatler*, and the Sunday *Observer* as well as the *Daily Express*. She did not need a J. Walter Thompson to tell her—she herself had already written—that "advertising no longer meant spending money in the advertisement columns of the newspapers. The gossip columns were the best and surest medium of attraction, for social names were the surest bait to catch the wealthy suburban worm." (Today Cartland counts Suzy among her best friends.)

Cartland was now perfectly positioned to revitalize her next account, the Embassy Club on Bond Street, once the headquarters of London's smart set, where the table to the right of the entrance had been permanently reserved for the philanthropy-professing, fun-loving Prince of Wales. She redecorated the club in romantic opulence, then invited the pick of her celebrity friends to play there so she could package yet more gossip plums for wormy suburban consumption.

Barbara Cartland: prodigious, prolific, persistent, and *positioned.* By now she had worn the hats—all of them named "Barbara"—of gossip columnist, novelist, journalist, publicist, philanthropist, and wife. (In 1927 she had met a Scottish gentleman of proper lineage and demeanor who almost immediately asked her to marry him. Her virtue was at long last to be rewarded by—she believed—lifelong security, for her fiancé had promised her a house in Mayfair and her own Rolls-Royce as a wedding present. One of her early novels she had titled, simply, *For What?* Now real life had given her its answer: For a house in Mayfair and a Rolls-Royce, that's what! On St. George's Day she married her betrothed, wearing a Norman Hartnell freebie, and that night he relieved her of the pangs of chastity.)

It would soon be time not quite to take those hats off, but to keep them juggling in the air while putting on the respectably rewarding hat of Society Mother. For the daughter that Barbara had produced, and prized, was growing up and needed to be promoted—the little girl whom she had titled "Raine," a Gaelic name as self-consciously original as that of any Barbara Cartland heroine—or cow, for Cartland had named the milking cows in her country herd after the leading ladies in her romantic novels: Lalita, Tain McSpean, Mona Vivien, Cornelia, Maxine, Lady Diana Stanlier.

"I am delighted with my daughter, who is the most photographed child in Mayfair," Cartland gushed to a *Vogue* writer, and, as she had hoped it would, the next issue of *Vogue* gushed back: "Five-year-old Raine's mantelpiece is covered with invitation cards and her engagement diary must be almost as full as mother's." (Mother's appointment calendar was *so* full that had Daughter been asked whether she was related to Barbara Cartland, in her fifth-year precocity she might well have replied, somewhat matricidally, "She's a very distant mother.")

Shortly after Raine's sixteenth birthday, Cartland decided to "produce" her as a beauty and make her the most sought-after deb of the day. That way, Cartland could, as it were, take her daughter to market to buy a fat cat—a duke would do very nicely, but the plot when it thickened would involve a prince of the blood, the Prince of Wales.

So Raine came out, became "Deb of the Year," and the next year had the obligatory "Wedding of the Year," marrying Gerald Legge, eldest son of the heir presumptive to the Earl of Dartmouth. She had, as they say, "come out noble." (Divorcing Lord Dartmouth and in 1976 repledging her troth to Edward John, eighth Earl Spencer, retired Equerry to both Queen Elizabeth II and her father, King George, godson of both the Duke of Windsor and Queen Mary, and Lady Di's dad, Raine would shoot Mother Cartland into the very kernel of the kingdom.)

With public motherhood behind her, Cartland determined to trade in all her hats for a proper crown. She formed the National Association for health and became the president of it, crowning herself, in effect, "England's Queen of Health." Publicizing and promoting, though not as yet producing, vitamins and health foods (later there would be Barbara Cartland stress pills, Barbara Cartland brain pills, and a mail-order health-food business), she made royal progresses from one rim of the realm to the other. Health turned out to be the most useful platform she had ever mounted. If the public adored her as journalist, novelist, and public mother—and they did, they did—now they positively worshiped her as health queen.

And Barbara Cartland luxuriated as never before in the image she'd created. Her toque-shaped Freddy Fox fur hats, her brightly colored Hardy Amies dresses (for there was color television to think of now), her pink-dyed Delman shoes, high-heeled and open-toed, exposing pink-polished toenails, her winking jewels (a bracelet round her royal wrist, a strand of pearls round her royal throat), her furs, and her trademark white Rolls-Royce all spelled GLAMOUR and HIGH ROMANCE—and, naturally, HEALTH—and, preternaturally, healthy WEALTH.

This is the role that Barbara Cartland at eighty-one is still performing today.

Barbara Cartland: prodigious, prolific, persistent, positioned, and *ever-productive*. In addition to the writing of those three hundred novels, the promoting of those platforms, and the production of that daughter, Cartland has produced a quartet of autobiographies, one of which is titled *The Isthmus Years,* a name that doesn't exactly sing; several cookbooks—*Barbara Cartland's Health Food Cookery Book, Food for Love,* and *Recipes for Lovers*—all of which, since she cannot cook, her cook helps her to write; three books listed under "Sociology" on Barbara's Brag Sheet—*Be Vivid, Be Vital, Look Lovely, Be Lovely,* and *Men are Wonderful;* and two plays—*Blood Money,* which she later rewrote, or rather, redictated, as a novel titled *Sawdust,* and *French Dressing,* about, no doubt, her salad days.

Then, on top of her career dressing Cartland portioned out a spoonful of sweet: *The Magic of Honey,* her book on the one substance she insists can do anything short of restoring virginity. According to Barbara's Brag Sheet, the book single-handedly emptied all of England's health-food shops of honey. And naturally it filled Cartland's coffers with layers of paper currency, for when the owl and the pussy cat went to sea in a beautiful pea-green boat, they took some money and plenty of honey wrapped up in a five-pound note.

To the spoonful of sweet on top of her career dressing Cartland now added a dollop of Devonshire cream: "Barbara Cartland's Album of Love Songs," on which, backed by the Royal Philharmonic Orchestra the octogenarian herself, her voice doctored for the record with an injection of RNA (a little nonsurgical plastic surgery for the voice), was able to produce what one critic described as "a tiny dew-drenched sexy" sound.

Cartland has also written the biography of her nonagenarian mother, the plucky Pershore plum packager of yore, to which she gave the nursery-talk title *Polly My Wonderful Mother*. (Barbara's Brag Sheet, which among other self-serving things gives a year-by-year account of Cartland milestones, beginning with a 1901 birth, lists under "1976" the following lines, chilling in their juxtaposition of loss and gain: "Polly her wonderful Mother dies aged 98½. In February visits Antigua, Martinique and Barbados. April Greece; May, Promotion visit to USA, 5 TV shows, 9 live broadcasts in eight days. Raine becomes Countess Spencer. Brings out 'The Dream and the Glory' in aid of the St. John Ambulance Brigade. Starts the Library of Love in England and USA.")

In 1980 Cartland, characteristically transforming one vehicle of self-promotion into another, put out Barbara's Brag Sheet in book form by amplifying its contents and illustrating them with memorabilia. Thus the *Barbara Cartland Scrapbook,* published by and partly in aid of the Royal Photographic Society (and partly in aid of Barbara Cartland).

The book looks and reads like an elderly *Brooke Book.* (Not only do Cartland and Brooke Shields have virgin-worshiping in common, they also have books that are instruments of blatant self-hype.) A few pieces from the jigsaw, a few scraps from the *Barbara Cartland Scrapbook* heap, will illustrate—better than a thousand pictures worth a thousand words apiece—why Barbara Cartland is the Empress of Hype:

> Caption to photo of Cartland and newborn daughter Raine: "This was hailed as the most beautiful picture ever photographed of a mother and baby." *** Caption to photo of Cartland and daughter Raine glad-handing the elderly: "The poor old ladies in a home in Hatfield have never had a Christmas party. I arrange one with cake, a glass of port each and crackers. Woolworth's gives me brooches, necklaces and bracelets for them and they glitter like Christmas trees! This became an annual event." *** "There is a fuss about Teddy boys in the newspapers and it is argued they run wild because no one seems to care. So I ask a Teddy Boy to tea. He is charming!" *** "With the makers of Sarakan Toothpaste which I always use." *** "I introduce the 'Brain Pill' (Celaton CH3 Tri-Plus) to Great Britain on TV. Because I was taking it I doubled my output of books. It has a fantastic effect on old people who are going senile." *** "I launch the Dona Magdelina in a Glasgow shipyard." *** "In 1979 I make Antigua

an important part of 'Love at the Helm' which I wrote with the help and inspiration of Lord Mountbatten." *** "I visit America to celebrate the sale of my 100 millionth book. On the Donahue Show in Chicago I was seen by 40 million viewers. He was a charming, very exciting interviewer." *** And, the scrap heap's wintry coda, a line that comes as close to being a cry from the heart as anything Barbara Cartland has ever written: "I have now refused to be photographed except in a studio."

In addition to the *Barbara Cartland Scrapbook* (though it doesn't seem possible there *can* be an addition to a hype tool as compulsive as that), there are other Cartland productions and promotions percolating, including a Barbara Cartland Health and Happiness Club; a mass-market magazine, *Barbara Cartland's World of Romance*; a syndicated comic strip, "Barbara Cartland's Romances," that appears daily in almost one hundred British and American newspapers; and Barbara Cartland World Tours, which, in conjunction with British Airways, carry herds of travelers hungry for romance to Turkey, Egypt, France, Germany, and of course Earl Mountbatten of Burma's India.

2

A Command Performance

Last year Barbara Cartland, Queen of Romance and Empress of Hype, descended on Manhattan like some missing Gabor sister, like the Dolly Parton of romance fiction, her false eyelashes batting as true as her healthily beating heart, to promote yet another Barbara Cartland product: Barbara Cartland Fragrances.

Cartland had been very effectively presold; there were queues of interviewers standing for hours on end outside her hotel suite.

One unfine day—the sky gunmetal, goosegray; the wind in a huff—an intrepid interviewer set out for Cartland's hotel through the garbage-struck, traffic-snarled streets of the city. As he walked, he rehearsed the questions he had thought up to ask her: Miss Cartland, have you ever experienced lust in your heart? Do you have corns? Do you suffer from gas? What disease are you most afraid of getting? What is your greatest hate? It's a well-known fact that these days people can't trust their servants not to have snag nails, so do you wash your own stockings or what? And do you, like the Queen Mother, use talcum powder for cleaning white fox? What is your view of Zsa Zsa Gabor? Isn't it true that Earl Mountbatten of Burma was queer and, tell me, didn't Countess Mountbatten of Burma fancy black men?

Oh, the intrepid interviewer had ever so many questions to ask the Empress of Hype!

At the storied St. Regis he was shown into an anteroom of "The Governor's Suite." Presently, the doors to the make-do Royal Chamber were thrown open. The interviewer saw her then as in his mind's eye he will always see her: the Queen of Romance holding court in a voluminous flame-pink dress and platinum hair helmet—hanging on by her pink claws to what is left of the British Empire.

Beside her was a table leaped high with complimentary copies of her latest romance, *Love Wins,* each wrapped in flowered pink paper and tied with a hot-pink ribbon. Every copy was promiscuously presigned—with a pink felt pen—"Love, Barbara Cartland."

Alongside the books was a bric-a-brac of objects, a veritable pyramid of Barbara Cartland paperweights, containing (as the intrepid interview discovered when he picked one of them up and saw printed on the back): "A leaf from the pages of history. This leaf has been picked from the OAK planted by Queen Elizabeth the First of England on the spot where she killed her first stag circa 1550 in the beautiful grounds of Camfield Place, Hatfield, Hertfordshire, the home of the famous authoress, Barbara Cartland. Preserved forever in 22-carat gold." This mumbo jumbo mound of freebies had just been upset, having been dived into by Queen Cartland for a present for the latest journalist who had been to see her.

Upon the intrepid interviewer's arrival at "The Governor's Suite," the retinue of the Queen of Romance and Empress of Hype had scattered, dispersing to their duties. All except one: Joseph of the Public Relations Department of Helena Rubinstein, which had produced the Barbara Cartland Fragrances that Barbara Cartland was here to promote. Joseph lingered, like cheap cologne.

BARBARA CARTLAND: I'd be so delighted if you had some new and original questions for me.

INTERVIEWER: Aren't we going to be alone?

BARBARA CARTLAND: Go sit in the other room, Joseph.

JOSEPH (*To interviewer*): Why? Am I making you nervous?

INTERVIEWER: No, but bugger off, will you! We two lovebirds want to be alone.

BARBARA CARTLAND (*To the exiting Joseph*): Shut the door, darling. It makes a draft. (*To interviewer*) Come on now, let's get right down and do it.

INTERVIEWER: Right. Let's get the perfume hype out of the way first. In your latest book, *Love Wins,* there's a centerfold ad featuring an old photograph—or a newly retouched one—of you posed in a pink sequined tea dress "introducing the romantic world of Barbara Cartland Fragrances."

BARBARA CARTLAND: I *have* just come out with three scents bearing the titles of my three *most* romantic novels: *The Heart Triumphant, Moments of Love,* and *Love Wins.* They're all aphrodisiacs—you fall in love the moment you put them on. Now the last one, *Love Wins*, I think is slightly nasty—I mean the smell, not the book—and you know how everything *I* am is romantic. But a lot of women adore its woodsy scent. And, my dear, the boys all say it's absolutely marvelous as an aftershave. You see, I'm onto something totally original here—unisex scent. The man uses it for an aftershave, the woman uses it as a perfume—they both smell the same. Like a garden of gardenia, jasmine, carnation, rose, narcissus, heliotrope! (*Reaches for "The Heart Triumphant" and sprays on interviewer's collar and cuffs*) I always apply perfume at pulse points—back of the neck, wrist, crook of the arm—because the blood is closest to the skin there. Isn't the fragrance divine?

INTERVIEWER: Pew! (*Gulping, unknots tie and pulls coat sleeve over shirt cuffs*) It does have the sweet smell of success, however—just give a book's title to a perfume so the perfume's name can ricochet back to the book, then insert an ad in the middle of the book for the perfume and increase sales while cutting advertising costs.

BARBARA CARTLAND: And we'll have *two* best sellers with the same name! Isn't it divine? Helena Rubinstein brought me thirty scents to choose from. I told them *my* perfumes had to be, number one, romantic; number two, inexpensive—one is not allowed to say "cheap" in your country—so my paperback readers can afford them—remember, it's not the high end I'm milking; and, number three, they had to last, because I was sick to death of spraying French perfumes on and by the time I got downstairs I didn't smell! Mine really do last. Like true—*licit*—love. And look at the quantity you get for seven-fifty—one and a half ounces! That's *very* cheap. And look, each perfume is packed in a different box, with a different French Court painting on it. They're *all* really worth having.

INTERVIEWER: What else do you have that's worth having?

BARBARA CARTLAND: I'm very fussy. I've got personal involvements with only twenty firms. I do everything myself. If my name is on it, I want it to be me. There's Barbara Cartland wallpaper, of course. I went to an awards reception at Rockefeller Center last night for the wallpaper trade; there were four hundred entries and *I* was the nominee—and the *winner*—for the traditional group of wallpapers, which I think is jolly clever of me in a foreign country. I wore the most divine dress you ever saw to accept my award—rhinestones and *coq* feathers, draped in front and scooped into a delicious demibustle. Of course, last year I received the "Achiever of the Year" award for my line of furnishings from the National Home Furnishings Association at Colorado Springs. Now let me see, what else do I have. . . .There's pink porcelain Barbara Cartland tableware, which I introduced during my "Decorating with Love" display at Macy's. There's Barbara Cartland curtains, Barbara Cartland towels, Barbara Cartland desk sets, Barbara Cartland calendars, Barbara Cartland greeting cards, Barbara Cartland coat hangers—

INTERVIEWER: Wire hangers?

BARBARA CARTLAND: Pink satin, my dear. Needless to say, I'm having terrible fights with you Americans because you *will* paint everything down—you have no color sense here. I like it *this* color pink. (*Displays sequined tea dress: piercingly pink*) That's my color—Cartland pink. There's also Barbara Cartland sheets. I'm waiting to see *those*.

INTERVIEWER: Of all your best sellers, Barbara Cartland sheets can least afford to be off-color. Have you ever considered coming out with a Barbara Cartland candy? It could be hard candy to suck on—striped pink like a candy cane. Or it could be in the shape of a heart and have pink syrup in the center. There could even be a Barbara Cartland theme candy—a chocolate-covered cherry! And why has there never been a Barbara Cartland doll? It could come with a toy white Rolls-Royce. And what about a line of Barbara Cartland scented toilet paper?

BARBARA CARTLAND: They suggested that, and I said no—no vulgarities.

INTERVIEWER: You said please don't squeeze the Charmin.

BARBARA CARTLAND: I said no vulgarity! I'm *Ro*mance. I'm Charming Ro*mance*!

INTERVIEWER: Aren't you afraid that—

BARBARA CARTLAND: I'm not afraid of anything! Now don't you start being negative. Just before I left England last week to come over here, a man came to write a piece on me and asked nothing but negative questions: "Aren't you afraid of being rejected by your readers? Does the competition from Silhouette Romances, Harlequin Romances, September Romances, First Love, Candlelight Ecstasy, and Second Chance at Love worry you? Does the projected competition from Bantam's Circle of Love, Ballantine's Love and Life, New American Library's Adventures in Love and Late Love, and Avon Books' Looking for Mr. Right frighten you? What is your greatest hate? Whom do you dislike the most? What do you regret most in your long life?" I said "Oh, *shut* up. I'm always looking forward, I'm always *enjoying* things, I'm not afraid of *anything*." Then I waited a second and said, "Except I do have this horror of what I call 'beige people.'" You see, darling, he was wearing a light brown suit.

INTERVIEWER (*Wearing a brown tweed suit, beige shirt, tan wool tie, brown shoes, and brown socks*): But maybe the best things in life *are* brown.

BARBARA CARTLAND: I don't like *anything* beige. I hate beige clothes, I hate beige cars, I hate brown books, I hate brown cows, I hate beige rooms, I like *bright* colors. And now the doctors all say that pink is a very good color from a health point of view. If you're difficult *or* hysterical and you're put in a pink room, it calms you down and you become a charming, loving person. This is doctors—not Barbara Cartland—speaking, so you see I really *have* made a very wise color choice.

INTERVIEWER: Do you dream in bright technicolor, and what violent sex fantasies wake you up in the middle of the night?

BARBARA CARTLAND: Yes, I do. I often dream in bright pink. I dream I'm flying and that if I crash I'll have a heart attack and die—I haven't done *that* yet. Of course, I had my own glider, you know, back in 1931—"The Barbara Cartland." It was towed by an airplane from Manston Aerodrome to Reading carrying mail—the first airplane-towed glider-borne mail in history!

INTERVIEWER: When you're not flying air mail, you're stationary in a twenty-seven-room house just outside London, which your brag sheet—I mean your résumé—says was built by Beatrix Potter's grandfather. Do you really live in the house where every child's favorite story, *The Tale of Peter Rabbit*, was written?

BARBARA CARTLAND: Her grandfather didn't *build* it, you silly, he *bought* it, in 1867—and *re*built it. He pulled down the old Tudor structure and made an enormous Victorian house. Beatrix lived there as a young girl, yes, and Peter Rabbit hippity-hopped in the woods behind the house and raided the garden of that nasty old Mr. McGregor for lettuce. I was lucky to buy the house, Camfield Place, from the estate of old Lord Queenborough who'd had two American millionaire wives who'd put in the most beautiful mantelpieces and Georgian cornices and parquet floors and, my dear, *ten bathrooms*. And now *I've* got *twelve*, so no one need be dirty in *my* house.

INTERVIEWER: Twelve bathrooms would take an awful lot of Barbara Cartland scented toilet paper.

BARBARA CARTLAND: My daughter Raine has *fifty-three* bathrooms. And her dining-room table seats fifty-four. She's mistress of Althorp House, the most wonderful, beautiful, treasure-filled Georgian stately house. Not that she married Johnny Spencer for his house, mind you, *or* for his wonderful pictures—twenty Van Dycks, *think* of it! My son-in-law said to me the other day, "You know, Mother, Althorp has become a shrine.

Everybody absolutely adores Diana and comes from miles and miles to see the house where she grew up." My dear, business is booming—five thousand visitors a week, at three dollars a head—up from a hundred fifty before Diana's engagement to the future King of England. And Johnny and Raine have invited the sixty American fans on the twenty-two-hundred-dollar Barbara Cartland Romantic Tours to lunch with them. Now you Americans may not know that every stately home in England open to tourists has a little souvenir shop. And now Althorp's is *besieged* by people. Raine has been so very clever—instead of having all those boring things the National Trust has, like wastebaskets, *she* sells champagne and everybody buys bottles to drink Diana's health. Also Johnny's set up a wine shop in the stables and the bottles all bear the Althorp crest. My clever, clever daughter also sells statuettes, glassware, matchboxes, and rape whistles—all with a picture of Althorp on them—and the *most* marvelous false jewelry.

INTERVIEWER: What was your first piece of important jewelry?

BARBARA CARTLAND: On my honeymoon in Paris in 1928, I got a diamond bracelet, my first, from my husband. A real corker. Both my husbands had the same surname, you know. They were first cousins and—at one time—best friends. But during my first honeymoon, I discovered I'd married the wrong McCorquodale.

INTERVIEWER: McCorquodale! Isn't that the breed of dog favored by your stepgranddaughter's mother-in-law, the Queen?

BARBARA CARTLAND: Those are McCorgis, I mean *Corgis*!

INTERVIEWER: Whatever, McCorquodale is the least romantic name I've ever heard. It's the name of a man who would wear a tan suit.

BARBARA CARTLAND: Just what do you mean by "wear a tan suit"? The McCorquodales are very Scottish and frightfully grand. They trace their family tree right back to Duke Rollo, grandfather of William the Conqueror.

INTERVIEWER: Did the second McCorgi give you diamonds as well?

BARBARA CARTLAND: Certainly he did. It's a man's privilege to decorate the woman he loves with precious stones. Now, of course, I've had all my jewelry copied. It's just not worth all the bother of putting it in safes and taking it out. A friend of mine went to a ball last year here in New York—dressed to the teeth and jeweled to the eyebrows—and after the ball she realized a man was trailing her out on Fifth Avenue, so she slipped her enormous ruby ring—it's a *real* corker—into her girdle. It made such a big lump. The man never discovered it but, I mean, who wants a lump in their girdle? A girdle is supposed to take lumps *away*.

So when I come to New York, I bring nothing but false jewelry. I arrive here saying, "It's false, it's false!" in case they think it's real. On the other hand, these days you can get bonked on the head for good paste copies.

INTERVIEWER: Aside from writing three hundred fictions, you've written the biographies of some real people, including Elizabeth Empress of Austria and Josephine Empress of France—your two favorite heroines from history. Odd that you admire Elizabeth of Austria. You've said in print many times that you totally disapprove of women who diet obsessively, and the Kaiserin Elizabeth was the first anoretic in recorded history. She gloried so much in her Diana figure that she starved herself to keep it—went on every kind of cranky diet. One doctor put her on a sand diet, another on a diet of just six oranges a day, but when she got advanced anemia, she had to drink sheep's blood with the orange juice. Her waist was an almost inhuman eleven inches or something.

BARBARA CARTLAND: Elizabeth was the first woman who slimmed, yes, and I admit she slimmed badly. But *oh*, she was so romantic. She was the most beautiful woman in the world. And she was *so* unhappy, poor darling—her wicked mother-in-law was absolutely cruel to her. Lord Mountbatten adored Elizabeth because she was the most wonderful horsewoman. There's never been anyone who rode as wonderfully as Elizabeth of Austria. She was taught by her father, Archduke Maximilian, to ride like a circus rider. When she died, her distraught husband, Franz Joseph, destroyed every photograph of her on a horse.

INTERVIEWER: But by the end she couldn't ride anymore, she was so weak. She didn't have the strength in her legs to hold onto the horse.

BARBARA CARTLAND: Don't count on it, darling. As Picasso once said, the rich ride and the poor walk toward the angel of death. When I was writing my biography of her, I asked Lord Mountbatten to ask Prince Charles, whom I didn't know in *those* days very well, if I could reproduce the drawing of Elizabeth riding, which hangs in his bedroom in Buckingham Palace. And of course he said yes, the dear. Think of it, the only reason he is where he is today—occupying that bedroom in the Palace— is because his great-aunt caused the greatest scandal for love that there ever was. My dear, it toppled a crown! I met Wallis when she first came to live in England as Mrs. Ernest Simpson. I'd always known Ernest. The other day I found a letter I'd written my wonderful mother after coming back from one of my first tea dances, in Surrey. I wrote, "Ernest took me home and tried to kiss me in the taxi. Such cheek!" My first impression of Wallis, who went on to be acclaimed the world's best-dressed woman, was that she was rather *badly* dressed. She also had a rather bad complexion. And she was so aggressively American. I watched the television series *Edward and Mrs. Simpson* with Lord Mountbatten and he pronounced it all terribly accurate. You know, Lady Diana Cooper still maintains that Wallis wasn't a bit in love with the little prince. Well, the fairy tale is all over now, so why should we fuss? She's gaga, poor thing, and completely in the hands of this French lady lawyer, Maître Suzanne Blum, who's clever and tough—she represented Rita Hayworth in her divorce from Aly Khan, and she's had other Hollywood clients: Charlie Chaplin, Darryl Zanuck, Jack Warner. They say she's locked the gates to the Windsors' Neuilly house and is going to publish all the Duchess's letters. I don't think Wallis will see any of the money, do you?

INTERVIEWER: Okay now, let's hear your hype for Empress Josephine, your other historical favorite. What kind of chaste case can you possibly make for *her*? She was powerfully sexed and slept around a lot. She even took a lover to Italy—which you have to admit was pretty stupid of her as empress. Just what is it about her you admire so much? Her black teeth? Or her green thumb? Wasn't she a passionate rose buff? I think there's even a rose called *"Souvenir de Malmaison."*

BARBARA CARTLAND: She *was* promiscuous, but she was always a fascinating woman. She inspired some of the greatest love letters of all time—the love letters Napoleon wrote her. You see, I collect really really beautiful lovely lovely letters from history. Josephine did have great love affairs—they weren't always very satisfactory but they were very romantic. Look, you're getting me wrong. I don't mind what people do when they're older. The cause I am fighting for as a woman is to preserve young girls from being pressured into losing their virginity. When *I* was young, I had forty-nine marriage proposals before I got engaged, and nobody ever said, "Come to bed." No girl went to bed before marriage, she just didn't. I never even knew what deep and passionate kissing was. You see, I always kept my lips sealed. The first time someone did kiss me passionately, deeply—it was in the Isle of Wight, on the beach, under a full moon—I was shocked.

INTERVIEWER: No wonder the good burghers in those days ran off to whores or other guys, or took to drink and gambling.

BARBARA CARTLAND: Ah my young men! I had my first proposal nine days after I left school. He was a middle-aged colonel with a rather common red mustache. I do hate mustaches. Another suitor flew me about in his private Puss-Moth—we had to wear helmets and goggles. And then there was Terence, Terence Languishe, the only son of Sir Hercules Languishe of Knocktopher Abbey—he was always known as Pingo. And Elmley, of course, Viscount Elmley, who's the real-life model for Lord Brideshead, Bridey, in *Brideshead Revisited*. Waugh wrote the novel about Elmley's house, Madresfield Court, an absolute dream house, with a ghost and a moat. But they filmed the television series at Castle Howard instead. When I saw Elmley's wife the other day, I said, "They've done you out of thirty thousand pounds!" Anyway, there used to be an enormous gap between the lady and the prostitute, and now there's *no* gap, they've joined up. Today the boys all say, "Let's have sexual congress," and the girls all say, "Yes, *let's!*" Well, I mean, it's too much. (*Bats her false eyelashes and blushes like a virgin*)

INTERVIEWER: Your sanctified war against the seducers of virgins can't help but be a losing battle.

BARBARA CARTLAND: But I'm *winning* my battle against young people being promiscuous! Fortunately, I don't have to fight east of Suez, where every man has always insisted on a virgin bride—it's in the bloody contract. The world, you see, is returning to love and purity. England and America are the only loose countries. The girls there get bullied at school into being promiscuous—which degrades the soul, affects the character, the glands, the personality, the complexion, everything!

INTERVIEWER: Right on!

BARBARA CARTLAND: Look, I'm sincere. I write entirely sincerely. I believe what I say, and that is why my books ring true, and that is why they sell. This year I reached the two-hundred-million mark.

INTERVIEWER: Did all the publicity you attracted in conjunction with your connection to Lady Diana's conjugation with the prince of Wales increase the sales of your books?

BARBARA CARTLAND: I don't honestly think it made any difference. Oh, maybe it gave a tiny push to my latest nonfiction, *Romantic Royal Marriages,* published on Charles and Diana's wedding day. A nine-ninety-five trade paperback, one hundred twenty-eight pages with forty black-and-white photos and one hundred fifty color illustrations—you get a *lot* for your money. My daughter and I got "stick" from the press simply and solely because we'd promised the Palace and we'd promised Diana, who, incidentally, reads my novels, that we wouldn't talk about *the* romantic royal marriage of the century. Naturally, the press expected *me* to talk, since I've never *not* talked to the press. So they explained my silence to their readers by saying I was keeping terrible secrets from them—which I was not.

INTERVIEWER: It's a lot like the plot of a Barbara Cartland romance, isn't it? The dashing, worldly prince and the lovely, inexperienced young girl. *Was* Lady Diana a virgin bride, by the way?

BARBARA CARTLAND: Mmmm.

INTERVIEWER: Although *you* were a steadfast virgin bride—like the heroines of all your novels—you must have distributed your affections rather widely to get forty-nine proposals.

BARBARA CARTLAND: Look, love isn't a cake which if I give a slice to you I can't give a slice to someone else. How about a biscuit? That's a fancy English name for cookies and crackers. Mrs. Austin! Mrs. Austin is a great friend of mine. (*Mrs. Austin enters, with biscuits, bowing and scraping.*) And she also does my hair. I can't cope with New York hairdressers—they simply never arrived on time, and I was always waiting to go on television with my hair undone. That's why I travel with my hairdresser, who I must say spoils me. (*Smiles upon Mrs. Austin; Mrs. Austin scrapes and bows*) You see! I appeal to something in people which is always the highest and best of what they're looking for. I met a woman in Los Angeles the other day who had just been to see Mrs. Billy Graham, and evidently both Mrs. and Mr. Graham were reading my books. Mrs. Billy Graham said they had helped her to get well when she was in hospital. Mind you, I get letters like that all the time from all over the world—"I was down, I was out, I was miserable, I was suicidal, and *you* saved my life." That is my mission. I do do good.

INTERVIEWER: You do do well. I read somewhere that Madame Sadat is also a great fan of yours, and that President Sadat was, too.

BARBARA CARTLAND: Yes, he always read me. When he came to America and was asked how he relaxed, he said, "I read Barbara Cartland."

INTERVIEWER: And Mrs. Gandhi, I gather, reads you, too. You've certainly infiltrated the Third World at its highest levels.

BARBARA CARTLAND: Ah, Indira is so dear. I spoke to her for an hour on the phone the other day because I'm going to India again next year and I don't want to come into town cold, so to speak. The last time I was there, Indira introduced me to President Giri, who declared that all seven of his daughters and four of his daughters-in-law had read all three hundred of my novels except for two. Lord Mountbatten had given me and my sons, who always travel with me, an introduction to the Maharajah of Mysore, who had us to stay—my dear, we had twenty-seven servants to wait on us and we watched tent pegging. I *first* visited India when Lord Mountbatten was there as our last viceroy. He took me to lunch with Nehru—

Lady Mountbatten was having a love affair with Nehru at the time, so you can imagine how frightfully exciting it all was—and Nehru's little daughter was there. She was very shy, very much under the thumb of Daddy. And I became great friends with her then, and have been ever since. Indira is a very, very great friend of mine and I love her—I love her very very very much.

INTERVIEWER: How would you judge Mrs. Gandhi's handling of the so-called emergency in India, when she imprisoned people right and left?

BARBARA CARTLAND: I never think you should judge any country by its politics. I think that's the greatest cheek. Everyone has his own problems. And—between us, dear—Indira hasn't done anything the British didn't do for three hundred years. India's a divine country—everyone has such intense spiritual experiences because the air is so dry. Have another biscuit, won't you? They're very good for you.

INTERVIEWER: Mmmm. As president of the National Association for Health in Great Britain, you must have a position on women joggers. But I'm more interested to hear what your stand on them is as a woman. You once wrote that you've "yet to meet a man who didn't like a handful." Now you can't not have noticed that women joggers end up with sinewy, hermaphroditic bodies. They lose their adipose tissue, their fleshiness—the softness and curves seem to go. And when body fat drops below a certain percentage—I think it's between five and seven percent of body weight—a girl can lose her period. Apparently, though, she can still ovulate.

BARBARA CARTLAND: No vulgarity!

INTERVIEWER: There's one woman of about thirty who runs about eighty miles a week who hasn't had a period in about two years. On the other hand, a forty-year-old woman who runs a hundred twenty miles a week has the biggest flow you ever saw.

BARBARA CARTLAND: *Please!* I'm *Romance*, I'm *Romance!* It's Barbara Cartland you're talking to, not some dish of indecency and perverted dirt! I daresay I watched all those idiots jogging this morning in Central Park as I was being driven to *Good Morning America* by Mrs. Austin. (*Mrs. Austin, bowing and scraping, grins.*) The American television interviewers all ask me, "Miss Cartland, how did your granddaughter know she was pregnant?" And I always say, "First of all, she's *not* my granddaughter and, second of all, we don't talk about those things in England." What do they *expect* me to say—she missed her period? I watched those joggers this morning, poor things, in their warm-up suits and running shoes, and they're really all middle-aged, you see. It's so *stupid.* Jogging upsets the heart, and I'm an expert, dear, on the heart—what it *cannot* take is all that stop/go. If they knew what was good for them, they'd be at home eating honey. Honey is the source of all energy. It's the *most* important factor in keeping people sexually competent. I know couples in their eighties on honey who make love several times a week. And sex is healthy for older people—good for heart, lungs, and blood circulation.

INTERVIEWER: Having eaten all that honey for all those years, they must be virtually glued together by now. Speaking of beeswax, I read that you're a recent addition to one of London's greatest tourist attractions, Madame Tussaud's. *Mazel tov.*

BARBARA CARTLAND: I went round to see myself. I'm rather badly done. I hate to think that's the way people will remember me—I look *hideous*! And I don't want to look hideous, I want to look *pretty*. Why couldn't they have made me look as pretty in wax as darling Twi-Twi, my white lion Pekingese? At Madame Tussaud's he sits at my feet. He's *so* grand. I wrote my two hundred seventy-sixth romantic novel, *The Prince and the Pekingese,* for him. Prince Charles is just awful. Mrs. Thatcher is not too bad. The Queen is *very* bad, *ghastly*. The whole point about Madame Tussaud's is being able to recognize the famous waxworks, but Sophia Loren you'd *never* recognize—they've given her a completely different face for some reason. Hitler is good. So is Idi Amin. Oh, Mrs. Austin, bring me my vitamins. My voice is going away and I've got two television shows to do this afternoon. I take seventy vitamin capsules a day, you know—ten vitamin Es, one hundred milligrams each, ten vitamin B$_2$s, ten milligrams each, plus a special kind of herb. One man who took it lived to two hundred fifty-six—this has been authenticated by the Peking and French governments. *I* don't want to live to be two hundred fifty-six, though my readers might want me to. I'm also on to a new thing called W-5, which takes away the lines on your face and makes you look young. It's not on the market yet, but I managed to get some samples from the laboratory and, my dear, it's almost as good as plastic surgery and, naturally, much less risky. When one grows old, she must keep either her face or her body. I selected my face. And put the little pot of honey in my bag, *will* you, Mrs. Austin, like an angel?

INTERVIEWER: Two television shows this afternoon! How can you keep up all this promoting? How long can you keep the writing and packaging up?

BARBARA CARTLAND: As long as I can make money for my children, because of course I *want* to make money for my children. Why, I can go on indefinitely. When I was born, the doctor asked my father which he wanted saved, his wife or the baby, then he threw me on the bed saying, "That's dead." But I lived! And I shall go on living—and writing—and making money for my children. There's plenty of relaxation in the grave. But also, think of the enormous amount of employment I'm providing. I've got fifty publishers over the world. Germany is now bringing out a book of mine a week—a *week*! They *were* bringing them out one a fortnight. And twenty-four books a year wasn't enough for America and England, they wanted *more*. That's when I got the idea to start and edit Barbara Cartland's Library of Love, and I followed that up with Barbara Cartland's Library of Ancient Wisdom. And now NBC has filmed one of my novels, *The Flame Is Love*. It's my very first film—all very exciting. I flew to New Orleans for the launching. It's the story of a young American virgin in Paris who falls in love with a poet but is forced to marry a duke and is very nearly sacrificed by Satanists. Linda Purl plays the virgin.

INTERVIEWER: She must have recycled herself then, because in her previous film, *Little Ladies of the Night*, she was a teenage runaway who became a prostitute and I don't think a virginal one.

BARBARA CARTLAND: Well, the film wasn't exactly what I wanted, anyway. And it had only twenty-two million viewers. But a very clever man did come to see me last week to propose making Barbara Cartland feature-length animated cartoons. You know—like *Snow White and the Seven Dwarfs*. I think that would be lovely, because then my dukes would look like dukes and my virgins *would* look like virgins. Walt Disney always used to say that every time a pornographic film was released, he made money, and I'm convinced that Barbara Cartland cartoons will, too. *I'm* the answer to pornography—*up*lift!

INTERVIEWER: How right you are! Just the other day, a movie house off Times Square—the World Theater, to be exact—a place dirty with oral, anal, and auricular sex, in fact the very theater where a decade ago the lubricious sex flick *Deep Throat* opened—opened wide, as they say in the trade—was turned into a family film house, and guess what the first movie they showed was? Walt Disney's *Robin Hood*!

BARBARA CARTLAND: Such a marvelous film. That's what I call *healthy* family entertainment. Thank God for my two sons. They are a great help in *all* my enterprises. They spend every weekend at Camfield with me. Glen, the younger one—he's forty-two now—is named after an old beau of mine, Glen Kidston, the famous aviator who was killed on—

INTERVIEWER: You named your son after an old beau? How did your husband feel about *that*? He wasn't jealous, having your beau around all the time in the name of the son? Why not? Because you'd never gone to *bed* with your beau?

BARBARA CARTLAND: Yes, that's it. My older son, Ian, travels with me on all my business trips. Here he is now. (*Ian McCorquodale enters.*) He's just been made chairman of Debrett's, which publishes *The Peerage,* the Social Register of Great Britain—haven't you, darling? In fact, he's been getting more publicity than his mother lately. Naughty boy. Jean Rook of Fleet Street just wrote this big personality piece on Ian. Here, have one. (*Hands interviewer a Xerox copy; Ian McCorquodale beams*)

INTERVIEWER: There are rumors of a current duke in your life.

BARBARA CARTLAND: Here's a *snap* of me with my duke. Duke, my Black Labrador. (*Hands interviewer color photo*) Lord Mountbatten gave him to me. He comes from the Queen's kennels at Sandringham. He's Kimberly's nephew. You know—*Kimberly,* Lord Mountbatten's favorite dog. Duke never leaves my side except in the shooting season. When he sees a gun, he goes.

INTERVIEWER: Mmmm. Duke is a bit hard to spot in this snap.

BARBARA CARTLAND: Now don't *you* start. Duke's got a little problem, you see—he's black. Every photographer who comes to do me says, "I'd prefer not to shoot the black dog, he won't come out well," and *I* always say, "That's racial prejudice. He can't help being black, poor darling. You're *upsetting* him." But then the photographer always says, "I'd really much rather snap the white dog." Little do they know that darling Twi-Twi snaps at strangers. But the minute he does, I send him straight back to bed. He sleeps in *my* bed, naturally. It's the most beautiful thing you ever saw: a scarlet and gold antique four-poster covered with flame-colored brocade, with a gilded angel spreading his precious wings above the bedhead. Duke is *not* allowed on the bed. I make him sleep in a basket on the floor. Racial prejudice again! I always spray my room with scent first thing in the morning because I *have* had two dogs sleeping with me. That's the *real* reason I've just come out with this nice cheap perfume. You don't want an expensive one if you're going to be spraying a room to get rid of doggy smells. With my seven-dollar perfume you can be really extravagant.

INTERVIEWER: To judge from the number of dog snaps in the *Barbara Cartland Scrapbook,* you must really love dogs.

BARBARA CARTLAND: I do. I do. My grandson William has a horror of them—very un-English of him. He gets it from my daughter. She was once bitten by a Cairn, and brought her children up to hate animals. And oddly enough, William hates flowers, too. (*Joseph of Helena Rubinstein peeks around the door and pops in, bowing and spraying.*)

JOSEPH: How are you doing?

BARBARA CARTLAND: Lovely, thank you. And William my grandson is coming to take me to a lunch party. Oh, here he is now. (*Enter William, Viscount Lewisham, the Earl of Dartmouth's sun and air out of Raine, and, at thirty-two, Barbara Cartland's eldest grandchild, who lives and works in New York and who is a microchip off the old Cartland block: The morning of the official announcement of Prince Charles's engagement to Lewisham's stepsister, Lady Diana, Lewisham rang an American friend to ask jokingly, "How can I get leverage in New York off my new royal connection? I must be able to leverage off it somehow. Good-bye, John Bowes-Lyon—Hello, William Lewisham!" [An amusing reference to another royal peripheral, quite a distant relative of the Queen Mother, who has carved a career in New York out of being accousined to the Queen.] Almost instantly, the* New York Times *accommodated Lewisham; its "Notes on Fashion" column began, "The week began with Lord Lewisham, the thirty-two-year-old grandson of Barbara Cartland and the stepbrother of the Princess of Wales . . ." Lately Lewisham has been getting name leverage off the fact that the royal baby was christened William.*)

VISCOUNT LEWISHAM: Hello, Granny, how are you? Hello, hello.

BARBARA CARTLAND: I was out last night until ten, which is three in the morning to me—for those damned wallpaper awards. But I'm having a very nice interview now. Joseph, go fetch a *very* special Barbara Cartland gift. And Mrs. Austin, offer the very nice interviewer another scrumptious biscuit. I really *am* an expert on interviews. I have at least one a day, you know—it really is every single day, and in every single language now. Except Chinese. Chinese next! They've done me in Icelandic, Greek, Swahili, Turkish, Arabic, and Hebrew, which goes the *other* way. (*Joseph presents a blue plush box to Cartland, who then presents it with a flourish to interviewer.*) Here is a truly special present for you because I love you.

INTERVIEWER: A key ring! Can't I have a paperweight?

BARBARA CARTLAND: A Barbara Cartland key ring is *better* than a Barbara Cartland paperweight. It's a very, very nice present. You'll be jolly pleased—*you'll* see. The key ring is *lucky*. The last interviewer I gave one to went off to the races and had five winners. He now goes to bed with it. And look, on the ring there's a twenty-two-karat gold acorn, picked from the oak at Camfield which Queen Elizabeth the First planted on the spot where she killed her *very* first stag. It's a little nut from the pages of history, dear. If you pierce it—and sooner or later, they all *do*—you'll find a real acorn inside. Each one is a different size. These key rings have become so terribly expensive to produce that I only give them to very *spe-*

cial people like you. When interviewers ask me bloody silly questions, I jolly well push the Barbara Cartland key rings under the sofa and give them the Barbara Cartland paperweights instead. You must understand, I'm the only person in the whole world who can give you this ring. And I want you to always remember that no person in the whole world has exactly the same as yours. That oak is *fantastic*, by the way—my grandson can tell you. Don't you hate his mustache? I think it makes him look common. He had a beard last year. *That* was ghastly. I wouldn't let him kiss me, I wouldn't even speak to him. Prince Michael of Kent came to stay with me last weekend at Camfield, and I said to him as he arrived, "I don't like your beard, *Sir.*" The children said I was rude, but really, I think it's unnecessary for young men to rush into beards. (*Hands interviewer a bottle of "Love Wins" and exits spraying "Moments of Love" on William her grandson's mustache*)

INTERVIEWER (*to Joseph*): What am I going to do with a bottle of cheap perfume?

JOSEPH: Do you have a cleaning lady?

3

Cartland Calling!

The bejeweled, befurred, beribboned octogenarian that is Barbara Cartland is so much a creature of her own inflation that one could stumble far afield searching for an image to sum her up—an image, that is, which would not fatten the very disproportion she embodies. And yet the key to her corporate kingdom lies, for us, close to home—in America, the United States of Advertising. For Barbara Cartland is a glorified version of the Avon lady, that jolly greeting card—that relentlessly cheerful cartoon—of healthy American enterprise.

She's just the extreme stage of those pseudorefined women who, using Avon's marketing gimmick of door-to-door peddling, ring doorbells—trilling in saccharine tones "Avon calling!"—and then hard-sell, softly, beauty products: love in a potion.

When Barbara Cartland comes calling—"Cartland calling! 'Love for sale,/ Appetizing young love for sale./ Love that's fresh and still unspoiled,/ Who will buy?/ Who would like to sample my supply?/ Who's prepared to pay the price/ For a trip to paradise?/ Love for sale . . .' "—she carries a kit containing such quaint items as novels of romance, sheets of romance, towels of romance, wallpapers of romance, hangers of romance, and now, of course, perfumes of romance.

Ding dong! "Avon calling!"

"Come in! Come in!" the suburban housewife calls back—at least she did in the days when bellringers, when they weren't Avon ladies, were sure to be Christmas carolers or Western Union boys, not knife-wielding muggers dressed to kill as Christmas carolers, Western Union boys, or even Avon ladies. "Come right in!" she called, for Avon was part of the suburban housewife's happy, gin-soaked day.

Like Barbara Cartland at the St. Regis in her isthmus years—that is, between this world and the next—the Avon "reps" carefully lay out all their products, which have names every bit as cloying as the titles of Barbara Cartland romances: "Dew Kiss" (moisturizer), "Wild Country" (shower soap), "Rainkissed Rose" (lipstick), "Timeless" (perfume), "Sandcastle Beige" (foundation), and "Dry and Delicate" (deodorant).

Happily for Avon and for *our* Avon lady, Barbara Cartland, both are Number One. The former, whose products are sold in thirty-one countries, is the leading beauty company in the world. The latter, whose products are sold in just as many countries, is the best-selling author in the world.

During Cartland's recent visit to New York, she called the Dial-It Services of the New York Telephone Company direct ("Cartland calling!") to suggest that they hire her to do a daily sixty-second love-line—"Dial ROMANCE." "I'll give out the lovely plot summaries of my latest romances," she told a telephone company executive, adding, "You know what's happening all over the world, don't you?—how they love my books, how they adore *me*. I'm a wildly marketable commodity. And I'll do the dial-it service cheap—I mean inexpensively. I'll do it for *you* at cost because I *love* you."

She was rejected and, with her broken heart on her sleeve, rushed back to England to plan, package, franchise, and promote 1,001 romantic questions for a new computer word game, including "The French Emperor Napoleon crowned as his Empress _____" and "King Edward VIII abdicated the British throne for the woman he loved. The American lady is _____."

Until the day Barbara Cartland dies—but as she cautions, one mustn't be negative, so, until the day Barbara Cartland goes, in Melville's phrase from *The Confidence-Man*, to her "long home"—that is, to what will be her home for a long time—she will go on adding to her line. Then, with all the additions incorporated in her résumé, Barbara's Brag Sheet will be so bulky with hype facts about Cartland Productions and Cartland Promotions that *it* will need its own Rolls-Royce.

Barbara Cartland, more than any other public person in contemporary life, is synonymous with strenuous self-promotion, the prerequisite for acclaim in our time—a time in which every one of our ennobling values has been shaved down to one bald rubric: whether one is famous or not. Singers such as Frank Sinatra have long been "famous for being well known." Writers such as Norman Mailer are equally famous for being equally well known. And now convicts such as Jack Henry Abbott get famous for being the well-known favorites of famous novelists, and acquire social, romantic, and even moral status by "symbolizing" society's ills. Radicals such as Abbie Hoffman are famous for being notorious. And even *very* famous actresses such as Sophia Loren give their waning careers shots from the hype hypodermic by voluntarily serving very promotable jail sentences.

But Barbara Cartland is the whole kit and caboodle. As Empress of Hype, she rules all the rules of self-promoting, self-aggrandizing, self-marketing, self-merchandising, and self-franchising.

Like her friend Suzy, Barbara Cartland forged a career as a society columnist who gave the lowdown on the high life.

Like Cheryl Tiegs, who followed Stan Dragoti's promotional instruction—GET AN ISSUE, Barbara Cartland followed Lord Beaverbrook's—GET A PLATFORM.

Like Bobby Zarem, Herb Schmertz, Howard J. Rubenstein, John Springer, and Christina Bellin, Barbara Cartland forged a career as a successful press agent—mostly for herself.

So, like Dr. Thomas D. Rees's résumé, Barbara's Brag Sheet is bulky.

And like Howard and Christina Bellin's bloated newsletter, Barbara's Brag Sheet banners the bragger's home phone number. Barbara's is Potters Bar (77) 42612 and 42657. Obviously, she wants all two hundred million readers to give her a ring.

Even more successfully than Cheryl Tiegs, Suzy, Dr. Thomas D. Rees and Dr. Howard T. Bellin, and Kenneth, Maury Hopson, and Way Bandy, Barbara Cartland sells RITZY ROMANCE.

Like Kenneth, Barbara Cartland earns her living in part by stroking virgin hair.

More than Dr. Thomas D. Rees with his Flying Doctors of East Africa, more than Cheryl Tiegs with her stationary African elephants and her African elephant stationery, more than Dr. Howard T. Bellin with what has become for him *his* "Six Day War," Barbara Cartland has used her good works to advance herself.

Like Dr. Howard T. Bellin and his Porsche Turbo, Barbara Cartland has a signature car. Hers carries an initial recognition in its license plate, BC 29: an initial recognition that precedes both Cheryl Tiegs's and Peter Rogers's, for B.C. precedes C.T. and P.R., just as it predates A.D.

As Cheryl Tiegs once had in Beverly Hills, and as Philip Johnson still has in New Canaan, Barbara Cartland has a signature hype house, the perfect private setting in which she can be the essence—the perfume—of her public self.

Like Elaine and Bobby Zarem, Barbara Cartland made a private club for people to be private in public in—the Embassy Club. In effect, she made her own Elaine's.

Like Peter Beard with Cheryl Tiegs, Peter Rogers with his great friend Claudette Colbert, Dr. Denton Cooley with Norman Mailer and Donald Sutherland, and Elaine with Everybody-Who-Is-Anybody, Barbara Cartland with Earl Mountbatten of Burma made an alliance for publicity and performed it in public, seizing every "photo opportunity" in sight.

Like Cheryl Tiegs, Barbara Cartland commands an imperial business empire, teeming with franchise operations.

Like Cheryl Tiegs, and like many of the stars in the old Hollywood system, Barbara Cartland employs the men in her life as supers, appointing her sons her star supers.

Like superstar Elizabeth Taylor, Barbara Cartland could enter the *Guinness Book of World Records*—were it accepting new categories—on the sheer strength of the number of supers she employs to sustain her own solar system.

Like Peter Rogers's "Legends," Barbara Cartland knows that a superstar must be reborn and reborn and reborn. But were she to be asked to become a Blackglama "Legend," she would have to demand that the mink be Cartland pink.

Unlike her American "Legend" counterparts, Barbara Cartland possesses—and thus profits from—a connection to the British throne, itself an engorged organ of stupendous self-celebration.

And finally, like hype itself, English aristocratic Barbara Cartland, though ancient, endures.

EPILOGUE

A LESSON IN MORAL STYLE
FROM MRS. TRILLING

But surely the way in which taste is exercised—every kind of taste: in art and architecture and decoration, dress, food, manners, speech—is the firmest clue we have to how someone pursues his life in culture and therefore to the style of moral being he would legislate for us, if he had the power. Merchandising recognizes this when it presents our choice in jeans or in running shoes as a choice in moral style.

—DIANA TRILLING, *Mrs. Harris*

[Mrs. Trilling] is obstinately moral, setting standards that perhaps few writers other than she can live by.

—*Vogue*

Shortly after the publication of Diana Trilling's book *Mrs. Harris*, a magazine commissioned me to interview the author.

Mrs. Trilling, a literary, social, and cultural critic long associated in the public's mind with such bastions of high intellectual endeavor as Columbia and Radcliffe and with such repositories of cultural interpretation and analysis as *Partisan Review*, *Encounter*, *Commentary*, *The Nation*, and *The American Scholar*, had taken the literary world by complete surprise when she signed a contract to write an account of the murder of the Scarsdale Diet doctor, Herman Tarnower, by his faithful lover of fourteen years, Jean Harris, headmistress of the fashionable Madeira School.

Mrs. Trilling had further startled the literary world by finishing her 150,000-word book within a year—a sensationally short time even for a seasoned reporter, which she was not and which a competitor, Shana Alexander, was. Although Alexander, a more obvious writer for the subject (she had recently chronicled the Patty Hearst saga), had signed a contract with Little, Brown to do a book on Jean Harris months before Mrs. Trilling had signed with Harcourt Brace Jovanovich, when Mrs. Trilling's book appeared in the fall of 1981, Alexander still had nine months' more work to do on hers. On finishing it in June 1982, she found herself with yet another obstacle to overcome: Little, Brown was postponing publication of her book, having calculated that its appearance on the originally scheduled pub date, coinciding as that would with the release of the paperback edition of Mrs. Trilling's book, would serve to hype—indeed, to sell—the latter.

It was with the expectation of an agreeable encounter that I made my way to Mrs. Trilling's apartment on Claremont Avenue, the "little-known" street near Columbia University, whose name she had borrowed for the title of the first of her two collections of acute essays, *Claremont Essays*.

I had met Mrs. Trilling once before. Years ago, the poet William Meredith had invited me to dinner with the biographer Francis Steegmuller and his wife, the novelist Shirley Hazzard, to meet the legendary Lionel Trilling, critic, novelist, and professor of literature and criticism at Columbia, and his wife, Diana. I was thrilled. Like everybody else who had ever read a book of his—*The Liberal Imagination*, *Beyond Culture*, and *Sincerity and Authenticity* sat centrally on every English major's bookshelf, and Trilling's courses on the Romantic poets and the Victorian novelists had achieved a fame beyond the precincts of the Columbia lecture halls—I was in awe of Lionel Trilling's sovereign and spacious intelligence.

379

White-haired, with hooded eyes, he spoke intensely that night of E. M. Forster and Matthew Arnold and—though his voice was soft and his manner guarded—skeptically of the recent student uprising at Columbia. Mrs. Trilling spoke with amused disdain both of *Making It*, her husband's old student Norman Podhoretz's advertisement for himself, which had just been published, and of Mrs. Arthur Goldberg, who had recently turned to her at a party saying, "Here comes the Justice." "*I* don't say, 'Here comes the critic' when Lionel walks into the room," Mrs. Trilling laughed. I found the rigor of her judgment, combined as it was with the great warmth of her person, most attractive.

In the years that had passed since Bill Meredith's dinner party, Lionel Trilling had died, ravaged by cancer. Diana Trilling, I heard, was numb with grief. But the seventy-six-year-old woman who opened the door to me on Claremont Avenue was as warm and vigorous as I remembered.

Inviting me to sit beside her on the sofa in her comfortable living room, she popped up to make instant iced coffee, suggesting that a scoop of chocolate ice cream added to it might be very refreshing—it was a hot October day.

When Mrs. Trilling returned with the two iced coffees, I asked whether her husband with his "magisterial exigence of taste" (Lionel Trilling's own phrase for a Columbia colleague) would have approved of her writing a book about such a sordid crime of passion as Jean Harris's.

"I think he would have loved the idea that I was doing this book," she answered, her brown eyes warm with affection, "because he would have known that I would write a good book—rather, he would have had the *faith* that I would write a good book, although—would you like me to give you a little nugget here?—I don't think my marriage could have sustained this past year. I worked fifteen hours a *day*. And while intellectually Lionel would have been all for it, on the other hand he was used to having me cook and run the house. My mind was always first for my family and my home—and *then* came my career. This week I have been asking myself: Would I still say what I once said absolutely truthfully— without hesitation—that I would rather be complimented for the good meal I'd just cooked than for the piece I'd just written? And I decided that I'm not going to say that anymore. Because, in the first place, I can't cook that well anymore. I'm out of practice—I haven't done it for five years very much, not since Lionel died."

And so—brightly, captivatingly—she talked on, about Dr. Tarnower's (to *her*) incomprehensible appeal to women, about "back street" wives, about Mrs. Harris's need for abusive love, about people who have "holes in their superegos" (that is, convenient consciences), about the Madeira School as a "patrician zoo," about how Dr. Tarnower "with his dry strivings and worldly salvations" was a contemporary Gatsby—interrupted by the insistent ringing of the telephone: the *Los Angeles Times*, the *Washington Post*, the publicity department at Harcourt Brace Jovanovich, all requesting more than a moment of her time.

When after a couple of hours the doorbell rang and I stood up to leave, I asked Mrs. Trilling to autograph my copy of *Mrs. Harris*. She wrote in her sure script: "For Steven Aronson, With my warmest greetings—October 1981."

Some weeks later, the interview appeared in *Interview* magazine's thick Christmas issue, whose cover—to almost everybody's cynical surprise—featured Nancy Reagan in Adolfo red. It was ironic to see *Interview* banners tacked up on newsstands advertising the issue with "Nancy Reagan . . . Diana Trilling," since the two were such incompatible political bedfellows. (That it was the First Lady's own daughter-in-law, Doria Reagan, who had transcribed my Trilling tape for *Interview* was a coincidence I felt sure would not have gone unremarked by Mrs. Trilling—had she known.)

Like many of its readers, though unlike several critics, I admired Diana Trilling's *Mrs. Harris*. I described the book as "blazingly intelligent . . . social history, political history, and cultural history of the most compelling kind."

Two months after my piece appeared, Mrs. Trilling left a message at *Interview* for me to call her. I was surprised, when I finally reached her on the telephone, to hear her say, "I have a favor to ask you—something that's very important to me. I would like—and would value—your advice. May I come to see you, or would you, could you, come to *me*?" I said that of course I would come to *her*, and made a weak joke about its being hot-toddy-with-hot-tea rather than iced-coffee-with-chocolate-ice-cream weather—it was the middle of a fierce March. She said good-bye, promising to lay on high tea.

Naturally, I was curious. In what possible way could I be of help to Diana Trilling?

A couple of days after our phone conversation, I took a cab all the way to Claremont Avenue again. I saw as the door opened that Mrs. Trilling had indeed prepared a high tea. Cucumber sandwiches and petits fours were set out on a tray by the sofa. We skimmed waterbuglike over the surface of a variety of subjects, as people do when they hardly know each other, until Mrs. Trilling asked me pointedly, "Aren't you *curious* about why I've asked you here? I want to ask you a question. Do you think I've been unfairly dealt with in the press and, if so, *why*? And what can I do about it?"

Before I could respond, she handed me the current issue of *Commentary*, open to a review of *Mrs. Harris*. There I read the following:

> Her enthusiasm seems to be limited to the assertion of a certain moral posture, which can be summed up roughly in this paraphrase: This is a Significant Trial (which is the only reason I deign to report it), significant because the people who take part in it are almost without exception lacking in taste, and thus morally worthless. Furthermore, their moral defects both make up and illuminate the Spiritual Corruption of our Time. You may best understand all of this if you attend closely to my Insights, which will make it all clear, for I follow in the footsteps of my mighty predecessors, Fitzgerald and George Eliot and Flaubert and Tolstoy. . . . She tells us that her fellow reporters are "ankle-deep in prejudgment," that the defense attorney is a snob, that Dr. Tarnower is vulgar and without generosity of spirit, that the defendant is obsessed by social status, that the middle class is culturally pretentious. Each and every one of these charges is more accurately made against this book.

As soon as I glanced up from reading what must certainly have been a painful review for her, Mrs. Trilling began to tell me of an even more recent assault. "A young man from the Harvard paper called, begging to see me," she complained, "and even though I'd stopped giving interviews by then, I agreed to see him. And *now* look—in his piece he talks of my *grand* living room. It's totally unjust. I mean, look around—*this* isn't grand. Don't you see that this has been a witch hunt?"

I agreed that for the most part she had been dealt with harshly in the press, though—I hazarded—not entirely unfairly. Surely she could understand and allow for some genuine objection to her book—she had, after all, set herself up as a moralistic judge in her own right. (Even her old friend Mary McCarthy was to remark in the Vassar alumnae bulletin that Mrs. Trilling's phrase "moral style" was an unpleasant one. And Jean Harris herself would gleefully call Shana Alexander's attention to the *Commentary* review with its excoriation of Mrs. Trilling for her moral stance.)

I also knew that some saw it as uncharitable, if not downright hypo-critical, of a woman who had herself gained status through a man to be so unsympathetic to Mrs. Harris's need to lean heavily on a powerful male for both self-definition and social place. Also—just possibly—Mrs. Trill-ing was being made to pay a price for being Mrs. Trilling; her husband had been an arbiter of literature and society, a cultural figure not only respected but feared (perhaps because he was so discerning, so dispas-sionate, and so uncompromisingly right so much of the time), and now she was a lightning rod to attract any storm still rumbling in the wake of his judgments.

And then, of course, there was the political issue. Mrs. Trilling had at one time or another been a Communist fellow-traveler, a neoconserva-tive, an anti-Communist, and an anti-McCarthyite; and in the sixties she had been opposed to counterculture, which in its anarchical spirit threat-ened the Arnoldian culture that both Trillings passionately advocated. Perhaps she was being punished now for her own announced and stren-uously articulated ideological convictions.

Finally, I added, some of the vituperation aimed at Mrs. Trilling that had greeted the appearance of *Mrs. Harris* could perhaps be attrib-uted to simple envy. Her covering of the trial had itself made news, and her book when it was published had generated tremendous publicity. Mrs. Trilling appeared on the *Today* show and *Good Morning New York*, and became, perhaps inevitably, gossip-column fodder; her staid name was mentioned more than once, and in rather frivolous company, in both Suzy and Liz Smith. Moreover, everyone had read that the California in-dustrialist and art tycoon Norton Simon had optioned *Mrs. Harris* for a million dollars for the movies as a comeback vehicle for his wife, the ac-tress Jennifer Jones, whom Mrs. Trilling would describe to *Interview* as "a darling girl, darling woman . . . a very serious person."

(A year later, envy was still percolating. At a party, Shana Alexander complained to me about how her former boss—she was the editor of *McCall's* when Norton Simon owned it—had gone and optioned Diana Trilling's book and not hers, which had been announced *first*. Re-minded that Simon had recently dropped that option and was now free to option *her* book, she replied testily, of one of the world's richest men, "He couldn't afford it." Alexander, incidentally, had once been married to—as Mrs. Trilling put it—"Lionel Trilling's most brilliant student of all time": Everything connects.)

So, I told Mrs. Trilling, one could see how people might perceive her as a custodian of certain values who had now stepped over into the immoderate world of public relations, big money, and big fame.

"The only thing you can do to set the record straight, as *you* see it," I advised her, "is to write an article explaining what your intentions were when you wrote the book, and your confusion over the critical reaction."

"No, I *can't* do that," she shot back. "One must never defend oneself in print. But *you* could write the article. I'll help you with it, but I wouldn't want anyone to know *that*."

Taken aback, I said, "I can't. I'm finishing a book."

"*Oh*," she said. "What's it about?"

"Hype," I replied. "The process of inflating careers and reputations—by almost any means."

"That's a *fascinating* subject," she commented, her preoccupation momentarily put aside. "I hope you'll do full justice to it."

Returning to the issue under discussion, I offered to suggest to some magazine editor or other that a story be commissioned on what Mrs. Trilling saw as—and indeed had termed—a "witch hunt."

"No!" she said. "I don't want that. It could backfire—turn out unfavorable to me. I have to know that the writer will be sympathetic. Why do you think *you're* here?" she laughed. "I loved what you wrote about me."

I was flattered, of course. And now I could ask her what she thought about being in the same issue of *Interview* as Nancy Reagan and what, indeed, she thought of the magazine itself.

She answered, amazing me, "It's a very serious magazine."

"Serious?" I protested. "Oh, I think *not*. Amusing, certainly."

"No—*serious*," she repeated. "A very serious magazine. I wonder if you know Renata Adler."

"I've met her many times," I said. "I just had a long talk with her at a dinner party."

"Oh, whose dinner party?"

"Bobo Legendre's."

"*Really!*" Mrs. Trilling exclaimed. "Bobo! What a silly name. It reminds me of all those Madeira names—Buffy, Muffy, Bopsy, Mopsy, Boopsy. You know, Renata would be the perfect person to write this piece on me—for *The New York Review of Books* or *The New York Times Magazine*, or even *The Voice*. Only, *I* can't ask her. But *you* could ask her for me. Only, you can't tell her—or anybody else—that this was my idea. You'll have to say it was yours."

I was made uneasy by the terms of Mrs. Trilling's request. I said that I might be willing to suggest to Renata Adler that she write such an article but that I couldn't pretend the idea was mine.

Taking another sip of tea in order to change the subject, I said, "I heard something very, very interesting the other day, and you can probably tell me whether it's true or not. Evidently, Dr. Tarnower was known to have frequented Court Street, a very short street in White Plains infamous for homosexual car cruising. Evidently, he used to pick up men there. Evidently, he had a longterm but sporadic homosexual relationship with a middle-aged executive he met there, who describes him as 'a lonely old man.' And evidently, Mrs. Harris knew all about the doctor's duality of taste but refused to allow her lawyer to bring the subject up in court. All this I heard from a very reliable source."

"I knew it!" Mrs. Trilling exclaimed. "I *suspected* it! Remember in my book I say that perhaps the doctor's more tender passions had never been meant for the opposite sex? When anybody plays women off against each other in that kind of public way—so that each knows about the other—there is always the implication that this is not quite the way heterosexuals behave. It's very cruel. And it's boastful, a little extravagant, a little ostentatious—parading his masculinity, saying 'Look how potent *I* am, I can handle all of these women at once!' You begin to say, 'Hey, what are you talking about, what are you protesting so much for?' "

"Then why," I asked, "were you so elliptical in your book about the possibility of this womanizing doctor's being a practicing homosexual?"

"Because I had no *proof*! Early in the trial I did get a call late at night from some man claiming that Tarnower used to hang around subway urinals, but I couldn't *use* that because the caller wouldn't give his name. But now *you* can get all the facts for me from your reliable source. I want to get this into print someplace before Shana's book comes out. What I'll write is that I had this information all along and sat on it—I'll think of why. So you see, it's two favors you can do me, not one. Now what can I do for *you*?" she laughed.

"Well," I said, laughing now myself, "I brought my copy of *Claremont Essays* for you to autograph."

"You *did*? How charming. Of course I'll autograph it."

In her sure script Mrs. Trilling wrote: "To a new old friend, Steven from Diana, March 1982."

A few minutes later, in the cab taking me from Claremont Avenue, the book's inscription of accelerated affection burning my hand, I recalled Charles Ryder's words from a *Brideshead Revisited* episode I'd watched on television. After Lady Marchmain, in an effort to win her son Sebastian's friend over to her side, inscribes on the flyleaf of a special book her name and his, the date and place, Charles reflects, "I was no fool; I was old enough to know that an attempt had been made to suborn me and young enough to have found the experience agreeable."

I, too, was old enough to know that an attempt had been made to suborn me—for Mrs. Trilling had just tried, in effect, to turn a writer who had honestly praised her work into a hack flack—but I was, by now, too consciousness-raised by the book on hype I was writing to have found the experience agreeable.

It went without saying that Diana Trilling was no Cheryl Tiegs posing in a fishnet bathing suit. Nor even a Lilliam Hellman posturing in a Blackglama coat. (When I'd asked Mrs. Trilling whether *she* would ever agree to be a Blackglama "Legend," she had answered, "I just *couldn't* do a thing like that. You see, in my book *Mrs. Harris* I talk about moral style, the relation of taste to larger moral issues . . .")

Nevertheless, Mrs. Trilling was prepared to say in print that she had possessed all along the information she had just been given about Dr. Tarnower's sexual imbroglio, and that she had been sitting on this scoop because—well, she was also prepared to find a reason for having sat on it.

To the extent that sexual passion was a theme in Mrs. Trilling's book, should she not have acted on her hunch and tried to discover the variousness of Dr. Tarnower's sexual passions? Another sort of writer than Mrs. Trilling, having received that anonymous late-night telephone call informing her that Tarnower was homosexual, would have acted on the tip and gotten in touch with every woman the doctor had ever had (God knows, it wasn't hard to find them) and asked that telling question—then tried to find the men.

And now, didn't Mrs. Trilling perceive that claiming after the publication of her book that she had known from the outset that Dr. Tarnower had had homosexual liaisons would retroactively flaw her psychological portrait of an aging woman driven by heterosexual jealousy?

Apparently not, for Mrs. Trilling was bewitched by the scoop mentality. As bewitched as I might have been by it myself, for one is as imperfect as any other pilgrim in today's hype progress, I could still judge in disappointment the ironic lesson in moral style Mrs. Trilling had just delivered. And my disappointment was all the more keen because I had hoped here to find the heartbeat—regular and stern—of American intellectual probity. Instead, one now had to reexamine Mrs. Trilling's many declarations of a life lived in moral fervor.

Puzzling over my final encounter with Mrs. Trilling, as I continued to do for several months, I came to understand, with a sense of weariness, that what she had done that cold March afternoon was write an ending—the only ending possible—for a book on hype.

Index